PERGAMON INTERNATIONAL LIBRARY
of Science, Technology, Engineering and Social Studies

The 1000-volume original paperback library in aid of education, industrial training and the enjoyment of leisure

Publisher: Robert Maxwell, M.C.

Dialogue on Wealth and Welfare
An Alternative View of World Capital Formation

THE PERGAMON TEXTBOOK
INSPECTION COPY SERVICE

An inspection copy of any book published in the Pergamon International Library will gladly be sent to academic staff without obligation for their consideration for course adoption or recommendation. Copies may be retained for a period of 60 days from receipt and returned if not suitable. When a particular title is adopted or recommended for adoption for class use and the recommendation results in a sale of 12 or more copies, the inspection copy may be retained with our compliments. The Publishers will be pleased to receive suggestions for revised editions and new titles to be published in this important International Library.

Other Titles of Interest

BOTKIN, J., ELMANDJRA, M. and MALITZA, M.
No Limits to Learning
Bridging the Human Gap
A Report to the Club of Rome

COLE, S. and LUCAS, H.
Models, Planning and Basic Needs

FELD, B. T.
A Voice Crying in the Wilderness
Essays on the Problems of Science and World Affairs

GIARINI, O. and LOUBERGÉ, H.
The Diminishing Returns of Technology
An Essay on the Crisis in Economic Growth

LASZLO, E.
The Inner Limits of Mankind

LASZLO, E. and BIERMAN, J.
Goals in a Global Community
   Volume 1: Studies on the Conceptual Foundations
   Volume 2: The International Values and Goals Studies

PECCEI, A.
The Human Quality

TÉVOÉDJRÈ, A.
Poverty: Wealth of Mankind

NOTICE TO READERS

Dear Reader,

An Invitation to Publish in and Recommend the Placing of a Standing Order to Volumes Published in this Valuable Series.

If your library is not already a standing/continuation order customer to this series, may we recommend that you place a standing/continuation order to receive immediately upon publication all new volumes. Should you find that these volumes no longer serve your needs, your order can be cancelled at any time without notice.

The Editors and the Publisher will be glad to receive suggestions or outlines of suitable titles, reviews or symposia for editorial consideration: if found acceptable, rapid publication is guaranteed.

ROBERT MAXWELL
Publisher at Pergamon Press

Dialogue on Wealth and Welfare

An Alternative View of World Capital Formation

A Report to the Club of Rome

by
ORIO GIARINI

PERGAMON PRESS

OXFORD · NEW YORK · TORONTO · SYDNEY · PARIS · FRANKFURT

U.K.	Pergamon Press Ltd., Headington Hill Hall, Oxford OX3 0BW, England
U.S.A.	Pergamon Press Inc., Maxwell House, Fairview Park, Elmsford, New York 10523, U.S.A.
CANADA	Pergamon of Canada, Suite 104, 150 Consumers Road, Willowdale, Ontario M2J 1P9, Canada
AUSTRALIA	Pergamon Press (Aust.) Pty. Ltd., P.O. Box 544, Potts Point, N.S.W. 2011, Australia
FRANCE	Pergamon Press SARL, 24 rue des Ecoles, 75240 Paris, Cedex 05, France
FEDERAL REPUBLIC OF GERMANY	Pergamon Press GmbH, 6242 Kronberg-Taunus, Hammerweg 6, Federal Republic of Germany

First edition 1980

British Library Cataloguing in Publication Data

Giarini, Orio
Dialogue on wealth and welfare.
– (Pergamon international library).
1. Saving and investment
I. Title   II. Club of Rome
332'.0415   HB501   80-40439

ISBN 0-08-026088-8 (Hardcover)
ISBN 0-08-026087-X (Flexicover)

Printed in Great Britain by A. Wheaton & Co. Ltd., Exeter

Preface

SCIENTISTS say that in our corner of the universe life began on Planet Earth of the solar system perhaps some four billion years ago, and forthwith started diversifying and multiplying itself in thousands of ways, adapting by trial and error to different and changing environments. Its texture spread slowly but surely to every nook and cranny of the globe, pervading and transforming that thin skin of soil, water and air which envelops it — the biosphere.

This evolution proceeded steadily until an extraordinary fact occurred just about only one million years ago, when the last of the great mammals, *homo sapiens,* appeared in the family of hominids. It is not yet clear whether with him Nature produced her masterpiece or just an unexpected freak, but what is sure is that this million years, or ten thousand centuries — a brief moment on the clock of evolution — sufficed for man to climb to stardom on Earth.

For much of the time, this new creature was struggling with other protagonists for a niche in the common habitat, so man's ascent was slow and faltering, helped by a few primitive tools. But then an epochal change eventually took place, just over 100 centuries ago, when man ceased to be merely a hunter and fruit gatherer and learned how to till the land. This cultural evolution triggered off profound transformations of all kinds not only in man's own condition but also in life at large on the planet. With more security and leisure, man undertook to record his mores and deeds; this was the start of what we call historical times. His tribes, up to then a few, loosely-linked assemblies accounting altogether for perhaps 2 or 3 million people, began to settle and numbers began to grow. Man's relationships with Nature changed, too, as he soon discovered that on many counts he could easily gain the upper hand. Thus it was that he subjugated or decimated many other species which stood in the way of his conquest of the world.

All these processes were boosted, quickened, and at the same time made more complex, by the industrial and technological revolutions that man somewhat heedlessly unleashed in the last two centuries, wave after wave. Though we are still unable to grasp the full depth and meaning of the ensuing changes as yet, ever new and more radical ones are in the offing. Even in the last couple of decades — a fleeting instant in the time-scale of man's history — unprecedented events have taken place, rendering all that is human oversized, precipitous, hectic and unpredictable. This accelerated change heralds a new sweeping mutation, fanned by the headlong advance of microelectronics and biological technologies, for which our generation is totally unprepared.

Recognizing the importance of these developments, The Club of Rome has been issuing warnings and stressing three concepts. The first basic concept is that of the *global problematique*. There are no longer separate economic, political or social problems which can be judged even remotely on their own terms and be dealt with individually, at leisure, one after the other. All problems intermesh and interact and tend to put out roots and ramifications across national or geographical boundaries. Humankind is thus faced by dynamic clusters of problems and must seek solutions no longer by the linear and sequential methods of yesteryear, but by the systemic approaches which it has to devise in order to coordinate its actions *vis-à-vis* the various parts of the problematique.

The second concept is subsumed in *The Limits to Growth** which launched the international debate on the human prospects on our finite planet. The rationale is that, as in all evidence there are biophysical, institutional, political and managerial limits and constraints to population and economic growth, a transition is inevitable from growth to a stable state of dynamic balances both within the human system and between this and the world ecosystems. Either humankind itself will learn to pilot the transition or this will be forced upon it by factors beyond its control, probably with great human suffering.

The third concept, the *predicament of humankind*, is a corollary of the previous two, for human society, grappling inordinately with an over-

---

*The first report to The Club of Rome, by Donella Meadows, Dennis Meadows, Jørgen Randers and William Behrens III, Universe Books, New York, 1972.

whelming tangle of problems and wrongly placing its faith in material growth, is in serious trouble. Despite amazing techno-scientific progress, the overall condition of society is worsening. The Club of Rome has indicated that enough facts and symptoms exist to show that this has actually occurred during the 60s and 70s. If our generations, who are fated to live at this hinge of history, let present trends continue unchecked, the advent of a dark period of decline, suffering and humiliation for our proud species is inevitable.

If on the contrary we act responsibly, the adverse tide can be turned and the human course again steered safely onwards. We must understand, however, that essentially we have two kinds of assets at our disposal and we must learn how to make good use of them. One, human intelligence, is within ourselves; the other is the global environment. Both derive from the original natural endowments of *homo sapiens* and of our pristine habitat, which our ancestors metamorphosed in a most profound manner during centuries and millennia past. At present both these assets are very badly utilized, or neglected, or even wasted for a variety of reasons, including ignorance, prejudice and miscalculation, yet both have a latent potential which can and must be deployed fundamentally to improve the human lot.

The Club of Rome has already taken a stance on the primary need to learn how to develop and use our prime asset, namely, our universal capacity for comprehension, vision and creativity and the moral energy that is innate in all human beings. With that of the sun, this is our most precious resource and, if properly groomed, is a self-renewing and self-reinforcing resource, indispensable for building a liveable and governable world. The first step towards creating awareness of the immense opportunities lying dormant within ourselves and of triggering off a world debate on how to make capital out of them was taken by the publication in 1979 of the report *No Limits to Learning: Bridging the Human Gap*.* The way of "learning" can and will be the way to shape a better future. UNESCO and a number of nations have already declared their intention of adopting it as a guideline for their activities during the 80s. Soon, another trail-blazing project, called *Forum Humanum*, will hopefully be launched with a view to mobilizing the greatest force ever for envisioning and forging a worthy future: the young.

*By James Botkin, Mircea Malitza, Mahdi Elmandjra, Pergamon Press, Oxford, 1979.

Dialogue on Wealth and Welfare is conceived in this general frame of ideas, the aim being to open up a road leading to a more insightful and appropriate understanding of goals and the learning processes. It focuses in a very broad sense on economics. It points out that the current paradigms of economics and the philosophy underpinning the notions of wealth, welfare and value derive from a cultural experience that originated in Europe a couple of centuries ago and was later adopted in the so-called developed countries. Whatever its merits, it can no longer offer orientation and support to the heterogeneous community of nations of our time, which, despite the growing global interdependences and the planetarization of problems, is characterized by a great diversity — and richness — of cultures and by profound cross-purposes. Human power, itself skyrocketing beyond the wildest expectations but, alas! spearheaded by the power of self-destruction, demands not only a fresh, diverse concept of ourselves and our world, and of our place and responsibility in it, but also a vision of our economy, as new and revolutionary as the Einstein cosmology was in comparison with the Newtonian concept.

This book tries to bring our economic thinking a step ahead in this direction. A few basic facts must be recognized. The world's ecological systems are being steadily degraded. Their condition, already seriously impaired, is going to become substantially worse before remedial action can be implemented on a large scale. Nature is being overexploited and wounded, and nobody has yet figured out what the evental consequences may be. However badly a scientific theory or assessment of the Earth "outer limits" and "life supporting capacity" may be needed, none exists, not even in outline.

Quite obviously, if society's reckless race towards further expansion remains in the present limbo of unknowingness and indifference, the result cannot but be disastrous. A radical change of outlook approach and behaviour is imperative. Only by a comprehensive assessment of the ensemble of human needs and demands over a long-period — well beyond our generations — will it be possible to ensure the intelligent combination, use and conservation of whatever resources are available. It is manifestly evident that, without a rigorous global management of resources, the needs of an ever more demanding multi-billion society can never be satisfied.

These tenets of conservation and good management concur with ethical principles whereby the Earth's natural endownment, the "common heritage of humankind" of which we hear so much, is held as something for which each generation is a trustee for those to come and only a *pro tempore* or income beneficiary.

All this forms, or rather should form, the very nucleus of a real "new economics". The most important point dealt with in this report to The Club of Rome is the recognition of the natural environment in "economic" terms. It says that a synthesis between economy and ecology is needed; that the two are not separable; that there cannot be wealth in an ecologically unsound world; and that the strategies for wealth production should be centred around this Earth endowment — which it calls "dowry and patrimony".

The whole question of value is also refocused — around two notions. Value is what humankind can and does produce — which means that value can also be negative, and this is indeed the case when destruction is the outcome of human activity, however scientific this might be and however much it might add to the GNP.

The other notion is that this production can and does usually take place both inside the "monetarized" system (which is economic's conventional, if not exclusive, field of enquiry) but as well outside it. Using these two notions, a new discipline, concerned with optimizing value, can be created. Moving from the restrictive interpretation of value given by current economics to that of utilization value, and shifting the accent on life cycle of products and services, it again puts man — with his needs and wants and his potential for satisfying them — exactly where he belongs, in the centre of the picture.

Capital requirements of the future world will be immense, and capital formation difficult and uncertain, but it is human capital which must first be formed. As we are now beginning to perceive, monetary capital without adequate human development will produce little or nothing and may even be counterproductive. As this report stresses, capital (in the classical sense) is *per se* nothing more than a tool to mobilize human action, and is productively usable only in so far as it helps to organize human endeavour better. Which brings us back to the imperative of learning, of apprehending how to control the direction of our course in a world which is showing an increasingly more disastrous tendency to get out of hand.

Dialogue on Wealth and Welfare is itself a tool — a tool to update and uplift our understanding of things economic in the new planetary and ecological setup which is our new habitat, so that we may have a reasonable chance to extricate ourselves from the present predicament and then organize a better quality of life for us and our successors.

AURELIO PECCEI

Contents

3 Dossier for an Analysis of the Foundations of Wealth: Dowry and Patrimony (D & P) and Capital   168

4 Dossier for an Analysis of the Monetarized Accumulation of Dowry and Patrimony (D & P): Some Issues in World Capital Formation and Needs **248**

Introduction

"Our simple problems often grew
to mysteries we fumbled over
because of lines we nimbly drew
and later neatly stumbled over."

(Piet Hein, Denmark)

"When a problem resists us in
spite of great research efforts,
we must doubt about its major
assumptions. Imagination is then
more important than knowledge."

(Albert Einstein)

The initial stimulus for this report came from a phrase in a discussion with Aurelio Peccei in Geneva. "Imagine our planet in twenty or thirty years from now, when total population will be about 7 billion people. All these people will need houses, food, education: what an immense effort of ingenuity and investment will be needed."

Yes, the potential "demand" for investments needed to face this challenge is clearly enormous. And even today, with the 4 billion population mark having been passed only a few years ago, we are still far from having overcome poverty and organized a satisfactory world plan for adequate investment.

The Quest of Carl Madden

But investment of what and investment for what? Is it just a problem of having enough money? And even if enough money is available, will something additional be required? It was in Spring 1978, during a luncheon in

Washington with Carl Madden, lasting almost three hours, that the first basic ideas for this report were structured, and in particular those which now appear under Chapter 2. This was a one-and-only encounter: I had never met him before and he died suddenly a few months later.

I would like here to express my gratitude to his memory and my profound regret: had he survived, this report would have been better. In fact, I might quote here what he, himself, wrote in 1976 for the Joint Economic Committee of the Congress of the United States on the very subject of "Capital formation: an alternative view"[1], and which constitutes the most pertinent lead-in to the key points of this report.

"Debate about capital requirements, in important part, turns on a deeper question of the possibility and desire for economic growth which affects growth problems, prospects and patterns."

The idea that growth is merely as "an increase of output per head of population" is absurdly too simplistic. Both logic and empirical evidence suggest a new concept.

"The evidence supports the hypothesis that, despite the complex causation of growth, the advance of science was the great innovation propelling the astonishing growth records of the last two centuries. However, economists have neglected study of the impact of science. Now, evidence abounds that science itself in the twentieth century is undergoing a revolution. Its form is to supplant earlier basic scientific assumptions about the nature of time-space, human life, and its origins, the nature of organisms, the structure of matter—energy configurations, the structure of the universe."

Carl Madden was ready for what Prigogine calls the new encounter or reconciliation of the "two cultures" (identified by the "natural sciences" on the one side and by the "human sciences" on the other).* In fact . . .

"The central concepts of twentieth-century science do not interpret reality as collections of material objects independently and indentically existing in absolute time or simply located in space. Instead, reality is

---

[1] Madden, Carl H.: "Towards a New Concept of Growth: Capital Needs of a Post-Industrial Society", Studies of the Joint Economic Committee, Congress of the United States, Washington, 1976.

*See Prigogine, I. and Stengers, I.: *La Nouvelle Alliance*, (The New Alliance), Paris, 1979.

seen as patterns and configurations of wholes, of systems whose parts can exist and be identified only in relation to the whole . . ."

"Economic evolution is hardly a subject fit for conventional discussion. Apart from a small handful of intellectual giants, economics remains dominated in conventional thought and study by mechanistic ideas that are analogies to eighteenth-century physics and mathematics. They depict activity in terms of mechanistic balancing of forces, of "equilibrium states" of self-identical systems. Indeed, the logic of "limits to growth" models itself suffers from difficulties precisely associated in other sciences with the logical fallacies that have eventuated in anomalies, in observed behaviour inexplicable in terms of the pre-twentieth-century theories or models of behaviour."

It is clear that: "The twentieth-century revolution in science is a revolt against the earlier world view of René Descartes". In fact "To envisage wealth as a growing pile of self-identical objects affixed in given configurations as through sub-periods of time and space may be adequate for some measurement purposes. It is utterly misleading in understanding what wealth is, how wealth has been created and how wealth will be created in the future" . . . "Basic economic concepts need to change in content . . . Our concepts of wealth, income, cost, and productivity are all in for changes in content. . . . It is not self-evident that our present ideas of fundamental economic inputs — capital, labour, land and management — are much more astute than the Greek view of the basic elements as earth, air, fire and water."

And finally, concerning investment: "Changes in the structure of investment, both public and private, are likely to be as radical, if not more so, in coming years than in the past two centuries. Public policy, therefore, which subsidizes existing or traditional industrial investment through a mistaken understanding of growth processes will inhibit productivity gains and retard the growth of wealth."

"Capital availability is perhaps the major constraint on the rate at which the new goals of the post-industrial world can be reached. These include: achieving an adequate standard of living for people throughout the world; providing useful and meaningful work opportunities; protecting the earth's natural capital through a safe and clean environment; developing new and renewable sources of energy; and conserving scarce materials."

"Lacking the right kind of capital capacity, we have to face up now to the need for changes in the pattern of investment in the next decade and beyond."

And the basic source of capital, for Carl Madden, was "knowledge and enterprise."

The Structure of the Report

Which capital requirements for *what*, then?

This report does not try to make an original contribution aimed at quantifying the world's financial capital needs: a general answer — within the framework of conventional economic theory — is already given and is continuously being given by many important economic studies made and published by private and public institutions everywhere. Some of their results are summarized and commented upon here. Furthermore, much more detailed studies would be necessary to recommend specific action, case by case, country by country. Some of the main financial problems are also summarized in this Report, mainly in Chapter 4: here again a wealth of expertise and knowledge is available around the world. At this stage of the research, it was essential to try and pin-point at least the key issues. However, the main goal of this report is to undertake an introductory analysis to provide answers for more basic questions, such as:

— What is real growth? What is economic value? and What is wealth and welfare?

— Under *which conditions* does investment produce real wealth? and *Which type* of investment?

Asking such questions seems essential since many of the basic assumptions about what should be done to increase wealth and welfare do not apply as they did in the past: more investment *does not* necessarily lead to more employment and or more wealth; more unemployment does not necessarily lead to less inflation; more solvable demand does not necessarily lead to increased availability of real wealth and enhanced welfare.

A better understanding of the main economic variables (and their redefinition) and of their interrelationship with non economic factors may help in a better allocation of the world's resources. In fact, a basic hypothesis of this report is that contradictions and limits of modern economic life are not such because of reality, but because of the distorted ways in which this reality is perceived. Its main goal is, in fact, a "return to reality", or — otherwise expressed — comprehension of economic facts in such a way that it will be possible to act with greater confidence. Nevertheless, it should also be remembered that there is always an element of dream or even of utopia in any attempt to apprehend reality.

As in the natural sciences, any important change in the time and space dimensions is a change in quality as well as in quantity. As far as time is concerned: the Industrial Revolution, which started in Europe in the eighteenth century, is losing most of its traditional connotations, be they cultural, philosophical or technical. The "Western" way of thinking, its "model" of the economy have been moulded by this reality. A new problem complex now requires a new model.

As far as space is concerned: the world is now less and less the extension of a one-sided, "universal" (essentially eurocentric), culture or power. It is a global, interreacting system which will inevitably produce a new culture and — by consequence — a new economics.

Within such a perspective, this report cannot be but "introductory": as Karl Popper would say, it is there to be "falsified", to be proved inadequate and even wrong by better insights and evidence and by deeper study. Its objective is to reopen the debate in regards to the assumptions underlying the conventional perspectives of economic analysis.

One of the main difficulties in drafting this report, was to find a compromise between the need to be succinct and comprehensive and, at the same time offer an analysis which lends itself to operable guidelines, whilst necessarily embracing so many fields.

In order to highlight certain ideas and problems, the first Chapter is presented in the form of a dialogue, supplemented by a series of graphs designed to provide a sort of visual glossary.

This introductory dialogue thus constitutes a lead-in to the main ideas which are then analyzed more deeply in each of the three following "dossiers"; and, in this way, it tries to at least stimulate the formulation of better questions in the human quest for wealth and welfare.

The first "dossier" (Chapter 2) aims at a review of the major factors which made the Industrial Revolution a success: it scans rapidly the cultural and philosophical underpinnings which provided the vision for action; the political and social structure which provided the historical basis for the development of industrialization, and the science and technology which provided the specific tools. The notion of value and its definitions are central to this analysis. An attempt is made to formulate a new concept of value — as a reference and measurement tool for defining wealth — which corresponds to the transition of the economic system from the Industrial Revolution into the post-industrial and planetary era. The role of technology, and, in particular, the phenomenon of the diminishing returns of technology, is proposed as being essential in explaining this transition.

The second "dossier" (Chapter 3) proposes a discussion of the foundations of the wealth of nations today: the key element is the notion of "Dowry and Patrimony" (D & P), defined as the stock of natural, biological, cultural and monetarized resources that are available to us and constitute our means of survival and our tool for the enjoyment of life. The concept of "capital" is integrated and interrelated to that of D & P. It is necessary to insist on the fact that the "monetarized" economy and capital form together a system which is not separate, in the Cartesian way, from the rest of non-monetarized production activities. It follows that mobilizing resources for the production of real values (or utilization values) is something different than simply investing on the basis of an exclusively monetarized analysis of the economy: the notion of value deducted is proposed as a means of measuring those investments which increase *monetarized* income, but do not increase *real* wealth. This notion of value deducted is probably the most significant theoretical tool which allows the much sought-after integration of (non-market) use values with exchange values. It is also essential in the construction of the notion of "Dowry and Patrimony" (D & P).

The third "dossier" (Chapter 4) then returns to the monetarized "subsystem" of "D & P" — i.e. "capital" — and tries to elaborate on the major problems in monetary capital needs, formation and transfer in the world today. Subjects are discussed here which are more familiar to the realm of current economic analysis. The discussion proposed in the previous "dossiers" and "dialogue" is thus to be used as a reference for organizing optimum allocation of the "monetarized D & P", or capital, with a view to facing up to the tremendous task of meeting the needs of a rapidly growing world population.

The Report in a Nutshell

In order to resume what this report is all about, the comment received from one of the readers and commentators* of the draft report, is reproduced in full, below.

"We expect the world's population to increase by at least 50% — to around six billion persons — in the next 20 years. If their requirements for capital are looked at from the conventional point of view of industrial growth, there is likely to be a considerable shortfall; with the current changes in the amounts, types and prices of different forms of energy, it appears even less likely that sufficient capital (savings) will be available for many of the developing and any of the poorest countries; nor will adequate supplies of energy be forthcoming, if these countries try to follow the path of industrial growth of the Western nations. This has forced us to reconsider what the meaning of savings and capital requirements should be for societies of different types. When this is done, it turns out that the Western nations have followed a very specific line of development, that of the monetarized economy. As its name suggests, the aim is to increase economic efficiency through specialization of tasks. Each such specialization involves the transfer of a human activity previously carried out without pay but with social and cultural obligation — in what we term the non-monetarized economy — to a paid activity in the monetarized economy, thus increasing its measure, the GNP. No society in the Western world has, however, ever succeeded in completely eliminating the informal or non-monetarized part of its economy. For example, in Canada the value of the contribution of housewives' work has been estimated to be one third of the GNP when costed at the level of unskilled (sic!) labour."

"Thus, the future capital requirements of any society cannot be understood unless one considers both the total of the monetarized and the non-monetarized sectors, which we term 'dowry and patrimony'; and the rest

*Simmonds W. H. C.: National Research Council of Canada, Ottawa, Canada.

of this book is devoted to the future of different societies in the world as seen in those terms. It will be obvious to the reader even at this stage that, if the patrimony of the western nations is greater than their GNP, how much more true this is for the developing, etc. nations. Years ago, Gunnar Myrdal pointed out the absurdity of using GNP in relation to Third World countries with their large, non-monetary, agricultural sectors. His criticism is even more valid today, but the onus is on us, not to criticize the omission, but to find ways of bringing in and beginning to appreciate (Sir Geoffrey Vickers' useful phrase) the value and impact of the non-monetary as well as the monetarized sectors of each economy. The reasons are very clear since it is probable that only by understanding and expanding the non-monetarized sector can such a sudden expansion of the world's population be successfully coped with. This is not to devalue or de-emphasize the importance of conventional economic growth in the industrial and technological areas, but rather to realize that this kind of growth must match and complement similar growth in the non-monetary parts of the economy, especially in the LDCs. The curtain of silence around unpaid activities must be drawn back and their real value appreciated, not only in economic terms but in their contribution to human satisfaction, social stability and cultural survival. It is our dowry and patrimony, not a GNP, which must be 'optimized' and 'satisfice' us."

List of Contributors

The following have contributed to this report:
*— with written texts which have been integrated totally or partially in the report**

- Henri LOUBERGE — Economist, Geneva — Chapter 4, paragraph 3

- Anders MUNK — Biologist, Copenhagen — Chapter 3, paragraph 1

- Patrick TEZIER — Sociologist, Lausanne — Chapter 3, paragraph 1—3

- Robert TRIFFIN — Financial Economist, Louvain — Yale — Chapter 4, paragraph 3

— with comments, criticisms and editorial suggestions on the intermediary drafts

- Archie BAHM — Philosopher, Albuquerque
- Agustin BLANCO-BAZAN — Social Scientist, Buenos-Aires/London
- Gerhart BRUCKMANN — Social Scientist, Vienna
- Bernard FORTIN — Philosopher, Geneva
- Bas de GAAY FORTMAN — Economist, The Hague
- Hazel HENDERSON — Futurologist, Gainesville, Florida
- Felipe HERRERA — Economist, Rio de Janeiro

*The author accepts full responsibility for the interpretation, erroneous presentation and use or possible misuse of all contributions received. As stated in the Introduction, special gratitude is owed to the late Carl MADDEN (Economist, Washington) for his decisive contribution at the very first planning stage of the report.

- Ranjit KUMAR — Third World Training Expert & Economist, Don Mills, Ontario

- Giuseppe LONGO — Information Theorist, Trieste
- Pentti MALASKA — Economist, Turku
- Donald MICHAEL — Psychologist & Urban Planner, San Francisco

- Firmin OULES — Economist (fiscal policy), Lausanne
- Howard PERLMUTTER — Social Architect, Philadelphia
- Michel de PERROT — Physicist, Geneva
- Eduard PESTEL — Science Minister, Hannover
- Juan RADA — Social Scientist, Santiago de Chili/ Geneva

- John M. RICHARDSON — Applied Systems Analyst, Washington

- Manfred SIEBKER — Physicist/Ecologist, Brussels
- Clive SIMMONDS — Industrial Economics Analyst, Ottawa
- Walter STAHEL — Industrial Economist, Geneva
- Dan TOLKOWSKY — Business Executive, Tel-Aviv
- André VAN DAM — Planning Economist, Buenos Aires

— *by organizing a seminar or a session at which this report has been presented during its preparatory phase*
  - The Tenth Anniversary Assembly of the Club of Rome (Rome, Accademia dei Lincei, July 1978).
  - The Spanish Chapter of the Club of Rome (Granada and Madrid, October 1978).
  - The International Conference of the Club of Rome (Berlin, October 1979).
  - The U.S. Chapter of the Club of Rome (New York, November 1979).
  - The Association "Futuribles" (Paris, November 1979).
  - The World Social Prospects Study Association (Dakar, January 1980).
  - The European Management Forum (Davos, February 1980).

— *Special acknowledgement is also due to*
  - The Graduate Institute of European Studies, University of Geneva

which, since 1971, has made it possible to organize a seminar on subjects closely linked to this report.

- The International Association for Insurance Economics Research, Geneva which has provided the opportunity of benefiting from its research programmes on risk, uncertainty and vulnerability in the present phase of economic development.
- Our grateful appreciation is extended to Susanne Hagemann and David Reed for their contribution in the tremendous task of editorial and linguistic revision, and to Mrs Rita Robadey who has borne the secretarial and typing burden.

CHAPTER 1

Dialogue on Wealth and Welfare

1.1. How to get More from Less — Economics and Industrialization

I. Currently in the world, there are about 600 to 800 million people who are absolutely poor. By the year 2000, the world's total population will be between 6 and 7 billion people: low- and middle-income developing countries will, by then, have a population of about 3.5 billion[1].

   This makes a lot of people who need, and will need more and more shelter, food, health care, education: in other words, the demand for freedom to live a human life is great and is increasing enormously. The world's major problem today and for the coming years is clearly to stimulate economic growth in order to provide as much wealth and welfare as possible for all. Don't you agree?

Y. I would formulate the problem differently: the main issue is to increase wealth and welfare as much as possible and for as many people as possible. But first, we must always be sure to apply a method — consistent with the goals of economists — by which we are certain to get more from less.

I. Isn't it the same thing as saying that we must stimulate economic growth everywhere and increase the Gross National Product (GNP) rates as much as possible?

Y. Not at all. In some cases — in more and more cases — so-called economic growth does not produce real growth in wealth and welfare. It sometimes even leads to situations in which one gets less for more.

[1] World Bank: Annual Report, Washington, 1978. To introduce a deeper discussion on various issues associated with the demographic dilemma, see Tapinos G. and Piotrow P. T.: *Six Billion People*, 1980s project — Council of Foreign Relations, New York, 1978.

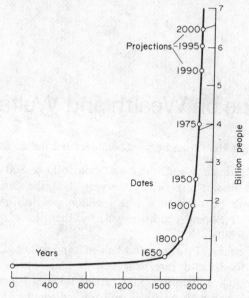

FIG. 1.1. *World Population Growth*

I.   Are you serious? This is playing with words. Are you going to try and tell me that economic growth, industrialization and the Industrial Revolution have not brought an immense increase in wealth and welfare to human-kind, which would otherwise have been impossible to achieve? You should just compare the living conditions of the average people in most of the industrialized countries today with those of, say, 50, 100 or even 150 years ago. If you make such comparisons honestly, you can only wish for the whole world to industrialize as quickly as possible and for everybody to continue or even accelerate growth as much as possible. Of course, I know what you will say: the process of industrialization cannot take place without some problems of adaptation and some negative side-effects, such as pollution. But the overall outcome of industrialization, and the economic growth it has produced, has been overwhelmingly positive in the production of wealth and welfare. You are certainly not going to deny that. . . .

Y.   It is obvious that two centuries of Industrial Revolution have con-

TABLE 1.1. *Poverty in the World in 1976*

Undernourished (i.e. below suggested calorie protein levels)	570 Million
Adults illiterate	800 Million
Children not enrolled in school	250 Million
With no access to effective medical care	1,500 Million
With less than $90.00 income per year	1,300 Million
With life expectancy below 60 years	1,700 Million
With inadequate housing	1,030 Million

Source: Basic Human Needs: A Framework for action by John McHale and Magda Cordell McHale.

tributed largely to the wealth and welfare of at least a part of the world's nations. It is also natural that most other countries aspire to reach a similar level of wealth: their apparently limited strategy is then essentially one of catching up, in one way or the other, with what is commonly presented as the great wealth and welfare achievements of the highly industrialized nations. The level of TV-set or automobile ownership, the number of miles travelled during holidays and the luxurious consumption of food products are all presented as the true symbol of achievement and wealth without their real cost being fully realized.

I.   I know what is coming now. You are now going to say that people do not like taking holidays (which were, any way, impossible 50 years ago), or that they dislike automobiles, or that they buy and eat sophisticated foodstuffs only because they are forced to do so by publicity.

Y.   Not really. However, one might remark that this increased consumption of goods and services in the privileged regions of the world, entails increasingly high costs for the present and for the future. These costs tend to have a greater and greater negative impact on the overall level of real wealth and welfare even for those directly consuming the goods and services in question.

I do not accept that the activity normally identified with economic growth does necessarily produce *under all circumstances,* a net addition to wealth and welfare. In certain cases, it will even produce a net real reduction in wealth and welfare.

I. It is obviously contradictory to say that economic growth can diminish wealth and welfare: economic growth means growth of wealth, even if − I admit − in some cases the indicators of wealth, and in particular the level of GNP, may be no more than an approximation.

Y. Very often the GNP is much less than a significant approximation. An increase in GNP does not necessarily represent an increase in welfare, because it is only one of the constituents of welfare and its real effects has to be measured only after verification that its increase has not diminished other sources of welfare.

I. Your point looks like a verbal sleight-of-hand. GNP is an economic indicator and economics is about welfare, or − more specifically − economics is concerned mainly about utilizing resources in order to satisfy human needs in the best possible way. If important elements of wealth and welfare are left out as you assert, they can be "internalized", which means that they will sooner or later be taken into account. Fundamentally, then, economics is the science of the Wealth of Nations.

Y. Here is where we diverge. Economics, as it has developed, is not the science of wealth (by the way, I would prefer to call it discipline, rather than science). Economics is the discipline of the industrialization process and specifically of the Industrial Revolution, which started in Europe more than two centuries ago.

I. But the Industrial Revolution started precisely as a means to increase wealth. Adam Smith's *The Wealth of Nations* is the basic book in the history of economics and was published as long ago as 1776.

Y. Exactly. The Industrial Revolution has been a major tool in the process of increasing, at least, material wealth. Until now, the identifi-

cation of increasing wealth with industrialization has proved acceptable, because, in most cases, it has proved correct.

However, it is interesting today to ponder the fact that economics,
as a new, independent discipline, really took off in the climate that
reigned at the beginning of the Industrial Revolution. In practice,
economics has been the discipline of industrialization; it could be
viewed as dealing with the global problem of wealth in so far as
industrialization was its prime mover. Internalization has never been
complete and, in the final analysis, was limited to priced goods.

I. I agree that the intellectual climate of the Industrial Revolution was
the cradle for modern economics as an independent and significant
"social science". However, to identify economics with the industrialization process is incorrect: from Adam Smith to Gary Becker[1], via
Alfred Marshall[2], not to talk of Karl Marx, economic thinking has
always expressed the ambition to analyze all the practical, economic
activities of life. Marshall, in the first pages of his major book, went so
far as to state that human life has only two basic dimensions: spiritual
life which is the domain of religion; and practical, material life which
is the domain of economics. Becker, today, is studying 'economic'
behaviour in fields which go far beyond what seems to be your restricted view of economics.

Y. I am conscious of these efforts and I consider them a stimulating
effort to expand the domain of economics. But it is therefore even
more important to verify what I say, i.e. the fact that the basic
paradigms or rules of economics are derived essentially from the
experience of the industrial mode of production[3] : as such, they put
clear limits to the ability of current conventional economics, even
when "expanded"[4], to embrace the whole problem complex of
wealth, in a situation where the industrialization process is not, or is
no longer, the only or the absolute priority for all ways and means of
wealth formation.

[1] Becker, Gary: *The Economic Approach to Human Behaviour,* Chicago, 1976.
[2] Marshall, Alfred: *Principles of Economics,* 1890, reprint, London, 1949.
[3] Hazel Henderson comes to the conclusion that "economics" being the offspring
of the industrial revolution, the new post-industrial era means also "The end of
economics" (see *Creating Alternative Futures,* New York, 1978).
[4] McKenzie, Richard B.: The Non-Rational Domain and the Limits of Economic
Analysis, *Southern Economic Journal,* Vol. 46 (1), July 1979, 145–157.

1.2. The Limits of Investment – when one gets less from more

I. I have the impression that our discussion is getting too philosophical. Our problem is to find the best way to allocate resources and therefore to invest: no economist will ever pretend that *any* investment is good. There must be, and there is selection.

Y. Yes, but by which criteria is this process of investment selection carried out? I propose that we examine a specific case: investment to increase fish production. You can see in the following graph the simulated analysis of fisheries exploitation.

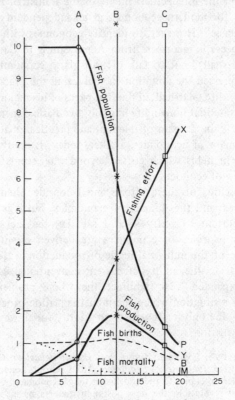

FIG. 1.2. *Simulation of Fisheries Exploitation*

From: Giarini, O., Loubergé, H. and Schwamm, H.: *L'Europe et les Ressources de la Mer,* Editions Georgi, St. Saphorin, Switzerland, 1977, p. 56.

Up to the situation A . . .

I.   . . . the first vertical line, starting from the left . . .

Y.   . . . yes; you will see that by increasing the level of effort (man hours, better tools) in fishing, fish production increases although at a slightly slower rate. It is the normal demonstration of the law of diminishing returns: when you put two people instead of one to do a job, they will do it faster and better (all other things being equal), but not quite really twice as fast or better than one. When you run 400 meters, you are not capable of covering the distance in just twice the time required for 200 meters; it will take a little *more* than twice the time.

I.   However, if you use a bicycle and then a car, you will do it faster and faster.

Y.   Yes! However, you have introduced two stages of technological advance, each of which entails a larger and larger investment. To run you do not even need a pair of shoes. A bicycle will need a given level of investment and a car an even larger one.

I.   And after you have attained the maximum speed possible with the car, you will have to move on to an aeroplane to improve your performance, although — I admit — you cannot *use* for practical purposes an airplane to rapidly cover the 200 meters between two given points.

Y.   The problem is also that the improvement in the final results might not be as expected. Let's go back to our fisheries: at point A, we can observe a sharp increase in the fishing effort and investment (indicated by the curve X), so that fish production (curve Y) increases until point B — the second vertical line is reached. At this level of investment, *total* fish production start diminishing and additional investment leads to catastrophe: to point C and even further.

The reason is that a fundamental equilibrium has been upset: the fish catch obviously depends on the total amount of fish available in the seas and lakes (the fish population). The more "efficient" the fishing process the more it will tend to destroy the total fish population. Worse still, the more the fish catch tends to diminish, the more advanced technology and investment will be used to maintain high levels of production for as long as possible.

I.   Catastrophe is not inevitable: investment in new fishing technology will prove less and less productive and therefore, at some point, additional investment will be halted. Normal, sound economic analysis will help a return to equilibrium.

In addition, we can intervene by further research and by the adoption of international agreements on measures to restore the optimal fish population.

Y. Nevertheless, repopulating seas and lakes will — one way or another — entail additional costs and, therefore, diminish *ex-post* the real yield of the total investment effort. Secondly, at the point at which the situation becomes acute, considerable investment will already have been made to improve fish catches and the capital equipment will continue to be used at least until total costs have been amortized. Thirdly, when normal investment starts to have a low or negative yield, pressure will be exerted for the allocation of subsidies (e.g. from the State) to maintain the fish catch as high as possible.

Fourthly, in all the investment calculations, the elimination of "inefficient" and traditional fish production is not taken into the calculations: a large part of this scattered production for local and for the fisherman's own consumption is not even accounted for. The displaced fishermen, in the best of cases, are now taken care of by unemployment or retraining programmes.

I. However, when all is said and done, our example of fisheries is a special case of free resources which are internationally distributed and where activity is largely uncontrollable. This means that problems in this area are largely of a political nature.

Y. Every economic problem is, to some degree, conditioned by political situations and constraints, and the example of fisheries is fully representative of many free goods such as air, water, land, etc. which contribute to welfare and which are, so often, destroyed by industrialization.

I. Such goods do not disappear. The outcome is that they just become scarce: they are therefore priced and have a defined value. The price mechanism is the guarantee that they exist in an optimal quantity.

Y. Here lies the major contradiction: the system which started out to produce more in order to add to wealth, is then, in such cases, simply producing more scarcities. Goods which have become scarce have *less* value in terms of real wealth, than when they were in virtually unlimited supply.

I.   But as something becomes scarcer, its price increases and, in this way, scarce goods or resources are conserved. "Internalizing" costs is a normal economic way of solving our problems.

Y.   Yes, making something very expensive is a way of protecting it. But the traditional economic system does not help in this degradation process that commences when free goods start being destroyed and continues on until they are priced. Their real *value* is not recognized by definition.

I.   It can be recognized, for instance, via the introduction of a fiscal policy which can help conserve free goods in instances where the market system would not react quickly enough.

Y.   Something like this can and is done. However, we still lack a way of accounting for values which are not priced, and we still continue to talk of "added" value in cases where the value is, in fact, "deducted" — it measures then essentially induced scarcity. As far as fiscal policy is concerned, when an equilibrium system (e.g. fisheries) is at, or reaches such a level of complexity, there is less and less likelihood that costs will really be borne by their originators.

The real problem is to promote a situation in which investment is halted before point B on the graph is reached. In fact, there comes a point somewhere between A and B (not to speak of the area beyond point B in which world fisheries had apparently already penetrated by 1970) where the process of getting less from more actually starts.

I.   In my view, the problem is essentially one of the poor functioning or organization of a market system which impedes the normal internalization process (i.e. making scarce resources more expensive). This is particularly true for fisheries.

Y.   I continue to believe what you say is important but secondary. The main problem is that: the *original* fish population was never accounted for as an economic value; its decrease or destruction is not accounted for as an economic cost; the effort of the simple fisherman producing for his own or for local needs is also of no economic value. While the basic resource — the fish population — is infinite or is not in decline, there is no problem in increasing *production* by any means and in making all forms of investment.

The fundamental problem is that the possibility of getting less from more is not only a theoretical perspective, but more and more a verifiable fact, for fisheries as well as for many other sectors.

1.3. Capital for Investment

I. In generalizing the example of fisheries to world development as a
    whole, I have the impression that we are back again to the first
    report to the Club of Rome, and the absolute limits of growth!

Y. I hope that, after our discussion, we will be somewhat further
    advanced.

I. Towards disaster?

Y. No, towards a better understanding of the limits and capabilities of
    our economic tools, the world's capital, dowry and patrimony, and of
    science and technology.

I. Frankly, it seems rather difficult to offer hope by saying that our
    world is limited. This is, in any case, a fallacy: the price mechanism
    solves the problem. In fact, when a resource becomes more scarce, its
    price increases, its use diminishes and investment is made in substitute
    products. This is elementary economics. We also know that science
    and technology — which provide new substitute products — have
    never been so powerful as they are today; and I still believe in human
    capability and ingenuity.

Y. Clearly, the real point is that we can have access to more only if we
    increase our knowledge of how to organize science, technology and
    human society itself. Knowledge and science are not scarce in absolute
    terms, but they are built up through a long and difficult accumulation
    process. The trouble with your "elementary economics", is that no
    price mechanism can really modify this process and produce new
    fundamental discoveries and inventions as soon as they are "needed",
    no matter what price is set for scarce products.* They cannot just be
    conjured up. If hope in our modern world is based on the concept
    that science and technology can work wonders, it means that super-
    stition has also been "modernized": and this is the real road to
    disaster.

I. Obviously, science is and must be separate from superstition. But we
    are once again returning to a philosophical discussion. The real
    priority is a practical one, namely of developing real wealth and of
    selecting investments well.

---

*For an illustration of this point see *Mankind at the Turning Point,* by M. Hesarovic
and E. Pestel, New York, 1974 (Second Report to the Club of Rome).

Y. I agree that science and technology *must* be separated from superstition. However, in practice, they are very often not separated: only too often the image of science is the image of a *belief* in human "supernatural" power over things that are not really understood.

I. But what has this to do with investment and growth?

Y. A great deal, because if the image of science and technology is often such that it promotes the belief that "all technical problems" will be overcome, as you also imply, then all investment policies, in fact any economic policy, will be conducted under the assumption that technology will always adapt to economic requirements. All you have to do then is to organize "demand", "investment", and "saving": science and technology "will necessarily follow", because they are so "powerful".

I. Historical evidence is against you: economic science has developed, until very recently, without feeling obliged to study directly the mechanisms of science and technology. And in most cases it has worked.

Y. Historical evidence is the other way around: from almost the beginning of the Industrial Revolution until the last two or three decades, the mechanisms and progress of science and technology were *underestimated*. Their level of development and their accumulated potential were such that this "factor of production" could be assumed as expandable at will. Demand pressure has been, then, the essential stimulus for every new cycle and development of the Industrial Revolution. The last great period of accelerated growth was the period in which the total available potential was put into action. We are now in a period where the potential of science and technology, in economic and other terms, is *overestimated*.

I. This is something that has to be proved and is not what we normally perceive when we read about developments in electronics, space research, biology, and dozens of other fields. You seem to be denying the evidence.

Y. I say it again. The question is not to deny the enormous efforts and achievements of science and research in general. The problem is that the "image" of science and technology has gone further than the reality: this is, in any case, counterproductive for science itself. Moreover, from an economic point of view, it shows that an economic analysis of the scientific and technological process is badly needed and must be integrated into general economic thinking and theory. It is a precondition for learning about supply elasticity.

I.   You propose then to consider, when deciding investment policies, the constraints imposed by the limitations of technological factors. This is common practice and I do not feel that anybody will readily invest without having adequate knowledge of the technology into which he is putting his money.

Y.   Of course, the engineer is normally aware of the processes in his field that are tried and tested but this has not prevented numerous ill-conceived investments. In addition, a number of large companies have made disastrous investments in new fields of technology precisely because they overestimated their own research and development capabilities. The further we move from those actually and directly involved in production and development work towards the public and private institutions which do "economic planning", the greater becomes the influence of "ideas" or of "images". The engineer who has to set up a textile mill, forsakes ideas and theories when they do not fit the functional needs of a weaving loom or of a spinning frame. However, when going from the particular to the general, much more time and effort are required to simply verify that a general scheme, theory or idea does not work. And even when this becomes evident, there is always the possibility that the undesired or unexpected results are due to "external factors" which are "unforeseeable", "uncontrollable" and/or "transient". This is why adaptation of economic theory to reality seems so difficult today.

I.   We all know how many years it took Maynard Keynes to get his ideas accepted during the great depression of 1929. If those ideas had been adopted earlier, much suffering and economic waste would have been avoided.

Y.   Yes. However, the trouble is that Keynesian policies could then benefit from considerable accumulated and underestimated technology. The case today is quite different; but we still normally approach the problem of world capital requirements as if the generation and expansion of wealth were determined essentially, not to say exclusively, by growth in national income which has to grow to permit more investment which will, in turn, permit further growth in the national income, and so on. Just look, for instance, at the following table (p. 14).

I. All these studies simply show that the essential method of stimulating development is to accelerate capital formation. Moreover, it is obvious that the present economic crisis in the developed world is due essentially to a lack of investment. Only a voluntarist policy aimed at encouraging savings and investment would permit growth rate to rise, absorb unemployment and, finally, achieve a higher level of wealth. I hope you don't deny the importance of stimulating savings and increasing capital investment.

Y. Of course not, provided one is producing *real* wealth and provided one is really increasing productive and useful employment. Even these forecasts are valuable as a very rough help when starting to discuss the problems of wealth generation. They do give a rough quantitative estimate of the problem, but they also can be misleading. My point is that one needs specific and usable criteria to organize investments in such a way as to produce "more". And in order to find such criteria we must inevitably revise the notion of economic value.

I. Value and Capital are basic notions in economics. But before we get deeper on this point I would like to comment on Hamilcar Herrera's forecasts on capital requirements in Table 1.2. One thing which does not figure in this table is that his study has also assumed that there could be a period of diminishing returns of technology.

Y. Yes. He further assumes that if technology productivity decreases, even more capital will be necessary. Here lies a basic misunderstanding. Capital investment needs to increase faster or at least in proportion to the increase of national income (or to total company sales), particularly at a time of important and exploitable technological advances which produce increasing returns. Diminishing returns of technology mean diminishing returns on capital, less capital needs. Here, by the way, we have one basic explanation why capital investment is lagging behind, particularly in the developed countries.

I. In fact, many economic studies show how in the seventies, the interest rates of countries such as the United States, Japan, Federal Republic of Germany, France, and the United Kingdom were very low in real terms. In all cases, in 1976 for example, the real rate of interest after

TABLE 1.2. *World Capital Requirements as Presented in Various Studies*

Study	Goal	Means	Investment
HERRERA/ A WORLD FOR ALL	Satisfy world basic needs in the year 2000.	Increase GNP growth rate of developing countries to 10–12% per year and of developed countries to 4–6% per year (Bariloche Model).	Increase to about 25% of GNP for dev. countries. Keep between 12 and 29% in developing countries, in inverse proportion to technological advances.
UNIDO	Achieve the Lima Target (the developing countries' share of world industrial production should be increased to 25% by the year 2000).	Increase manufacturing investments by 13% per year in developing countries.	Manufacturing investment in the year 2000 in developing countries of 492 billion dollars (constant 1972 $) out of total dev. countries investment of 1348 billions and world total investment of 3.441 billions.
WORLD BANK	Scenario Projections 1975–85 (Base scenario).	Increase GDP by 4.2% in developed countries per year and by 5.7% in low-income, and middle-income countries.	Increase gross investment by 5.3% per year in low-income and middle-income countries (with a gross domestic investment between 19.1 and 26.4% of GDP in 1975).
LEONTIEFF – UNO SCENARIO FOR 1999	Scenario Projections and investment levels to satisfy internal demand.	From 1970 to the year 2000, increase gross domestic product per year by: – – 3.3% to 4.9% for Japan, USA and Western Europe – 4.9% to 5.2% for Eastern Europe and USSR – 6.3% for developing, centralized economies – 7.2% for developing, market economies (UN MODEL)	Increase between 1970 and 2000, from 20% to 41% in the Middle East and African oil producers, from 17–20% to 31–33% in Latin America, from 15 to 23–25% for non-oil producers in Asia and Africa; the model shows that 4 to 6% growth is linked with a 20% investment, 7 to 8% with 30% investment, 9 to 10% with 35–40% investment.

deduction of taxes, was negative and this situation was particularly marked in Japan and the United Kingdom.

Y. There are many "structural" and also "contingent" reasons for this but, in my view, one critical reason is the diminishing returns of technology. If technology had the same reserves of productivity as twenty or thirty years ago, it could easily absorb many of the other "structural" or "contingent" constraints[1].

I. It is true that, in spite of cheap capital and even widespread unemployment, there seems to be difficulty in stimulating the investment needed to attain our major economic objectives: i.e. to absorb unemployment, use savings profitably and control inflation.

Y. True, one would "normally" expect that the availability of cheap capital — at least in the developed countries — and of large amounts of unemployed labour would together stimulate "growth". However, the problem is that real resources (such as oil, minerals, etc.) must be economically available and/or that technology must be able to quickly provide adequate and cheap substitutes. This is the crux of the matter and we will not find solutions using methods which *presuppose* an extreme technological flexibility.

I. Are we then condemned to stagnation and recession? Are you just pleading for the acceptance of inflation and unemployment?

Y. Quite the contrary. If we start looking at such problems from *another* angle we have a better chance of finding new ways to produce wealth and welfare.

I. Let's leave aside generalities: we need practical suggestions for solving, for instance, the employment problem.

Y. I think it is possible to propose a specific example which summarizes in practice many fundamental issues.

[1] See Kristensen, Thorkil: *The Nature of the Present International Crisis,* IFIAS, Copenhagen, 1978. In his study, T. Kristensen explains the basic economic difficulties of the modern economies, as being due to the growth of institutional market rigidities. There is clearly a link between such phenomena, but if technology could be expandable at will, all such rigidities (which essentially concern demand) would have a much less marked effect.

1.4. Investment for Employment

Y.   An international research centre has done a study aimed at identifying new ways to stimulate employment and save energy[1].

   The research has selected two industrial sectors in France: the building industry and the automobile industry.

   A first important fact identified by the study is "the general rule that about 75% of the total energy necessary to produce a product is consumed in the base material phase and 25% in the manufacturing phase; whereas for the input of man/hours this proportion is approximately reversed".

   This means that the more we privilege and optimize production rather than the whole utilization cycle, the more the system becomes energy intensive and labour saving.

I.   This does not mean that available resources have not been used in the best economic way. Or are you or the study suggesting that productivity be reduced in order to use more labour? This is nonsense: by diminishing productivity the quantity of wealth produced is actually diminished and at the end everybody will be the loser.

Y.   Well, let us have a look first at the following table, making a comparison between a 10 and a 20 year life-time car in terms of energy consumption and labour use.

   The study says that if we used an automobile for twenty years on the average, rather than only about ten, we would save 72% of the energy used to manufacture the car, per year of utilization.

   The study also states that, for a twenty-years car instead of a 10 years car, the total amount of labour necessary for manufacture, maintenance and reconditioning, would be 56% higher per year of car utilization.

I.   This table is misleading, in the sense that if the cost of labour is too high in comparison to the cost of energy, it is obvious that in terms of wealth production we are better off producing cars in a system

---

[1] Reday, G. and Stahel, W. R.: *The Potential for Substituting Manpower for Energy — A Study for the European Community*, Battelle, Geneva, 1977. This work was financed by the Commission of the European Communities in Brussels, as part of its Program of Research and Actions on the Development of the Labour Market and is published by Vantage Press, New York, 1980.

TABLE 1.3. *Comparison of Energy and Labour Input for Production and Maintenance 10- and 20-year Life-Time Car*[1] (excluding operation)

	10-year life-time car (Today)		Δ*	20-year life-time car (Possible future)		Δ 20-year life-time car / 10-year life-time car	
	1	2	3	4	5	6	7
For the average European car	per car	per car/year	Δ*	per car	per car/year	per car (%)	per car/year (%)
ENERGY CONSUMPTION	(in toe)**	(in toe)		(in toe)	(in toe)	(%)	(%)
In basic materials (57%)	0.85	0.085	20	1.020	0.051		
In manufacturing (43%)	0.65	0.065	10	0.715	0.035		
TOTAL ENERGY CONSUMPTION (transport was ignored as it represented a low %, i.e. 3 to 4%)	1.5	0.150	16	1.735	0.087	+16	−72
LABOUR	(in man-years)	(in man-years)		(in m-y)	(in man-years)	(%)	(%)
In basic materials	0.03	0.003	10	0.033	0.0016		
In manufacturing	0.11	0.011	20	0.132	0.0066		
In production	0.14	0.014		0.165	0.0082	+18	−71
In maintenance & repair	0.03	0.020	50		0.030		
In reconditioning	—	—			0.015		
Total Labour		0.034			0.0532	+56	

Source: Battelle, Geneva.   *% increase of column 4 over column 1.   **toe = tons of oil equivalent

[1] See also: Fuhrmann, E. The Long-Life Car, *Futures*, June 1979.
Davis, J. A Study on the Long-Life Car, University of Loughborough and ITDG, London, 1979.

which takes into account the effective market costs of all the production factors.

Y. This logic is only apparent and short-term. It is apparent because a lot
of costs are normally not included in such an analysis. For instance,
the cost of destroying old cars: this is never taken fully into account
and therefore the real costs of choosing a production system favouring
shorter life-periods, in fact does produce less global real wealth than
normally calculated: shorter-life products mean more recycling,
disposal and pollution costs. Then we also face a short-term problem:
the production system chosen might well be rational at the moment
of the investment decision. Nevertheless, one must not forget that an
investment such as an automobile factory is not limited to a few years:
the factory will still be there many years later by which time the cost of
energy may have risen significantly, so much in fact, that it would
later justify a different investment policy. But by then it is too late.
The rigidities of long-term investments, in a situation in which new
technology cannot compensate rapidly for new scarcities in energy
and raw materials, will have a negative effect on the real production of
wealth. Pressure will grow to save wherever possible: Labour — because
of its mobility — will be the first item affected.

I. Once again you are expressing your pessimism as to the ability of
technology to adapt itself to change.

Y. After the energy crisis of 1973, I did not see modern science and
technology providing the type of answers you seem to expect.

The realistic assessment of the true potential of available technology is a key factor of dramatic importance. Probably we already
have a lot of unnecessary problems that derive from wrong solutions.
A typical example is attempts to solve the employment problem by
investing in a new automobile factory, even though to justify the
investment it is necessary to expand the market by any means. So for
example, it is currently a temptation in market research to double
sales by halving the useful life of the product.

I. I really do not see the point. It is obvious that if I build a new automobile factory, I increase employment . . .

Y. . . . provided you can count on flexible and developing technology
in the future. If not, you are just increasing present and future
demand for energy and raw materials for which you cannot predict

future prices and availability. On the employment side, you employ less people than if you had instead developed an automobile with a longer *service* life.

I. But you must leave people the opportunity of choosing the car they want, and people like to change their cars much more often than every 10 years.

Y. Of course. But it seems to me that a product with a longer life will entail *less* uniformity, not more, and can be traded in on better terms. Moreover, the individual has to make his choice after due consideration of all the real costs. The problem is to optimize the utilization value and period not only of cars, of course, but of many other products as well.

In a period of stagnating real productivity of technology, stimulating an economy so that it invests more in *production,* rather than in actual utilization of products, becomes a self-defeating exercise. One must invest to use more, which does not coincide with producing more.

I. There is still a contradiction: if one produces products of longer life, they will cost more.

Y. Yes, their price will be higher *per unit* of product, and this is also a favourable point in facilitating the transition. But the price will be lower in reference to the period of utilization. Furthermore, this opens the way to the development of a very constructive energy policy, which could constitute the key component of an energy-saving programme.

I. I am not so sure that the overall saving would be very great, here.

Y. It could be, but obviously it would be necessary to evaluate such approaches more closely: nevertheless we do have some pointers that suggest that the results could be staggering.

I. Such as?

Y. *Per capita* energy consumption in the USA is three times higher than that in Switzerland, at comparable levels of *per capita* gross national product.

I. I see that, for once, you are referring to a "traditional" measurement of wealth.

Y. Yes, but only to illustrate the magnitude of waste, because in my estimation, the real value of the "value-added" used to measure wealth in the GNP, is lower in the USA than it is in Switzerland. But coming back to the energy problem, it is clear that at least part of the huge amount by which American energy consumption exceeds that of Switzerland is due simply to the organization of the economic system and is unrelated to wealth formation. I might, perhaps, express it differently: the United States have been the world's most efficient promoters and developers of the industrial mode of production. Being more "advanced" than others, they are in a worse position than others, when the industrial society is no more what it used to be.

When a process is in a situation of diminishing or even negative returns, efficiency simply adds to the negative acceleration. In this sense, energy consumption in the USA can be seen as a "negative" indicator of wealth, instead of looking — in the traditional way — at *per capita* energy consumption as an indicator of "development" or of "wealth".

I.   That sounds like a paradox.

Y.   Let's say, rather, that it is intuitive. However, to return to the subject of investment and labour, let me quote from the Governor of a Central Bank, "The problem today is not the quantity but the quality of investment". I have tried to extend this notion of "quality of investment", which does not apply only to such aspects as: investment security, adequate political and economic environment, good management. "Quality" of investment also relates to a basic reorientation of economic policy aimed at increasing wealth.

I.   In simpler words, this boils down to stimulating more activities which are more labour intensive.

Y.   Where capital intensive investment tends to show itself to be an inadequate tool for increasing wealth, there is no justification for augmenting its use. If one continues to do so for political or other purposes, one runs the danger of diminishing overall wealth. Perhaps I can propose a more fundamental analysis on the basis of the following table (p. 21).

I.   I do not quite agree with what you are saying there. In the final analysis, in purely economic terms, if labour is underemployed, it means it is too expensive. I do not see how, by developing a more labour-intensive economy, as you propose, you can overcome this contradiction.

Y. The contradiction is also in the fact that capital is very cheap and that, although many investments are made, merely to save labour for political and not just economic reasons, there is still abundance of it. The point is that, since the situation has not been assessed in terms of the real returns of technology, economic policies are still orientated as if we could count on a period of high returns of new technology, which could absorb, on the one hand, higher wages and, on the other, higher capital returns. This not being the case, the result is inflation. Furthermore, investment made to save 'labour' is offset by the increased social costs of unemployment. Under such conditions, monetary investment is like malignant growth: cell multiplication loses its initial constructive aim, because it does not fit the other environmental conditions. We have to return to the basic evidence, that labour − in different forms − produces wealth and that it can be substituted by investment and technologies only to the extent that the costs, in real terms, of these direct-labour substitutes, are lower than those that direct labour could otherwise achieve. The following table will perhaps help make this point clearer.

TABLE 1.4. *Capital Requirements: Labour and Productivity*

1. In the *pre-historical World,* men's labour to survive is performed essentially with their own body tools (hands to catch and fight, legs to run, etc.).
   Here labour (L) leads directly to a product (Y)

$$(a) \quad L \longrightarrow Y_1$$

2. In the *pre-industrial,* essentially agricultural societies, more and more labour is devoted to the production of *tools,* which contribute subsequently to improving overall performance. These tools were of various sorts, e.g. the wheel, agricultural tools, bows and arrows, animal domestication, etc. and were developed and accumulated essentially without monetary investment.
   However, more and more labour is already being diverted to an intermediary (indirect) manufacture of tools (Pc = cultural dowry and patrimony)

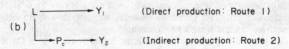

(b)
L ⟶ Y_1 (Direct production: Route 1)
⟶ P_c ⟶ Y_2 (Indirect production: Route 2)

Clearly L will be diverted through Route 2 so long as the effort and resultant yield proves more satisfactory and sustainable than with Route 1.

3. In the *industrial society,* two fundamental events take place:

    I   Tremendous new developments take place in tool-making capabilities as a result of advanced and, subsequently, science-based technology.

    II But the new technology needs unprecedented quantities of labour to be diverted from direct and traditional production. The accumulation of money (= CAPITAL) is the way to solve this problem (and this is why, since the beginning of the industrial revolution, the *monetarized* economic system has grown more dynamic and potentially dominant).

The indirect production Route (2) next gives way to a new major bifurcation (3) leading to development of modern technology thanks to capital accumulation (C).

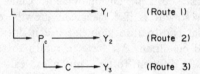

The greater the advances in technology, the greater the need for capital, so that:

- In the 18th century, capital investment in the "modern" sector represents about 5 to 6% of sales
- In the 19th century goes up to 12 to 14%
- In the 20th century goes up to 25% and more.

Currently, a single "machine" will increasingly cost over 1 billion dollars (such as a nuclear reactor or an offshore oil rig).

Obviously L will also continue to be advantageously diverted to Route 3 (= increasing the capital intensity of the economy) so long as its efforts and yields prove more satisfactory and sustainable than in the case of Routes 1 and 2. In such evaluation, the increasing costs of coordination and management must also be taken into consideration.

4. In contemporary society, capital needs are related to:

    (1) Replacement of worn-out capital equipment (i.e. the situation in a steady-state economy).

    (2) Investment in advanced technology, which makes existing equipment obsolete and allows a real net increase in productivity. This has been the prime growth factor of the Industrial Revolution. If technology is in a period of diminishing returns[1] and capital tends to have a low or even negative rate of return,[2] real yields will not improve by developing capital intensive projects. Direct human labour can then again become "competitive" in real-wealth production.[3]

    (3) Geographical spread of investments, in particular where the limits of (2) have not been reached and where other development factors (cultural, political, organizational) can profitably assimilate and benefit from the technological–industrial revolution on the basis of real utilization value.

1.5. The New Economic Structure – The Service Economy

I. We have been talking of changes in the economic structure: after all most people now recognize that we live in a post-industrial society. So I do not understand why you insist in saying that the reference point is still industrialization.

Y. True, there has been a lot of talk about the post-industrial society. In simple terms, it means that when we pay 100 dollars for a product or service, the actual production cost is often less than 20% of the final price. The remainder is accounted for by various types of services: transport, storage, distribution, marketing, insurance, etc. The real *access* to the product or service is determined by the functioning of services which are cost-decisive.

I. The problem of storage and distribution has always existed, today it is just more developed. And everybody knows about figures showing that services have become in most advanced countries, the major sector of the economy, and agriculture has been very much reduced. All this is clear.

Y. Well, I do not think that this concept is as clear as it seems. Moreover, the subdivision of the economy into three basic sectors – agriculture, industry and services – is both inadequate and misleading. This also is a subdivision inherited through a form of economic thinking linked to the experience and philosophy of the Industrial Revolution. The reasoning behind such a subdivision is that in a pre-industrial world, the economy is essentially based on agriculture – which is right and proper. This is the primary sector. You have then the industrial sector which is the focus of the economic development process, and which means developments in the manufacturing sector. Since, in any economic situation, not all activity is limited to these two sectors,

---

[1] Giarini, Orio and Loubergé, Henri: *The Diminishing Returns of Technology,* Pergamon Press, Oxford, New York, 1978.

[2] Kristensen, Thorkil: *The Nature of the Present International Crisis, op. cit.*

[3] Vester, Frederic: *Ballungsgebiete in der Krise,* Stuttgart, 1977. Vester shows that in Germany, 100 billion marks investment have "produced" employment for an additional 2 million people in the period 1955–60, 400,000 in the period 1960–65, *MINUS* 100,000 in the period 1965–70, *MINUS* 500,000 in the period 1970–75. In terms of "real" wealth produced by the apparent increase in capital productivity, one has to deduct the costs of Government subsidies, taxes and social security expenditures necessitated by the readaptations. See also the other tables and discussions on "value".

there is a further category — the "tertiary" or "service" sector which is considered a kind of *residual* activity, in the way that an etcetera is put at the end of a sentence to refer to things which exist but which are not worth specifying. It is enough to look at an econometric model to see how far this "residual" category is really treated like an "etcetera".

I.   Much effort and research is now being carried out to define this tertiary sector. For instance, the transportation sector is more and more considered in isolation and specified in its own right.

Y.   Yes, but the "etcetera" is still large, growing even larger and larger and also continues to cover numerous activities which, in many classic textbooks on economics are referred to as "non-productive". Such a debate is, in passing, a most useful indicator of how far, the "real" focus of productive activity is the secondary or industrial sector, both in theory and in practice.

I.   You are just pleading for the service sector to be given a higher grading than is normally the case. Are you not knocking at a door which is already open?

Y.   The doors you are talking of are still very frequently firmly closed. First because this "residual" service sector is still labouring under the idea that at least in part it is not productive of wealth and welfare. This is the natural consequence of a notion of value which is historically and conceptually linked to industrial production.

Furthermore, the subdivision of the economy into three (or four, or five) sectors misses the point that "service" operations are involved not only in the "tertiary" sector, but also, and very often more so, *within* the industrial and even the agricultural sector. Visit a large chemical company and try to find how many employees really do "produce" and how many are involved in "service" activities such as planning, organization, distribution, finance, safety, insurance management, storage, maintenance, etc. You will soon find that a modern "industrial" organization, is essentially a "service" or tertiary organization. The "tertiarization" process has taken over the "industrialization" process.

I.   Alright, but service organizations, on the other hand, are using more and more machines.

Y.   This is exactly my point. The "Industrial" Revolution has led to an economic organization where the production of wealth and welfare, whatever the type of activity (the production of food, machinery or insurance policies) has changed to such an extent that a "vertical" subdivision of the economy into agricultural, industrial and service sectors, makes less and less sense. Even so, it is staggering to see that an activity which accounts for less than 20% of a product's price, is still the starting point of economic considerations for investment aimed at stimulating growth.

I.   Even if services are so important, they cannot service anything but a real product.

Y.   I can reverse this proposition: a product is usable not because it exists but because it is available and it works. When we reach the point where the "organization of availability" is the greatest cost, something has changed in our priorities.

I.   However, if we take the case of the Great Depression of 1929, products were still available, but demand — solvable demand — people with money to spend, did not exist. Most economic textbooks give the example of people going hungry whilst food was being destroyed — even live pigs — and not distributed free since this would have depressed the market. Availability means "demand" and having money to buy the products that exist.

Y.   That is only partly true. In particular, it is not true for cases where the most "advanced" industrial system is adopted in situations where the local infrastructure and culture tend to aggravate the problems. In all cases, and not only in industrially advanced countries, a better attempt could be made to comprehend the problems of developing wealth if we tried to fathom the real value of things. Moreover, this value must be something that can be used profitably under *given* conditions, i.e. it must have *utilization* value.

1.6. Utilization Value

I.   You say "utilization value": you probably mean utility or use value. There is no such concept as "utilization value".

Y.   I use this word intentionally, in order to make a clear distinction with the different ways the notion of value is normally used in economics. The first point is that utilization value includes goods and services which are both free (available at no monetary cost) and priced (available from the market at monetary cost).

I.   The introduction to Samuelson's[1] textbook of economics contains the statement that economics is, in fact, about exchange values, whether they are expressed in money or not.

Y.   Looking back at the history of economic thinking and at Samuelson's book itself, it is quite clear that the whole of economic thinking is centred on monetarized activities: non-monetarized activities are considered as separate cases which can be analyzed by *analogy* with the monetarized system. By contrast, "utilization value" tries to define wealth by a *combination* of monetarized and non-monetarized elements.

I.   What is the difference? In principle, at least, you can add the two.

Y.   The point is that such an addition does not give a result which corresponds to the sum of the two. The monetarized system does not develop without affecting the non-monetarized system and its yields. This is obvious when one reflects that in some poor countries one can survive on 50 dollars per month; with the same amount of money in a "rich" country, one can only die. This means that a certain number of free utilization values are still available in the "poor" country, whereas many of them have been destroyed or transformed into "market" value in the "rich" country.

The "rich" country, therefore, has not increased its riches in real terms in proportion to the growth of its monetarized economy.

I.   Alright, but the monetarization of the economy has favoured industrialization and has, as such, increased the general level of wealth.

Y.   This has often been the case, but giving absolute priority to the development of the monetarized economy, hides the fact that this development does not necessarily always represent a net addition to real wealth. In part, at least, it represents *substitution* of a "free" value that has never been accounted for. Sometimes the net gain as measured by monetarized value can represent a net loss in terms of real utilization value: in this case the so-called "added" value is in reality a "deducted" (or substracted) value. It means that the new value which has been created does not make up for the lost values consumed or destroyed in the process.

[1] Samuelson, Paul A.: *Economics,* New York, 1970. Introduction.

I.   This is quite paradoxical. Could you give me an example?

Y.   With pleasure. Think of the money you have to spend if you want to go for a swim in a swimming pool which has had to be built on the seacoast, because the seawater is so polluted it is dangerous to swim in.

I.   If you have money, you buy the ticket for the swimming pool and you enjoy it: isn't that a form of wealth?

Y.   I do not see why you believe you are richer now than you were when the sea was unpolluted and you could go swimming for free. The fact is you are paying for a deducted value — an original natural value, whose utilization has been destroyed — and you have to pay not as evidence that you are richer, but as evidence that you are poorer. A real net added value, or a real increase in utilization value, would have occurred if the resources used to build the swimming pool had instead been used, for instance, to build houses for the homeless.

I.   Resources will be allocated to house building rather than to swimming pool construction when people express their preference in another way and, therefore, give up using swimming pools.

Y.   There is a difference in the preferences, as you say: building a house when there are not enough houses is a net real addition to wealth. Building swimming pools because free utilization values have been destroyed is a "preference" which is generated by the negative costs (or deducted values) of the economic system. In terms of your concept of value, you make no distinction: the price structure is the unique reference point. With the concept of utilization value, you have to start by verifying how much priced values are indicative not only of net added values, but also of costs to the non-monetarized system.

I.   This is an impossible exercise. *How* could you do it? *Who* would do it?

Y.   That is a difficult, but not an impossible exercise: the key is to start defining, evaluating and measuring economic value differently from the way it is normally done. If we can reach agreement on this point, the "how" to do it and "who" will do it, will be easier to discuss. In any case, from my point of view, the present notion of economic value is not only approximate — I doubt that we can ever achieve anything better than a good approximation — but it is now more and more misleading as a reference for defining and organizing real wealth and welfare.

I.   I think that there is something misleading in what you say: you seem
     to imply that there is a basic, unique notion of value in economics.
     This is untrue. The notion of value has changed a lot in the course of
     economic history.

Y.   Yes, it has changed, but one fundamental factor has remained as a
     cornerstone: the possibility of measuring value through the price
     system. In fact, the very real problem that confronted economics, in
     its attempt to become a "science" was the need to identify measure-
     able phenomena, in imitation of the natural sciences. In the study of
     temperature, speed, matter, weight, light, etc. it is relatively easy to
     define such phenomena and then measure them. In any social science,
     the major and often unresolved problem is, first, to isolate a pheno-
     menon and then to measure it. Economics was, in fact, able to
     become one of the most advanced social sciences precisely because the
     price system seemed to offer a real possibility of measuring, with
     maximum objectivity, a specific social phenomenon, i.e. economic
     value.

         Looking, in perspective, at the fundamental contribution made
     by Adam Smith at the birth of economics, I would say that it was
     firstly that of having linked the notion of value to a price mechanism
     which allows its quantification. Secondly, it was his having clearly
     identified the onset of industrialization as the real source of new
     wealth; this recognition is all the more important since it is precisely
     this industrialization process which little by little transformed the
     traditional, dominant, non-monetarized economy into a predominantly
     monetarized one.

I.   I would prefer to say that the importance of Adam Smith lies in his
     analysis of the free market system which guarantees optimum resource
     allocation: all traditional economic liberalism goes back to his clearly
     stated defence of free trade as the basis of the wealth of nations.

Y.   From my point of view, this aspect of Adam Smith's analysis is less
     important than that of his having defined a concept of value based on
     the industrial production process and quantified by the price
     mechanism.

         In fact, it was possible for Karl Marx to develop his economic
     theories — which are utterly opposed to economic liberalism —
     merely by following and appropriating for himself the core of

classical economic theory — in particular the concept of value and of "productive" (essentially industrial) labour, that had been developed since Adam Smith.

I.   This is an over simplification, but it is true that a great part of Marxist economic theory is derived from classical economics. To come back to your utilization value though: how does it relate to the classical concepts of value, or as Hayek has called them "the old cost-of-production theories of value"?[1]

Y.   I would first observe that the picture of a production process as one ending in the output of "final" goods and services is a very incomplete one: the real final step of any production process is the transformation of an original quantity of raw materials and energy into a quantity of waste, part of which — but only part — is or can be recycled as raw material.

I.   You must be joking! The goal of the production system is not to produce waste.

Y.   Whatever the goal of any production system may be, the final result is invariably waste. This is the reason why the value of goods and services cannot be related to the increasing number of products, or to the rapidity of the transformation process. This value should be related to the frequency and *period* of time a given product or service is available for use.

I.   We do at least agree that there is no value in waste! But I still do not see why you cannot speak of use values instead of utilization values.

Y.   First, because the concept of use value is linked to the separation of what is monetarized and what is not, as if wealth — as I mentioned already — could be the simple sum of the two.

I.   In fact, since Adam Smith, many economists have written about use value, including for products which are free, or — as you say — non-monetarized.

Y.   Yes, that is true, but they finally came roughly to this conclusion: either use value is free (for instance the use value of air) and as such it is not a problem in terms of producing more wealth; or it is rare and in such a case it is part of the market or priced system and the word 'use' of a product becomes almost a synonym of its destination (for

---

[1] Hayek, F. A.: *The Pure Theory of Capital*, London, 1941, reprinted 1976, p. 10.

TABLE 1.5. *The Classical Economic Concept of* $\boxed{VALUE}$
in the Industrial *Society (The example of an automobile)*

The *EXCHANGE* VALUE: one sells a car for 10,000 dollars

The *10,000 dollars* are the *Exchange Value* of the car

The *ADDED* VALUE:

> *Costs* of extraction of *Raw Materials* to build a car such as iron, glass, rubber, etc.

+

> *Costs* of various *Transformations* necessary to build the components: engine, wheels, seats, etc.

+

> *Costs* of assembling the car, and of making a *final,* usable *product*

+

> Costs of distributing the car: delivery, storage, publicity, marketing, selling, etc.

= TOTAL *ADDED* VALUE (= ADDITION OF *COSTS*)

The *VALUE PARADIGM* in "classical" economic equilibrium:
Total added value   (= Production costs of supply) must match
Exchange value   (= Price paid by demand)

In the "FREE MARKET" System:
- *IF* exchange value is higher, then new competition will contribute to reduce it
- *IF* total added value (costs) is higher, then the production will be obliged to stop (go out of business)

In the SOCIALIST System (Centrally planned economy):
- The state controls and organizes this equilibrium

In the "SOCIAL MARKET ECONOMY":
- A compromise is attempted between the free-market mechanism and state intervention

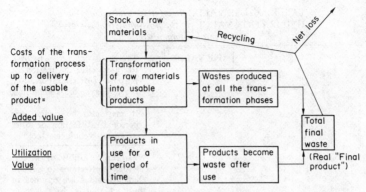

FIG. 1.3. *The Real Final Outcome of the Production Process*

instance the use value of bread is for eating). It was inevitable — when price is *the* reference for measurement — to abandon in economic practice the notion of use value as a basis for defining wealth.

I.   But still, classical economics could live and develop quite well without trying to put use value, or, as you call it the "utilization value" at the centre of the analysis.

Y.   Of course. The notion of exchange-added value was adequate in a situation in which industrialization was making real progress and adding to real wealth. Even if many costs — in terms of real utilization value — were not taken into account, the net final result has, in the main, been positive — and sometimes very positive. The evidence helped to identify, in good conscience, the strategy for increasing wealth with the strategy for increasing monetarized added values.

I.   Why and when then do you start proposing a concept of value which, as you say, should integrate monetarized and non-monetarized sources of value?

Y.   The fundamental change occurs when economic activity measured in terms of value added, starts giving signs that this increased activity is counterbalanced by its negative effects in the overall non-monetarized sources of wealth. Worse still, when in some cases, more added values means less available wealth. It is the moment when we observe the "production" of deducted values: the utilization value then starts

TABLE 1.6. USE VALUE *(in an industrial society) and*
UTILIZATION VALUE *(in the post-industrial society)*
The example of an automobile

| USE VALUE | = | • The car is *bought* to be *used* for a specific destination or purpose (for transportation, for holidays, for commuting, etc.)
• It may also be *bought* for personal satisfaction or other reasons (psychological, etc.) |

BUT, — Whatever the utility of the car, all such motivations to buy are elements which are resumed in the fact that a price is considered acceptable or not.

SO, — The *use value,* in traditional economic terms, *is finally included* and absorbed *in the* mechanism which determines the *exchange (added) value.*

The UTILIZATION VALUE is the utility gained from a stock of products or services for the *period or duration of their life time* whatever their destination, and *regardless of the fact that they are paid or not.*

Examples: — An Automobile with which one can drive 200,000 miles in its lifetime has *twice the utilization value* of a car lasting 100,000 miles.

— A cotton bed-sheet which lasts through 50 washings, has *50 times more utilization value* than a disposable bed-sheet which is thrown away after one period of use. In fact, its value is even higher because an old cotton sheet has still a long life as a house-cloth, whereas a disposable, plastic impregnated cloth is much less suitable for secondary utilization.

— The housewife's domestic labour has a *utilization value* even if it is not paid for.

— The water of a polluted lake *has negative utilization value* for drinking or swimming.

— Many ancient roads and houses have an obvious utilization value even if they are completely amortized.

— Works of arts and literature have great cultural and educational utilization value in themselves (beside the value of the paper or other supports to transmit their message) even when the author no longer receives royalties.

— A destroyed city has *no utilization value,* even if by the very fact of being destroyed (by any natural or man-made catastrophe) it offers the possibility of producing — via reconstruction, anti-pollution equipment, etc. — a lot of "value added".

THE UTILIZATION VALUE IS THE MEASURE OF REAL WEALTH AND
WELFARE

diminishing. It is the moment at which *real* zero or negative growth starts even if the GNP indices are still positive.

I.   Even if one admits that real growth is now very low and in some cases negative, the real problem is to explain why all this is happening today. In other words, we still do not know if we have to face fundamental changes or simply business cycles adaptations.

Y.   My hypothesis is that a large part of what is happening is linked to deep changes, the most important being the modifications in the relationships between technology and economic development.

I.   Which are then — in your opinion — the technological preconditions for a strategy of industrial growth?

Y.   The preconditions are that existing free resources remain unlimited and that new technology increases the net yield of all resources. More specifically, all the time science and technology have a global, positive effect, and are the source of continuing increasing returns for the economic system, there is no problem. Even if this is never totally true, one can consider the "free" resources world as separate from the world of monetarized rarity and concentrate on the latter, assuming that if *within* this one, one produces more, one gets an *overall* beneficial effect.

   The trouble begins when we start observing more and more increases in scarcity which is essentially the recognition of a situation of diminishing returns of technology.

I.   Could you give me an example in order to clarify what you mean?

Y.   In the last ten years, technological development has not been able to catch up with the increasing demand for energy, and offer a technical solution to energy shortage by inventing quickly new sources of energy or new processes so as to at least maintain the price of energy at what it was ten years ago. Furthermore, the whole pollution problem is clearly related to the utilization of modern technology and is an example of costs which have been produced by this technology and which have often been neglected at the moment of the investment decisions. We can now often find cases in which the more powerful the technology, the greater its potential to produce deducted values. This brings us back to the necessity of identifying real utilization values.

I.   The notion of utilization value would then be closer to the classical

TABLE 1.7. *The Real Costs of (Utilization) Value (Taking into consideration* monetary costs only*)*

THEY ARE *ALL COSTS** INCURRED AS A CONSEQUENCE OF USING A STOCK OF PRODUCTS OR SERVICES *DURING THEIR LIFE-TIME*

For an automobile used during 10 year, they would be:

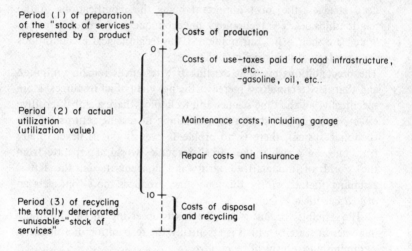

Period (1) of preparation of the "stock of services" represented by a product

Costs of production

Costs of use–taxes paid for road infrastructure, etc...
–gasoline, oil, etc..

Period (2) of actual utilization (utilization value)

Maintenance costs, including garage

Repair costs and insurance

Period (3) of recycling the totally deteriorated –unusable–"stock of services"

Costs of disposal and recycling

Whereas, the shorter the utilization period (2), *the greater* the global costs of preparation (1) to face accelerated substitution, and *the greater* the recycling and disposal costs (2) as a result of accelerated waste.

In a period of no environmental limitations and of increasing returns of technology, the gains in production costs (1) can more than compensate the loss of utilization value of period (2) and the additional costs of period (3). It is a period of net real value increase due to the industrial revolution.

In a period of environmental limitations and of diminishing returns of technology gains in production costs (1) are not sufficient to prevent a net loss of real (utilization) value.

---

*Of course, to be even more precise, also the costs of accidents, pollution, road wear, health effect, etcetera, should be taken into consideration, and their variation with the lifetime of a stock of products, or services.

notion of value, in that it is more concerned with the formation of value on the supply side.

Y. Yes. I would like to present the following hypotheses: for the major part of the Industrial Revolution, the process of science and technology has not been analyzed as such by economists, but rather taken for granted as an expression of general human ingenuity.

The experience of its adaptability has been such that, the interest of the economist, both at the practical and the theoretical level, has tended to be concentrated on the demand side. It is clear now that if the hypothesis of diminishing returns of technology is even only partially true, it should have an appreciable effect on both economic theory and practice.

I. You would dismiss, then, the idea that "utilization value" is just another word for "utility".

Y. Yes, "utility" in economics is a very wide concept that covers the global and general subjective motivations behind economic behaviour. Obviously this is an important problem. However, I have always wondered why a theory of subjective values does not start out by analyzing the whole field of psychological, psychiatric and even neurological research. Tibor Scitovsky[1] and a few others have at least ventured in this direction which is inevitable in any attempt to develop an economic theory of subjective behaviour.

I. Then, utilization value has nothing to do with individual choices and motivations?

Y. It certainly has. However, I would give economics the priority task of researching the conditions under which it is currently possible to increase the availability of real wealth. The fight against scarcity is first and foremost a problem of adequately developing the "supply" side, or, simply, the worth of goods and services produced.

I. You are not for zero growth, then.

Y. That is not the point. I do not think growth exists when costs grow regardless of what happens to real utilization value.

Moreover, I do not believe that the normal standard of GNP growth actually measures real growth. If the GNP increases by 3% per year and this percentage increase is, in fact, absorbed by what I

---

[1] Scitovsky, Tibor: *The Joyless Economy,* Oxford, 1976.

have defined as values deducted (costs for pollution, for instance), the outcome is that we are already in a situation of zero growth.

Let me reiterate what I have already said: the real problem is to redefine wealth and welfare, and to reorganize the strategy for making the best of the possibilities available.

1.7. Utilization Value – A Reference Paradigm for Industrially Developed and Developing Countries

I.   This discussion about limits of investment, diminishing returns of technology and utilization value is all very well, but it looks very much like a discussion for privileged countries. The developing world has much more down-to-earth problems.

Y.   The problem of producing real economic values is at least as acute in the developing countries as it is in the industrially advanced countries.

I.   Are you now going to plead for the "noble savage" or some other sort of Rousseauesque utopian felicity?

Y.   Not quite, although it is probably safe to say that at least some bush-men live better and are probably happier than some people living in the slums of "rich" industrialized cities. But this is not the central point. The real problem is always one of how much *more* wealth and welfare can industrialization bring to people in the rest of the world.

I.   At least you admit that they have to industrialize . . .

Y.   Not always and not necessarily. Particularly when one discovers that the concept of and skill for industrialization is often directly linked to essentially "northern" cultures and needs, and that it cannot be separated completely from those cultures without starting to produce negative values *quicker* than it has done in the "developed" world.

I.   Here we are . . . Now you are going to tell me that bread production depends on culture, and that if you are not a descendent of Shakespeare you have a different type of hunger.

Y.   I am certainly convinced that bread – or rather the basic food best fitted to any given condition (which is not necessarily bread) is a net value-added for absolutely everybody. But when, in a developing country I am producing it with super-modern machinery operated by skilled foreign workers and, in order to pay for it, have to export a lot of other good food, I am not sure that the total amount of "real bread" which is left is always a net gain.

I. There might be some aberrations of the type you describe, but one can avoid going too far.

Y. This is not merely a problem of measure or of common sense. The nature of industrialization based on the traditional notion of value can be conterproductive not only in developed nations but also — and sometimes even more so — in developing countries because of the logic which development too often generates in the international exchange system.

I. What do you mean?

Y. The excess in the development of the dual economic system in the developing world. It goes like this: you start by planning for "modernization" and therefore you buy foreign "technology". In order to buy it, it is necessary to have money — foreign currency: therefore you stimulate national production for export. Obviously the export in question will be goods used in other countries at a different economic level and with a different demand: therefore, the export industry will often be producing products of limited interest to the domestic market. In contrast, the large industrialized nations started by producing for their domestic market and then built up international commercial strength with the production that exceeded domestic demand. In some "developing" countries, the process has been inversed: the "modern" sector develops first to satisfy international demand with the object of obtaining foreign currency. However, as a result, domestic production for local needs is very often relegated to second or even lower priority. Consequently many peasants — for instance — become poorer in real terms because what they produce for their own consumption is not improved and some may even be eliminated in order to permit the production of goods for export.

I. Nevertheless, these same peasants will, in time, use imported technology, such as tractors or fertilizers, which will also add to their consumption needs.

Y. This sometimes happens, but the reference is not the utilization value of each economic system, but the exchange values of the world system. In fact, the junction between the initial effort of producing for export and the subsequent benefit of increased real value, does not work that often.

I. You are, therefore, against development of world trade. This is obscurantism.

Y. I am by no means against trade in a system which can improve the overall level of wealth. No international trade and no economic activity can last for long if, on the one side, the production of waste is increasingly a part of the economic "value" of the "advanced" nations and, on the other side, the development of the rest of the world is bound to a strategy feeding such waste.

I. Are you not exaggerating?

Y. We have a clear example before our very eyes: there are, on the one side, the advanced industrial nations and in particular the United States with an energy consumption attributable largely to a system of intensive waste production. On the other side, the world's economic development (and even the world's monetary system itself) seems to be linked to the soundness of the US economy and to its "growth" even though such growth entails even higher levels of energy consumption (and waste production!).

I. All this is paradoxical, but you forget that Europe too, during the first phase of the Industrial Revolution, and even up to very recently, had to undergo many adjustments which were not so different from those the rest of the world is experiencing currently.

Y. The situation is not quite the same. Remember how I explained that the Industrial Revolution in Europe was able to start when the economy increased monetarization. It was possible for this to occur in closed circuit, limited to a given region of the world, especially since responsibility for money emission was split among a number of institutions and the result was virtual chaos not subject to external control. This means that it was the Europeans who were the first to use money in larger quantities and were then ready to handle the new system; they could also rely, to a large extent, on their own capabilities and local resources. Internationalization of trade and capital movements, as we know them now, intervened, on a large scale, only later. Western society had time to adapt and also organize the movement. Even so the wars and social upheavals that have occurred since the French Revolution till the present day show how difficult and how costly this adjustment has been.

I.   Would you not agree, then, that the Western world has had the prior experience which can now be transmitted to the rest of the world and which will spare other countries enormous efforts as they pass through the various phases of the Western Industrial Revolution?

Y.   There is clearly some truth in what you say, but it is far from the complete truth. You do not learn technology in a vacuum, you do not use modern machinery merely because you are able to do it personally; the whole of society is involved — and this takes time.

I.   Alright, but is there not a contradiction in the fact that most of the developing countries just want to industrialize as quickly as possible?

Y.   Their attitude is justifiable as evidence of their wish to increase their wealth and welfare. It is also clear that, in many cases, imported knowledge and techniques help to achieve some of their goals. However, the problem is not an abstract one based on general definitions, or rather, preconceptions. The problem is to know whether, in such cases, there is an increase in "real wealth" and real utilization values for their people since utilization values are determined, at least partly, but nevertheless consistently, by the culture to which they are linked, in terms of both "supply" and "demand".

I.   Give me an example!

Y.   First, the production of good cloth on a modern loom entails the ability to operate and maintain the machine in an adequate manner. Second the finished products must have utilization value at the place and in the way they are consumed.

I.   Are you sure you are not pleading for a world where the advanced countries stay advanced, and the other countries remain underdeveloped?

Y.   The very term "underdeveloped" is not an acceptable one. It means underdeveloped with respect to a unique model of development, which is derived in practice from the dominant or reference culture. If production "value" is the standard of reference for everybody, then everybody is, of course, playing a game in which there will be a large number of late starters.

I.   They can catch up.

Y.   It all depends on what they are supposed to catch up on. If it is to achieve health standards and life expectancies similar to — or even better than — those of the advanced countries — so much the better.

However, is industrialization — using the traditional measure of added value — the sole means of achieving these objectives?

We should mediate upon facts like this one: do you know that in Sri Lanka life expectancy is as high as in the state of Washington which has a *per capita* national income which is more than 35 times higher? You have understood correctly: 35 times.

The general principle I want to propose is that the very value concept linked to the major development period of the Industrial Revolution in the Western — or, more exactly, Northern — world is an inadequate one for both the mature industrial countries and the developing world. First, the added values are more and more concealing negative contributions to wealth and welfare. Second, the costs of adapting the Industrial Revolution and industrial technologies to other cultures, and vice versa, are clearly higher if artificial short-cuts are taken. Furthermore, the hyper-concentration of industrialized towns in many parts of the developing world shows that the developing countries sometimes catch up more quickly in the production of deducted values than in the production of real net added utilization values.

I.   But the crux of the matter is to ensure adequate technology transfer.

Y.   It all depends on what you mean by adequate. Very often the debate on the transfer of technology is the result — in the form of a backlash — of superstitious Western attitudes to science and technology.

I.   But wouldn't you agree that not everybody has access to the best available technology?

Y.   There are always "political" problems in any transfer and in any negotiation. This is clear. But the main problems do not always lie there. There are too many misconceptions playing a negative role.

The first is the result of what we have already discussed. The myth is that the more modern the science and technology, the easier it is for everything to work: change will be more rapid, efficiency rise more markedly, wealth increase more noticeably, productivity expand better, control become easier, manipulation become simplified. In many cases, all this is wrong. One forgets that, even in the most automated and "advanced" production processes, control, manipulation, maintenance are related to and dependent on the ability of the worker or the engineer to really *dominate* his machinery. In addition, the result must be "useful". The best type of technology transfer is one in which one takes a machine and tries to copy it. This is not very expensive in money terms and has the advantage of providing an education and training experience.

I.   Are you proposing the infringment of patent and licence rights?

Y.   Not really, but it is a waste of time buying a licence for a machine which you do not know how to handle, repair, maintain, adapt and, if necessary, *modify* to meet one's own needs.

Only when such performances are accomplished, can we say that a real transfer of technology has taken place, to the advantage of the development of self reliance. Only in this way, can the production system be adapted and modified to the skill and needs of a specific culture. One will also know better whether one really needs such or such a machine or tool and be freer to decide whether to abandon it or not. The problem is always the same: the worth is not that of having a chemical plant, but of running the plant to produce products that add to *local* wealth and welfare.

I.   Are you then for limiting the flow of modern technology to the rest of the world.

Y.   I didn't say that at all. Technology — i.e. machinery and processes for producing products and services — must not be simply "transferred" regardless of their local utilization value. Otherwise, you also then need to transfer the man-power and the technicians who operate the plants and — in some cases just to have a rational "order" — one is even tempted to transfer the consumers! Take the cases of so many development projects: they would have made such wonderful examples of rapid adaptation to advanced technology if only one could have replaced the local population . . .

Definitely, "transfer" is not a simple thing; it is more a question of selection and assimilation. Instead of imperilling a culture by introducing technology and habits from other countries, you can make it stronger by ensuring it understands and assimilates what it has chosen. In this way, interdependence is based on real self-reliance and development. But the development model must be an open one, not just the replica — more or less imposed — of what the Northern world has already experimented for itself and its own needs and conditions.

I.   Don't you fear that you will then get a great plurality of development methods, solutions and schemes?

Y. Why fear it? Pluralism is the guarantee that no one scheme, produced inevitably by one person or one group — be it a chemical plant or an ideology — imposes itself on others. Plurality of solutions is a guarantee that the wealth conditions developed are adapted to the natural, geophysical and historical factors that exist in different parts of the world. Multiplicity of approaches offers greater probability of finding better roads to the future. If the Third World could really improve their own strategy for wealth and welfare, it would be a *net* gain for all. In a true global perspective of the world, uniformization is wealth destructive. Diversity, based on a multiplicity of *values,* is the condition of the planet's welfare. A more thorough discussion of the concept of wealth and welfare is, then, essential since the traditional concept of added *value* drawn from long matured "Western" or "Northern" culture tends to exclude anything not *determined* "scientifically" by an "objective" price system. In fact there is nothing really "objective" or "scientific" about it; it is the one-sided view of a single culture, whatever its merits.

1.8 The General Sources of Wealth and Welfare —
Our Dowry and Patrimony (D & P)

Y. We should now try to analyze more closely the question of wealth and welfare and where it comes from. To this end, it is necessary to introduce and define the concept of "Dowry and Patrimony", or D & P.

I. Dowry and Patrimony? D & P? What's that?

Y. We need a term to define the stock of natural, biological and man-made goods and services we have available to us and from which we derive our welfare in the largest sense.

I. Can you be more specific?

Y. First of all, we all benefit from a stock of "goods" produced without *any* human intervention: the earth, with its water, air and different climates, and a certain number of biological assets.

  All this natural stock is available without the intervention of human labour, and if yielded enough products to meet human needs without human effort of any kind, it would constitute very much to the image of the Christian paradise. It is amusing to think that such a paradise, in current economic terms, would be the equivalent of a society of extreme poverty.

I. Another paradox.

Y. Less of a paradox than you think. Whatever the wealth of this natural wealth — infinite for the heaven and great, but limited, on earth — its economic "value" in terms of national product is zero. Much less than that of any "under-developed" country. If there is no incentive for mankind to take the natural D & P and transform and exploit it, there is no production — on the basis of current criteria — of any added "value". Yes, the "poorest" of the worlds is heaven.

I. By contrast, what would hell be then?

Y. Oh, Christian hell is probably the richest world of all. If we persist with our parallel between GNP and energy consumption, we probably have a very good indicator: apparently, hell is a very large energy consumer (in the form of fire) and, therefore, by current standards it must be very rich. I suspect that the value added there is enormous — one might say almost infinite in view of the paucity of the D & P.

I. What do you mean by that?

Y. Clearly, the less the natural D & P is sufficient to provide usable goods and services, the more the added value that one has to produce. The poorer the D & P — which by current economic criteria has no value — the richer the world or the country.

I. Hell and heaven are two extreme situations.

Y. Yes, the reality is that we live in purgatory, where wealth and welfare are composed of a combination of natural D & P and human effort. The problem is how to achieve a gainful balance in accounting for them.

I. But our D & P has been *given* us and therefore it is not necessary to account for it. On the contrary, it is necessary to account for the human labour in order to make a societal organization possible.

Y. This reasoning is apparently, but only apparently, right. It presupposes that two things — in this case, natural D & P and human effort — can be added and that the sum is equal to the combined values of the parts. This reasoning is tricky: it is a negative heritage of European Cartesianism.

I. Are you against Cartesianism?

Y. In this context, definitely yes. The result of human effort is not necessarily beneficial: it has all sorts of impacts on our natural D & P. It is necessary to measure or at least estimate the extent to which human action has increased or decreased the wealth and welfare derived from our "free", natural D & P.

I.   Now you are going to tell me how bad is the effect of human intervention on nature!

Y.   Not really. I have spoken of modification of the natural D & P: human intervention can and does play a role which may be either positive or negative. There can be positive or negative synergy. The problem is to know when and under which conditions the negative results exceed the positive ones.

I.   For instance?

Y.   The development of agriculture in history can be considered as one of mankind's contributions which has greatly added to the natural D & P and the net total result is that wealth and welfare have improved significantly. The growth of the ancient civilizations, was due largely to positive synergy — a happy combination of factors.

I.   You accept this outcome for agriculture, why not for the industrial civilization?

Y.   Before entering upon a discussion of industrial civilization, it is essential to recall that even agricultural societies produced situations of negative synergy. Deforestation, which was initially required to increase the area of cultivated land and also to ensure a supply of firewood resulted and continues to result in soil erosion — clearly a case of negative synergy; some civilizations, in fact, disappeared because of it. The task was not one of increasing activity to get more from poorer and poorer soil, but rather of optimizing the general capacity of producing wealth and welfare taking into account the natural D & P and the amount of labour necessary to guarantee the optimum equilibrium. This is the process we discussed earlier when we examined the simulation of fisheries exploitation.

I.   You have spoken of human effort and knowledge. Isn't this also a type or part of D & P?

Y.   Absolutely so. Humankind contributes through knowledge and labour to the production of wealth and welfare — operating within the given natural D & P and in symbiosis with it*. The rapid increase in the use

---

*The education policy is therefore crucial, and the realization of a bad or inadequate policy in this field can have a negative effect on the human D & P, leading to a deterioration of this D & P.

of money, prior to the Industrial Revolution allowed a more rapid mobilization of human labour; this together with the spread of monetary exchange permitted the development of a new form of accumulation essential for launching the Industrial Revolution.

I. You are talking of the development of capitalism.

Y. The Industrial Revolution and the development of capitalism are the same thing. The political answers as to how to mobilize or utilize money circulation may differ but industrial revolution cannot be anything but capitalistic, whatever the political regime. Accumulated money is the key tool, in conjunction with advanced technology and science-based technology, to organize and mobilize natural and human resources to increase wealth and welfare. Of course, like any tool it can be used in many ways, but this is an issue closely linked to human nature, which goes beyond given historical conditions.

I. Are you not exaggerating the role of money? After all there have been many rebellions against the constraints of money.

Y. Slaves existed because you could not otherwise build pyramids or develop large plantations without sufficiently developed exchange and monetary systems to facilitate organization of work. Money is, of course, a constraint, but it also provides the wherewithal to diminish the type of constraints which society builds up when there is no money.

Of course, money can produce new types of constraints and have its own deducted values: but the point is again one of achieving the optimum equilibrium situation. You can decide whether money is right or wrong in specific situations, you cannot decide whether it is right or wrong in general.

In the final analysis, justice concerns the distribution, control and access to D & P and not simply to capital.

I. So money is also a type of D & P, in your opinion?

Y. It is a tool that can be used to increase D & P. So far we have seen that D & P can be natural — the earth and nature available without human intervention. Now we can consider the contribution of humankind in terms of culture and labour. A major part of this latter D & P becomes monetary D & P in the course of the industrial revolution.

Total D & P is the product of four components (natural, biological, cultural and monetarized resources), but that total is not the simple sum of the four.

Total D & P is a stock of wealth, and welfare is measured by its actual utilization.

This has nothing to do with the concept of wealth in traditional economic terms.

I.   Are you referring to the fact that the traditional notion of economic value is based on flow and not on stock?

Y.   Precisely!

I.   In the final analysis, all what you say sounds rather materialistic. You criticize traditional economics but, in the end, you are still an "economist", concerned with material wealth and welfare. What about spiritual D & P?

Y.   Although this analysis of D & P starts from considerations of material utilization value, I think we are in a better position to take account of non-material wealth and welfare.

I.   How?

Y.   First of all, once we have introduced non-monetarized goods and services and concepts such as culture habits and preferences, the definition of wealth and welfare goes beyond a pure materialistic one.

However, what one has to do is eschew the belief that one can really separate (and then eventually add together again), the material and the non-material aspects of wealth.

I.   Are you not introducing confusion?

Y.   No. On the contrary. We must admit that reality is complex and that there are no clear-cut boundaries or subdivisions between different aspects of wealth and welfare. If, for the needs of research or analysis, we momentarily simplify the picture by isolating some limited aspect, it does not necessarily constitute an advance in scientific method. On the contrary, it is proof of our inability to embrace total reality.

We can try to extend or improve our knowledge but must realize that greater knowledge in one direction can obfuscate understanding in another. The Cartesian pretension that we can "pile up" knowledge bit by bit, is the basis which explains how value added can still be considered the way of piling up wealth bit by bit, excluding non-

TABLE 1.8. *The Dowry and Patrimony (D & P)* – The Source of Utilization Value

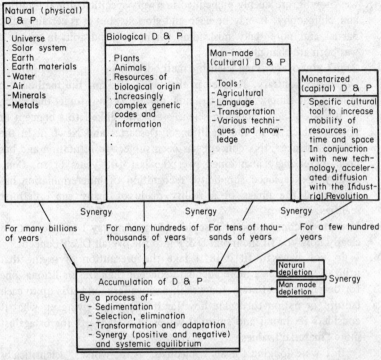

- Each element of D & P has a different time factor of accumulation
- The capital accumulation process is new only in terms of its velocity (time factor)
- All elements of D & P are interdependent
- The formation of D & P depends on *positive* synergy between one element and the rest of the system
- The Industrial Revolution has produced real added value when it has increased *the utilization value of total D & P.* Example: new technology in food production combined with the necessary capital investment has led to an increase in the food potential of our natural, biological and cultural (i.e. rough agricultural technology) D & P
- The Industrial Revolution produces negative added values – or *deducted values* – when increases in production in the monetarized sector destroy other components of D & P so that the *total* utilization value has been reduced. Examples: soil erosion following forest destruction because of excessive use of wood; the case of overfishing (see graph on page 6)

Synergy:
"Association of several organs to accomplish a function, in a process which stimulates the contribution of each"

monetarized values and their interactions. The roots of economics as we know it, are deeply embedded in a very specific cultural tradition and philosophy. It may be deep and glorious, but it is certainly also partial and potentially misleading when the conditions in which it was born are changing.

I.   Aren't you overlooking scientific method?

Y.   Quite the contrary. It is clear that science is not the method "to know", but simply "to try to know more". Do not forget that much of the social and economic sciences are still linked to a concept of science which is in the tradition of Descartes and Newton. In the natural sciences, this concept has been subject to refutation and has been increasingly abandoned over the last 100 years or so. Complexity has replaced simplicity, recognition of indetermination has supplanted the image of a reality made of many small definite realities.

I.   You are becoming too philosophical here. Anyway I still do not see clearly how you fit the moral D & P into the overall D & P concept.

Y.   I do not have to fit it in. I take the precaution of saying that utilization value is a more adequate concept than the traditional one for developing a strategy for wealth and welfare, and it is up to each culture or nation to decide how far it can go in giving up what it considers its moral and spiritual values in a trade-off for or against more "material" values.

If I were looking for an "objective" — or, worse, "scientifically determined" — and unique concept of value, I would simply create the base for a new era of one-sided cultural domination for those who would take power and organize so that they could lay down the "right" interpretation of the "right" value. Two centuries of the manipulation of science as revealed "truth" and of "scientific" ideologies are enough.

I.   Would it not then be better to completely exclude the concept of moral and spiritual values from your concept of D & P?

Y.   It is impossible and unrealistic to pretend that one can really separate the material and the spiritual.

On the one hand, we can define many "concrete" actions which are clearly legitimate and needed if we are to increase "material" wealth and welfare; on the other, many needs and actions are of the type that medicine calls psychosomatic interreactions. Many illnesses and pains have a psychic and moral origin, certain emotions also produce material changes in our body and vice versa; we must therefore guard against any attempt at developing wealth and welfare which covers only non-monetarized material goods and services. In particular, we must also consider our own discussion simply as an attempt to achieve a workable approximation, and not as a new form of definite truth.

1.9. D & P Accumulation and Capital Accumulation

I. You have defined D & P as a stock of goods and services which are accumulated from different sources. Finally, this is a sort of fixed capital incorporating many monetarized and non-monetarized assets.

Y. I do not think that "fixed capital" is an adequate definition. The idea of capital is linked, in economics, to investment goods. Many of the constituents of D & P are so-called "consumer goods".

Secondly, D & P is never really "fixed"[1]. All its components are continuously subject to a process of accumulation and depletion. To better grasp this reality, we must view it dynamically and not just as a photographic image.

I. The notion of accumulation, in economics, has been the subject of detailed analysis.

Y. Yes, but almost always as a specific "monetarized" economic phenomenon. Capital accumulation is, in fact, just a specific case of a much wider phenomenon which is all around us in different time and space dimensions.

I. I hardly see how you can speak of accumulation of free natural resources, for instance.

Y. All the "natural" resources currently available are the result of a long accumulation process.

I. But the air we breathe?

Y. The earth's atmosphere is not something static: it accumulated in a

---

[1] The concept of fixed capital goes back to the distinction made by Adam Smith, between fixed and circulating capital. The former comprises machinery and buildings as opposed to small tools and raw materials which constitute the latter. Fixed capital, like D & P, is of course also subject to depletion.

given way, at a given place, and a given quantity over a very long period of time. Accumulation must clearly not be dissociated from selection, however. Accumulation is, in a certain sense, the mechanism of piling up a stock, but also, at the same time of selection and elimination of what does not fit into the general equilibrium of this stock. The amount of oxygen, which allows those special types of energy machines — which are our bodies — to work, is available in the air not as a "given" situation, but is the result of an equilibrium derived from a process of natural accumulation and selection.

I. A coal mine will be the same thing, then.

Y. Exactly. It is the result of what we can call the natural accumulation process, which presupposes, in this case, the previous accumulation of the vegetable life from which coal is derived.

I. You extend, then, the same concept to biology.

Y. To everything. The biological accumulation (and selection) process is the one through which information, which means new and more complex characteristics, is developed and transmitted in living cells. The evolution of living species is the result of this long and subtle process of genetic accumulation and selection.

I. Would you also speak of cultural accumulation?

Y. Well, this is the phase that follows immediately after when some biological entities start to have a "cultural" behaviour, that is, when they are able to influence, by an act of decision, their own evolution.

After having accumulated all the knowledge necessary to hunt, the human species developed agriculture, ideas, religions, forms of communications and arts which are all processes of accumulation and selection.

I. Up to now, you have given three clear and distinct examples of accumulation: physical, biological and cultural.

Y. Once again, let us avoid the word "distinct". Although they develop at different speeds and in different forms, all the forms of accumulation interreact with each other.

I. What do you mean?

Y. You have given the example of the formation (accumulation) of a coalmine. This accumulation must be combined with the cultural accumulation of humankind which will not have access to the coalmine until it has discovered the uses of coal and how to extract it.

D & P in this case is not the coalmine alone, but also the cultural mechanism which provides access to it.

I.   Exploitation of a coalmine, or of any mine for that matter, is in reality conditioned by a relatively advanced technology.

Y.   This is a further step. In primitive cultures, the available technology made it possible to use only those pieces of coal that were readily accessible. With time, increased knowledge gave rise to the development of more powerful technology, this interactive process is also a kind of accumulation. We can understand and appreciate the gap between technological/cultural accumulation and natural accumulation when we discover a source of energy very deep into the earth, which is inaccessible in our present state of knowledge.

I.   In fact, many geologists say that the earth's crust contains enormous quantities of all sorts of raw materials.

Y.   This realization is of no real consequence even in terms of today's economics. What counts is the access and the real costs of the access to them. And access is the key to utilization.

I.   In any case, in your concept of D & P accumulation, you have excluded money.

Y.   No. Money is also a "cultural" tool. The monetarization of economic activity is a technology by which goods and services can be accumulated and distributed in time and space more efficiently than without it. When we travel, all we need to take with us is money: if we needed to take all the goods and services we planned to use during our journey, we would not get very far. Money was of vital importance for the Industrial Revolution, since modern technology could not be mobilized unless goods and services were more easily — and efficiently — transferred in time and space, by using money. Money, then, also changes the degree of access for utilization purposes.

I.   So, you admit that monetary accumulation has been essential for the development of the Industrial Revolution and for the industrialization process in general.

Y.   Yes, but it is perhaps better not to look at this process in isolation. Accumulation is a normal, general process. Cultural, technological accumulation, at a given moment, needed the input of monetary accumulation to interreact and initiate the period of new development in wealth and welfare that occurred in the Industrial Revolution.

I. I remember an economist − I think it was Hayek[1], who made an analysis of capital and pointed out that money capital covered a variety of real goods and services, that are not homogeneous in time and space.

Y. Yes, but in my view, Hayek's analysis is upside down. It is not a question of discovering, after having achieved a monetary accumulation, that real goods and services can be mobilized with different delays and inertias in time and space.

Rather, the essence of the monetary phenomenon, is − starting from the great and diversified natural and cultural inertia in the mobilization of goods and services − to develop a system, where non-differentiation in time and space becomes increasingly better and more efficient.

I. One might perhaps interpret the essential evolution of money utilization and production as increasing the mobility of goods and services in time and space.

Y. Yes. The first thing to understand though is that monetary accumulation is a new form of an old and wide-ranging process, and that it interacts fundamentally with all other accumulation processes.

What I would like to make clear is that monetarization of the economy was an essential step in expanding the possibility of accumulating wealth in money form; this wealth had to be sufficient to cover the cost of the new machinery and technology of the Industrial Revolution.

I. There are numerous books and treatises about capital accumulation.

Y. I am proposing to look at the problem in another way though. Most of the books you are talking about, start from the assumption that the "economy" and the "monetarized economy" are essentially the same thing. Such an assumption is misleading nowadays. The accumulation process is a phenomenon or process which has always existed, from the point of view of both nature as well as specific human cultural characteristics.

Money makes possible accumulation in a form suitable for the development of industrialization. First by extending the use of the capital accumulated and then by promoting ways of accelerating and

---

[1] Hayek, F. A.: *The Pure Theory and Capital,* London, 1941, reprinted 1952.

facilitating its formation, through banks and various forms of financial intermediation.

But monetary accumulation is only one form of accumulation, strictly linked to the phenomenon of industrialization and increasing use of technology which is more and more capital "hungry".

The onset of the Industrial Revolution was a time in which many factors essential for developing a new era in the production of wealth and welfare, were present simultaneously and started to interreact with each other.

I.   Agreed — but, in any case, there is progress in accumulation of global D & P.

Y.   Not necessarily.

1.10. D & P Depletion and Value Deducted

Y.   Accumulation is one side of the coin. However, D & P is also subject to disaccumulation, depletion and destruction. Synergy and interdependance between different forms of D & P, may have a negative outcome.

I.   Such as?

Y.   The oxygen content of the atmosphere is changing, as it did in the past when nitrogen and ammonia were much more important constituents. These changes do, of course, occur over a very long period of time. Biological accumulation and selection are modified accordingly and, at the same time influence the natural D & P: most oxygen is a yield of the biological D & P itself. On the other side, the composition of the atmosphere may be changed by natural and man-made catastrophes.

I.   Such developments have such a long time-span that they are almost beyond our appreciation.

Y.   The probability of such changes taking place over a very long future space of time is high, but not infinite. The point I wanted to make, is to underline the importance of time. The time "available" and how time is used are fundamental issues. Man's intervention and, in particular, modern technology accelerate the accumulation and depletion of D & P. Are we sure we can manage time correctly?

I. Would you apply the notion of depletion and disaccumulation to living species as well?

Y. Of course. Cancer, for instance, is a proliferation in which accumulation cannot continue in a positive way because the process of selection or elimination of diseased cells no longer functions correctly. Over longer periods of time, it may be found that many species do not have the right type of accumulated properties for them to survive; consequently, they will "degenerate".

I. However, as far as human culture is concerned, we have the means to record and preserve our knowledge in order to better protect and transmit it.

Y. This is probably an illusion. Real knowledge and real culture are the *capabilities* of knowledge and culture exploitation. We can write whatever we want and store all knowledge available: but this will not guarantee its "survival". Human beings will always need to have *intelligence* in order to *use* tools or information.

I. In some cases, however, the computer can substitute intelligence even.

Y. Talk of the computer's intelligence is closer to superstition than to science. Evolution, development, survival depend very much on the formation of *new* questions based on the need to react to new conditions. When conditions are really new, formal pre-existent knowledge is of no determinant help. We must "learn". The idea of a perfect and ultimate computer, containing *all* knowledge and fabricating learning, may perhaps be just a very modern definition of God . . . of a rather techno-animistic type!

I. Dark ages may occur, but they have not been definitive.

Y. This is an assumption of those who live in a culture which could apparently escape ultimate disaster. But the rise and fall of entire civilizations is there to demonstrate that the type of accumulation they represent, can be fully annihilated by the depletion process.

"Western" culture too, has lived through tremendous periods of depletion — and not so long ago either.

I. For instance?

Y. The Industrial Revolution was the offspring of a period of new cultural, scientific and philosophical accumulation which has its origins in the Renaissance and more particularly the Copernican revolution, Descartes and Galileo.

I. Was not this a type of new cultural accumulation?

Y. Yes, but it was not so new. What was said and "discovered" by Copernicus and his followers, was already described by the Greek Aristarcos*; it took almost 20 centuries merely to reach this same point of departure.

Cultural decadence, and decadence in wealth and welfare in the largest sense, are always possible.

I. Are we not better able to prevent decadence today than we were in the past?

Y. I hope so. But a negative accumulation process does not readily reveal its true nature since it may at first look like a positive process. When a process appears to produce value added, whereas it is really producing larger and larger quantities of value deducted, cultural adaptation is needed for the truth to become apparent. This sort of adaptation may not take place rapidly enough. The computer itself, if it is not mastered by a really conscious civilization, might play the role of the ptolemaic theory of the universe. It all depends on whether mankind uses the computer to produce more knowledge, or as barrier to promote ignorance.

I. D & P is then something very indeterminate. Can we really do anything with such a concept?

Y. In practice, we have to process progress by approximations, and always remember that they are such.

What must be remembered is that D & P is a stock in a state of changing equilibrium. Each element has a different behaviour in time, and each element interacts with the others. The real problem is to maintain D & P in the best possible condition; it is the source of all utilization values. Utilization may contribute, in part, to its depletion although not necessarily; for instance, a better education can diminish the monetarized part of D & P, but increase the non-monetarized part of it in such a way that in the overall equilibrium, there is a net gain.

I. But the normal concept of capital is somewhat diluted in all this. Money must be saved in order to invest and to continue to produce new goods and services. I don't see the link between the practical problem of organizing capital investment and your philosophy of D & P.

*Koestler, A.: *The Sleepwalkers,* French Edition, Paris, 1960.

Y.   The link is a simple one, and I have explained it before. Capital investment does not necessarily add to wealth and welfare *per se*. It can
contribute to the equilibrium of D & P, and to wealth by reinforcing
its accumulation behaviour. But it can also accelerate the depletion of
D & P itself — just think of our example of fisheries exploitation.

Recognition of this fact will also provide us with an understanding
of the reason for the world's social turmoils both today and in the
past. The message is that, in many cases, in view of the enormous
problems that confront us, capital can be economized and put to
better use. Money and capital are precious development tools, and
their misuse is most regrettable.

I.   A key rule?

Y.   Capital investment must contribute to the utilization values of all D &
P. Negative effects should and can be detected and analyzed within
the framework of the specific and different aspects and structures of
utilization values in different parts of the world.

I.   Monetary equilibrium has a logic which must be respected. Otherwise
it will not function correctly.

Y.   Sometimes it may function even less well if no allowance is made for
real value problems and societal situations. The history of the twentieth
century is paved with huge investments annihilated by revolutions and
wars, by mere changes in Governments, by mishandling and by
"unforeseen" and "unallowed-for" environmental factors.

The real new investment problem is one of adequacy of capital
investment in conditions of real net increase of wealth and welfare,
or real value.

For this we must find ways of identifying, in particular, those
actions which lead to net value deducted in our D & P, i.e. to a
reduction in total wealth and welfare even though these actions may
appear as an increase in the "Value Added'.

1.11. How to Measure Wealth and Welfare — The Indicators

I.   You have just admitted that in addition to defining and applying the
concepts of "utilization value", "value deducted" and "D & P", it is

also necessary to find ways of measuring these concepts. If you abandon "national income" as an indicator, with what do you replace it? You will have no quantified references whatsoever to work with.

Y. I agree: we must solve the problem of measuring, of giving at least appropriate "weights" to our concepts. But we must not fall into the trap, of considering important only what is measurable by common standards. This would be a positivistic aberration and the source of many problems in economics: it leads to "objective" blindness instead of "objective knowledge", as is sometimes claimed. We have to quantify all that is quantifiable for the very reason that our understanding of things must be as complete as possible, in order to form judgements and organize action. When dealing with a non-quantifiable factor, we must, at least, verify whether it has an effect on a quantifiable one: the study of this *interrelation* is fundamental.

Having said that, I would also add that there are many indicators that, in my view, have far greater use than the indicator of national income.

I. Are you referring to such "social" indicators as "quality-of-life indexes" and "social accounting"?

Y. Yes. Much work has been done in this direction, over the years. For example, instead of measuring how much money has been invested in health services, it is much better to monitor people's health status. When a hospital bed in a developed country costs 100 dollars per day and more, this amount of money does not measure a level of health or of wealth, rather it measures the system's inefficiency in producing wealth.

Life expectancy and infant mortality; type, quality and quantity of food available and consumed; type, quality and quantity of shelter and clothing available and used; education level and access. All these are examples of commonly used "indicators".

I. Nothing very new there, The problem is that there exists no commonly accepted view of how to calculate and use them.

Y. The reason for this is that, in most cases, they have been seen as a simple outgrowth of sociology or of peripheral research in economics. The diversity of their nature and use has been such that these indicators are still seen as a sparse, scattered way of collecting information without any general reference theory.

I.   This is clearly so[1]. Almost everybody using some type of indicator has a different formula, and one has the feeling that they really do not go very far. If they are too different, they are useless for making comparisons and, therefore, for helping in decision-making.

Y.   I do not quite agree.

First, you can make comparisons in time, using the same indicators in the same place.

Secondly, you can make a limited number — but this is not a negative point — of comparisons in space. The fact that people in certain very "rich" areas have a life expectancy similar to that of people in some poor areas is rather significant.

Thirdly, indicators *must* be different in order to measure wealth and welfare in different parts of the world. In fact they are tools for measuring utilization values, and the utilization value theory of wealth and welfare can be the reference point to give them a more general significance.

I.   How so, if they are different and therefore incomparable?

Y.   Utilization value is *different,* once you include in the D & P all cultural and geographical characteristics. For instance, an automobile has a very low utilization value where there are no roads. One has to start by admitting that utilization values are measurable on the basis of different components and different criteria in different places and cultures. Then you can also study these differences and learn about the mechanism of D & P equilibrium.

I.   But you never really get a general reference point such as that of GNP.

Y.   One should first be very careful in interpreting the type of general reference provided by data on GNP and traditional national accounting. They are not net indicators of wealth, they are not indicators of net value. They are diffused and penetrate the economy in the wake of industrialization: they indicate essentially the degree of penetration of modern industrialization, and not necessarily the real value it adds to wealth.

I.   This is what you said earlier, when you put forward the curious idea that economics started as the discipline of industrialization and is

[1] Nordhaus, W. and Tobin, J.: *Is Growth Obsolete?,* National Bureau of Economic Research, New York, 1972.

still limited by the conditions of its birth in analyzing real total-wealth-producing activities. However, this still does not offer an answer to the point I made that although GNP and national accounting measurements have certain shortcomings, they are still a general measurable reference point, and as such they are useful.

Y. Yes, they can be useful too, in so far as world development cannot avoid certain degrees of uniformization in certain specific and limited areas. But the present use of GNP indicators is such that I wonder if getting rid of them would not be more beneficial than keeping them. GNP, especially when used for indicating level of wealth and development, is not an acceptable reference level at all. It makes horses and chickens alike because it paints them all in a single colour — and in so doing it is often misleading and deceptive. Take for instance a northern country where the climate is rather cold and it is necessary to develop a large industry to manufacture heating systems for private and/or public buildings. The cost of operating this industry and the fuel consumed will be accounted for as a contribution to the national income and considered net welfare.

I. Is it not welfare to have your house warm in winter?

Y. Of course it is, but if you lived closer to the Equator and had no cold winter, the natural D & P would take care of the problem of keeping people warm.

I. Well, so much better for them, they are saving money.

Y. Yes, they are in a position to have less reliance on monetary D & P for the same utilization value. But they will still be poorer in terms of GNP, because they have no need for an industry to build heating systems. Therefore, they have "lost" an "opportunity" to industrialize, and to become "richer".

I. Nevertheless, they may need more refrigerating systems and that gives them the opportunity of catching up.

Y. True, they can "catch up" partially there — but refrigeration in a hot country is not as essential as heating in a cold country. What I wanted to draw attention to is that the normal measure of wealth once again fails to provide a valid reference precisely because it claims to be universal. The situation, of course, becomes dramatic when heating systems are produced and marketed where they are not needed. At this point people exist for the economy and not vice versa, and the growth concept has definitely developed into a cancer destroying wealth and welfare.

I. Are not the indicators themselves perhaps wrong if you measure wealth by the number of units of heating equipment, for instance?

Y. Quite sure. You cannot isolate the object of measurement from its environment, from its culture, from *specific* objectives.

I. You have included education and cultural development as indicators. Where do you take the reference there?

Y. The reference is that the culture and knowledge of humankind is made of the cultur*es* of its different populations. In a sense, the plurality of cultures is in itself a major human asset: it implies a plurality of adaptation capabilities under different conditions. Differences are a fundamental means of reducing vulnerability and of opening up greater perspectives for the future.

I. Are you pleading in favour of strictly separated cultures, in order to preserve this multiplicity?

Y. On the contrary; a separated and isolated culture is as much in danger as a state of humanity where everybody is an exact replica of everybody else.

Culture is a matter of equilibrium, of dynamic equilibrium. This concept is perhaps not satisfactory for those adopting a cartesian approach, who like things clearly separated, isolated and well defined. The real issue is to guarantee and stimulate differentiation and confrontation, continuously. In this way the real D & P of humankind can grow, by accumulating and by selecting, in a continuous process. All attempts to make it "rational" easily become potentiators of all sorts of cancers: it leads directly to "modern" forms of "irrationality".

I. Fundamentally, you do not think it normal that, in a developing country, when a child goes to school he starts by learning the national history of a Western country, for instance.

Y. Exactly. And this process goes much further than we normally recognize. Even in most developed nations, how many people really learn, at school, about the history of the city or the region in which they *live,* instead of the history of those factors of importance in the development of their nation state? Very often, these two aspects of history do not coincide.

I.   You cannot study only local history.

Y.   Of course, one must attempt to achieve a balance between local, national and international history, in such a way that one's own *personal* patrimony and consciousness have better chances of developing.

I.   But what then of the indicators of education?

Y.   They must incorporate many references and not be a way of measuring, as a priority, access to a unique, perhaps important but often foreign, cultural model, to the exclusion of everything else. "Ignorance" very often contains much more knowledge than is currently admitted, and vice versa. There is "open" ignorance and there is "closed" (educated) ignorance.

I.   This is another paradox; can you give an example.

Y.   Easily. Take the case of the jungle "medicine-man" who is often presented as the symbol of total ignorance and superstition. Recently, it has been "discovered" that many of the "powers" such people have to "cure" certain illnesses, are linked to their ability to select and use various specific plants. Their knowledge is not intuitive: it is the sedimented outcome of long periods of trial and error over many generations of such "medicine-men". Pharmaceutical companies have "discovered" these points as a source of natural chemotherapeutic agents and have called them "living laboratories".

Clearly, in such cases, although "advanced" cultures considered these people exclusively "ignorant", this judgement was (and is) reversible. In the meantime, the advance of modern "civilization" has destroyed many of these "living laboratories", and it will never be known how much of our global human D & P has been lost with them.

I.   Nevertheless, there has, at least, been some — admittedly delayed — recognition of such facts. Moreover, one should not overestimate the total impact of such cases.

Y.   Such examples are, in any case, indicative of the possible negative effect of the mechanism of "modern culture" which the positivistic nineteenth century has passed on to us, together with a faith in the fact that it was "right" and "better" in absolute terms and in all conditions.

I.   Let us go back to our indicators; we have mentioned the indicators of wealth and welfare. Should we not also speak of indicators of need?

Y. Yes. This is the "demand" side in our enlarged analysis of economics, where D & P is the stock supplying utilization value.

Here again, we can recognize general basic and absolute needs of people, which depend on their biological constitution, and we can also differentiate needs with other natural or cultural origins.

I. The problem is, that the more you give people, the more their aspirations will grow. We have seen, in the most advanced countries, that economic growth seems to imply increased frustrations and needs although people are now much better off than they once were.

Y. This psychological judgement is only partly true. Frustration and unsatisfaction are not, as they seem superficially, an expression of growing needs. In more and more cases, they are the reaction to the fact that the "value" received has not grown in commensurate measure with the monetary added value.

Let us return to the matter I have already mentioned so often before: even when a family today has an income which, in real monetary terms, is double what was common 20 years ago, this income does not satisfy twice as many needs.

I. This is a matter of choice of how you spend your money.

Y. Not really: if we look closer at how money is spent — and consider only net figures — we will be able to identify many expenditures which have no real added value, in comparison with earlier situations.

I. Can you be more specific?

Y. Think of household appliances. Initially, the purchase of a washing machine and a tumble dryer was a net addition to welfare. However, subsequently, when, because of our economic structures, it becomes necessary to buy a machine to compact and destroy the enormous quantity of waste (often more than a kilo per person per day, that we each produce in a "developed" country), we see that the situation has changed and we are faced with needs that are induced by the functioning of the system and that were not "needs" at all before. This is the "needs" aspect of deducted value.

I. One is not obliged to buy a compacting or incinerating machine.

Y. But one is obliged to pay taxes to cover the costs of the municipal or communal services dealing with the problem for you. The "service" becomes collective — but the results are the same: the servicing of *negative induced* maintenance costs.

There are many such "needs"; pharmaceuticals consumed because of overeating; refrigerating fans working when the central heating makes a modern building too warm and one cannot open the windows; the "need" to buy a second car to go to work or to commute two hours per day because of the distance between home and workplace. It is a simple exercise to observe around us just how many needs are simply the result not of real demand but rather a maintenance need just to keep things going.

I. I remember Ivan Illich once demonstrated paradoxically that even when we have a car, we do not move any faster nowadays, if we trade off the time spent driving the car against the time spent immobile earning the money to buy the car.

Y. There is a great deal of truth in that — but not in all cases, of course.

I. However, you are not suggesting measures which act contrary to individual freedom of choice?

Y. The induced costs I am talking about are related to choices which are really not so free: you *must* clean a lake to swim in it again and to use its water; you *must* commute two hours a day if you want to get to work; you *must* pay taxes or buy machines to cope with waste production.

All these are concrete aspects of "needs" attributable to deducted values. This, I maintain, is why people often "feel" so unsatisfied — the reasons are very plain and understandable. One does not need to consult Freud or Maslow. It is enough to ask the question: how much are economic values "worth", and which "needs" are we talking about.

I. I still have the impression that what you say is true but limited in real significance. Why was this misconception of "needs" not "discovered" earlier?

Y. Do you not remember our earlier discussions? It is only when industrialization reaches maturity and the diminishing returns of technology occur that the phenomenon of deducted values takes on importance and becomes apparent.

I. What then of the developing countries? They do not yet even have enough washing machines!

Y. This is one reason why industrialization can, in many cases, yield better net wealth results there. Nevertheless, this does not obviate the need to bear in mind all the deducted values there too.

I.   Would you then suggest that conflicts for the appropriation of resources and their redistribution could disappear if a strategy for wealth and welfare were based on what you call "utilization value"?

Y.   Conflicts will not disappear. However, a more adequate notion of real value could be introduced into all economic policies, and we could at least avoid exerting greater efforts and consuming more energy and raw materials for the pursuit of "deducted values". In this latter case, injustice in the distribution and use of world resources really goes hand in hand with nonsense.

1.12. The Distribution of Wealth

I.   Let's talk a little bit more about justice. At this point I agree that it is important to consider capital and D & P formation as a basis for wealth and welfare development. But you have to admit that this issue does not solve the problem of justice and of an equal, or at least fair, distribution of wealth. In many cases, justice and fairness are the real priority: the mechanism of accumulation is one thing, but the redistribution problems are another. About *whom* are we really talking when we talk of wealth?

Y.   Your question shows that I have not yet, apparently, got my ideas across to you. In our previous discussion, I tried to explain that the problem of justice is linked to the degree of everybody's access to D & P.

I.   If everybody had enough money, or at least if money were better distributed, access to D & P would also be easier.

Y.   Not necessarily. It depends if, with your money, you increase your wealth or if you are compelled to have more money just to pay for what we have called here "deducted values". As I said previously, if you live two hours from your working place, you will need to spend more money to go there every day, as compared with somebody else who is just five minutes walk from work. You need to be "richer", in conventional monetary terms, to pay for your daily travels. In our terms, you are "richer" in the second case, even if you do not earn the equivalent amount of money necessary for the daily trip! In fact, you have more time available, you can choose to travel for your pleasure, you are not *bound* to. You suffer less from a situation of what a physicist calls increased bound energy — what we could call "increased personal entropic state".

I.   You would conclude, then, that being "richer" can be measured by the fact that many activities simply do not have a monetarized value? The paradox would be that the more people do things for free, the wealthier they would be. What about the work of housewives? And what about the work of all those who are underpaid or who are not paid at all, even if they would like to be paid?

Y.   You are still trying to fit the concept of wealth and welfare based on D & P, and the notion of access to D & P into the old framework of conventional economics.

I.   You escape the answer by too general a statement.

Y.   The point is that both the monetarized and the non-monetarized systems and *the way they interrelate* are the key to the justice game. You can distribute to a part of the population enough money so that you can declare that you are just, and not take into consideration all the free work which helps make the whole system work. This free work includes compulsory work in concentration camps and work imposed by society, like that of housewives or other "economically" marginal groups.

    You can also play the game the other way around: you can preserve privileged access to D & P, simply by using price barriers. The sea is most often free and no payment is requested for sailing on the free (non-monetarized) waters. But you must have a boat to have *access* to this free D & P. By the way, this also applies to access to underwater resources in non-territorial waters.

I.   Would you admit that justice is a problem which does not specifically relate to your analysis of wealth and welfare formation? That it applies either to the monetarized system or to the non-monetarized?

Y.   Quite the contrary. My conclusion is that, by separating the two concepts (the monetarized and the non-monetarized activities), one is bound to fail to achieve a programme of justice because, in fact, the two concepts are interrelated in practice, and the game is falsified when only one facet is presented. The problem, again, is not only to have more or less money; the real problem is to know under which conditions we can have better and more just *access* to D & P, considered as the real reference of wealth and welfare. In this way, we are also bound to evaluate better what the real contribution of every human being is through his activity, monetarized or not, to the general increase of wealth and welfare. If economic value is limited to the monetarized part of wealth and welfare production, we are, in fact, organizing injustice against those who are not producing monetarized goods and services, and who are considered at most ancillary to the industrial society. Try to imagine all non-remunerated activities stopping right away: the monetarized world would not survive for a minute. But it is also true that a sudden disappearance of the monetarized activities would produce the greater disaster in history.

I. The real point you are trying to make, then, is not only that the non-monetarized system is an essential part of "economic" activity, but also, and even more, that both the monetarized and the non-monetarized systems are strictly interrelated.

Y. That's it. And that a strategy for justice is clearly one where freedom of access to D & P — which includes the effects of such access on its formation and depletion — is the key reference. The key reference of the industrial revolution has been "redistribution" of the added value: we see now how such redistribution may become not only unsatisfactory as a goal but also unfair, when limited to an exclusively "monetarized" logic.

1.13. Conclusions — A Question of Human Quality

I. When we originally started this discussion we agreed that we were facing a dramatic world situation in which the global population would increase by about one billion additional human beings every decade for the next several decades, unless major catastrophes — surely the most bloody ever — occurred to interrupt this trend. This "new" world will be one of tremendous needs, not to mention the hundred million of extremely poor and literally undernourished.

Y. It is for this very reason that we can no longer tolerate a situation of waste, and that we have to develop a strategy of world capital formation — *within* the main objective which is *world D & P* formation.

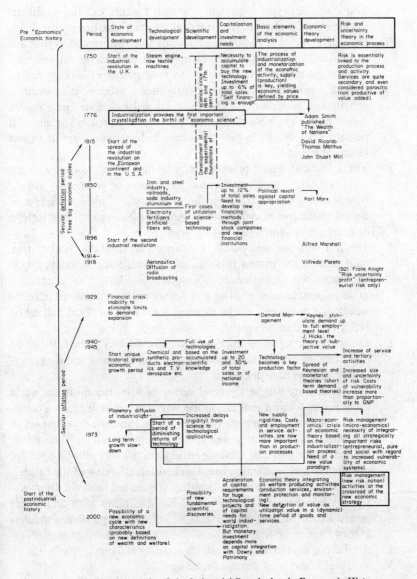

	Period	State of economic development	Technological development	Scientific development	Capitalization and investment needs	Basic elements of the economic analysis	Economic theory development	Risk and uncertainty theory in the economic process
Pre "Economics" Economic history	1750	Start of the industrial revolution in the U.K.	Steam engine, now textile machines	*science since the 16th and 17th century*	Necessity to accumulate capital to buy the new technology. Investment up to 6% of total sales. "Self financing is enough"	The process of industrialization and monetarization of the economic activity; supply (production) is key, yielding economic values defined by price.		Risk is essentially linked to the production process and activity. Services are quite secondary and even considered parasitic (non productive of value added).
	1776	Industrialization provokes the first important crystallization (the birth) of "economic science"					Adam Smith published "The Wealth of Nations"	
Secular deflation period / Three big economic cycles	1815	Start of the spread of the industrial revolution on the European continent and in the U.S.A.		*Development of the experimental foundations of*			David Ricardo Thomas Malthus John Stuart Mill	
	1850		Iron and steel industry, railroads, soda industry aluminium ind.	First cases of utilization of science-based technology	Investment up to 12% of total sales. Need to develop new financing methods through joint stock companies and new financial institutions	Political revolt against capital appropriation	Karl Marx	
			Electricity fertilizers artificial fibers etc.					
	1896	Start of the second industrial revolution					Alfred Marshall	
	1914–1918		Aeronautics Diffusion of radio broadcasting				Vilfredo Pareto	1921 Frank Knight "Risk uncertainty profit" (entrepreneurial risk only)
	1929	Financial crisis: inability to eliminate limits to demand expansion				Demand Management	Keynes: stimulate demand up to full employment level J. Hicks: the theory of subjective value	
Secular inflation period	1940–1945	Start unique historial great economic growth period	Chemical and synthetic products electron-ics and T.V. aerospace etc.	Full use of technologies based on the accumulated scientific knowledge	Investment up to 20 and 30% of total sales or of national income	Technology becomes a key production factor	Spread of Keynesian and monetarist theories (short term demand based theories)	Increase of service and tertiary activities. Increased size and uncertainty of risk. Costs of vulnerability increase more than proportionally to GNP.
	1973	Planetary diffusion of industrialization / Long term growth slowdown	Start of a period of diminishing returns of technology	Increased delays (rigidity) from science to technological application	New supply rigidities. Costs and employment in service activities are now more important than in production processes	Macro-economics: crisis of economic theory based on the industrialization process. Need of a new value paradigm	Risk management (micro-economics) necessity of integrating all strategically important risks (entrepreneurial, pure and social with regard to increased vulnerability of economic systems).	
Start of the postindustrial economic history	2000	Possibility of a new economic cycle with new characteristics (probably based on new definitions of wealth and welfare).		Possibility of new fundamental scientific discoveries	Acceleration of capital requirements for huge technological projects and of capital needs for world industrialization. But monetary investment depends more on capital integration with Dowry and Patrimony	Economic theory integrating all welfare producing activities (production services, environment protection and monitoring). New definition of value as utilization value in a (dynamic) time period of goods and services.	Risk management (new risk notion) activities at the crossroad of the new economic strategy	

TABLE 1.9. The Megacycle of the Industrial Revolution in Economic History

I. You don't deny the importance of what I would call the traditional assessment of capital requirements and capital formation.

Y. Of course not. It is obviously important to integrate and exploit any serious and constructive analysis, at either national or international level, in particular with reference to mechanisms of savings, capital markets, international debt management, balance of payments deficits and surpluses, etc. All these are quite delicate and complex questions which, nevertheless, have to be analyzed in detail; it is perhaps advisable to bypass them here and examine them in a more technical report.

I. Yes, I think it would be useful, as a starting point, to deal with the major problems we have discussed, in a form of preliminary report; this would include further analysis, at least, of the basic issues of capital needs and world problems. Among these issues, the principles of fiscal policy should not be forgotten.

Y. This is a very practical point. It is easy to see how the fiscal system, built around the notion of value in the traditional economic sense, aggravates the distortion of a situation in which the "economic" value is sometimes a positive and sometimes a negative addition to wealth and welfare — not to mention the effects of fiscal policies on D & P rather than on capital.

I. Let us try then, to produce such an introductory report. It will be important to check the reaction — be it criticism or indifference — to the ideas we have discussed.

Y. The initial step will be a general survey of what has made the world economy and world civilization the way it is today. We have a fundamental need for a complete overview of, at least, the development of the Industrial Revolution and of its present mutation. Then if our general hypothesis can survive verification, the way will be open for specific research and action based on a sustainable view of the future.

I. This sounds as if you are not definitely committed to world disaster.

Y. I don't know if world disaster will happen: many facts and trends justify all sort of pessimism. But there is a form of pessimism which is at least "action optimism".

I. All this is a kind of wager on human capacity and quality, isn't it?

Y. Yes, that is just what Aurelio Peccei said:
    "The question is one of human quality, and how this can be im-

proved. It is only by developing adequately human quality and capacities all over the world that our material civilization can be transformed and its immense potential put to good use. This is the human revolution, which is more urgent than anything else if we are to control the other revolutions of our time and steer mankind towards a viable future. However forbidding, this unparalleled task is not an impossible one, provided that we realize what is at stake and recognize that the business of becoming better is something that we have all to learn anyway in order to be modern men and women in a true, lasting sense."*

*Peccei, Aurelio, *The Human Quality*, Pergamon Press, Oxford, New York, 1977.

CHAPTER 2

Dossier for an Analysis of the Contribution and Limits to Wealth of the Industrial Revolution

"It has become increasingly apparent that the economic crisis of the last years is not only a crisis for economic theory.... In such a situation there is always a movement back to the sources. ... What are the fundamental changes which are taking place in the structure of our economies and in the functioning of economic life which are invalidating the theories that served us reasonably well in the post-war period?"

From a report of the European Trade Union Institute, Brussels, 1979 on *Keynes plus a Participatory Economy*.

2.1. The Industrial Revolution: The Triumph of Cartesianism

2.1.1. THE SEARCH FOR WELFARE THROUGH THE INDUSTRIAL REVOLUTION

Growth, and more specifically economic growth, is not limited — as a social phenomenon — to the historical period dominated by the Industrial Revolution.

For instance, between the year 1000 and the beginning of the Industrial Revolution in Europe, it has been estimated that production *per capita* almost tripled, in spite of wars and disease epidemics.[1] Such growth, however, is so diluted in time that short-term cyclical phenomena appear as being more important than the long-term movement. The perception of economic development remains of the type described in the Bible: after seven fat years, seven lean years will come and bring the level of prosperity practically to the starting point of the cycle. In such conditions, material welfare depends much more on territorial conquest than on increased productivity: in parallel, more energy can, in some cases, be devoted to contemplation and/or to religious activity. It is easy to perceive, then, how the perspective of sustained material growth over a long period has been something really revolutionary.

Industrialization was the tool of this revolution, and it gained a fundamentally *new* momentum after the middle of the eighteenth century in Europe.

Many authors have studied and written about cases of industrialization that occurred before the eighteenth century, [2345] implying — or in some cases, clearly stating — that what is known as the Industrial Revolution is not a unique phenomenon, or else that this term should not be limited — as is the convention — to the period starting around 1750.

This is an interesting question: but the important point is not whether or not elements of industrialization occurred in specific periods of history before the eighteenth century. The potential for a given historical development is always present to some degree in all societies. The real problem is to understand and monitor the growth of a particular phenomenon which is the most powerful of the forces commanding the continuous adaptation of society, as a system, at ever different degrees of equilibrium.

The speed and the size of such long-term economic progress, can be only roughly estimated. The average growth rate* during the whole period of the Industrial Revolution in those countries where this type of development** has been diffused, is estimated at under 3% per year, in terms of gross national product. This rate is then the "normal" one for the industrial revolution, even if today it is often considered as a sign of economic crisis. Such reactions to the present situation are due to the fact that during the limited period of thirty years following the Second World War, the industrial world has known a unique period of growth: in

---

*It should also be noted that the notion of economic growth itself is relatively new in economic science: many economists have started to analyze in depth the history and theory of growth only in the last decades, probably impressed by the striking performances after 1945. Simon Kuznets with David Landes (*op. cit.*) is one of the most reliable references in this field and we suggest that the interested reader refer to the publications of these authors for a thorough analysis of growth in the Industrial Revolution. See Kuznets, S.: *Economic Growth and Structure,* London, 1966, and Kuznets' various other publications on the subject of growth.

**Every time the word developed or developing country is used in this report, it must in fact be understood as *industrially* developed and *industrially* developing.

terms of gross national product, the rate of increase has been on the average between 5 and 6% per year. Although the GNP as an indicator does not correspond to real added wealth, it is clear that — thanks to the industrial revolution — there has never in history been such a period of sustained increase in real material wealth and welfare for so many people and for at least a part of the world's nations. This can be confirmed easily by all sorts of indicators: improvement in life expectancy, diminishing infant mortality rates, food and shelter available *per capita*, new products and services available for transport (trains, automobiles and aeroplanes), for information and entertainment (telephone, television, etc.) for leisure and for education.

All such accomplishments are essentially of a material nature, but it should not be forgotten that they are the result of human culture and ingenuity. The criticism against the "materialistic" culture that economic growth represents, could better be diverted into criticism against our cultural and intellectual inability to master all available *instruments* in order to achieve real advancement of wealth in its widest sense. Strictly material wealth, as such, can help considerably in the search for human freedom, although not *necessarily* so.

If the Industrial Revolution has and still is mobilizing so many efforts and energies, this is because it appeared and, in most cases, still appears as the principal instrument in the search for wealth.

It is this last assumption which now requires verification to determine how far the industrial revolution still is and might continue to be the major factor adding to real material wealth in most circumstances. Nowadays it is quite readily admitted that industrialization must not be applied in all cases and indiscriminately: however, such cases are essentially considered as exceptions to the rule and as normally due to the "inability" of given environments to adequately exploit and benefit from the yields of industrialization.

Most readers will agree that industrialization is for the first time really becoming a worldwide phenomenon, that technology has developed characteristics totally different from those at the beginning of the Industrial Revolution, that the world is being looked at as a space vessel of limited size, and that so many different cultures and political structures are bound to play a more important role on the world scene. In such a situation it is perhaps legitimate to check which are the *present* major conditions for and constraints on the promotion of wealth and welfare, and — even further — to verify the very notions of wealth and welfare themselves.

When all is said and done, the Industrial Revolution was produced in the cradle of European culture and behaviour. Industrialization presupposes a certain outlook — or ideology — and a certain social behaviour. It has its roots in a certain way of developing and using science and technology, in certain methods of accumulation of capital and, even more fundamentally, in a certain philosophy.

We therefore propose in the following pages to stimulate discussion on these major issues, because having seen how they are related to specific cultural conditions, and having accepted that wealth and welfare are also matters of social preferences, one should be better able to make a contribution to world strategy for wealth in the next decades.

2.1.2. THE TECHNOLOGICAL PERFORMANCE

Invention and utilization of technology as well as formation and utilization of capital are two essential factors conditioning the development of the Industrial Revolution.

As far as technology is concerned it is important to distinguish between two distinct phases: the first one, with no contribution and the second one, with full contribution of scientific discoveries.

The first Industrial Revolution is associated with the spread of new technology: the flying-shuttle loom and the steam engine are the main symbols of the new industrial era.

This technology was in no way associated with science. It was the result of the improved knowledge of the engineer, based on practical experience and common sense. The steam engine was developed when science did not yet know what water was: the observation of how water is converted into steam by heating and the fact that the volume of the steam produced is much larger than the volume of the water is something anybody can easily make without a laboratory. The same was true of the new looms: instead of using a hand to push the shuttle, why not just use a hammer, which struck the shuttle with the energy provided by the engine? The ability to develop this kind of technology is that of the engineer, or, more simply, of somebody possessing practical ingenuity and an ability to make things work.

The basic technology of the First Industrial Revolution was the last step in the technology which man had been evolving since prehistoric times. The engineers of the Stone Age were those practical people who knew how to cut a stone, the same type of people who, in the Iron Age, knew how to smelt certain types of earth to produce iron, without knowing scientifically what iron was in terms of chemistry and metallurgy.

This non-science-based technology reached an unprecedented level of development in the course of the eighteenth century.

The second Industrial Revolution, starting sometime in the middle of the last century, is based on technology which exploits, for the first time in history, scientific discoveries. In this case, many practical applications derive from the fact that physics, chemistry, biology and other natural sciences, had produced new knowledge of the structure and formation of materials and of natural phenomena, so that it became possible to enlarge enormously the potential of technical applications.

The first type of technology did not need more than an artisanal organization. The new one requires a complex, organized technological – scientific organization. In 1920, the number of laboratories in the USA was 350 and had increased to 1800 in 1933: the number of research workers rose from 8000 to 42,000 in the same period.

During the sixties the number of research workers exceeded one million. With the *second* Industrial Revolution it becomes possible to establish a parallel or correlation between investment in research and development, birth and expansion of new products and even of new industries, and general economic growth.

The following graph shows the results of an analysis made by Professor Freeman of the University of Sussex of the period 1935 to 1958 in the United States and the United Kingdom. It concerns 17 industrial sectors and shows that, in this period, the more research and development, the more growth. In the United States, for instance, for this overall period, the aeronautical sector invested in research and development about 40% of its net product and had a growth of over 6000%. The relative figures for electronics are 25% of net product invested for a growth of 1000%; for the chemical sector, 8% for a growth of 400%; for the textile industry 0.2% for a growth of 60%.

1. Aeronautics
2. Electronics
3. Instrumentation
4. Chemical industry
5. Other electrical industries
6. Machinery
7. Rubber
8. Nonferrous metals
9. Metalworking

10. Automobile
11. Cemented glass
12. Pulp and paper
13. Foodstuffs
14. Ferrous metals
15. Other manufactured goods
16. Textiles
17. Wood

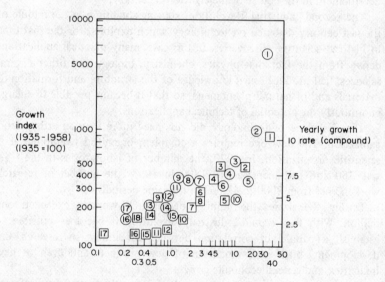

Research expenditure as a percentage of net product per industry in 1958.

○ = USA   □ = Great Britain

Source: Duckworth, W.: *New Scientist,* London, December 8, 1966, p. 564.

FIG. 2.1. *Relationships between Research and Development Expenditures in Percentage of net Product in 1958 and Increase in Industrial Sectors between 1935 and 1958.*

It is interesting to note in this graph, that:
— the influence of technology on growth is even more striking when industry is broken down by sector: the newer the industrial sector (in certain cases it is a sector created by the new technology itself, as in the case of aviation and electronics), the higher the research costs in relation to other production costs;
— note should also be taken of the stimulating role of the newer and most dynamic sectors: growth in the traditional sectors is normally much lower and is, to a large extent, a consequence of the impulse and spin-off from the most progressive branches.

Science and technology have had tremendous effects in the course of the second industrial revolution: in fact the period up until the 1960s may be designated as the period of the greatest success of science and technology in producing wealth and welfare ever.

2.1.3. THE ESSENTIAL CONTRIBUTION OF CAPITAL

New technology and science-based technology, however, would not have succeeded in becoming a useful tool for the production of wealth and welfare if it had not proved possible to mobilize them through the economic mechanism of capital formation and capital investment.

This has been an essential phenomenon which has developed parallel to the technological one, from the primitive era of the beginning of industrialization at a very small scale, up to the present huge investment needs, where a single "machine" may cost more than one billion dollars.

Going back to the times of the "new" steam engine and of the "new" flying-shuttle loom, we find the testimony of Adam Smith. In his *Wealth of Nations,* he writes:
"In the opulent countries of Europe, great capitals are at present employed in trade and manufactures. In the ancient state, the little trade that was stirring, and few homely and coarse manufactures that were carried out, required but very small capital."[6]

The capitalistic function of money starts to be clearly perceived. The new technological development can be exploited only if there has been a development in the use of money as a medium for transferring goods and services in an undifferentiated way over space and time more rapidly and efficiently than could be achieved by any complex system of transport and storage.

Money and the development of industrial technology are closely inter-related. Specialization, one of the cornerstones of industrialization, would be impossible without a money-based exchange system which overcomes the individual producer's problem of not being able to produce all the kinds of good he needs, allowing him to concentrate on those which — in principle, at least — he can produce better.

Money, and the consequent monetarization of the economy, are there-fore essentially signs of the increased complexity and development of a society. This view is much less generally accepted than its obviousness would lead one to suppose. There are a number of reasons for this.

In the pre-industrial world, money was very limited in quantity, and, as we shall see in later chapters, also very diversified in form. It was an auxiliary instrument for certain market dealings and was generally used only for settling differences in value between what was bought and sold in a very simplified market. The great majority of goods produced and consumed in a pre-industrial society were never objects of monetarized trade. At that time money was of little importance in the economic organization of society since a society which is not industrialized does not need capital. Money was often regarded as a symbol of wickedness since it was a sign of wealth but not of *productive* wealth; it was not even necessarily an instrument of economic exploitation since, in agricultural societies, the fiscal system could effectively harass the peasant without the use of money.

With the advent of industrialization, money came into its own as an instrument, since it constituted the embodiment of capital, the key instrument for the promotion of production and wealth, by the use of new "costly" technology.

But cultural inertia is not rapidly overcome. The cultural tendency to relate money to sin persisted, and has even been perpetuated in many of the great works of Western literature. Moreover, it has traditionally been under attack in many religions.

The basic cultural revolution supported by Adam Smith was precisely that of treating money (and particularly capital) as an instrument deserving *moral* approval: "Capital is increased by parsimony, and diminished by prodigality and misconduct".

The early socialist opponents of capital continued to fight against money as being a means of exploitation. Some of the famous utopian socialists made many attempts to devise community structures in which there was no place for money.

In all these cases, it may be suspected that this approach was symptomatic of the problems involved in adapting a traditional agricultural society to the wider use of money.*

Industrial society has admitted that money in itself is one of man's positive achievements and a useful tool for society; the real problem has been that of adapting and controlling the use of money. The invention of money and the extension of its use for capital formation was at least as important as that of genetic engineering. It is scarcely fair to condemn a tool just because it is being used badly. Moreover, when it is subject to indiscriminate attacks, its correct use is even more difficult to organize. If a society really believes that everything relating to money is bad, the virtuous will tend to hold aloof and the unvirtuous to predominate. Like many "predictions", this too becomes a self-fulfilling one. Even Marx, following some youthful hesitations, finally rejected socialist proposals for a money-less society.

How is money able to become "Capital"? The answer is extremely simple. Let us take the traditional textile industry, as it existed in England at the beginning of the eighteenth century. The peasant's spinning and weaving tools were often so simple that he could make them himself – as can be seen from a visit to a museum of ethnography in any part of Europe. Crafting the tool was an integral part of the job, and many of the pieces are decorated and are virtually small works of art. No money is needed to produce "machines" such as these.

A major change took place when, as a result of new technology, it became possible to produce mechanical looms which can be assembled and operated by a single man, since the new looms could be driven, at least partly, by a static prime mover – the steam engine.

This marked the beginning of the concentration of production, opening the way to industrialization. At the same time, it broke up the system of home manufacture. The peasant became a "worker" and had to work away from home, handling the new machines. Factory construction and operation, machinery building, the provision of power to drive

*See on this point Chapter 3, paragraph 3.3.1.

the machines — all required a different type of money to that used in the trading of consumer goods: as production becomes more technologically advanced, more investment capital is needed, which requires more and more saving. Money, as a reservoir of value, has facilitated a form of saving, which could much more easily be transferred in time and space. Without a stock of money unrelated in time and space to any specific type of goods, this process would have been impeded.

As the process of industrialization created a demand for bigger and faster machines, more concentrated centres of production, etc., the amount of money capital needed, obviously increased. Even though, during the initial stages of the Industrial Revolution, it seemed to Adam Smith that the amount of capital employed was very large, it was in fact relatively very small by modern standards. In any case, it was sufficiently small for indiviuals to promote a very scattered Industrial Revolution (and Adam Smith never wanted development that exceeded this capital requirement or technological scale).

The textile industry was closely associated with this initial stage of the industrial revolution. It was to be 200 years before the single-family pattern of capital formation began to be relegated to the past. By the end of the Second World War, many of the mills in certain European textile regions continued to operate on a family, self-financing basis even though a fair degree of concentration had taken place in the two preceding centuries. This was possible because the rate of investment needed was rarely over 5% of total sales, and the absolute cost of machines was not too great. It confirms Landes' statement[7] that "The ratio of net capital formation to income did not go above 5 or 6% through most of the eighteenth century, rising to perhaps 7 or 8% in the last decade, when the Industrial Revolution was in full swing (in England)."

In the last thirty years, the textile industry has undergone a techno-logical revolution which has disrupted this system. This case also brings out a particular feature in the development of the Industrial Revolution, i.e. the succession of break-throughs in different sectors, each providing the impetus for the next.

It also accords with the analysis made by Schumpeter, who detected clearly the long-term cycles in the development of the Industrial Revolution.[8]

During the nineteenth century, the Industrial Revolution progressed, largely due to the stimulus of railroad development. John Stuart Mill pointed out "Many undertakings require an amount of capital beyond the means of the richest individual or private partnership"[9] and this became increasingly possible with the spread of a major new invention: the joint-stock company. Nevertheless, by the middle of the century capital requirements were still small by current standards. According to Landes, "By 1850, mining, heavy industry, and the railway network were all expanding rapidly: even so, the rate of net capital formation for the two decades 1850–70 averaged less than 10%."[10] The liberation and free-flow of capital were essential. Finally "Continental Europe became the scene of the spread of the Industrial Revolution and began to approach that mobility of capital that Britain had achieved half a century before."

But any new step forward is never a mere copy of previous events, even in another geographical area. The joint-stock company provided a way of pooling the resources of several individuals in a joint undertaking, but there were limits to what could be done by this means. For this reason, the period also saw the beginning of the modern financial intermediation system, through the joint-stock investment bank. Banks had, of course, existed for centuries, but their essential function had been to finance trade. The financing of industrial production was an interesting innovation but involved considerable financial risks. Hence, the development of the financial intermediation system for the industrial revolution occurred only after a century of delay, when capital accumulation and investment had risen to extremely high levels.

Marx, on the wave of this phenomenon, perceived the process essentially in terms of the old-fashioned individual entrepreneur with money capital, and saw the whole production system becoming concentrated in the grasp of fewer and fewer incredibly powerful hands. The fortunes of some renowned families become legendary just as the feats of the military commanders of the Thirty Years War had become legendary in Europe.

No matter what judgement is reserved for it, the financial intermediation system, invented for the continuation of the Industrial Revolution, clearly provided many new flexible tools for the progress of industrialization.

With these new tools available, industrial societies were prepared for the unforeseen acceleration of the Industrial Revolution that resulted from new technology based on the direct exploitation of scientific knowledge. If we compare the total volume of capital formation in major countries today, with that of last century, we can appreciate the continuous, both absolute and relative, increase in the part played by capital in modern economies.

As can be seen from the following diagram,[11] in the most industrialized nations, capital formation has been in recent years at a minimum level of 18% of GNP up to about 35%.

Even though these figures are not exactly comparable with those recorded for previous centuries, it is obvious that we have come a long way from the capital needs of the textile mill at the beginning of the Industrial Revolution, described earlier.

What are then, in terms of capital requirements, the outlook and the perspectives for the future?

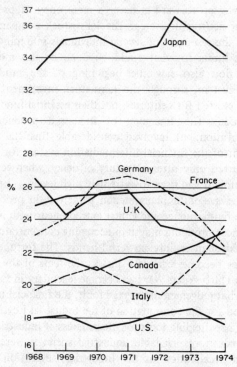

FIG. 2.2. *Annual Growth in Gross Fixed Capital Formation as a Percentage of GNP.*

One might be tempted, in order to answer this question, to retrace the development of capital requirements at earlier stages of technology and extrapolate for recent technological developments.

The following three factors would indicate then, that in the next few decades, world capital/capital requirements could be at a fantastically high level:

(a) The world's population increase, and the demand which will be generated as a consequence;
(b) The extension of industrialization to the rest of the world;
(c) The extrapolation of past trends in the capital needs of new technology.

But, at the same time, we have also to bear in mind that every major new step forwards in the Industrial Revolution has been accompanied by some fundamental structural changes. Are we sure that the future will bring something similar to the passage to the era of science-based technology, which amplified enormously the need for capital? How far can general conclusions be drawn from the fact that many industrial units (e.g. a nuclear power station or an oil rig) currently require an investment of the order of a billion dollars a piece? Is investment in production still as vital to economic development as it was in the past? To what extent is technology increasing net productivity, so that the increase in investment is really adding to net wealth?

It is likely that some of the past trends at least will continue in the future, but it is the task of economic thinking to try to verify how far the industrial model of adding to wealth for the present and the future world really match the new challenges.

Let's then turn to another event, of a cultural nature, whose official "birth" took place in the middle of the take-off of the Industrial Revolution: economics, or economic "science".

2.1.4. THE INDUSTRIALIZATION PROCESS AND THE MATURATION OF ECONOMICS: THE NOTION OF VALUE

Certain economic observations, and even some preliminary theories on economic activities, were established in times more ancient than the middle of the eighteenth century in England. But it was the development of industrialization into a prominent social and economic phenomenon, that produced the real birth of cristallization of economics. As Alfred Marshall remarks: "Modern economic science owes much to ancient thought indirectly, but little directly".[12] The underlying philosophy of economics is very much related to values and theories that stem at least from the time of Copernicus. But the specific object of enquiry of economics is essentially a new system of thought, a new tool of analysis adapted to and stimulated by a new problem complex: industrialization, which gained unprecedented momentum during the life time of Adam Smith.

This parallel between a new, important social phenomenon and the development of a new discipline is an important subject for research. It implies that if the object of analysis undergoes change and its essence is eventually modified, the relevant tool of observation will need to change accordingly. Marshall also states that "If the subject matter of a science passes through different stages of development, the laws which apply to one stage will seldom apply without modification to the others".[12]

Such remarks are not without important consequences: they underline the fact that social "sciences", are historical sciences.* The scope of their objectivity is not only limited — as is any other discipline or science — by the imperfection of available knowledge, but they are also limited in time by their changing historical relevance. In other words, the time and space of their validity are limited.

If this is true, it would mean that the present validity of standard economic theory is linked to the fact that industrialization persists in being the essential economic phenomenon stimulating society. This might happen even if entire branches of economics do not study directly the industrial system and its development, which in any case is the prime indirect mover of any other kind of economic activity.

We have the advantage today of observing two phenomena, the Industrial Revolution and the birth and development of economics, from horizons of more than two centuries of experience. We can therefore have a perspective of things which could not be available to the first founders of economics.

---

*Some economists have utterly different views: "For historians each event is unique. Economists however, maintain that forces in society and nature behave in a repetitive way. History is particular; economics is general" (from Kindleberger Charles P.: *A History of Financial Crisis*, New York, 1978, p. 14).

We can observe more clearly, for instance, how if on the one hand economics did develop under the impulse of the new industrial mode of production, it was still largely influenced, on the other hand, by an environment which remained essentially an agricultural one until our century, even in the most "industrialized" nations.

Marshall recalls that the "first systematic attempt to form an economic science on a broad basis was made in France about the middle of the eighteenth century by a group of statesmen and philosophers under the leadership of Quesnay, the noble-minded physician of Louis XV".[13] The intriguing thing is that Quesnay, on the one hand, felt the need to systematize economic activities (among other things he is even considered the forerunner of the input—output models). On the other hand, he naturally wished to apply his "model" to the "reality" of production. However, at the beginning of the Industrial Revolution, industrial production was an activity of limited economic importance, as compared with agriculture: the Wealth of Nations, for Quesnay, was then based almost exclusively on agriculture.

A man who had travelled from Scotland had the opportunity of meeting Quesnay and discussing economics with him; his name was Adam Smith. When he wrote and published *The Wealth of Nations*,[14] he produced the first great cristallization of economic thinking, the official birth of economic "science". It was Adam Smith who gave order to the main elements which allow a systematic analysis of the developing economic systems based on industrialization. This was in 1776.

And yet, although Adam Smith perceived and analyzed a society in evolution, sustained by the optimistic rationalistic philosophy of the XVIIIth century, he still did not perceive completely the consequences of what was really going on. He did not see the Industrial Revolution! As Heilbronner remarks,[15] "his system is based on the idea of the possibility of increasing wealth under the assumption that the Great Britain of the XVIIIth century will statically remain the same society. No qualitative change is foreseen. No great attention is given to the formation of the first industries. He does not really believe in the future of the new economic organizations raising capital and called corporations (joint-stock companies). His objection is that individual ingenuity will suffer from being submitted to an anonymous organization, controlled by a plurality of shareholders."

Still later, the influence of a predominantly agricultural society was to form the basis of further economic analyses; nevertheless, in fact, those analyses always prepared or favoured the ground for the development of the industrial system.

Ricardo's theory of rent and the law of diminishing returns take agriculture as their example.

Malthus, who was a contemporary friend of Ricardo, even though a much less practical business man, analyzed the limits of agricultural production versus the growth of population. Some twelve years after his publication, events showed he was *right*: many countries in Europe did experience a real period of famine (around 1840). Later, however, events also showed that Malthus could be wrong too, especially when the new crops from the Americas (potatoes, tomatoes, etc.) contributed to pushing back the limits of agricultural production, even before the Second Industrial Revolution really started to increase productivity through mechanization and the use of artificial fertilizers.

Economic theory, then, although constantly stimulated by the industrialization process, has also been constantly conditioned by the agricultural environment, for most of its history.

In our view, even today, contemporary economic theory has not completely ridden itself of some assumptions implicitly derived from the agricultural tradition — the most important one being the time-organization of economic activity.

The normal time-organization of agriculture is in fact dictated by the seasons and by the solar year. We shall come back to this point later on. But we would like to note here already that it is probably because of this sedimented experience that economic thinking has often had a tendency to privilege the short-term whereas modern technology is introducing new types of inertias with longer reaction times.

Why then was Adam Smith's *The Wealth of Nations* so important? As Marshall says "his chief work was to combine and develop the speculations of his French and English contemporaries and predecessors as to value . . . his chief work was to find in the theory of value a common centre that gave unity to economic science".[16]

This notion of value is essential from many points of views:

(a) It is a philosophical and even a moral justification: value is produced by the labour of man. What man produces has a value. Man is the source of value: in the final analysis, we can recognize in this definition the humanistic ambition and idealism.

Reading the classics in economics, at least as far as John Stuart Mill[17], it can be seen that this notion is the real key to the whole theoretical construction.

(b) Value is the basis of the production system. Smith, Mill and others, all insist at length on the notion of productive and non-productive labour, mixing together practical and ethical concepts. Productive labour produces wealth: producing bread, producing cloth, i.e. producing goods, means producing wealth. Those who do not produce goods, do not produce wealth. Evidence (or supposed evidence) is combined with the image of man obliged to leave Paradise and to work in order to *earn* his livelihood.

Exclusion of the broad category of "non-productive" labour, was the very simple decision — whatever the motivation — which was to make value the exclusive paradigm of the *production* system and in fact of *industrialization* as a whole.

(c) However, these premises were not enough to found the new economic science, and leave behind the generalities of a social philosophy. The decisive step was the establishment of a system for *measuring* productive value. Modern rationalism stipulated that a phenomenon, in order to be analysed, had to be measured. How does one measure value, in the same way as one counts flowers, people, or measure speed, weight, heat, etc.? In the latter cases, the objects were measureable by themselves: they had an "objective" existence. How was it possible to measure value in an equally "objective" way? It was here, in the quantification of value, more than from any other point of view, that Smith's market theory was of importance.

The market, by the mechanism of demand and supply (with a more or less "invisible" and, therefore, supposedly "objective" hand), attributes a price to the results of man's productive labour. Value then is measurable by price. In this way, economics at last had at its disposal a means of measurement and, upon this basis, it soon began to claim it was the first social science to be "scientific".

For our purpose, it is essential to note that value (and its quantification by a price) is the real founding element of the new economic "science".

(d) The combination of the concepts of productive value and price had not only the direct effect of fertilizing the first cell of economics but also the indirect effect of providing the framework for the definitive characterization of economics as the "science" of analyzing industrialization.

Although agriculture, as we have seen, was the predominant activity until the end of the nineteenth century and beyond, it was, for the most part, not monetarized and did not need to be until money was required for the purposes of agricultural *industrialization*.

When economic theory developed a paradigm of value based on price (defined in money terms), the liaison was established between economics on the one hand and industrialization on the other, even though the fathers of such fertilization were, to some extent, unaware of it.

We can then resume this notion of value in the following way:

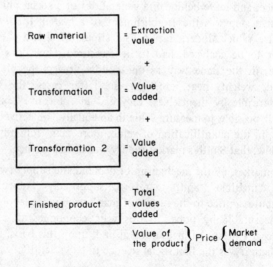

TABLE 2.1. *The Value Added*

On the basis of this chart we start, for any form of production, from the raw material which has no "value" in itself. The value of this raw material is equal to the cost of extracting it. The raw material passes through one or more conversions before becoming a finished product. In each phase, a value is added which represents the cost of the additional labour used, directly or indirectly (under the form of "capital").

The price set by the market (for the sake of simplicity, we have taken this at the level of the final product) is the unit of measure which will be the reference for quantifying value.

This concept of value, determined by price in the market and referring to a production system, was adopted in full and extended only slightly by Karl Marx, although with new political significance.

In fact, since the theory of value is based essentially on the concept of labour, which has both biblical and humanistic connotations, capital itself is nothing more than the accumulation of the labour required to produce a machine, for instance, in a previous phase. Marx simply introduced (with violence, however) the concept that the producers of capital, are those who furnish their labour in the production process, but who are deprived of at least a part of the value they have added. Money, although necessary for the functioning of the economy, through a complicated system of circulation,[18] is the tool by which the value of labour accumulated in capital is finally appropriated by those who control money.

There is undoubtedly a certain logic in this reasoning, provided one starts from the classical concept of value. But this logic is possible only if another seed of classical theory is taken for granted: namely, the concept of unproductive labour, to which we shall revert later. Marx may also be read as one of the first writers on financial intermediation: he offered certain explicit analyses of what today is known as the quantitative theory of money (by linking the level of prices to the quantity of money in circulation) and, on this point at least, he is linked to even the Chicago School of Milton Friedman (although for the Chicago School, it is the quantity of money which determines the level of prices and not vice versa).

In economic theory, in particular in classical economics, services such as banking and insurance are not linked directly to the production process, and may easily be classed as unproductive or even parasitic labour: they are outside the value paradigm. Certain nineteenth-century socialists and utopians often dreamed of a society without money. Marx clearly rejected such a hypothesis, but service/financial activities have continued to be stigmatized with the original sin of being of "no value". Even though he admitted the usefulness of the monetarized system, Marx did not see clearly how the industrialization processes and the development of technology and monetarization were, in absolute terms, facets of the same problem. In an era of industrialization, a socialistic system may try to better redistribute the yields of the economy; by promoting the industrialization process (as has since been the case for all socialist countries), then it will inevitably develop, through monetarization, *capitalism of one sort or another.*

Thus, we are currently confronted with two sorts of "impasse": on the one hand, the basic paradigm of classical economics theory has been in some way "captured" by Marxism; on the other hand, socialist states, in as much as they are involved in promoting industrialization, are caught in the logic of "capitalism".

Even from this angle, we see that the process of industrialization is the fundamental reference point for different regimes and for different economic traditions of thinking.

We have seen then, how the classical concept of economic value has concentrated on the supply/production aspects. This was also due to the deeply ingrained idea that, in a world of scarcity, there would always be demand for whatever was produced. The economist Jean-Baptiste Say, from Lyon, formulated this idea into a Law.

In his pioneering work, Alfred Marshall[19] gave a fundamental impulse to research on *demand* in economic theory. In this way, he helped to open the breach through which numerous attempts have been made to find a new basic concept of value, which would replace or at least complement the classical concept.

This evolution of economic thinking has produced relevant results on several grounds.

On the positive side, one can put the efforts, such as those of J. R. Hicks, to establish a subjective theory of value.*

*Hicks, J. R.: *Value and Capital,* Oxford University Press, 1939 and 1974. This tendency to stress subjectivism has led economic theory almost to invade the field of behavioural sciences such as psychology or psychosociology. Tibor Scitovsky, for instance, deals with Psychology and Economic Motivations, in his book on *The Joyless Economy,* Oxford University Press, 1976.

The importance of demand in theoretical analysis as well as in practice, had its most successful proponent in John Maynard Keynes.* When most modern economists, whether they are "monetarists" or "keynesians", speak of preferences, utility, demand management and investment, their vocabulary and analytical procedures are most often clearly related to a value paradigm which is essentially demand-orientated.**

Although paradoxical, this is nevertheless a confirmation of the immense success of the Industrial Revolution and its science-based technology: it has been demonstrated for such a long time now that supply can be increased even beyond expectations, that the main concern in the economic management has become that of controlling demand.

This brings us to the main questions: how far can we rely, for the future production of wealth and welfare, on the same industrial premises that have been applied over the past two centuries? Are the value concepts adopted in the various economic theories fully adequate; especially since the formulation of these theories has been influenced by specific conditions of industrial development?

Perhaps we should return to what Marshall has called the "indirect sources of economic thinking and of industrial development". The Industrial Revolution has clearly been the greatest material achievement of a philosophical and cultural revolution which has its roots in European rationalism. As such it has been the triumph of Cartesianism.

Let us first try to be more explicit about these "indirect sources" and then attempt to verify how far Cartesianism has determined current concepts of economic value and whether these are, today, consistent with a world strategy aimed at maximizing wealth.

---

*When, for instance, Keynes produced evidence that, in certain cases (e.g. when there is excessive saving), the key economic measure for achieving full employment is the stimulation of demand.

**See, for instance, the Chapter on the evolution of values (expressing human preferences) in the OECD report *Facing the Futures* (Paris, 1979) which are discussed as referred to the demands. The basic reference to demand-created values is still maintained in some of the new economic research concerned with the non-monetarized economic system as in the recent book on *Unpriced Values – Decisions without Market Prices,* by Sinden, J. A. and Worrell, A. C. (New York, 1979).

2.1.5. THE PHILOSOPHICAL BACKGROUND TO THE INDUSTRIAL
REVOLUTION

When Copernicus died in 1543, at the age of seventy, the reigning
"ideology" was based predominantly on religion: the principles of truth
were derived essentially from dogma and controlled revelation. The first
Renaissance had started but was not yet undermining the fundamental
ideological beliefs on which society was based. During Copernicus' lifetime,
this can be identified in the blossoming of pictorial art in Italy (e.g.
Raphael) and elsewhere: the vast majority of Europe's painters' themes
were inspired by the Christian religion. Following the end of the medieval
era, as symbolized by Dante, the only aspiration of secular power was to
be separate from the church; however, the principles of legitimacy were
still derived essentially from religion.

In this framework, authority, religion and the principle of deductive
thinking went hand in hand. The Reformation, which took place during
Copernicus' life span (Luther was excommunicated in 1520), was a first
attempt at introducing at least some latitude in the interpretation of
dogmas and revelation, thus leading to a restriction in the number and
content of dogmas.

The problem with religious thinking which, by deduction from the
Bible and other "given" sources, provided explanations for many aspects
of physical reality (e.g. that the earth was the centre of the universe), was
that it could not bear verification, without feeling that its legitimacy was
being attacked. For this reason, when Copernicus discovered that the
planets rotate on their axes and around the sun, he did not dare to dis-
seminate his ideas during his lifetime. Instead he admitted publication of
his famous treatise only a few months before his death. His work came
under condemnation by the Catholic church, which was not revoked until
the nineteenth century!

Clearly, if research was to be carried out, areas of competence had to
be delineated to provide protection from accusations of attacks on
religion.

When Bacon and subsequently Descartes developed the concept that
research must be strictly inductive (based on visible and materially
experimentable facts), they not only developed a specific philosophy, but
also took the fundamental step to gaining a minimum of space for the

free application of human reason to the study of human and physical phenomena.

The philosophical and *political* nature of such an attitude was obvious to all the new "rationalists". Some of Galileo's letters[20] are very revealing in showing his constant affirmation of Christian faith and even his attempts to convince the church that if Christianity would insist in claiming to define reality by the authoritative/deductive method even when its definitions were contradicted by experimental evidence, there would be a very negative backlash effect. The essence of religion was something else — he insisted — from that which would be shattered by scientific discovery. In a more or less nuanced way, Galileo tried, in practice, to tell the church how to defend its interests in a better way. However, this could not be appreciated since, in the final analysis, the religious authorities were but human. . . .

Galileo was condemned by the Church in 1633, and as in many similar trials the accusation was a rather complicated one — revealing the embarassment of the accusers; on some points, it was even correct, stating for instance that Galileo was wrong to affirm that the tides were determined essentially by the sun — which shows how complex the path of research and evidence can be.*

Galileo's condemnation was felt bitterly by Descartes, and showed how delicate it was to defend the new principles of rational research. Initially, Descartes stopped working on his philosophical treatise. Friends insisted that he should summarize at least some of the ideas, and finally four years after Galileo's trial, he published the *Discours de la méthode.***

The *Discours* can be read in many ways: it may be taken as a pure

*Arthur Koestler, in his book *The Sleepwalkers* tends to criticize Galileo on many grounds and in particular on the fact that he finally "provoked" the church which was much more open-minded than normally recognized. But this interpretation is very much determined by Koestlers' implicit ideology. He thinks that both Religion and Science research "truth", and therefore should work hand in hand: in fact, Religion and Science are two forms of Religion and this is the proof of how far modern rationalism has its roots in an (anti-) religious "universal" thought. Other ancient Marxists, like Garaudy, will follow a similar path.
Galileo is then condemned for having been tried and condemned. . . .

*In 1637, nine years earlier, he had already written the *Règles pour la Direction de l'Esprit* (Rules for Controlling the Mind), which show — among other writings — that his thinking was more complex than is presented here in a necessarily simplified version, but which is still meaningful in terms of the today's operational significance of "Cartesianism".

philosophical treatise, a revolutionary pamphlet ("Il suffit de bien juger pour bien faire", good judgement suffices to ensure good actions), or a disguised conservative document ("Ma troisième maxime était de tâcher toujours plûtot ... à changer mes désirs que l'ordre du monde", my third rule has always been to change my aspirations than the world's order).

In his *Discours,* Descartes delivers a number of important messages, sometimes logical and based on good will and good sense, but also sometimes fanciful and even irrational. However, it must be read here in relation to the significance that it had for the further development of Western rationalism. The following points are relevant here:

— Descartes wrote the *Discours de la Méthode* in the vernacular and not in Latin as most of his other philosophical works, thus showing his desire to be "modern" and make a "breakthrough" in public opinion. As such he was a revolutionary.

— A psychometric analysis of the *Discours* would show that this small document is essentially a confirmation of Descartes' Christian faith containing, as it does, much reiteration of dogma. Galileo had provided the necessary lesson and he succeeded, in this way, in being accepted by the Catholic theologians, in spite of some problems at Utrecht University, which did not however lead to an official condemnation.

— The inductive method is clearly stated in four rules:

(1) Accept only factual evidence (theologians themselves could accept this as innocuous since, having excluded everything related to religion from the realm of verification, such a rule ends as a tautology).

(2) Break down all complex natures into their constituent simples so that each can be examined separately and in depth. This second rule is probably the most significant in the development of rationalism because it implies:

  · that the subjects of research can be divided into *separate* subclasses without losing elements of their explanation;

  · that subjects of research can be divided into *distinct* and *determinate* space/time units. Problems can be isolated by specific boundary conditions. This assumption will nevertheless stimulate the subdivision of knowledge into "disciplines" and, thus, produce quite positive effects;*

*See note opposite.

that — and this has wide-ranging philosophical implications — the separation of *discrete* units involves both the body and soul. This is contrary to Aristotelism and contrary to the essence of some of the Church's fundamental dogmas (e.g. that of the Nicean Oecumenic Council of 325, establishing the unity of spirit and matter through the Dogma of the Trinity). It also has a "practical" consequence: the conquest of an area of independent, rational research at least as far as the "material" world is concerned. Nevertheless, this was considered by the theologians as a rather limited breakthrough and of little consequence since, as the pre-eminence of the Church's dogmas was still accepted, it should, at any time, have been possible to reduce the sphere of "factual" enquiry.

Today, it is obvious that the principle of distinction and separation of problems into their individual components is a commonsense tool for most study and research as far as this is practically feasible; this is admitted by Georgescu Roegen,[21] in particular for that specific areas of research that Kuhn calls "normal science".**[22]

However, this rule cannot be considered an absolute general *principle*: as such it implies the existence of a philosophical or ideo-logical counterdogma (the total "objectivity" of reality), to which we shall return later. To ensure that Descartes' second rule was not intentionally dogmatic, thought should be given to the historical and political situation in the seventeenth century. The key objective was to gain as much space as possible to advance in the pursuit of knowledge. Even philosophical ideas are not born in a void: they are tools for human advancement and in a certain sense they are political tools (expressing the will for the advancement of knowledge).

---

*Certain negative effects can also be detected. The existence of Two Separate Cultures (seen in the Human "soft" Sciences and by the Natural "hard" Sciences) also has its roots here. This separation is, among other things, "a cause of the failure to make politics more responsive to the environmental crises", see Brett-Crowther, M. R.: *Cultural Values and Environmental Problems,* Réseaux — Revue Universitaire de Science Morale, Mons (Belgium), 1979, No. 35–36, 157–182.

**Normal science, as Kuhn defines it, means scientific investigation within the phenomenological context of a particular paradigm; most of his examples are reductionist because most science has been reductionist. It can be argued of course that this need not be so.

It is probably this second rule that turned Descartes into a symbol, perhaps the major symbol, of Western rationalism: it was not just an idea, but a practical "mot d'ordre" to open the breach that would subsequently be continuously enlarged, and through which scientific research and method would pass to start moulding our present world.

Descartes' importance does not rest on the fact that he was "right", but that he devised the necessary tools at a particularly significant period of history: here again, society was evolving in such a way as to incorporate these tools as a major element of its own development.

(3) The third rule of Descartes was that of synthesis: the addition of several parts of analysis, whose total was equal to the sum of each part.

This third rule is the corollary of the second, based on the "discrete" separation of subject-matters.

The practical application and usefulness of such a rule is, at least today, much more limited than the second one. Notions like those of synergy and of system are in clear contradiction to it, and we shall return to this point later.*

(4) The fourth rule, was that of careful verification in any analysis to ensure nothing is omitted.

Here, again, it should be supposed that there are certain systems which can be studied in their total** number of facets. Once again there must be clear-cut boundary conditions and determinate realities. This applies only, and even here some doubt exists, to a certain number of realities (a table, a water molecule) which are objective, material realities. The principle of indeterminacy, which applies to all social sciences, and which, at the boundary-condition level, also applies to natural sciences, is a clear contradiction of Descartes in this sense. Moreover, even where "objective" realities

*In his "Rules" No. 11 and No. 12 of *Règles pour la Direction de l'Esprit* the notion of interdependence is still more complex, but it is also significant that, in the *Discours,* he chose to be more clear-cut.

**When David Hume acknowledges the impossibility of making predictions on the basis of an ever incomplete number of facts, he destroys — as B. Russell so desperately said — the basis of empiricism, with its consequent negative effects on scientific research; this is one of the many negative effects of "Cartesianism".

For a discussion on this point see Karl R. Popper: *Objective Knowledge,* Chapter 1, Oxford, 1972.

exist, they are considered such because human judgement can easily define (as a result of its perception) the limited nature of the object. In fact, even a molecule of water can be described as a separate system, but it never exists in a total time/space vacuum.

We see here that, if we take this rule, as the preceeding ones, as a pragmatic principle, as a first approach — acceptable even though fundamentally inaccurate — we can all agree.

However, when these pragmatic principles are based on a philosophical, tendentially universal and even metaphysical explanation, they create, more or less consciously, the basis for a counter-religion. From extreme deductivism to extreme inductivism, we move between two dogmatic poles.

In the final analysis, it was not the Reformation which finally built a new religion: today, it can be seen that its achievement was the introduction of variations and some liberalization.

The subtitle of the *Discours,* is very revealing of what was really at stake with the new ideas. It reads "for properly guiding the Reason in the *Search for Truth in the Sciences*". Ambiguity continued to accompany the "scientific movement" and, *up to the present day,* this ambiguity has even increased: it lies in the search for "truth". As mentioned, Descartes explained that his work was about inductive truth, and that he respected religious deductive truth. However, as soon as the clear division between the material and the spiritual becomes progressively blurred, the method for finding "objective" truth will increasingly appear to be the method for a modern religion. In the case of philosophical materialism, the spiritual is not eliminated but rather completely absorbed by the material, where the metaphysical promise that objective truth can be *added* up by scientific method, is simply the mirror image of Christian revelation.

In fact, starting from the Cartesian proof that God exists, since God is perfection in contrast to the imperfection and limitation of human knowledge, it will be enough to extrapolate from the concept that science is providing *total* knowledge in a specific well-defined system, and use Cartesianism as a tool for reaching God by additional units of truth, via the "scientific" method.

Maybe it was inevitable, in order to compensate for dogmatic, conservative religion, to plant the seeds of a counter-religion. However, nowadays, we are suffering from the dogmatism of inductivism, rather than from that of deductivism. The justification of authority based on "facts" is a relatively common "sleight-of-hand".

If Descartes had written, in the subtitle, that this method was to be used in searching for *"more* truth", and that the inductive method was an efficient tool for learning *more,* and not simply for "learning", he would probably have weakened his case, and by not providing the scheme of discrete and separate realities, he would paradoxically have been more likely to incur condemnation.

But the fact remains, that – probably unwillingly and surely unwittingly – he, together with the other rationalists, not only provided important elements for the great advancements and developments that were to be made in the modern world of yesterday: the seeds he sowed produced a strong tree of knowledge *and beliefs,* some of which though, have now become somewhat sclerotic and are probably at the origin of the difficulties that our culture is currently experiencing in adapting itself to the post-modern world.

The excesses of Auguste Comte. The ambiguity of the seeds of rationalism can be clearly detected in the intellectual adventure of Auguste Comte, the father of positivism.

Some of his sentences are clear cut, and obviously derived from the rational tradition: "Observation of facts is the only solid basis of human knowledge."[23] "Any proposition which cannot be reduced to the simple description of a fact would have no real and intelligible sense". In his theory that the evolution of human thought and knowledge passes through three main stages (theological, metaphysical and scientific or positive), he insists that the only truth or reality is the "objective" reality of facts. He adds that the positivistic state is the *definitive* state of man. Rationalism, or rather, positivism, as a "scientific" method, after having achieved "many conquests, has, today just simply to absorb (he uses the word 's'emparer') the social ideas". For Comte, certain methods of rationalism were no longer simple tools, and he states that "There is no possible improvement for the spirit of man other than through the division of labour".[24] "Specialization" was a principle of what he called the "new spiritual power system". In the first part of the nineteenth century, Comte was able to throw off the residual limitations of considering rationalism as a counter-religion, corresponding to the "real", "inevitable" state of modern societies, where the revelation of facts, once accomplished, will be the moral and spiritual basis of the new order. He clearly states[25] that his goal is "to demonstrate the necessity of the institution of a spiritual power, distinct and separate from the political power, and to determine the main characters of the moral organization most appropriate to modern society". He dreams of the creation of a "priesthood, which would devote themselves to be the clergy of Humanity"[26], and formed by positivistic Philosophers, who would have first completely adopted five main principles, defined by the new Pope, Auguste Comte himself.

In the exaggerations of Auguste Comte, one may wonder how far "a society based on facts" verified by experimentation (by whom? under which criteria?) can lead to the formulation of a religion.

This is the distortion which stems from underestimating the fact that even when Copernicus, Descartes, Bacon, Galileo and Newton started their research and enquiries, they were moved by motivations which were *human,* and probably of the type that many would call spiritual. They clashed with other, older and in part sclerotic and even diverted, "spiritual" motivations, so that their battle was a battle of *ideas* on the *interpretation of truth.* The battle of science was and still is a subtle one, in which a hypothesis can quickly become a dogma, where a verification can quickly become an exercise in confirmation of predetermined truth.

The matter is even more complicated today if we accept that even dogmas sometimes can be a specific type of hypothesis, and if submitted to verification lead to discovery and knowledge.[27] Some of the extreme inductivism derived from Descartes has today been partly moderated by the wide-ranging debate on the function of both deductivist and inductivist attitudes in the progress of knowledge. However, it is not our goal here to enter into this debate but rather to introduce some of the philosophical elements which help to explain the birth of economics, and of industrialization, and of which they constitute the profound basis.

It is clear in fact, that the fundamental paradigms of economics, as well as of the industrialization process, are essentially specifications of Cartesian rationalism.

The principle of factual evidence is the basis which leads us to search out in economic reality, *that part* which can be most easily defined and quantified: priced goods are in this way a better "fact" than a free, less definable asset, like the "value" of air.

The principle of separating elements in order to better understand them is the principle of specialization which leads to the economic laws of comparative advantages. From the principle of specialization we have also the law of the economies of scale: the greater and the more specialized the production unit, the more efficient it is.

The principle of synthesis as the sum of the separate elements, will provide the necessary guarantee that, what produces more industrial growth will also add to *total* wealth.

The process is a simple one, of successive ameliorations through specialization, and accumulation of wealth through the supposed net additions brought about by the advances in the industrial revolution.

Such a vision of things is a simplified one; however, in particular in the economic system, it worked well enough in practice for over two centuries. It even worked better in this sector than it really has — since the last century — in the field of natural sciences.

In a certain way, then, the industrial revolution has been the last great triumph, in time, of European Cartesianism. It has been like a heavy branch of a tree deeply rooted in many centuries of Western, and in particular of European history, and fed by a sap made up of cultural attitudes, religious and ideological beliefs, and by specific historical experiences. No wonder then that when economic growth no longer works or no longer meets our usual expectations, when the Club of Rome makes a contribution to the debate on the "Limits to Growth", the debate itself becomes passionate: the whole tree feels shaken. It is not shaken simply by ideas, but by a new reality, where the search for rationality needs new roots other than those of "Cartesianism".

2.2. The Limits of Cartesianism and of the Industrial Revolution

2.2.1. THE LIMITS OF CARTESIANISM IN SPACE: LIGHT AND ELECTROMAGNETIC WAVES — ECONOMICS AND THE ECONOMY

"Economy" can be used as a word to embrace all sorts of activities, both human and natural, which contribute to the production of wealth and welfare. In this broad definition, ecology — for instance — can be considered a synonym of economy. By contrast, particularly in the industrial revolution, the meaning of economic activity is normally restricted to a limited part of the entire economic process aimed at producing wealth: i.e. "monetarized" activity. Let us take an example from the physical world to illustrate what we mean and its implication. Let us look at the phenomenon of electromagnetic waves and the way in which wavelength or frequency can be used to classify these waves.

We know today that light covers a specific spectrum of electromagnetic waves: i.e. the visible spectrum. These waves are not visible in themselves; however, by its nature, the *human eye* can detect this spectrum amongst the total range of electromagnetic waves.

Visible light may be considered an "objective" phenomena; however, the limits of the visible range of wavelength and frequency are set not by the phenomenon itself, but by the "technological" limitations of the eye. Nevertheless, the eye is a perfect organ for the purpose of seeing. As far as the "invisible" heat-carrying infrared waves are concerned, it is not necessary to see them; it is enough to *feel* them.*

To draw a parallel with man's economic activity (using, producing, transforming energy of all sorts, both physical and mental), we would suggest that *economics* has been that particular subsystem developed with the purpose of *looking* at the *industrialization process*: we have already stressed in former paragraphs the fact that the selection of basic paradigms of economic science was determined in relation to the industrialization process.

Here we would prefer to follow the development of economics as a part of a larger system (*economy* being as infinite as the wavelength system).

The quantitative and qualitative uniqueness of the industrial revolution was such that a new type of light was needed to comprehend this specific and particular historical phenomenon.

The analogy with the "visible-light spectrum" of electromagnetic waves is even more striking when one considers that "price" is the phenomenon which gives economic activity a specific "light". In fact, an economic science develops, in which price is the selective element of the

---

*It is interesting to note that heat, for instance, is carried by *both* visible *and* invisible waves. The heat we receive is the sum of the two, just like our welfare depends on priced as well as on "free" goods and services.

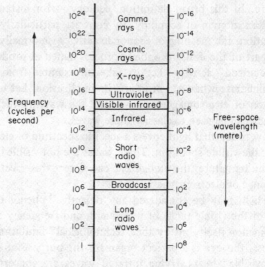

FIG. 2.3. *The Electromagnetic Spectrum*

phenomena considered, because pricing them makes them detectable, really quantifiable: in simpler terms, visible.

We have stressed in other paragraphs how money is the necessary financial technology which allows modern technology to develop and which in turn allows the industrialization process to grow. Money, technology, industrialization are the facets of the same developing system which, in theoretical terms, is appreciated and analyzed as "visible light".

Rationalism, even if tendentially a dogma, was necessary in practice, here: the visible-light spectrum of economics had to find boundary conditions for making the analysis more specific.

Boundary conditions were automatically furnished when price and monetarized activities were taken into consideration. Because industrialization is the most dynamic societal phenomenon in this long historical period, the inconveniences of what after all is an arbitrary way of limiting the analysis of economic activity, are more than compensated for by the practical advantages. As Kuhn would say, a new "normal science" paradigm was discovered, and it could be profitably researched.

The problem now is to see if this process of reducing man's economic activity to a monetarized subsystem, is still sufficient to provide useful explanations of problems (abstract logic is a game which can go on forever) of an economic nature.

It is here that the underlying rationalistic philosophy can be questioned: to what extent is the monetarized economic system subjected to more and more interferences from *outside* the system? The boundary conditions have been a practical convention (acceptable in as far as they were useful) but we may now be approaching a situation in which the interferences from other systems are greater and greater and/or the delimitation of the boundary conditions is being questioned.

At this point, "rationalism" is required to make a choice: if what has been a tool for promoting science becomes a firm belief, a theory becomes a dogma or even an ideology. Auguste Comte and his religious visions, are no longer a curiosity, but a symbol of the transformation of science into an ideology: the inductive method becomes an induced dogma. The other possibility is to revise the foundations of what is meant by "rational".

Let us pursue our considerations of the electromagnetic wave analogy and take the example of a large system with larger *provisional* boundaries: a system which would encompass *all* human activities producing material wealth (regardless of their being priced or not); in other words, not only the price-visible activities, but also the free-invisible ones which constantly contribute to our necessities of life.

One might admit that our total wealth (a term so dear to Adam Smith), welfare or wellbeing, is the result of all the goods and services we can obtain from both the monetarized and free-goods system (clean, freely available water and air, etc . . .). By analogy, heat is transmitted, for instance, by waves which are partly visible and partly invisible: the invisible ones are even more important. We shall return later on to the historical analysis of the monetarized and the non-monetarized economy. What we want to highlight here is that the sum of the material goods and services we obtain from both systems is really that which allows us to live: the growing importance of the monetarized portion of the economy in the last two centuries reflects the fact that the *industrial* organization of society has permitted enormous increases in the *total* welfare available.

Even if many sacrifices have been necessary — particularly at the level of non-monetarized activities (and we shall examine this point in more detail later) — the total progress achieved has undoubtedly been very large.

However, the monetarized system has never been completely separated from the non-monetarized one: the boundary conditions, strictly speaking, have always been a theoretical *fiction*. The functioning of many factories has been profitable only because certain resources could be obtained *free* (air for nitrogen extraction, water and many other "invisibles"). In other words, the price-visible subsystem has been capable of producing and developing thanks not only to the many factors we have defined, but also to a large reservoir of "invisible" economic goods and services.

The important point to verify in this interrelationship is not whether the functioning of the price-visible system and its production is, at any given moment, encountering limits which appear within the logic and space of its own development, but rather if it is encountering limits to the utilization of the outside free system.

Pollution is exactly the type of problem which confronts the monetarized system when it discovers that the non-monetarized support system has limitations and demands compensation, or replacement.

Furthermore it is conceivable that, in some cases, a gain in the monetarized system might be more than compensated by the diminishing available goods and services of the free system, which more than compensate for the visible gain. In other words, one can admit increased gross national product for a decreased *material* welfare.

Why and how both the price-visible economic system and the non-monetarized system encounter limitations is, in turn, linked partly to cultural attitudes and adaptation problems, but probably even more to the effective potential of science and technology to counter-balance this situation.

Here is where we discover once again the subtle links between science, dogma and ideology.

Having believed in the omnipotence of science and technology, humanity — or a large portion of it — is discovering or rediscovering that science and technology are no substitute for religion.

If "faith" in science has gradually drifted more or less consciously to the belief that science is "better" because it guarantees more miracles than our older religions, it is obvious that the discovery of the diminishing returns of technology (or of the limits to price-visible growth) will be viewed and reacted to as an attack on moral or ethical (not to say religious) belief.

Comte may have seemed excessive: but, in fact, everybody has at one moment or another hoped for a miracle from those people — the scientists — "we-do-not-understand-anything-about-what-they-are-saying" (like the priests of some old rite).

Our problem is probably now to dedogmatize science, to concede — and not with false modesty — that the realm of our ignorance is greater than ever before: in fact, we have never had so many questions to which we have no answer.* The path of science and knowledge, in general, is marked more by the overall increased capability of putting justified questions, than by the amount of answered questions. And science, in all sectors, is in fact now confronted with more basic questions than ever. Technology is increasingly demanding and time consuming: the lagtime between the start of development work and general use of the results is longer than ever.

Moreover, economic science has to discover whether the industrial process, from which it issued, is still really the same type of phenomenon to handle and struggle with, for the creation of real wealth, as it has been for the last two centuries.

In any case, once it is clear that the "economy" is a system far greater than the one normally analyzed by economics, the big question arises: do the different parts of this system positively add to its total performance? As the economists say: how far does the optimization of a part contribute to the optimization of the whole?

2.2.2. THE LIMITS OF CARTESIANISM IN TIME: FROM STATIC ANALYSIS TO DYNAMIC EQUILIBRIUM

The rationalist idea that a problem, to be more satisfactorily analyzed, should be defined in a definite, discrete space, has also been extended to time, particularly in economics. Again, this fiction can work well enough

---

*Pascal said "Knowldege is like a ball in a universe of ignorance. The more it expands, the greater the ignorance with which it is confronted."

under *given* conditions, and also make good sense from the practical point of view, in *some* cases.

As we have already mentioned, industrialization has been largely influenced by its period of transition from the agriculture-based societies. In agriculture, either the time frame is very large (major changes do not intervene in the course of an average lifetime) or it is linked to the variations of the seasons, repeating themselves every year. From the time-frame point of view, either phenomena are very long so as to be almost universal in time, or they change in the *short-term* (within one year).

This situation, in practice, linked with the philosophy of time-discrete space, favoured an economic analysis which has until now been essentially static.

The equilibrium of demand and supply, or of an input/output model, occurs essentially under the constraint of "a given moment in time".

The concept of the market, at the beginning of the Industrial Revolution, could but confirm this: bringing cattle to market for sale and the buying of a couple of chickens could be done quickly. The economy was simple and there were no problems of time and cost for the storage, transport and packaging of the merchandise comparable to contemporary ones. To build a wooden weaving loom was also not only relatively cheap but also it took relatively little time (a few weeks or months). Even the introduction of a new technical idea could occur rapidly in a civilization which does not know the wheel: as soon as the wheel is conceived as an idea, it can be built in a matter of hours or days. During the last century, building a whole carriage, including the design work, was a much quicker business — to go to the other extreme — than the construction of a space ship on the basis of a *known* technology — a ten years task.

Although not at all the same thing, short-term analysis and static analysis could, in practice, achieve a workable compromise.

Marshall, who studied the problems of trade-off between the short and long term in greater detail, observed that demand can react more rapidly than the supply can respond since the latter is often subject (and we can say, more and more subjected) to longer periods of adaptation.

Subsequently, some of the best known economists proposed theories of "dynamic" economics. In particular, Hicks, in his *Value and Capital* devotes[28] an entire section to "The Foundations of Dynamic Economics; in the same vein, Paul Samuelson, as early as 1941, wrote an article on

"The Stability of Equilibrium: Comparative Statics and Dynamics".[29]

However, here we have to face a verbal misunderstanding. The dynamics is here still dependent on the Cartesian discrete-time system. Situations of equilibrium are called dynamic, passing from one given and definite point in time to another. In fact two *static* time situations are simply confronted.

On the one hand, this can be called[30] an abstract time: it refers to the economic reality as if the boundary conditions were clearly defined, outside the flow of real, historical time.

On the other hand, time series, when they are of the analytical, causal type, do not represent a dynamic system in the systemic, cybernetic sense of the word. It is precisely what an engineer would call a sequential movement, where feedbacks are excluded: this is less and less acceptable in economics, as a social science where all action is continuously modified by its effects, and where each element has a different behaviour (inertia) in time.

The study of time and inertias and their introduction into the social sciences and into economics,* in particular, is probably one of the breakthroughs with the greatest potential for future economic research.**

For this reason we consider Forrester's[31] system dynamics, although not directly proposed for the economic theory study, as an essential step forward in current economic thinking. It is interesting to note that one of the reasons why his method — used for the first report to the Club of Rome — has been rejected by so many economists, is that real-system dynamics are only infrequently a part of the economist's research armamentarium.

2.2.3. THE INDUSTRIAL REVOLUTION AS A SYSTEM

At the time of Descartes, the interrelation of phenomena could be

---

*Research points more and more in this direction, when for instance analysis are made of the "Lifetime" of products or services.

**Anders Munk comments on this point: "An important parameter is the 'mental inertia' of a human population. As long as the material changes in society went on slow enough, the mentality of the population could keep pace with them spontaneously — From the very moment on when the acceleration of material change overtook the *maximal* rate of spontaneous mentality change, something qualitatively new emerged: A steadily increasing gap between the material circumstances and the 'mental equipment' of the population." See also his *Biologie des menschlichen Verhaltens,* Stuttgart, 1971.

perceived as a bias to maintain confusion in the minds of the people. Unified, dogmatic, authoritarian thinking was so all embracing, that separation of problems and clear identification of separate issues — as we have seen — were tools for further advances in philosophy and attitudes, leading ultimately to practical action. Therefore, when we criticize more specifically the "Cartesian" era, this is not intended as criticism *per se*, but rather an attempt to stimulate a reorganization of our mode of thinking *vis-à-vis* the *new* phenomena we are currently faced with in both economics and society.

The industrial revolution itself, in reality, has always been a dynamic "system",* where interrelations** of all sorts have always been at work. It has never been a very simple system, and science and technology were able to bring about so many positive changes, precisely because they could fit into the overall situation and culture.

A recent study[32] shows, for instance, that, during the fourth century, there was enough technical knowledge in the Roman Empire to set off an industrial revolution in the same way as occurred fourteen centuries later. This would probably have ensured the survival of the Empire and made it possible to introduce computer information systems in all the provinces by the seventh century. A likely scenario for the seventh century would have been one with ecological movements appearing as new political forces leading to the election of an Emperor from the "Green" Party.

But the type of "culture" needed for such a development was not present. Another of the system's very important preconditions needed for the development of modern technology can be found in William McNeill's Plagues and People.[33] Not until micro-parasitic equilibrium (resistance to major plagues) was achieved during the seventeenth century in Europe (with a great decline in the number of plagues), could cities really develop and provide a framework for the concentration of industry.

---

*There is of course a very important literature on the "Systems Approach". For an introduction to the capability of the systems approach to deal with complex problems see Simmonds, W. H. C.: "The Systems Approach", National Research Council of Canada, Ottawa, Canada, May 1979 (Lecture) and its bibliography.

**The growth of interrelations and interdependence has also stimulated in recent time many efforts in the field of philosophy. See for instance: *Interdependence, an Interdisciplinary Study* edited by A. Bahm, Albuquerque, New Mexico, 1977 and his various writings on "Organicism, the Philosophy of Interdependence", University of New Mexico.

It was not until the eighteenth century that the spread of the cultivation of maize, potatoes, tomatoes, peppers and manioc provided enough new types of food to sustain an increasing population and soaring industrialization.

Furthermore, until the eighteenth century, England was not rich enough and did not possess the institutions and social philosophy and structure needed for exploiting and developing new technologies and starting the process of modern industrialization.

So, even in the Cartesian era of the Industrial Revolution, reality was in fact complex, and each of its elements and factors were strongly interrelated in time and space.

What probably happened is that the dynamics of the overall system was such that, in fact, industrialization was one important point of equilibrium and that *its* development was, in fact, parallel to a positive development of the *overall* system. In other words, synergies had, in the main, positive effects. The problem today is to see how far, taking into account the enormous increase in complexity of industrialization itself and the modification of many other premises, the overall system can produce or develop more wealth.

It is therefore the interrelations of factors and their dynamic behaviour which — in our hypothesis — become more and more important: it is the behaviour of the total system which requires understanding before it is possible to determine what is the best strategy for real wealth. In order to illustrate what we mean, we would like to refer to other complex systems such as those studied by agronomy and by meteorology.

Let us take as an analogy a number of simple experiments that are described in any book on practical agronomy.

In pre-industrial times, experience had already shown that soil quality and crop yield could be improved by crop rotation. It was also known that plant nutrients could be replenished by incorporating in the soil various forms of vegetable, animal and human waste.

Agriculture benefited from the Industrial Revolution, by learning to apply existing methods more accurately and by developing scientific new procedures and was thus able to:

- control chemically, with natural and man-made products, the pH (acidity or alkalinity) of the soil;
- modify and control the mechanical structure of the soil more

efficiently than in pre-industrial times (e.g. by new agricultural machines);

· add plant nutrients in the form of fertilizers, with (thanks to chemistry) precise knowledge of the action of nitrogen, phosphorus and potassium;

· control the level and action of trace elements which regulate nutrient uptake and many important plant functions.

As soon as each of these new methods of soil treatment were discovered, there was a clear improvement in crop yields.

However, it was subsequently found that, for example, in the field of fertilizers, one cannot go on adding nitrogen indefinitely, without also adding other types of fertilizer: there is a limit to nitrogen intake which is dependent upon the interrelations between various fertilizer components.

Moreover, the fertilizer system itself is also interrelated with the structure of the soil and the type of crop – and this imposes further limitations.

In other words, as new means are applied to agricultural development, the individual performances of each product, machine or technique will be dependent on the use and control of interrelationship of each with the other. In an initial stage, things develop the easy way, but with time the equilibrium of this interrelationship may be even more important that the action of any specific component if modification of the equilibrium produces a result (either positive or negative) which offsets the action of a given component. At this point, we have a *practical* transition from "analytical" ("shot-by-shot") activity to a "systemic" approach.

Weather too is an equilibrium system, determined by a multiplicity of factors and *by the way they influence each other.* The fact that it is so difficult to make *exact* weather forecasts for the next 24 hours, and why it is still impossible to forecast weather several days in advance is due to two major factors.

Firstly, the enormous number of variables, of which many are difficult to measure, and others are difficult to even identify and define.

Secondly, one might believe that the problem is one of first determining the most important variables, and then of trying to measure them and their behaviour in the most accurate way. This is important. But what happens is that very often a quite secondary or almost undetectable factor, although being of very little importance at first, starts having an action on the equilibrium system of the major factors. By a series of reactions in the relative equilibrium system, it can then start a major, "unpredictable" weather change.

This is not very different from a minor switch in a political election where 100 votes or even a single vote can transform a majority into minority. Or, in the case of a revolution, a small minority also, can start a chain reaction which will prove determinant in changing the system. Looking at reality in a "systemic" way, we understand why important changes are very often unpredictable and how the belief in controlling scientific and societal development, derived from the Cartesian philosophy of piling up important factors one by one, by order of priority and importance can be totally inadequate. The same problem is apparent in economics, where "models" are still built around "important factors", whereas — in a period of great change — it is more important to analyze the interreaction system itself. This is why we have tried here to make it clear how the "economic" system has been isolated from the general economic producing activities in order to understand and organize this part better. But now, in a period of deep change, it is precisely at the interface between the monetarized and the non-monetarized systems that the main reasons for present disruptions and for future new developments are probably to be found.

The table 2.2 (p. 112), drawn from the work of Joël Rosnay[34] is presented in an attempt to clarify the distinction between analytical thinking and the systems approach.

It should also be stressed that the dispute between the "analytical" and the "systemic" approach is not an abstract "philosophical" or "theoretical" debate of no more than intellectual relevance. This shift in attitudes and approaches in favour of "systemic" analysis (no matter what the theoretical intricacies with which these approaches are presented) reflects a change in the *real* situation.

We can now try to see how the standard economic system has evolved and how its scientific and technological engine is involved in this change.

2.2.4. THE TRANSFORMATION OF THE INDUSTRIAL SOCIETY

We have considered the phenomenon of industrialization as an essential

TABLE 2.2. *The Analytical vs. the Systems Approach*

Analytical approach	Systems Approach
Isolate: concentrate on components	Combine: concentrate on component interactions
Consider the nature of interactions	Consider the effects on interactions
Base oneself on accuracy of detail	Base oneself on global perception
Modify one parameter at a time	Modify groups of parameters simultaneously
Independent of time; the phenomena studies are reversible	Integrate time and irreversibility
Validation of facts by experimental proof within the framework of a theory	Validation of facts by comparing the functioning of the model and that of reality
Models are precise and detailed but difficult to use for action (e.g. econometric models)	Models are not rigorous enough to serve as a basis for knowledge; but valid for decision and action (e.g. Club of Rome models)
Effective approach for weak, linear interactions	Effective approach for strong, non-linear interactions
Leads to a single-discipline (juxtadisciplinary) outcome	Leads to a multidisciplinary outcome
Leads to programmed action on details	Leads to aim-oriented action
Knowledge of details – poorly defined objectives	Knowledge of objectives – details unclear

indicator of two centuries of European and world history in the search for wealth. We have also considered the fact that, over recent decades, industrialization has really started to spread throughout the planet.

The lessons of the past should be learned if we are to understand the conditions under which the Industrial Revolution can really spread and be adapted to different cultural requirements.

However, the major point of concern in the next few paragraphs is the qualitative change which is taking place in the industrialization process itself, and which is best observed in the most developed countries. The same phenomenon can be detected in isolated cases in the developing countries where the most modern types of industrial processes have been introduced provoking other types of problems — which we shall also discuss later.

The qualitative change in the industrialization process is such that it might be concluded that a certain type of Industrial Revolution is over. Are we at the beginning of a new era, usually defined as "post-industrial"? Is this simply a matter of terminology or, over the next decades or even centuries, will it mean changes in culture, philosophy, ideology, of the same dimensions as those attributed to the Industrial Revolution? The dimensions might be those of a truly global, multifaceted culture and not just an extrapolation of the European or Western tradition.

The current reality of the production structure. In the previous paragraphs we have shown a simplified flowchart of the production system from the raw material to the finished product.

In most cases, industrial specialization results in an increase in the number of the intermediary stages between raw material winning and completion of the final product. Each operation and function is submitted to the "Cartesian" rule: it is subdivided into more and more subfunctions in order to improve the operation of the total mechanism. This mechanical system resembles, at first, a biological evolution from the simple, single-cell to the complex, multicellular organism. It is of course essential that this subdivision of functions is of overall advantage to the system. When this is the case in practice, the Cartesian approach can be adopted to break down the problem into its discrete components which after solution, can be rebuilt into the complex whole. When this is not the case, recourse must be had to a more comprehensive, non-mechanistic biological philosophy in which the improvement of a system component may contribute negatively to the functioning of the system as a whole. But let us remain at the first stage of our analysis and review our diagram (p. 114).

It will be observed that, in practice, the magnitude of n tends to increase as a function of specialization.

In this simplified situation, the price/cost of the product reflects costs at the different production stages.

The simpler the economy, the truer this is: I bake my bread in my shop every day and sell it to people who come to buy every day.

However, the introduction of specialization (bringing with it quantitative

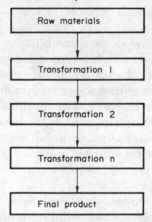

TABLE 2.3. *The Building up of the Final Product*

and/or qualitative production advantages) will, in most cases, also result in production concentration: thus confirming the classic law of economies of scale.

As specialization and economy of scale increase, concentration also increases: from the tens of *thousands* of cotton spinning mills in Europe over a century ago, to a few *dozen* polyester yarn mills of today. The increase in productivity has been immense.

Yet, this concentration movement modifies the type of action required to keep the system functioning. With a high level of production, the prime problem is to ensure a continuous inflow of raw materials: in my bakery, I can buy my flour even on a daily basis. However in polyester-yarn production, it is essential to have a sufficient reserve of raw materials, not only for current consumption but also to cover any interruptions which might occur in the input flow. The more distant the source of the raw materials and the more difficult the line of communications, the more vulnerable will the plant be to supply interruptions.

Storage problems exist not only for the raw materials, but also at each output level. With time, stock control grows in importance in relation to production control *per se*. The system becomes more and more efficient but more and more dependent on external factors (inflow, outflow and storage control). There is a problem of organization and technology in keeping the advantages of production efficiency ahead of the disadvantages of such dependency. Storage implies distribution and the distribution system must work properly at all levels. This includes the transport of raw materials and intermediate products, and the distribution of the final products (including marketing, publicity, etc.). The greater the extension of the storage and distribution system, the more complex the packaging system becomes (for protecting the contents and not just of sales-appeal purposes).

Storage and distribution are part of the service activities that become more and more essential in keeping the production system working, but which are not "production" strictly speaking. In addition, there are other types of very important services.

Advanced industrialization implies increasingly capital-intensive production. This means that machines are expensive and must consequently not remain idle for too long. This is why, over recent decades, the change-over from the traditional weaving loom, to the "shuttle-less" loom has favoured a change-over from the two-shift working day (16 hours) to the three-shift day (24 hours) with all its resultant social problems. In some cases, technology may add other constraints: many chemical processes (like blast furnaces in the iron and steel industry) have to operate continuously for technical reasons (this is called "fatal" production). This further complicates the logistics of production which are further aggravated by the demand constraints. "Fatal" production of fertilizer intermediates may clash with agricultural demand which is normally seasonal.

The greater and more concentrated the production, the greater the problem. In the case of fertilizers, the problem can and is alleviated by exporting to distant countries, thus exploiting the season inversion between the northern and southern hemispheres, for example. However, this may mean transportation costs (excluding packaging) which can be higher than production costs. In other words, advanced technology and increased productivity must not only contribute to cheaper production but also help compensate for transport and other service costs. Of course, technology can and does contribute at the service level too.

Maintenance is also an important factor: the more advanced the machine, the more carefully it has to be "prepared" and checked before starting production, and the more disastrous will be the results of a breakdown. During the nineteenth-century, opening a carriage door when the horse was moving would have passed almost unnoticed; in a modern train it would be dangerous, and in an airplane it would be catastrophic.

Furthermore, during operation, the machines and the systems have to be closely monitored and, where necessary, repaired. Repairs to capital goods have become increasingly expensive and delicate. Defective consumer goods are frequently disposed of since repairs are relatively expensive; however, in the case of highly expensive capital goods, repair work (although costly) is still a flourishing and increasing activity.

Growth in the service sector has been paralleled by growth in the financial and organizational sectors.

Organization, planning and insuring the maintenance of the investment activity is one aspect of the problem and insuring against damage of all sorts is another. The spectrum of operations needed to keep the system functioning (including training operators for the new machines) tends to reach enormous dimensions, undreamed of in our small bakery where *all these functions* exist, but mostly at an undifferentiated stage and where the low level of specialization is, nevertheless, sufficient to achieve the correspondingly low level of efficiency required to attain the objectives.

2.2.5. THE IMPORTANCE OF SERVICES AND THE GROWTH OF WASTE

(a) *The development of services.* If we return to our flow chart we might now add to the production line, a line that indicates all the service and maintenance activities.

It is essential to note that these service activities are accomplished both *internally* and *externally* to the production system. This may seem a self-evident remark; however, it clashes with the traditional economic separation of productive activities. Services are considered a separate (and often either insignificant and/or unproductive) part of the economy. As we have seen, Quesnay considered agricultural production to be the only source of wealth. Since Smith, industry has increasingly been the key sector, with minor allowances for some types of service (in the national accounting system of the Soviet Union, for instance, transportation is clearly now a value added).

Discussion on the growth of bureaucracy in the modern industrial society seldom provides any real help in understanding the importance of the service sector. Many grievances (sometimes justified) against

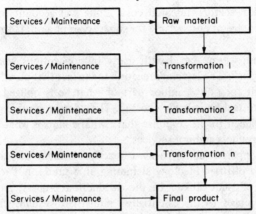

FIG. 2.4. *Services and Maintenance in the Production Progress*

bureaucracy reflect the Smith/Mill philosophy of productive and unproductive labour: they reflect the idea that industry is producing goods in
a vacuum and do not perceive clearly enough the growing systemic and
logistic constraints, which must be dealt with if the production system
is to work.

Many of the so-called "idle" activities can now be found within the
pure production phases; they are not all confined to the services or even
to pure officework. This does not mean that bureaucratization does not
exist, nor does it deny that some service activities favour it. It seems that
the debate on bureaucratization very often hides – probably unconsciously
– a deeper ideological debate about productive and non-productive labour,
as it has been sedimented in economic theory (together with its ideological
and moral implications). But in fact growth in "bureaucracy" is induced
as a necessary cost of the growth in industrialization.

Here we come to the key point in the relation between production and
services, which can be clarified by a very simple observation. If we take the
price of a product (be it an automobile, a carpet or a fertilizer), and try to
allocate, on a percentage basis, the cost of production, on the one hand,
and the cost of related services, on the other (including all the activities
we have indicated above), we will seldom find products with a true
"production" cost higher than 30%. In many cases, the figure would be
only 10%. In some sectors, such as aerospace or some chemical and

pharmaceutical sectors, research costs alone will account for by far the largest percentage of costs, rising for some types of aircraft to as high as 50 or 60%.

Here again, we are faced with many misconceptions when talking of "profit margins". The layman's reaction to the fact that pure "production" costs account for only a minor part of what he is obliged to pay for a product, is to feel he is being cheated. The "common sense parameter" is normally reduced to the response that "what counts is what we eat, drink or use, i.e. products and not services".

But this apparent common-sense reaction is today increasingly wrong and part of a diffused ideology stemming, in a subtle, but real way, from the notion of value linked to the production process, and to all the implicit references to the essentially "industrial" system, which are convergently proposed by both the liberal and the socialist tradition.

In fact, what is the value of a product that I cannot obtain (because it is too far away), I cannot use, I cannot have repaired or have replaced? We shall return later to this question in more detail.

We now need to make a further step forward.

(b) *The growth of waste.* There is another feature which accompanies this evolution towards greater industrialization: the accumulation, in time and space, of waste.

In our artisanal bakery, there is little waste, since most of it can easily be recycled by burning it in the oven.

Waste is a constant byproduct of any process of transforming energy or of converting materials.

Nevertheless, certain wastes may also have positive aspects: animal waste on the farm, mixed with vegetable waste, is a valuable natural fertilizer.

When the iron and steel industry on continental Europe had to process the low-grade high-phosphorus iron ore ("minette") from Lorraine to remove the phosphorus, it was found that this waste was a good fertilizer and subsequently developed an important industry based on this "waste". A similar situation occurs in the production of nylon in which one of the processes produces roughly as much waste ammonium sulphate as it does the chemical intermediate from which nylon is derived. This waste is once again widely used as a fertilizer.

However, the possibility of converting waste into a usable "by-product" is gradually diminishing. Specialization is also restricting the adaptability of waste utilization. Furthermore, qualitative and quantitative phenomena are interrelated here.

The concentration of production also means the concentration of waste and we once again encounter here the logistic problem of storage and distribution. Total increase in production means a total increase in waste. Scientists generally admit that the quantitative modification of a problem also brings about a qualitative modification. This is seen clearly, for instance, in the case of some chemical solutions: saturation occurs and it is no longer possible to dissolve a product (for instance nitrates in water) when the concentration rises above a given level.

Consequently, as industrialization develops and becomes more complex, waste disposal becomes a larger and larger cost factor.

The waste problem is complicated by the nature of modern technology* which entails the increasingly profound modification of matter. This tends, on the one hand to increase the number of dangerous waste products (plutonium is an extreme case), in addition to the production and storage hazards (such as that of liquefied natural gas). On the other hand, man-made materials are often less degradable than natural materials, for the very reasons for which they have been developed: greater resistance and less corrosion produces less-degradable products which, in turn, aggravates the waste disposal system. Here we encounter increasingly a situation in which "production" entails greater and greater investment and effort for waste control.

We shall return to this problem, when we examine the relationship between the monetarized and the non-monetarized economic system. In fact, the growing cost of waste disposal is the systems effect of the reduced capacity of the non-monetarized system (the sea, river and water, the wind, etc. . . .) to work "for free" in the same way as it does at less advanced stages of industrialization.

Here, particular attention should be paid to the third, new component

---

*Hence the efforts to reduce waste and monitor technological performance from this angle. See "Non-Waste Technology and Production", proceedings of the UN Economic Commission for Europe — Seminar on Non-Waste Technology, Oxford, 1978 (678 pp.).

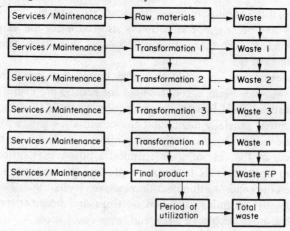

FIG. 2.5. *Waste and the Production Process*

of our production flow chart, namely the "waste production" factor that we have added to each processing stage.

It can be readily seen on the right of the chart how waste is produced at each stage of production.

As already mentioned, this is a phenomenon that has always existed, but that until now was of little importance (either on its own account, or because the non-monetarized economic system was capable of absorbing it without damage). Clearly, the economist's and entrepreneur's attention was concentrated on the production line.

However, it is now necessary to take into account this increase in the complexity of the industrialization process and determine whether the production system is still essentially such.

Another important factor is that the final product, after a period of utilization, also becomes waste.

Consequently, if we look at this chart not as a static picture of a situation at a given moment in time, but instead place it into a real time context, it is possible to view it as the description of a process by which a given quantity of raw material (RM) has been converted into a given amount of waste (total waste).

A lot of this waste will, of course, then be recuperated and reintroduced into the system as raw material and the problem then will be to see if the raw material stock and the total waste recycled are quantitatively the same.

This leads, on a very general time scale, to a discussion of the law of entropy according to which, inevitably, a certain amount of energy (or raw material) must necessarily be lost (becoming bound energy): the book by Georgescu-Roegen[35] is a very important reference for any discussion in this context, concluding as it does, that the acceleration of industrialization has the effect of accelerating entropy.

This is a fundamental problem which will, however, not be considered further for the moment, for the two following reasons:

— the entropy process has a time scale which is very large and beyond the shorter time horizon of this research. It might, in the end, provide the simple explanation of the inevitable end of the universe. This decisive fact also has a direct link with our present problems, if it is clear that we are at present accelerating entropy to a significant degree as far as the immediate future is concerned (i.e. for the coming centuries or even millenia).*

— nevertheless, although there is a clear *analogy* between our analysis of waste production and the entropy system, we are not sure that the two problems are identical. Our task is to analyze and provide a solution to the problems in the shorter term (the next few decades).

In the longer term, we are not sure that our current knowledge of physics is definitive enough; the entropy process — although verifiable — might, following a further step in our knowledge of physics, be circumscribed, and thus substantially modify our forecast of the end of the world.

2.2.6. VALUE ADDED, VALUE DEDUCTED AND UTILIZATION VALUE

We hope we have now prepared the ground for a first introduction to the notion of utilization value.

In the preceding flow chart, we saw that the production process may be

---

*"All mature industrial economies are in a process of transition from their maximizing of material production, consumption and 'throughput', based on non-renewable resources, to economies based on minimizing material throughput"; Henderson, Hazel: The Exhaustion of Economic Logic, in *Creating Alternative Futures op. cit.*

considered as a system converting raw material into a total amount of waste which is then, at least partially recycled; in this system, the growth of recycling costs has to be considered seriously and controlled carefully.

The real value in all this system is not the *production* value of the final product because *the real final product* of the entire process of production *is a total amount of waste.* What counts and what has *value,* is the *period of utilization* of the products and services: this is the positive part of the balance sheet.

On the negative side (costs), we have to count: production, utilization of services, waste disposal, maintenance and repair of the goods and services during utilization, cost of waste disposal after utilization. The whole economic process is a *cost* (of producing, servicing, waste disposal). We shall see later on, that *there is also a cost for the non-monetarized system.*

Value added and value deducted. Another way to introduce the concept of utilization value is through the notion of value deducted.

In the concept of value added, it is normally implied that the word "added" is intended to indicate an increase in the amount of total wealth and of welfare produced and available.

We transpose this idea in the following simplified graph:

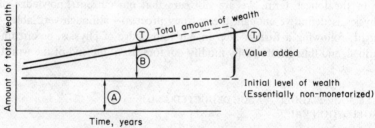

FIG. 2.6. *Value Added and Wealth*

In this graph, we start from the general assumption that the non-monetarized goods and services also have value (use value), but no exchange-added (monetarized) value. Industrialization strongly contributes to the addition of value through its action on rare resources: all such measured activity (through the notion of value added) is considered a positive contribution to the increase in total wealth.

In fact it is also admitted that not *all* the added value is a *net* increase in wealth: economists – during the heated debate which followed the first report to the Club of Rome – often said that zero growth (of added value) was leading to decadence and increased poverty. In fact, statistical evidence can be provided from some countries, where zero growth (of added value) has been the reality for a decade or more: the apparent level of the standard of living in these countries (as shown by social indicators) has decreased. This argument was used to combat the idea of *zero* growth as a perspective which would lead to *decreasing* wealth.

In fact, all that this reasoning and statistical evidence shows, is that the *value added,* as normally measured in economics, does not *totally* add to wealth, otherwise zero growth would mean stabilization in the level of wealth and not net decrease.

It is therefore, implicitly or explicitly admitted, that value added is a *gross* concept, and that if we want to measure real added wealth, we need to find a *net* concept of added wealth.

It is here that we can first introduce the concept of *value deducted,* which – in a first approximation[36] – indicates that part of the value added (production) which is accounted as a positive value, but does not add to real wealth. As we have already indicated, this concept should contain all the expenses and "value added" representing investments which are not real net values but – like the anti-pollution industry – constitute the cost of repairing damaged utilization values. In other words, and going back to the graph, we can accept the idea that the total amount of wealth T_1 is smaller than the sum of the A curve plus the B curve.

We thus return to our discussion of Cartesianism: the total is not the sum of the parts. But if we take a step further and consider where the negative value added (or value deducted) actually produced is located, we recognize that it concerns essentially that part of the free, non-monetarized system, the wealth potential of which has been diminished.

In other words, the deducted value is the notion which *links monetarized and non-monetarized activities.*

We are now better placed to appreciate the difference between the concepts of *utilization value* and of *use value.*

Use value. In classical economics, use value (everything that has a utility) and exchange-added (monetarized) values are clearly separate: starting from the Cartesian premise, it was simply impossible to integrate them into a single concept. Their separation highlighted how one concept (value added) was measurable whilst the other *also* incorporated all the goods which were, by definition, not measurable (using the exchange market standard). When price is therefore taken as basic standard to measure value, the notion of use value becomes "economically" useless, and as such will be practically abandoned.

We now see that, even though value deducted is difficult to measure there can, in fact, be no real notion of value unless the deducted value is accounted for. Economics can no longer overlook that part of values which, in practice, has been excluded from analysis and which was determined as free-use values.

We may have lost something in the way of obtaining a comfortable, specific measurement of value, but we have perhaps discovered a means of studying *real* value. Precise measurement is desirable, but provided it measures something significant!

The evolution of value deducted. We have seen how it is normally admitted that the notion of value added is not a net indicator of wealth; however even when values deducted are implicitly admitted to exist, they are still seen as a percentage of the value added. In other words, it is not yet normally admitted that the development of values deducted and their relation to values added varies in time and space and that this relation is of a systemic nature.

If one considers value deducted as a part of value added (exchange value added), it is clear that, at most, it will be equal to the value added itself.

However, if we recognize that the value deducted relates to the utilization value of the monetarized *and* non-monetarized patrimony (which we shall describe in more detail in the next Chapter), then there is the possibility that a given value added produces a value deducted which is greater than the value added itself. In other words, a given economic activity measured in terms of value added can yield a net *decrease* in real wealth and welfare.

In the first case (Fig. 2.7.) the relation of value added to value deducted may be seen in the following (hypothetical) way, i.e., where the sum of

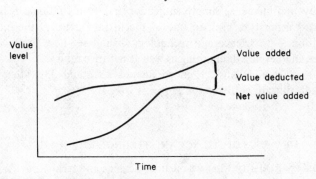

FIG. 2.7. *The Positive Applied Value*

the two is always greater or, at most, equal to zero. In this case, the non-monetarized values are completely omitted.

In the second case (Fig. 2.7.) it is clear that the deducted value, in reality, affects the general level of wealth and welfare — what we call the utilization value.

In this case, the value deducted may be greater than the value added from which it has originated, as is shown hypothetically in the following graph.

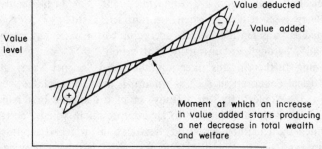

FIG. 2.8. *When the Value Deducted is Greater than the Value Added*

How does it occur that values deducted can vary in relation to the activities from which they are originated? There is obviously a subjective element of judgement concerning the definition of value added and value deducted. But we are most interested here in the objective origins and sources of the values deducted (many of which also explain what are normally considered as simply subjective and even irrational reactions). For this we must go back to one of the main sources of the Industrial Revolution — to science and technology — and see how these can also produce and develop diminishing as well as negative returns.

We shall then reconsider, in paragraphs 33.2 and 33.3, the general notion of utilization value.

2.2.7. THE MEANINGS OF SCIENCE AND TECHNOLOGY

Let us try to clarify what we mean by science and technology.

The words "science" and "technology" are used so often with different meanings that, before analyzing the diminishing returns of technology, it is essential to define the scope of these terms for the purpose of this dossier.

In most of the literature, the word "science" can advantageously be replaced by "discipline", e.g. a specific field of activity or of research, since we speak of the chemical sciences, legal sciences, agricultural sciences, economic sciences, etc.

This use of "science" instead of "discipline" in not unintentional; the objective is to persuade the reader that the document in question is "scientific", i.e. "serious", "objective" and "of high quality". This tendency is even clearer when, in contrast, a study or a document is defined as "unscientific" which, according to the case, may imply that it is "bad", "wrong", or "unworthy of attention".

Going further in this direction, the word "science" may also have ideological connotations such as when it is used to guarantee, beyond all doubt, the "objectivity" of a study, or of a doctrine. In this case, it is a label given to a theory or to an interpretation, where "certainty" is provided by a method based on "verification" which is supposed determinant and decisive, in the same way as it has been decided by the religious authorities to divide the gospels between those really inspired by God and those which are apocryphal. "Objectivity" is perceived as the concept that ensures ultimate certitude. This form of exaggeration is more common than is generally admitted; it has even been codified by such "scientific" authors as Auguste Comte for whom the positivistic/analytical theory — as we have seen — has clearly become a new objective "scientific" religion. Science is here equated with the search for "certainty" or definitive "truth": in the name of science, the scientific search can be clearly manipulated and utterly betrayed.

The word "science" is then a very difficult one to use; too often, it just attempts to create an aura of legitimacy, as if the use of this word could miraculously transform the quality of a discipline or a piece of research. Psychologically, it illustrates a profound and constant need of approval by the sources of given or revealed truth that man has lost in his rationalistic revolution: a loss, to which he has never become reconciled, apparently.

In practice, scientific method is simply a way of being as honest, as open to criticism, and as thorough as possible in studying a given problem. The scientific approach differs profoundly from revealed religion – just because it entails continuous doubt of the validity and the applicability of any given theory or explanation. God is a subject for religion in that one is seeking to convince people of his existence; whereas Einstein's theory of relativity is a subject for science in that research is devoted to demonstrating its limitations and, where applicable, its inexactitudes. A "scientific social" theory is therefore an ideology (a substitute for religion) if it employs the concept of "scientific method" to justify provisional assumptions as "objective" theories. On the other hand, "scientific" method starts by studying the principles and by assuming that they may be partly or totally wrong.[37]

European history is very ambiguous on this issue; in fact, the notion of "science" is at the crossroads of a century-old ambiguity, where all the above-mentioned definitions and attitudes meet. There was a moment in history when scientific research was on the point of proving that it was really the efficient method of obtaining definitive, objective knowledge: in particular, in the last century, fundamental, philosophical speculation, verified by experimentation, led to very important breakthroughs in our understanding of "objective" phenomena. Scientific research and the development of new instrumentation has since enabled us to gain enormous knowledge of the natural world around us, that would not have been possible by sensorial perception. In this way, a bacterium, a microbe, a molecule, an electron, etc. have become clearly definable realities in the same way as a table, a tree or a horse. The ultimate extrapolation of this process of making specific realities and phenomena visible and detectable is that the "whole" of reality – God himself – should be "discovered" sooner or later; conceiving the possibility of such a discovery may also lead someone to claim to have "the proof" (which in fact is a tautology) that God does not exist.

The principle of indeterminacy[38] (the fact that we can hardly enquire beyond a certain limit, without destroying or modifying the object observed) has placed new limits on the metaphysical hopes of analytical, "fact-based" research.* Today, once again, the most we can reasonably hope to achieve using the "scientific" method is to "know more" rather than "know".

However, the outcome of the enormous advances in scientific knowledge and observation that took place in the last century, and which have continued up to the present day, is that technology has been provided with tremendous new means for manipulating materials.

It should never be forgotten that technology is as old as man himself; in order to make fire, to hunt, to build or repair, man has had to apply technology. It is the combination of mental capacity and skill in the manipulation of existing objects to achieve better results: for instance, to fashion a piece of wood into an arrow.

As we have seen in an earlier paragraph (1.3.) the First Industrial Revolution, starting in the eighteenth century, witnessed the maturation of a technology based on "traditional" knowledge of matter.

The Second Industrial Revolution is by contrast the outcome of the "scientific" revolution since the "engineer" had expanded his range of materials beyond wood, or cotton fibre. The scientist discovers that a

---

*We refer here in particular to the new cosmology as developed in the last seventy years and more, since the publications by Albert Einstein on the Theory of Relativity (the first one in 1905). The ideas on economics proposed in this report represent an effort to be consistent also with this general framework. The "Cartesian", "monetarized" economics is clearly rooted in the Newtonian tradition, which presupposes time and space having absolute dimensions and where the force of attraction (gravitational force) is supposed to be istantaneous (a kind of equilibrium state similar to the one between the classical economics curbs of supply and demand). Since Einstein, time and space are considered in physics as a relative four dimensional continuum (three dimensions in space plus one time dimension). Furthermore, since and because of Einstein theories (and even against his philosophical and metaphysical preferences), the simple principle of linear causality is substituted by the principle of probability: events concerning a particle at the subatomic level cannot be predicted and described but statistically. The notions of "system" and of "uncertainty" are more and more crucial in scientific research since the Einstein revolution.

The non specialized reader can find a fair introduction to these fundamental ideas and problems in the book of Ronald W. Clark: *Einstein, the life and time,* London 1973. An updated version of this book has been published in French in 1980 — *Einstein, sa vie et son époque,* Paris.

fibre is composed of macromolecules and that these can be rearranged by chemical transformation; he then states that it is possible to convert oil into synthetic fibre. The conversion work is a task for the engineer, using the knowledge of matter which the "scientisit" has made available to him.

This is the real meaning of "science-based technology"; it is not, as so often understood, a technology developed by a particular "scientific method". Although this latter definition might at first sight seem correct, it is essentially wrong because, in the final analysis, it classes science, as such, as an efficient "rational method" which can produce "near-miracles". Science is not a method of technology. There are both serious and frivolous (adequate and inadequate) science and technology, related to each one's specific goal: science attempts to widen knowledge; technology to put knowledge to use. Science has increased our knowledge of matter, and technology ensures that benefit is obtained from it.

The reciprocal fertilization between science and technology, it must be remembered, is a special kind of inter-relationship which occurred for the *first time* in history during the second half of the Industrial Revolution. It remained unobserved by the classical economists who could, until the end of the last century, hardly even claim to have really studied it.

When authors like Marx speak of science and technology; they *never ever take this phenomenon into consideration.* The word "science" is used essentially for the *legitimization* of efficient technology or of specific sociological theories. The fact that scientific discovery has made technology so powerful has been interpreted as a confirmation of the principle of the "scientific" method, whereas it is in fact one of the greatest misunderstandings in the cultural history of Europe, and of the Western (and part of the Eastern) world in general.*

Only when the relationships between scientific discovery and technological achievement have been clarified, can we start to study how technology, in its developments, is conditioned not only by the social, economic or institutional environment, but also by the type of relationship it has in terms of scientific evolution and knowledge.

*It is not by accident that the function of technology as a myth is now more and more under scrutiny by economists, historians and psychologists. See for instance: London, Herbert: *Myths that Rule America* (Chapter on Myth of Technology), Arlington House, 1980; Michael, Donald: Technology Assessment in an Emerging World, *Technological Forecasting and Social Change,* p. 189–195, 1978.

2.2.8. THE DIMINISHING RETURNS OF TECHNOLOGY

As we already stressed this point in paragraph 2.1.2., it is then fundamental to distinguish two main phases in the Industrial Revolution: the first one, where the type of technology used did not presuppose a development of science. It was simply a higher development of techniques which man invented since he made his first tool. The second phase of the Industrial Revolution — exploiting scientific discoveries — started about one century later and an understanding of its development is essential if we are to properly analyze and comprehend the present situation.

2.2.8.1. A "future shock" or a "shock from the past"?

Certainly, technological performance, this century, has been bewildering. But the widely disseminated images of "future shocks" implying continuous and accelerated change due to scientific innovations, are often misleading.

The major confusion starts when the acceleration of the pace at which new products and services are marketed is taken as proof that technology can change things quicker and quicker. In the majority of cases, this is utterly false and it reflects the fact that, as Tolstoi said, changes are perceived when they have already taken place and not when they are underway.

The more a new technology is science-based, the more time is necessary to develop it. Physicists confirm that, today, andy new fundamental discovery in physics will take at least 20 years before it can be economically applied. Moreover, even when a new technology has been developed in a laboratory to prototype level, the industrialization of that new process or machine may take many years before it really "appears" to the public.

Let us take as an example the new generation of textile looms (so-called "shuttleless" looms). In the case of one of the major and most successful types of this new technological generation, the first ideas and designs were developed over a ten-year period from 1930 to 1940, the first prototypes being developed from 1946 to 1960. Sales started in 1960 and it then took 15 years for these machines to achieve about 10% of the total world market. What some traditional textile industries might still consider a "new technology", was designed as much as 40 years ago.

The public has been struck by such "sudden" changes because of psycho-sociological and social mechanism: in fact, at the technical level, new changes are much more difficult and time-consuming today than they were in the last century.

What is often presented as an acceleration is often simply a reduction in time needed for an industrialist to grasp the business potential offered by an available technology. In this way, photography took 112 years to be applied and transistors five. One must also take into account the existence of contradictory criteria used to determine the moment of discovery and the moment of application.

In any case, the "accelerating pace of technology" is, in most cases, more a social problem than a technological reality.

On the other hand, the difficulty of establishing a research and development policy and of estimating the economic relevance of the research is increased by lengthening lead times. The complexity and mutlidisciplinarity of research introduce a further element of delay.

Let us not forget that the first moon landing was accomplished using technology available ten years before, i.e. when the American space programme was prepared and approved.

2.2.8.2. The limits of science-based technology.

The idea that technology has unlimited beneficial effects and potentials has often been directly or implicitly admitted, particularly during the sixties.

Listed below are considerations which indicate how technology is itself subject to the law of diminishing returns;

(a) The first limitation comes from the fact that technological lead times do not fit easily into the supply—demand equilibrium. Economic theory says that when a product is in short supply, its price will increase in such a way as to discourage demand and/or stimulate the supply of a competitive substitute. It would appear, then, that this mechanism stimulates new technologies because it stimulates substitution.

But this equilibrium is conceived as essentially static: in practical situations it means that it is short-term. Most economic theory is based on static assumptions, where there is no room for dynamic factors. This was reasonable in more static situations than those prevailing after the Second Industrial Revolution.

Where substitution is subject to long delays, the supply—demand mechanism may even work the opposite way. Let us take the recent case of the energy crisis: the market price of oil reacted, at first, as if supply were inelastic. In reality, this inelasticity, because of technology, is a factor of time: in fact, we have an elastic supply situation, with a prolonged response delay. But because the market reacts in the short-term, technological adaptability looks more and more to be economic rigidity.

One could say that, because of the delay bias, science-based technology introduces, therefore, an element of economic vulnerability, in the sense that market supply/demand mechanisms can fall — in the absence of external intervention and under given circumstances — into a self-unfulfilling logic. The key problem is therefore to incorporate these dynamic, delayed factors into the supply/demand equilibrium. This difficulty is aggravated in cases where production concentration and market dimensions are gigantic, as with fertilizers. We have here a world market of over 100 million tonnes: consequently, a variation in supply or demand of less than 1% (which can be due just to delays in shipping or to a couple of weeks of exceptional rain in an important agricultural zone) will already involve a considerable volume of product, and as such can completely disrupt the price equilibrium; in fact, for very marginal quantities, the price may easily be doubled or halved. Here again, disrupted prices for marginal quantities can disrupt investment (justified on longer-term considerations) far more than is warranted by the quantities involved in the price upheaval.

Let us now look at the cycles of technological innovation itself.

(b) Technological change gives evidence of a series of superposed medium, long and very long-term cycles. Let us take the case of man-made fibres.

In the course of this century, we have experienced basically two large invention cycles linked to two fundamental ideas. First, the birth, growth and development of the so-called artificial fibres was based on the following idea: a natural fibre such as cotton is constituted of some sort of cellulosic material. Why not take cellulosic materials from other sources and, by submitting them to appropriate chemical processes, obtain other textile fibres? This basic idea lent itself to various solutions. Three or four of the best solutions succeeded each other, and were the key element in the development of this industry. At the end of the whole cycle, everything suggested that further development could not be achieved through a new type of artificial fibre. The new development had to be sought in a new basic principle, which would provide an answer to the following new question: Why use cellulosic material? Why not just use whatever other chemical structure we can build, provided it can be based on macro-molecules and have appropriate properties? We are now dealing with more sophisticated scientific knowledge; moreover, the raw material is no longer similar to a natural fibre (cellulose being related to cotton) — it has a very different source (oil) which has to be chemically rebuilt and transformed. And so, the synthetic fibres came into being.

Here again we can observe sequential cycles of four major* families of fibres (although the trade names give the impression that there are thousands), each of them giving a formidable impetus to industrial development.

This second major cycle came to maturity in the last decade: new families of fibres have been invented but their application is more and more marginal, and compared with the past successes of the big four, rather insignificant. The bulk of research has been more and more concentrated for the last fifteen years on the improvement of existing fibres.

We are clearly here in a situation of diminishing technological returns.

The question would seem to be: how can a new fundamental cycle be initiated? One answer has been research into non-wovens, but it has clearly failed to become a significant "locomotive". Moreover, it seems difficult to use our expanding knowledge of physics and chemistry to produce a revolutionary new approach, at least for the next decade. Of course one can argue optimistically and say: you can never predict fundamental changes, although this does not modify the time-lag problem. Or one can argue more pessimistically: we are more

*Polyamide, Polyester, Acrylics, Polypropylene.

and more coming to the point where science-based technology, at least in certain sectors, has exploited all the major possibilities made available by the scientific advances of the last century.

Analogies with the fibre-development cycles are easy to identify in other industrial sectors, such as aviation for instance, and in many chemical products.

At this stage, some viable opportunities still appear to exist in the electronics communication field and in biochemistry.

Very extensive research is necessary into the present situation regarding time lags and cycles over the whole spectrum of technologies in all sectors. Our point here is that technological production is not immune to its own law of diminishing returns, which is implicit in the whole history of discovery and invention.

But there are other ways in which technology, by its very development, can have the effect of diminishing economic returns.

(c) At the micro-economic level, the phenomenon of the diminishing returns of technology has already been experienced in some industries for more than a decade, at the level of the company body responsible for research and development investment.

The following graph gives an idea of the problem:

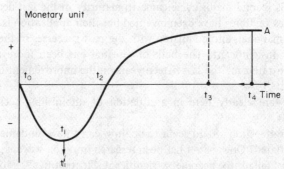

FIG. 2.9. *The Strategic Problem in Research and Development Investment*

A = Net amount of money spent (under the horizontal line) or earned (above the line) in any given moment in time. The *areas* (above and under the line) indicate the *accumulated* amounts.
— at time t_0 a new research programme is started: money is invested with no possibility of any return until t_1;

- at t_1, the new research programme has started to yield a new product which is put on the market, but research continues to improve it and expand its applications, so that for a period of time, income is less than outlays on continuing research and market penetration costs;
- only at t_2 does income match outlays; this marks the start of the period during which one must recover the deficit accumulated from t_0 to t_2;
- this deficit is offset at point t_3;
- the whole operation starts yielding net profit only after t_3;
- at t_4 another product is introduced on to the market, which makes the first one obsolete, and therefore the latter's marketable period is over.

This outline, of course, is simplified, but it helps to bring out the impact of trends which, in many cases, make the whole situation very vulnerable:

- it must be borne in mind that of all the projects that have reached point t_0 of a research programme, as a rule, less than 10% will prove successful. A company knows that of 100 million dollars it invests in research and development, 90 millions will simply be wasted. The successful part of the programme must therefore cover this net loss. In some industries, the situation is aggravated by the fact that the percentage of successes is diminishing, so that to make the probability law of large numbers operate, research — and therefore investment in it — must expand. There is a tendency therefore for point t_1 to be lowered towards t'_1;
- increased research costs mean that the period for recovering them must be longer or that the market must be larger; the whole programme becomes more and more risky;
- on the other hand, increased research means adding obsolescence to the products: substitution will be quicker and quicker. This does not happen because — as we have seen — results can be achieved quickly, but because parallel research in the whole industry will, as a consequence, lead to comparable solutions which will curtail the time available for exploiting the benefits of a research project. The drive for substitution, which in all sectors

has increased the trends towards shorter obsolescence time — or put more simply — which has resulted in products with a shorter and shorter life ("use-and-throw-away" products, from the handkerchief to watch) has become in many sectors a nonsense even in purely economic terms, as for instance the story of textile disposables (non-woven products) has shown. These trends are not yet completely widespread in industry as a whole, but they exist in those sectors of industry which have achieved maturity, and where a qualitative technological leap is out of the question for the next decade at least.

(d) Technology, in many cases, is a means of producing something better, faster and in larger quantities. There is a tremendous push towards specialization. In fact, a new machine very often produces, quicker and better and larger quantity of a more limited range of products than the machine which it has replaced. These improvements are often at the expense of range and flexibility.* A clear example is provided by the modern shuttle-less looms which have superseded the traditional loom. Each of the new methods offers an advantage in a more restricted application. Limits are reached when, for instance, a single machine is capable of producing 500,000 blankets per year very efficiently, provided they are all of the same type, from all the points of view: materials, colour, size, textile structure, etc. In cases such as this, specialization is economically attractive from the point of view of production, but an economic handicap from the point of view of product distribution and utilization.

(e) Decisive limits are of a logistic nature. The success of technology seems to lead, paradoxically in many cases, to a situation in which production becomes marginal to the economic process. In more and more cases, production has become an appendix of the distribution system for a great many products of our everyday life, and we have seen this point in an earlier paragraph (2.4.).

All this means that many mistakes can be made in preparing a cost/benefit analysis of a new product, at the manufacturing level. Apparent

---

*Efforts to counterbalance this tendency has often been a major goal of applied research. Positive results have been obtained in some specific cases, such as numerically controlled machine tools, which are particularly well-adapted to short production runs which in conventional machine tools would entail excessive set-up times.

gains at that level can be more than offset by the increased costs involved in the whole distribution system. Some years ago, considerations of this kind, for instance, prevented the chemical industry from stepping up the individual capacity of ammonia or ethylene production units.

(f) We have already mentioned the growth of waste production. With traditional technology, the problem of waste remained, in the main, limited.

With science-based technology, it is another matter, because science-based technological production changes the structure of materials and modifies the natural recycling patterns. The problem, of course, is aggravated, in a cumulative way, by the total increase in production.

Technology, in many cases, increases the life span of natural recycling: often the more a product has been transformed because of scientific knowledge, the longer the recycling period and the recycling costs. The treatment of uranium wastes takes this phenomenon to its most costly and dangerous extremes.

(g) Closely related to this latter development is the question of increased vulnerability of the economic system. This sounds at first like a paradox because one is accustomed to the idea that modern technology has a higher level or coefficient of security than traditional or primitive technology. An outer space vehicle is much more "safe" than a nineteenth-century carriage in term of the probability of malfunction. But, in fact, the system itself it much more vulnerable since, even though the frequency of a disaster is lower, the severity of a disaster is much greater and the available margin of error much lower. Insurance statistics and experience show that the decrease in the number of accidents (frequency), and the increase in the maximum possible levels of loss are an indication that the situation tends essentially to be unmanageable. There is a loss of control over events and this process is even more dangerous since failures are in fact due mostly to human error or to a human negative action. This is why the increase in the level of vulnerability is a negative problem in itself, beyond and apart from the simple accounting of probabilities of a mishap. This is rather obvious in sectors such as nuclear power or the transport and storage of liquefied natural gases (LNG). There are even some writers[39] who contend that, owing to the growing interdependence and complexity of social systems, all the very rare probabilities of producing disasters from *different* sources can cumulate and then, *de facto*, increase the total probability of a disaster.

It is obvious in any case that the control of such vulnerabilities is a cost — and an economic one — which contributes largely to the diminishing returns of technology.*

(h) One last point is the growing difficulty of adapting the most modern technology to the ability of those who have to handle it. In other words, although some of the technology normally used in the industrially developed countries clearly cannot always be properly handled in the so-called "developing" countries, certain very advanced modern technology may be beyond the operational capabilities of the "developed". The electronics industry is well acquainted with this problem.

All these points are not intended to prove that science and technology are condemned once and for all to the law of diminishing returns.** Many sectorial improvements are possible, some through the synergistic effect of one sector on the progress of another, as for instance the case of synthetic fibres offering a major opportunity for technological innovation in the knitting machinery industry. However, we have also seen that, on the one hand, the unique economic growth of this century has a very specific origin in the unique, historical marriage between science and technology, whilst on the other, there are obvious limitations which are all the more serious

*Anders Munk suggests one should speak of dependency rather than of vulnerability. For instance "centralization of energy production as in a nuclear plant means vulnerability, literally 'exposed to become wounded'; it is not necessarily pathological in itself. But physical dependency of non-renewable or limited resources is in itself pathological. Literal vulnerability *may* go right, physical dependency in such cases *will* go wrong".

In our view, the two concepts are interrelated: in order to counteract increasing dependency, more and more deducted values are produced and vulnerability levels are increased, in a vicious circle hidden by an inadequate notion of value. The absolute level of vulnerability governs society's level of dependency on security measures and behaviour.

**The discussion on the "Mature Entropy Stage" of the industrializing model is further discussed by, among others, Jean Voge, in *Technological Forecasting and Social Change*, Brussels, July 1979, and again in the last book by Georgescu-Roegen, Nicholas: *Demain la Décroissance*, Lausanne 1979.

because of the time mechanism involved in the science—technology—production sequence.*

2.2.8.3. A helpful criticism to the "diminishing returns of technology"

What we have described in previous paragraphs summarizes a series of empirical experiences which go back a little more than a decade. More detailed analysis and research on this very important issue are absolutely necessary and should be carried out systematically in all sectors of activity.

A contribution to such an analysis was recently published by a large private financial institution under the title *Business and Technology, Today and Tomorrow*,[40] which the press has referred to as proof that there is no "general weakness in technological innovation".

Many readers of that document will probably have studied at least the introduction, which summarizes the numerous analyses of specific technological sectors, and which is clearly optimistic in tone.

But when one studies the report in detail, the subtle ambiguity of our civilization towards the "facts" of science of technology appears quite clearly.

The facts given by this document almost all tend to indicate that *we are* in a period of diminishing returns of technology. The big exception is that of the microprocessor where the "revolution is just beginning".

Considering that this document was intended to *prove* just *the opposite* to what we have just presented, we think it provides an interesting reference point for readers.

Individual chapters of the report are devoted to separate industrial sectors and we have, in the following pages, extracted from each the concluding or key remarks on present and future prospects.

Technology and Business

Introduction
"The results of these studies made it clear that there is no general weakness in technological innovation and that technology has by no means lost its role as a driving force for economic growth. It is true, of course, that technological development does

*As to the future pace of scientific discovery see also: Rescher, Nicholas: *Scientific Progress,* Oxford, 1978, which discusses the reasons and implications of a deceleration of science.

not take place at an even pace and that the number of inventions commercially utilized by industry has been declining since the early seventies. This should, however, not be ascribed to stagnation in technological research and development but rather to the fact that new inventions do not reach the stage where they can be realized on a continuing basic and that the environment for commercial exploitation is not always favourable." (p. 5).

Energy

"Even presuming that the political problems coupled with nuclear energy can be solved, we must take drastic steps over the intermediate term to save energy, whereas the pent-up demand in the developing countries is not ever likely to be fully met. (. . .) At any rate, it could be a dangerous illusion to assume that the age of ample and cheap energy will ever return again." (p. 13).

Raw Materials

"Although the metal reserves located at accessible areas of the earth's crust are truly gigantic, the situation is considerably less favourable in regard to deposits with a high metal concentration. In the case of certain metals such as iron, copper, molybdenum, chromium and possibly nickel, it is feasible to work ores with lower metal contents but such exploitation requires substantial amounts of energy and extremely capital-intensive installations, they also significantly pollute the environment. As far as aluminium is concerned, it is possible to switch from bauxite to alternate ores, but such a substitution necessitates the consumption of vastly greater amounts of energy than before. The supply situation in regard to silver, lead, zinc, mercury, cadmium, tin, tungsten, antimony and perhaps cobalt gives rise to concern. (. . .) Society will, to a large extent, have to do without gold jewelry, silver cutlery, galvanized sheet metal, lead batteries and other items considered commonplace today". (p. 17).

Technical Materials

"The future of the materials employed in manufacturing and construction will be depending to a much larger extent on the raw material market environment than has been the case in the past. An increasingly crucial factor will also be availability and price of the energy needed to reproduce such materials. For these reasons it is likely that construction materials such as concrete steel and light metals will retain the leading role they play today". (p. 17).

Automated Production

"Any kind of automation calls for a significant increase in capital expenditure. For this reason alone, the goal of automated production can only be reached by employing a step-by-step approach. The development of modern production technology into automated production represents an evolution which will take its time." (p. 25).

Electrical Engineering

"Electrical energy technology, whose pronounced degree of reliability is its principle feature, is not the scene of spectacular events. Its evaluation is much rather characterized by slow but steady progress where time is measured in decades. The risks which an industrial society must shoulder when it introduces an innovative concept are truly enormous." (p. 29).

Mechanical Engineering
"Many signs indicate that the age of important and spectacular inventions in machinery construction has long passed." (p. 31).

Textile Fibres
"The future promises new fibre and textile technologies. (. . .) Major tasks also lie ahead in the finishing of fibre fabrics. (. . .) Processing technology and textile machinery also face a bright future. Advanced and less expensive constructions must be designed and the productivity of technical installations and equipment must be increased. As regards yarn production and the possibilities of automation in general, higher output must be achieved with less labour." (p. 34–35).

The Printing Industry
"It is interesting to note that the breakthrough of electronics in the graphic arts and the printing industry in particular has generated substantial capital investment although many firms were marked by overcapacity and the earnings situation was poor without exception." (p. 40).

Construction Technology
"The required technologies are widely known today, but they will have to be applied with great discrimination under the aspect of energy saving construction." (p. 44).

Defence Technology
"Integration of basic discoveries into defence technology is a complicated process and still takes several decades. (. . .) A weapons system conceived for a specific range of missions in 1977 will thus be based on scientific and technical knowledge obtained before 1970. The system itself, always provided that it is ever developed to operational maturity, will be produced in a prototype version towards the middle Eighties, to be followed – if it is ever to become operational – by quantity production some time after 1990." (p. 45–46).

Electronics
"The significance of the microprocessor as a technological force can best be likened to the Industrial Revolution of the eighteenth century. (. . .) It has been estimated that roughly one half of all microprocessor applications* in 1980 are still largely unknown today." (p. 53).

Scientific Instruments
"In any case, the revolution triggered by the microprocessor is only just beginning."*
(p. 56).

*The key point will be in this case not simply to determine the level of technological performance (speed, reliability, miniaturization, etc.), but the real value it adds to economic wealth and welfare. The relative slowdown of the chemical fibres industry in the last ten years has been accompanied by great technological innovations: but although it is possible to produce fibres resistant to 500°C, how much help has this been for the clothing industry?

Optics

"*Adoption* of this new technology over the next *ten* to *twenty* years would be clearly likely to be the starting point for a new and important branch of industry." (p. 59).

Photography

"The most important raw materials used in photography are silver and gelatine. The first is a metal which needs to be processed to the highest degree of purity, the second is a natural substance which comes in a great variety of different types. Despite intensive research, no substitute for either is in sight." (p. 63–64).

Computers

"This readily illustrates how makers and users of computers alike soon reach the ultimate ceiling if they try to make their tools do what they are not intended to perform. Genuine future progress in data processing does not lie in higher capacity or the elimination of some bottleneck or other, but in its more rational and purposeful application – in effect, in optimum management of computer operations." (p. 69).

Communications Worldwide

"It can already be foreseen that the fundamental problem for global communication will not be technology or its realization – technologically, almost everything imaginable can today be realized. The problem will lie in software, the programme that are necessary for the functioning of future telecommunications systems."

2.2.9. THE QUESTION OF ECONOMIC CYCLES

In the preceeding section we have emphasized the fact that important technological innovations proceed by long-term bounds and that, as from the end of the last century, advances in scientific knowledge gave rise to technology of quite a new kind.

The relationship between technological advances and the economic and industrial phases of expansion have been studied by a number of authors (looking, however, essentially at the effects of technology, rather than at the actual path of discovery, invention and technological development).

The most important of these studies is that by Schumpeter[41] who clearly attributed major expansion cycles to the creation of new markets and to the development of technological innovations. By stimulating new investment, it is these combined phenomena – and not savings – that are the real instigators of economic progress.[42]

Landes[43] makes several observations concerning the inter-relation between technological cycles and economic cycles: "from 1870, with the exception of a branch like steel, British industry had exhausted the gains implicit in the original cluster of innovations that had constituted the Industrial Revolution.... The marginal product of improvements diminished as the cost of equipment went up and the physical advantage over existing techniques fell." In our discussions of the diminishing returns of technology, it is our belief that the same type of phenomenon is now taking place for the cluster of innovations related to science-based technology.

The long-term technological cycles, recall the debate on the long-term cycles proposed by Kondratieff.[44] For Kondratieff, as cited by Landes "the upswing of the long cycle is associated with increases in both investment (due to new inventions, resources and markets), and money supply. ... Kondratieff does not look upon these concomitants of fluctations as causes, but rather as products of the conjuncture, and speaks cryptically of 'causes which are inherent in the essence of the capitalistic economy'."

In fact, advances in technology require more investment and an enlarged money basis of the economy, as we discussed in previous paragraphs. So all these factors clearly *appear* as concomitant. But if the new technology does not bring substantial advancement in productivity, the increase in the money supply will simply contribute to demand-push inflation.

The long-term cycles* are therefore the results of a subtle and complex interreaction of technological innovation "which is not constantly productive in time, but which has its own cycles", with the entire economic system.

The really important thing is not to consider innovation as an abstract function, equated with human ingenuity, and expendable and usable at will. Technological innovations have their own patterns of evolution, which can sometimes favorably influence the elasticity of supply and sometimes be a determinant reason for its rigidity. This is why it should be essential in economics to study the historical and systemic conditions of evolution of technological innovations and utilizations.

More recently the links between economic and technological development have been studied by Gerhard Mensch[45] who, in the graph on p. 144,

---

*The vision of cycles can be extended even further. Henderson, H. goes back to the late stone age (4000 B.C.) and identifies in the present "the confluence of at least six historic transitions of different periodicities" (The Coming of the Solar Age, *Resurgence*, July–August 1979, pp. 6–9).

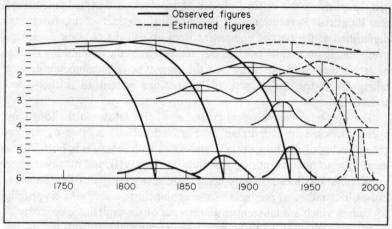

FIG. 2.10. *Cycles in Scientific Discovery and Innovation*

Review of the occurrence in knowledge transfer at six levels:
(1)   new theories
(2)   fundamental inventions
(3)   technical feasibility
(4)   start of development
(5)   innovation decision
(6)   fundamental innovations

demonstrates clearly the sequence of new theories, fundamental discoveries, applied research, development research, industrial utilization and economic development.

His book is a major contribution to the theory of innovation cycles and is based on thorough analysis and empirical verification.

Like Schumpeter, Mensch has also described the long-term cycles of the industrial system and their relationship to cycles of innovation.

However, his analysis tends to overlook a major factor: each major cycle is *different* from previous cycles. He attempts to establish a law that is valid in *general* time, whereas it seems to us important that the relationship should have been to *historical* time.

It is then also necessary to take into consideration super megacycles, above the long-term cycles, rather than viewing long-term cycles of the Kondratieff type as the highest dimensional unit of time.

This is why in this research, the start of the industrial revolution is considered as a point of major discontinuity, based on the growing importance of certain specific factors (industrialization as we try to describe it), which will influence the whole megacycle that spans over a period of over two centuries. Within this megacycle, we can even detect another major discontinuity — mainly the point at which technology itself began to be conditioned primarily by the use of scientific discoveries.

We would then propose that the Industrial Revolution itself be considered a megacycle which lasted for more than two centuries, subdivided into two very long major cycles lasting each about one century. The first being linked with the First Industrial Revolution and the second with the science-based technology in the Second Industrial Revolution.

This superimposition of cycles with different wavelengths is not just an intellectual exercise. In fact, each *type* of cycle is clearly and inevitably conditioned by its relative position with regard to the other types of cycle.

There is then superimposition of cycles, or — as Forrester[46] calls it — intercyclical relations.

It is something like observing the waves of the sea: from *our* relative point of view, we see or consider first a type of wave which is of the order of few meters. But looking closer, we often see on each wave a superimposition of small waves — of the order of some centimeters. Then we have the very long waves determined by the moon's attraction: the "tide" phenomenon. We can add to all this the very rare gigantic or mega-waves — which happen at irregular intervals — due to seismic or other catastrophic occurrences.

Each of these waves has a priority effect on a different type of system. They can also add their movement, or sometimes counteract each other.

This is probably also what happens for "economic cycles": many of the "irregularities" are due intuitively to the superimposition of different cycles, which react to different — although interrelated — causes and equilibrium changes. The diminishing returns of technology are then to be linked partly to long-term cycles — in the Schumpeter sense — in as much as they are oscillations about fundamentally the same "industrial" system or "industrial" megacycle. But they are also an element, or an indicator, of change in the megacycle itself, when the essentially industrial characteristics of this one, are themselves in a period of deep structural modification.

The way Forrester is studying intercyclical relations is rather different from what we propose here. He does not go back to the megacycles as defined by the agricultural society, later by the industrial society, and now by the start of a post-industrial society in the sense we have tried to define it. He goes back — studying essentially the American case — to the "very long term" cycles of about 50 years, which are intuitively proposed as determined by the length of human life.

In his interpretation, the major cycles are determined by the fact that fixed investment is, little by little, built up to such an extent that there is overcapacity. Only when such fixed investment, of long life, is worn out and has to be replaced, does a new very long cycle start. It is also obvious that such new capacity has to be built up after a war or any other type of catastrophic destruction.

But, in our view, the real significance of the new technology in the Industrial Revolution, has been precisely the fact that the fixed investment has become *obsolete*: in other words, that a better technology has made possible the substitution of existing capacity, not because it has worn out, but because a *new* investment could produce a gain in productivity of such a dimension that *usable* capacity was no longer economically efficient.

The diminishing returns of technology appear when, precisely, the development of *obsolescence* — substitution of equipment because it has become inefficient — has reached a level of saturation or even of negative productivity so that the very mechanism which has stimulated the Industrial Revolution has lost, at least a part, of its driving force.

In any case, there is a very important point in stimulating not only studies on different types of cycles, but also of their interrelation.

Finally, we would like to reverse some final considerations to the subject of cycles, referring to the second report of the Club of Rome entitled "Mankind at the Turning Point".[47]

In that report, the proposal is made to organize future growth as against past growth, as being an "organic" one instead of an "extrapolative" one. We would like to make here a further step in this direction.

In fact, all growth is organic: the chemical industry grows when new products start new mini-cycles *within* the bigger cycle of chemical industry development. We have seen how, in the field of fibres, there are successive, "organic", changes from natural, to artificial and finally to synthetic fibres.

We propose then to reformulate the "philosophy" of organic growth, in saying that when a cycle at a given level, has developed its major potentials, then it is time for a cycle of an upper level to take over the "running". Here is where the "organic" growth becomes a change from an "industrial" order to a post-industrial one. The point is not then to go from an "extrapolative" to an "organic" development, but to consider the change in the level (or cycles dimension) of the "organic" development underway.

2.3. New strategies for Developing Wealth and Welfare

2.3.1. THE PROBLEM OF DEFINING WELFARE

We have tried to highlight, in the previous paragraphs, the fact that the technological revolution, industrialization and the spread of monetarization (as the basis for capitalization in the form of private and/or public capitalism) are all facets of the same phenomenon. They are the reactive elements of a single system — the Industrial Revolution. This has permitted unprecedented growth in human material welfare, being at the same time deeply embedded in a specific historical and cultural setting.

We have also underlined how economics, as an important, new social science (=discipline), is largely an outcome of the same industrial revolution. Economics provides light for the analysis of social phenomena, in as much as they become "visible" and quantifiable by the price system.

But the fact remains that wealth, welfare, and wellbeing are all human aspirations which are not satisfied by priced products alone, *even if they are strictly material.* Furthermore, there are probably many aspects of welfare and of human needs which are a mixture of material and of "spiritual" nature, something like the psychosomatic diseases where there is no boundary between the imagination or mental attitude on the one hand and the physical body's reaction on the other. Even further, many would also add that numerous needs are purely spiritual. Monastic contemplation can also be a definition of wellbeing which is — at least in principle — completely excluded from a monetarized organization of society.

The notion of welfare (and of wealth, wellbeing, human needs, etc.), in its widest definition, allows infinite variations. It is something like the wavelength spectrum (see 2.2.1. p. 102). The visible light can be compared to visible welfare, expressed in monetary terms. The infrared and ultra-violet waves are not as visible as the light waves, but still relatively easy to detect (particularly infrared radiation which we feel when it transports heat): we could pursue the analogy by saying that in the economy, these waves might correspond to all those elements of *material* welfare, which are *external* to the priced or monetarized economic system. Furthermore, the short and long radiowaves become more and more imperceptible to our direct senses, but are still essential as carriers of sound: in the economy, we enter here a zone where connotations of material and spiritual wellbeing are more and more difficult to distinguish from each other.

Finally, since we do not know where the wavelength spectrum starts or finishes at either end, we are here in presence of a *boundary of knowledge* or even of the possibility of inquiry, which probably corresponds to the impossibility of setting any final boundary to reality.

The subdivision of the different types of wavelength and of the different types of welfare and needs, must be understood as a tool for better under-standing the problems, and *not* as a representation of reality: otherwise we would fall into the trap of "Cartesianism". In fact, the passage from one type of waves to another and from one type of welfare to another, is a continuum.

In its article on wavelengths, the *Encyclopaedia Britannica* notes that: "The various frequency ranges bear different names because of the different behaviour in the emission, transmission and absorption of the corresponding waves, *but they overlap* . . . and . . . there are no precise wavelengths accepted as boundaries between any of these continuous ranges".

Even here, we are therefore not quite in the "Cartesian" system of objectively distinct and separate frameworks.

So much more in the case of welfare and needs, where the subjective elements (the cultural and individual attitudes and conditions) make even more complex the relations between material and non-material welfare, between the monetary and non-monetary.

This subdivision is necessary purely to improve the degree of *approximation* of our analysis. It is not for the purpose of acquiring true know-ledge – rather just a little more knowledge (if possible). Experience with "Cartesianism" and everything that followed, as has been outlined in our previous paragraphs, should warn us of the danger of proposing new views which, when they are made a philosophical absolute, run the danger of transforming the element of knowledge into an instrument of modern-day superstition.

It must therefore be emphasized that when we propose here apparently clear-cut boundary conditions, they are a tool for a first-step analysis, but they are also an avowal of inadequacy linked to our mind's inability to capture a multitude of elements which exist simultaneously in reality, but which we cannot encompass due to *our* basic limitations. To understand this better, we just have to look in front of us for a moment: it is impossible to scan all the objects, shapes, colours and movements simultaneously. The eye will detect only a fraction of the reality. Reconstruction of this simultaneity of a complex picture is possible only with patient, *ex post*, detailed analysis and synthesis, owing to the inadequacy of our sensorial and mental capacities.

Let us return to our wavelength and/or welfare spectrum having now realized its inadequacies and limitations not just as a "*formule de con-venance*" but in a more basic sense.

Since total, human material and spiritual welfare and needs comprise an infinite range of possibilities, the traditional industrial economic system is the one which is motivated by the effort to increase *total welfare*, through the expansion of the social system which is organized around monetarized forms of relationship.

History has known periods of spiritual upheaval in which attempts were made to increase man's wellbeing by giving a priority to spiritual goals.

One specific period in human history, the Industrial Revolution, has — thanks to the combination of culture, technology, industrialization

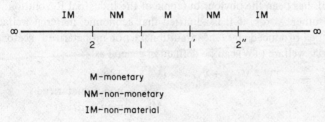

M—monetary

NM—non-monetary

IM—non-material

FIG. 2.11. *The Infinite Elements of Welfare*

and monetarization — had the historic possibility of reinforcing in an unprecedented way one part of the human welfare or needs equation.

The most important problem confronting the modern economy here, is to verify how far its *contribution* to total welfare, and in particular *to total material welfare* is still determinant, or at least important.

In the context of the diagram above, the task is to examine how far economics, concentrated in space 1 to 1′ (the monetarized zone of the economy) is now being more affected than in the past by the inter-relationships with the wider spectrum of *material* forms of activity producing the welfare comprised between 2 and 2′.

2.3.2. MONETARY AND NON–MONETARY ECONOMIC VALUES

Human (and even animal) societies have always been faced with "economic" problems: whenever there is scarcity and wherever action is taken to combat it, there is an economic activity, whatever its nature.

The Industrial Revolution has provided the human race with efficient new tools to combat shortages. Industrialization has become the priority so that even if economics is essentially the outcome of this phenomenon, it will still be sufficient for analyzing and for directing policy in the organization of welfare. It will provide added "production" value, which is supposed to add to the material welfare of any other non-monetarized type of activity, *but this applies under specific historic conditions.*

More than that, substitution of a non-monetary activity by a mone-tarized activity, even though entailing certain specific sacrifices, will finally be considered desirable: the productivity of the monetarized sector will more than compensate, in the long term, and often also in the short term, for any loss in the traditional, essentially non-monetarized sector.

This has been the obvious outcome of the Industrial Revolution.

In other words, if it is admitted that economic, material welfare may also be produced by the traditional, non-monetarized sector, total material welfare (TW) can be defined in general as:

$$TW = V_{NM} + V_M \qquad \begin{array}{ll} (V & -\text{value} \\ NM & -\text{non-monetarized} \\ M & -\text{monetarized}) \end{array}$$

A relatively high degree of non-monetarized values has persisted even in the most industrialized nations, e.g. non-remunerated work (housewives, benevolent activities), non-remunerated goods and services (unpolluted air and water). The *historic* evolution of monetarized and non-monetarized economics will be studied in greater detail in the next Chapter.

What should be emphasized here is that insofar as V_M is the really dynamic part of the question in adding to TW (where V_{NM} is particularly static and/or irrelevant), then the economist can and does normally assume that TW = V_M.

However, V_{NM} is *not* independent of V_M; V_M in fact reduces the field of the NM economy and/or transforms it.

As stated, it is normally assumed that any loss in the NM sector will be more than offset by the M-substitutive activity. In terms of value, gain in V_M will be greater than any loss in V_{NM}.

But it is only under such conditions that TW will, in fact, increase. The difficulty of analyzing such an equation is due not only to the problem implicit in evaluating non-monetary activities, but also to the concept of value in traditional economic theory, when this is equated with welfare. We have examined this problem under paragraph 2.2.6: we would like, then, here to stress the importance of the non-monetarized part of the economy.

If the notion of value is limited to the monetarized production process, we discover that, in fact, it implies that *any* production, which considers only prices boundaries, is producing welfare. This can happen – as we have seen – when the advantages of industrialization are overwhelming, indisputable and do not suffer from diminishing returns of technology. If the notion of value is based, as we proposed, on its utilization, it becomes a matter of common sense to identify welfare with the total *net* contribution of the non-monetarized *and* the monetarized economic system to the satisfaction of material needs.

In other words, the basic paradigm – the concept of value – of traditional economics (be it the Smithian concept, or the demand-based one), represents an obstacle to assessing the true net contribution to welfare by non-monetarized economic activity.*

*The literature discussing the shift in the economic paradigm is multiplying rapidly. See among others: Henderson, Hazel: Economics: a Paradigm Shift is in Progress, *Solar Age*, August 1978, pp. 18–21; Katscher, Ernst: *Wiedergeburt der Oekonomie*, Eisenstadt, Austria, 1979; Huber, Joseph: *Technokratie oder Menschlichkeit*, Berlin 1979; Siebker, Manfred: *Die unsichtbare Hand sichtbar machen*, Frankfurter Hefte, April 1979, pp. 21–26.

The following remarks may clarify this:

— a closer look at any production process reveals that, among the production factors, there are many inputs which are not monetary or not monetarized: the cost of the air for a company producing nitrogen through the liquefied air process, is nil, as are the large quantities of river water used by a paper or an aluminium mill.

— if this air or water is highly polluted, costs will be incurred in returning these "free" raw materials to their initial purity — the problem is intensified in that most advanced technology may not be able to avoid pollution emission, and may even tend to aggravate the total environmental control problem.

Consequently, in the initial industrialization phase, the industrial system will have many essential production inputs "free of charge". Subsequently they will have to be paid for: this transfer into the monetarized system does not indicate that a process is increasing total welfare, but simply that it is first of all increasing the total *costs* for producing welfare.*

The same examples can be drawn at the level of the individual: swimming in a non-polluted sea or lake for free is an element of welfare. Invention of the automobile led to an increase in total welfare by adding to the choice of places to go swimming. There is an obvious increase in total welfare (based on services available from the non-monetarized economy and from the monetarized one). In a third phase, the same industrial system which makes possible the production of automobiles, leads to the pollution of seas and lakes. Thus, there is diminishing welfare (utilization value): costs entailed in re-establishing utilization value of the water, will be "catching-up" costs and not costs adding to total welfare (or utilization value). We encounter here, once again, the concept of value deducted.**

*The problems of environmental costs and their discussion are, anyhow, stimulating economic thinking. In the study by the European Trade Union Institute mentioned at the beginning of this dossier, it is proposed to integrate environmental factors in a new "Keynes-plus Economy". The reference to Keynes is understandable as reaction against a resurgence of conservative liberalism in recent years, which tends to lay at the door of union policies most of the rigidities of the present economic situation in the industrialized countries. It is clear that, from our analysis, both neo-liberalism and keynesians are still largely prisoners of increasingly inadequate traditional economic paradigms.

**A similar notion has been proposed by Fred Hirsch in his book *Social Limits to Growth,* London 1976, where he speaks of "Positional Goods".

Starting from the *traditional* notion of value, it can be said that, in current economic accounting, a certain number of production phases (and a number of products) are not produced in order to increase added-value, but in order to restore utilization values which have been previously destroyed and which now have to be recycled or reintegrated at some cost, in order to permit the economic machine to run. If the rise in national income in recent years is due increasingly to the development of the anti-pollution industry (detection systems, chemical products, incinerators, compacting machines for domestic use, etc.), this production is not adding to the initial level of welfare but it is being used more and more to fight the negative effects of industrial expansion. The resultant added value is not a measure of added welfare: it represents the *cost* of previous consumption which now has to be paid in order to restore utilization possibilities. It is, in fact, a *deducted* value. The indicator of GNP as a sum of added values is in fact diverging more and more from an indicator of welfare: it is increasingly clear that it is rather only an indicator of cost. If, in the golden era of the industrial revolution, it could also be assumed as an indicator of material/economic welfare, it is because in a period of no real diminishing returns of technology, almost all the production costs become net real wealth. Now, an ever greater part of those costs represents a negative feed-back loop effect on the overall trend of the total *monetarized cost indicator* – the GNP.

2.3.3. THE TIME FACTOR IN THE NOTION OF VALUE

The idea of defining net value in a first approximation, as the differential between total gross added value (as normally computed), less the "deducted values", does, of course, present some problems.

The first is that deducted value represents a cost *in the past,* which has not been taken into account: the pollution of today is the result, in most cases, of negative accumulations in the past, which have not been eliminated. The present has been subsidized by the future: instead of preparing a world for the future generations, many costs have been, and are being, simply transferred in time. As mentioned in the previous section, we find here again a limitation of the static notion of time in economics: added value always seems to be net added value, because it represents a specific moment in time. In other words, if the notion of value is *static,* one can safely state that any production or any investment today — including that in pollution — tends to ameliorate the standard of living. The *future* pollution produced by *present* production will appear as a negative element only later. It may therefore continue to destroy future welfare and still give the impression, in the static analysis, that added value is a real thing. This is an obvious, paradoxical case, in which formal logic, within unverified boundary conditions, leads to absurdity.

As a consequence, a real challenge for economic thinking now, is to explore all possible ways of reviewing the basic notions in a real dynamic time dimension.*

All this leads to a basic concept, i.e. that of the general source of wealth and welfare, which we have termed "Dowry and Patrimony" (D & P).

The next paragraphs and Chapter are devoted essentially to this concept which is the basic reference for identifying not only deducted value but also the source of utilization value, as an indicator of real wealth.

---

*Discussion of "deducted value" also necessarily entails a reappraisal of the economic literature on externalities. Here are some major points:
— Internalization is not, as normally represented, a marginal economic phenomenon. Rather, in our perspective, it is a fundamental mechanism of the modern industrialized economy: it represents the transition of the economic activities from the non-monetarized stage to the monetarized stage. At any given moment in time, this process might seem marginal: but it is its *cumulation* in time which really creates the fields of action of "industrial" economics. The historical transition process should be better analyzed in order also to verify how much of the increase in "monetary" welfare represents simply a transfer from the non-monetarized economy and how much represents a real added value. We would not be surprised, if, when introducing this notion into national accounting, the real growth in GNP were diminished by something like 20 to 50% — even before taking into account the "deducted" value.
— There is a second aspect of internalization (termed by Simon Kuznets the "negative externalities") which is linked to the diminishing returns of technology:
— It is the moment at which the internalization of an economic activity is carried out not in order to increase total overall productivity (first case) but because the free elements or factors contributing to the monetarized production need to be restored, by investing money (i.e. investing for pollution). This is the case of deducted values (which remain deducted even when they are "internalized").

For a further analysis of externalities see E. J. Mishan *The Costs of Economic Growth,* Harmondsworth, 1969, as well as "The Post-war Literature on Externalities: an Interpretative Essay", *Journal of Economic Literature,* March 1971.

However, by now it should already be clear how the concept of utilization value has both a comprehensive time dimension (real-time continuum) and a space dimension (integration of monetary and non-monetary activities).

We can now add to the graph in section 2.5 (page 117) – in which the reasoning was limited to the monetarized economy – the dimension of the non-monetarized economy and consequently be able to make the following statement:

· *the utilization value of products or service is built up and guaranteed by a series of monetarized activities* (costs), such as:
  – production costs
  – storage and distribution costs
  – maintenance costs
  – service and repair costs
  – financial and insurance costs
  – disposal costs
  as well as of non-monetarized activities and stock of goods and services, such as:
  – free-labour activities
  – qualitative (cultural) performances of people
  – free flow of free goods (water for washing and drinking), derived from the natural and non-monetarized Dowry and Patrimony, *related to their life period.*

2.3.4. VALUE, DOWRY AND PATRIMONY (D & P) AND CAPITAL

We can now reconsider the notion of capital and of its utilization. Here, we concur partly with the views expressed more or less explicitly by various economists, such as Irving Fisher,[48] Georgescu-Roegen,[49] Daly,[50] etc. which highlight the fact that the value of any economic product is in fact the *stock of services* it represents. This stock of services is the real wealth (both monetarized and non-monetarized) available at any moment in time. Such a moment in time is to be considered a dynamic equilibrium situation, in a given moment or period. It should be added, in fact, that an important feature is not only the amount of "wealth" (stock of services) available in time (with the risk of introducing again a static element of analysis), but also the amount of costs (monetary and non-monetary) and the quality and quantity of services that such stocks will require and produce *in their future lifetime.*

It is clear that all "products", in this case, are considered a "stock" of services: an automobile represents a stock of services which have utilization value, and which will, during its utilization, cost a total amount of monetary and of non-monetary effort represented by production, repair, fueling, parking costs, nuisances, insurable damages, disposal and destruction of the automobile, etc.

The economic problem then, is not to optimize merely the cost of production, but rather to optimize the total utilization value. At least some of the non-monetary values will be quantifiable by future discounted values;* others could be determined by an effort/equivalent index. This is another point which demands thorough research.

The concept of "stock of services" is, in reality, the equivalent of Capital, if we reduce it to only monetarized goods, and to the concept of "Dowry and Patrimony" if we embrace both monetary and non-monetary goods and services together.

We can then put the former definitions in another way.

The growth of Capital (monetarized D & P) has been the essential feature of the Industrial Revolution, through which the yielding of services of the total D & P system has been vastly increased by its partial monetarization. The sense of the Industrial Revolution is that, by way of money, the total stock of services available for use to the human being has been enormously increased. Here too, the monetarization/industrialization process has, in most cases, been the key to the increase of global D & P

---

*Another fundamental aspect of research here is, of course, depreciation. A first survey of the literature and experience in this field shows that:
- The notion of economic depreciation itself is extremely vague and often inconsistent. It is even more difficult to clarify real production capacity, if one introduces the notion of obsolescence (which again, is linked to the real productivity of technology). Some studies by the Economic Commission for Europe are very explicit on this point. See for instance *Seventh Report on Production in Agriculture,* ECE AGRI/28, Volume II, New York, 1976.
- Financial depreciation follows patterns which seem to diverge more and more from economic depreciation: the "Hong Kong" amortization system (two to three years for the new Hilton Hotel in Hong Kong, and similarly reduced period of amortization for some oil installations).

There is a curious return to the non-monetary system when a unit of production capacity is fully financially amortized and yet is still producing, or capable of producing.

wealth; it was enough to look at the wealth-producing system exclusively from one side, the monetarized side, i.e., Capital.*

Our main proposal here is to look at Capital as a subsystem of a more global D & P concept: a subsystem which has been the key in the development of the whole system.

We would then underline again the fact that the relationship between the development of capitalization/monetarization and the development of a global D & P has been one of positive synergy, at least in those countries which are now known as "industrially developed".

The real problem today is to see if this positive synergistic relationship is not likely to give negative synergistic results.

This may occur in two cases:

(a) in the industrialized countries, where the phenomenon of diminishing returns of technology is probably indicating a situation in which this synergy between capital and patrimony has reached its upper limits, at least within the frame of a long-term Kondratieff cycle.

(b) in the developing countries, where the relationship between D & P and Capital is naturally much more difficult and much less likely to produce positive synergism, if one simply follows the models of the advanced industrial countries. Capital integration into the general D & P situation is very often initiated from the outside, not always really self-generated; consequently, the danger of negative synergy being produced is even larger within developing countries than within the framework of those cultures in which the Industrial Revolution commenced one or two centuries ago.

In both cases, the problem is not one of more or less industrialization:

---

*Another important aspect of research is, of course, linked to the fact that the sharp differentiation between savings (i.e. for future consumption) and present consumption on the one side and "capital" goods and "consumer" products on the other, is not quite the same in the "utilization value" perspective as in the "added value" one.

The capital problem becomes one of mobilizing resources with a view to maximizing production and utilization of the "stock of services" (for production maintenance, repair, storage, transport, financial services, insurance, waste management, etc.), taking into account, as far as possible, the contribution of the nonmonetary system. Saving means reduced use of the stock of services, in order to allow for greater utilization in time and space. Monetary, financial saving should be an instrument to make this process more efficient.

but rather of developing industrialization to the point at which it is a real added value to the total D & P situation.

From the point of view of a study on the future needs of Capital at world level, it means that, before extrapolating past experience in Capital use, it is necessary to see how far the point of maximum equilibrium can be achieved in using profitably all D & P resources, increased by those capitalization/monetarization production systems, which really are a potential improvement to *total* D & P "productivity".

It would be a real tragedy if, in a world of growing needs and population, the optimization between Capital and the global D & P stock were not a priority consideration: there is a great danger of provoking Capital waste. For future years, the main strategy should be to mobilize Capital *and* D & P jointly.

The strategic use of Capital and D & P. Recognition of the economic relevance of D & P and Capital, of the necessity of stimulating their positive, as opposed to their negative synergy might be of help in providing a more soundly based theoretical framework for a world economic policy combining solidarity, cooperation and self-reliance.

In fact, one of the main tendencies and advantages of Capital is to operate at a supra-local and at a supra-national level. It represents the accumulation of a monetarized D & P which, in principle, can be circulated as storage of value rapidly around the world.

Non-monetarized D & P, at large, is more often local (or at least circumscribed); an educational or physical resource is a patrimony which is characterized by its dispersion and diversity. Its accumulation and use depend on local history, local traditions, local accumulations and acculturations. Its yields are based on the potential of such diversities. Its total value is rarely represented by the addition of homogeneous elements. It is a value in itself, as one of the basic potentials for human survival under various climatic and cultural conditions. It is a counterweight to the vulnerability of mankind. It provides more probabilities of adaptive answers to changing environmental conditions. Variety of human cultures is in itself one of the major proofs of mankind's ingenuity. Monetarized D & P, then, represents that part of D & P which tends to overcome differentiated values in time and space.

A sound balance between D & P and Capital, between non-monetarized and monetarized economic activity, is obviously the condition for development. Even the most monetarized economy is today still largely conditioned by non-monetarized activities which ensure a consistent part of the daily utilization values. In some cases, excessive monetarization in highly developed countries is now counterbalanced by increased interest in non-monetarized activities. In several cases, especially in developing areas, the increase in welfare has been simply the expression of the transition phase from a non-monetarized economy to a monetarized economy without any *real* increase in *net* wealth being produced.* This likewise applies to the activities of the technologically advanced world, such as the case of a transition of a health system from a home to a hospital basis; this does *not necessarily* improve the patient's health but it *always* increases the cost in terms of the monetarized economy.

Practical experience has been the antidote to the extreme attitude of over-extrapolation of the obvious advantages of the monetarized economy. But the problems encountered have too long been dismissed as exceptions to the rule and not as the result of an unsatisfactory product of theories and attitudes on which the rules were based. Owing to this, not only has a lot of D & P been sacrificed without practical, positive or satisfactory results but a great deal of capital has been, and is being, wasted. There is probably a profound link today, between the dissatisfaction of those who speak of self-reliance with agressive overtones, partly justified by past experience, and the unsatisfactory way in which capital flows throughout the world and integrates D & P. The dominating philosophy has been too one-sided and, as a result, the monetarized/capital economy has been regarded as a challenge, or as the progressive alternative, to the patrimony/non-monetarized economy. In the final analysis, this opposition is nonsense. It leads to the legitimate defense of local cultures and D & Ps "against international capital" on the one side or against pollution on the other. In both cases, it is the defence of the D & P as material as well as cultural consistency, which is at stake. Obviously, political issues add their pressure to this picture and they are not simply dissolved by our analysis. However, a step forward could be made if at least the reasons for the conflict, which arise from inadequate understanding of the

*What we say here merely repeats what in other words Tévoédjrè, Albert wrote in *Poverty: Wealth of Mankind,* Oxford, 1978.

economic issues at stake, could be eliminated. Therein lies the whole difference between seeing in the present world turmoil a reason for despair or a chance for building the future.

Industrialization is now bound to undergo worldwide dissemination just as the nineteenth century saw the propagation of the Industrial Revolution from Great Britain to Continental Europe and to what might today be called a reduced OECD area. But at the same time, the structure of industrialized society is changing, and a deep process of adaptation is already in the making.

A basic reassessment of the mental tools required to follow this phenomenon might help in stimulating and understanding the interest of self-reliance, in starting a more conscious process of patrimony valorization, and in attaining a better allocation and use of Capital.

It must be stressed also that the same differentiation between D & P and Capital also applies to the activity of mankind itself: on the one hand, we have labour and personal effort (not paid for) and on the other we have employment ("remunerated" or monetarized labour).

The very difficult problem of unemployment for the world of tomorrow, may be better appreciated and better solutions may be found in terms of a strategy for developing a D & P, in which mankind and its labour are an integral part.

Therefore, before concentrating in the next dossier (Chapter 3) on the definition of "D & P" and "Capital", let us try to tackle the concept of utilization value from the point of view of the "employment problem".

2.3.5. LABOUR, EMPLOYMENT AND UTILIZATION VALUE

An International Labour Organization recent publication[51] has indicated that the present level of unemployment in the world is of the order of 300 million people and that, by the end of the century, it will be necessary to provide worldwide for more than a billion *new* additional jobs.

The classical question, in consideration of such problem is: "Will there be enough investment to absorb all this manpower?".

This is, of course, an obvious question at first sight, but one must wonder if it has really been put the right way.

In fact, to start with, is manpower as such really a "problem" or rather an "asset"?

It is a problem if it means merely that new "adequate investment has to be made," particularly bearing in mind that a modern economy is capital intensive as the following table shows.

TABLE 2.4. *Capital Investment per Job*

Industry	Capital investment per employee
Petroleum	$108,000
Public utilities	105,500
Chemicals	41,000
Primary metals	31,000
Stone, clay, glass	24,000
All manufacturing (average)	19,500
Food and kindred products	18,000
Textile mill production	11,000
Wholesale and retail trade	11,000
Services	9,500
Apparel and other fabricated textiles	5,000

Source: The conference Board, Capital Invested, Road Maps of Industry No 1799, New York, January 1977.

If we take an average figure of, say $40,000 of investment per job and we multiply it by 1 billion new jobs (a conservative estimate), we get the figure of $40,000 billions necessary *only* for the additional new jobs that need to be created by the end of this century.

This means that the world needs to invest up until the year 2000, every year, the total equivalent of the current (1977) GNP of the United States, merely for these new jobs, without counting investment for the renewal of present capital equipment. It can, of course, be said that investment per job in the developing world may be at a much lower level than that required in developed countries, say 20%; we may need "only" an *additional* $400 billions or so *per year.*

But *do* all these figures have a real meaning? Do they give an indication of the best strategy to follow? No! They are again simply the consequence of a strategy which has *already* been determined and assumed in advance and which states that one must, as far as possible, catch up with investment trends in order to create jobs.

There is, however, probably a more fruitful approach which consists in considering people, labour as an *asset*: the problem is, then, to stimulate, promote and organize an economic system in which all this human potential is not "condemned" to industrialization under any circumstances, in order to "work".

As we have seen in earlier sections, the problem with the "economics" of the industrial age, is, in fact, that productive — and organizable — labour is one which produces monetarized, "added" value.

Labour is thus strictly linked with this concept of value.

The trouble is that when, in a post-industrial world, the value produced may be "negative" (a deducted value), human activity can be organized and stimulated to produce waste too. In fact, the pollution industry also provides jobs, all the more so since all the economy becomes intensively waste-producing.

Using the traditional concept of value and investment strategy, it will be preferable to have waste and a resultant pollution industry and therefore more jobs, than less-polluting industry, a smaller anti-pollution industry and therefore — in total — less jobs. But the point is: with which system one *does* produce more *real* value?

Classical economics concerned with the problem of defining "productive" in contrast to "non-productive" labour, must be changed in order to distinguish between "wealth-producing" and "wealth-*destroying*" labour.

Once again we are confronted with the negative consequences of having restricted the economic analysis of labour purely to remunerated employment.

If more and more investment follows the logic of *adding* to added/deducted value, the pursuit of full employment has far from glowing prospects, if the remuneration of labour is, in a period of diminishing returns of technology, to be absorbed more and more by the *negative* gross national product.

Therefore, it seems essential, if we are to organize a valid strategy for optimal utilization of human assets, that the current concept of value be urgently modified and replaced by the utilization value concept.

We have already seen in the first chapter, in the dialogue on "investment for employment", how in practice the concept of utilization value can modify both the investment strategy and the better use of labour intended to increase *real* value of products and services. In a post-industrial society, and in particular at a time when the diminishing returns of technology make the trend to increasing capital intensity a source of negative value, it is necessary to aim at a new equilibrium and a new, more positive use of labour.

A second very fundamental aspect, discussed in detail in the dialogue on "investment for employment" concerns the strategy for ensuring that all non-remunerated activities are considered as a "value". An economic system which stresses the value of the remunerated activity will and inevitably does tend to substitute productive non-remunerated labour with remunerated labour even if it is less productive. The level at which the remuneration of a service no longer adds to total real wealth should be identified and never transgressed.

Specific economic and fiscal policies should be developed to stimulate the full potential of "free" labour. Until the economic success is measured in terms of value added and of national income, such real advances will never be apparent and taken into account. This is another reason why current national accounting should be put into a very large parenthesis and perhaps even dispensed with after a more adequate system of indicators has been determined, which must, above all, measure *real* value.

All this is linked to the recognition that the traditional economic measurement of value and development strategy is often inadequate. Many studies confirm this point; for example a study by the Battelle Institute,[52] states that:

"An analysis[53] which was made for the United States concerning the point of diminishing returns reached in terms of additional energy investments in the production of goods and services could also be true for some EEC countries . . . if the trend holds up, the end result of greater use of energy in industrial processes would be not a higher material standard of living, but a lower *quality of life* as the result of growing inflation, waste and pollution."

Some companies in United States basic industries have reached a similar conclusion and have accepted the first aim of the Clean Water Act (to make American waters "fishable and swimmable"); however, all companies object that the second aim (zero discharge by 1985) can be achieved only at crippling cost[54] and is not feasible.

"Quality of Life" as an abstract goal is gaining increasing attention in

Europe,[55] and some experts[56] claim that the quality of life has already *diminished* in some European countries over the last decade despite a rising standard of living!

All this boils down to something very simple: human activity should be stimulated to produce and to build now for the future. Remunerated work is a measurement of activity, but not necessarily of positive, non-destructive activity. The tool has lost the sense of the goal, if it is not orientated towards the increase of wealth, real wealth. Humankind produces value and, in the final analysis, *is* value.

The problem is clearly to review the strategy of labour's contribution to real wealth production.

2.3.6. CIVILIZATION AND VALUE

The traditional explicit and implicit definition of value linked with the Industrial Revolution, has also been at the core of the socio-political analyses and doctrines of the last few centuries.

A new definition of value and wealth can open new horizons in this area too.

We have no intention here of initiating a discussion which would need a complete new report, but we would like to submit some considerations for further debate and research.

Societies might view the problem of justice in terms of access to D & P, of which capital is part. It seems obvious that if the political and sociological debate is centred exclusively around the concept of capital and added values, this may lead, in many cases, to the paradox of appropriating and distributing what we have called "deducted" value on the one side, and net added values on the other.

Utilization value is a concept by which, behind each function, one discovers a plurality of human activities, whereas necessarily, "added" value gives a privileged position to the "capitalist" and/or the "production worker" (or his "representatives"). If then, real wealth and welfare depend on utilization value, we may perhaps become more aware of the fact that we are all producers, users and *consumers* of the world's D & P. The problem is one of making use of the widely disseminated *right (and duty) to produce and to consume* and to reach a socially acceptable level of justice. The story of the Industrial Revolution, which is the "story of added value" contains some considerable and indisputable achievements: we have to move on from here and not to go back from here. We *must* make progress. We *can* believe in progress.

However, it is also probable, that this period of history will become known as a period of human pre-civilization. Its historical deducted value has been very high and, as high as ever in history, particularly in the second part of the Science-based Industrial Revolution. The accounting of this deducted value is tragically simple:

World War I: 8.5 million killed during the conflict and 21 million dying after the War from "Spanish 'Flu", due partly to the perturbations brought about by the conflict.

World War II: 38 million killed (several millions of which in Nazi concentration camps) to which should be added 18 million deaths under the Stalinist regime, not to count the large number of other wars and massacres.

Intolerance has never been so great, both in absolute and relative terms;* apparently we are still barbarians: just of a more efficient kind.

A goal for future society is simple to define: the foundation of the first *real* civilization, the *new* cycle in world D & P formation, in which only a society respectful of humankind and individual values will deserve the qualification of being civilized.

Bibliography

1. LANDES, David: *The Unbound Prometheus – Technical Change and Industrial Development in Western Europe from 1750 to the Present*, Cambridge, 1969.
2. DOBBS, Maurice: *Studies in the Development of Capitalism*, New York, 1947.
3. TOUTAIN, Jules: *The Economic Life of the Ancient World*, London, 1930 (reprint 1951).
4. FRANZEN, Pieter: *Histoire de la Pensée Economique*, Bruxelles, 1978.
5. GIMPEL, Jean: *La Révolution Industrielle en Moyen-Age*, Paris, 1977.
6. SMITH, Adam: *The Wealth of Nations*, Harmondsworth, reprint 1977, p. 434.
7. LANDES, David: *op. cit*., p. 79.
8. SCHUMPETER, Joseph: *Theorie der Wirtschaftlichen Entwicklung*, Leipzig, 1912.
9. MILL, John Stuart: *Principles of Political Economy*, Toronto, 1965, Volume II, p. 135.
10. LANDES, David: *op. cit*., p. 79.
11. BARON, C. Donald: *Capital Availability*, SRI, Menlo Park California, 1977.
12. MARSHALL, Alfred: *Principles of Economics*, London, 8th Edition, 1920.

*Over its 150 years of activity, the Holy Inquisition was directly responsible for "only" 800 death sentences – a very artisanal endeavour.

13. MARSHALL, Alfred: *op. cit.*
14. SMITH, Adam: *op. cit.*
15. HEILBRONNER, Robert L.: *The Wordly Philosophers* (The Great Economists), Washington Square Press, 1970.
16. MARSHALL, Alfred: *op. cit.*
17. MILL, John Stuart: *op. cit.*
18. MARX, Karl: *Das Kapital*, Book II, 2nd Edition, Hamburg 1893.
19. MARSHALL, Alfred: *op. cit.*
20. Centre International de Synthèse: *Galilei. Aspects de sa Vie et de son Oeuvre*, Paris, 1968;
    de SANTILLANA, Giorgio: *Le Procès de Galilée*, Paris, 1955.
21. GEORGESCU-ROEGEN, Nicolas: *The Entropy Law and the Economic Process*, Harvard, 1971.
22. KUHN, Thomas, S.: *The Structure of Scientific Revolution*, Chicago, 1962.
23. COMTE, Auguste: *Du Pouvoir Spirituel*, Le Livre de Poche, Paris, 1978.
24. COMTE, Auguste: *op. cit.*
25. COMTE, Auguste: *op. cit.*, p. 284.
26. COMTE, Auguste: *op. cit.*, p. 345.
27. POPPER, Karl: *Unended Quest*, Glasgow, 1976.
28. HICKS, J. O.: *op. cit.*
29. SAMUELSON, Paul: *op. cit.*
30. HEILBRONNER, Robert: *op. cit.*
31. FORRESTER, Jay W.: *Principles of System*, Cambridge Massachusetts, 1968.
32. *New Scientist*, October 1977.
33. McNEILL, William: *Plagues and People*, Garden City, New York, 1976.
34. De ROSNAY, Joël: *The Macroscope: A New World Scientific System*, New York, 1979.
35. GEORGESCU-ROEGEN, Nicolas: *op. cit.*
36. GIARINI, Orio and LOUBERGE, Henri *The Diminishing Returns of Technology*, Oxford, 1978.
37. See the notion of falsification or refutation in Karl Popper's *Unended Quest, op. cit.*
38. HEISENBERG, W.: Das Naturbild der heutigen Physik, *Rowohlts Deutsche Enzyklopädie,* 1955.
39. HENDERSON, Hazel: Risk, Uncertainty and Economic Futures, *The Geneva Papers on Risk and Insurance*, No 9, 1978.
40. Union Bank of Switzerland: *Technology and Economics*, February 1978.
41. SCHUMPETER, Joseph: *Theorie der wirtschaftlichen Entwicklung,* Leipzig, 1912.
42. FRANZEN, Pieter: *op. cit.*, p. 367.
43. LANDES, David: *op. cit.*, p. 234–235.
44. KONDRATIEFF, N. D.: Die langen Wellen der Konjunktur, *Archiv für Sozialwissenschaften und Sozialpolitik,* LVI, 1926, p. 573–609.
45. MENSCH, Gerhard: *Das technologische Patt*, Frankfurt a.M., 1977, p. 249.
46. FORRESTER, Jay W.: *The Changing Environment for Industrial Enterprise*, System Dynamics Group, Paper No D-2667-2, Cambridge Massachusetts, March 1977.
47. MESAROVIC, M. and PESTEL, E.: *Mankind at the Turning Point*, New York, 1974.

48. FISHER, Irving: Income in Theory and Income Taxation in Practice, *Econometrica*, January, 1937.
49. GEORGESCU-ROEGEN, Nicolas: *op. cit.*
50. DALY, Herman E.: *Steady-State Economics*, San Francisco, 1977.
51. International Labour Office (ILO): *Employment, Growth and Basic Needs*, Geneva, 1976.
52. REDAY, G. and STAHEL, W. R.: Battelle, Geneva, 1976.
53. O'TOOLE, J.: *Energy and Social Change* (p. 20). MIT/Cambridge Massachusetts, 1976.
54. Warning Signals from Smokestack America, *Economist*, 2nd April, 1977.
55. See for example: SCARDIGLI Victor: Mode de Vie et Changement Social en Europe Occidentale, *Euroforum* No 4/77 Communautés Européennes, Brussels.
56. WITTMANN, W.: Freiburg, Switzerland, during a conference on the cost of prosperity in Zurich, February 1977.

CHAPTER 3

Dossier for an Analysis of the Foundations of Wealth: Dowry and Patrimony (D & P) and Capital

> "...opulent society grows sick on
> its riches ... and the abundance
> of the industrial nations disguises
> their increasing miserliness"
>
> Albert Tévoédjré,
> *Poverty, Wealth of Mankind*

3.1. The Process of Dowry and Patrimony (D & P) and Capital Formation

3.1.1. THE PHENOMENON OF ACCUMULATION

Accumulation is a universal phenomen which can be observed in the natural, cultural and economic order.

D & P (Dowry and Patrimony)* is a global stock or asset in a dynamic equilibrium state resulting from different, interreacting forms of accumulation, which can be both positive and negative (depletion, disaccumulation).

3.1.1.1. *Characteristics of accumulation*

(a) Qualitative and quantitative aspects. Accumulation is both *qualitative*

*The word Dowry has already been used by the economist Pentti Malaska: see his *Mankind's Dowry and Technology,* Turku School of Economics, Turku, Finland, 1979. It is used here in conjunction with the word Patrimony in order to ensure that the notion of "global assets" is sufficiently wide and fair as to both its feminine and masculine components and contributions to the earth's history heritage.

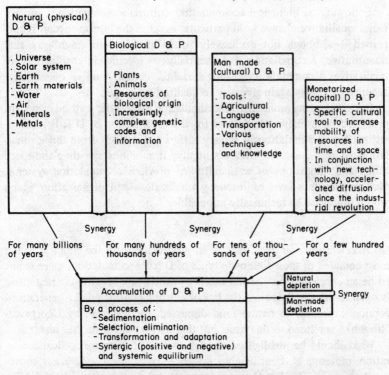

TABLE 3.1. *Dowry and Patrimony* (D & P) − *The Source of Utilization Value*

and quantitative. These two aspects intervene and combine at different times and at different levels.

The birth of the universe (the "big bang" or any other theoretical explanation of it) is essentially a qualitative phenomenon, and is the starting point for many specific forms of quantitative accumulation: galaxies, stars, planets, etc.

The transition from a pure "physical" world − i.e. where there is no "life" − as is probably the case with most of the solar-system planets, to a situation where a biological D & P begins to develop, is a qualitative change. Biological accumulation, its development and diversification, is also characterized by a series of quantitative and qualitative changes.

Following on biological accumulation, cultural accumulation is another major qualitative change — in particular as far as the human species is concerned — although not exclusively so. Intuitively, one might say that quantitative accumulation is essentially a specific intensification of qualitative accumulation: having reached certain limits, quantitative accumulation may again give way to qualitative change.

In our view, the monetarized accumulation is a specific method or system produced by a man-made culture for the organization of D & P accumulation. The accumulation of money differs qualitatively from the accumulation of real goods in that essentially, it modifies the time-and-space limits and conditions of availability of previous accumulation systems. Money permits a level of resource mobilization and organization which would otherwise be technically impossible.

(b) Acceleration and deceleration. In proceeding from the simplest to the most complex of these four main types of D & P accumulation, there seems to be an *acceleration.* Whether this is a positive or a negative characteristic is open to debate. Probably, the law of entropy considered as a generalized economic process in nature (and discussed, for instance, by Georgescu-Roegen),[1] is related to this issue, but this is a matter for further research.

What should be highlighted, though, is that, if there are cyclical acceleration movements, considerable evidence exists for *deceleration* movements as well. The latter probably occurs when the intensification of a specific accumulation phase — developing essentially in a quantitative form — is preparing the way for a major qualitative change and the start of a new cycle.

If we take "cultural" D & P and consider the evolution of Western society, it is possible to detect some "privileged moments" of accelerated "accumulation": for instance, the two megacycles of the Industrial Revolution and the feudal society at the end of the Middle Ages, which gave rise technically, artistically and in other ways, to the Renaissance.

Each of these periods represents a major cycle . . . subdivided in turn into smaller oscillations each of which has its own periods of acceleration and deceleration. This can be seen during the major cycle of the Industrial Revolution, for instance, in the emergence, maturation and deceleration of specific industrial activities which have, in turn, set the pace of development: the textile industry, railroad transportation, the chemical industry and now, probably, microelectronics. However, the global impact of the pace-setting drive provided by a smaller cycle will vary depending on the pre-existing general status of the overall system of industrialization (this being a higher level of cycle).

Currently, the deceleration trend in the major wave of industrialization is being counterbalanced only partly by an acceleration in the smaller sectoral wave represented by microelectronics or any other promising new technology.

A deceleration occurs essentially when the general law of diminishing returns predominates over forces introducing positive returns.

(c) Selection. Any form of accumulation presupposes a process or a mechanism of selection. Saving — which produces accumulated monetary resources, i.e. capital — is the result of a decision as to the way in which inflowing money is to be used. In this case, selection is a conscious process; however, it can also be unconscious, as for example when we look around us and select (by what the psychologists call our automatic "input selector") those events or facts which fit our personality (which also is a form of accumulation).

Selection is essential in the process of sedimentation: otherwise, we would have no deposits of specific raw materials.

This demonstrates how close the concept of accumulation is to that of evolution. Industrialization is clearly one specific form of cultural evolution, with its own selection behaviour.

(d) Synergy. The more complex *total* D & P becomes, the more each new form of accumulation will react with all other forms: vegetable life in the form of forests with their accumulated physical energy, becomes part of the earth's raw-materials D & P, in the form of coal. Agricultural land — which is part of the natural D & P — is extended or enriched by human, cultural D & P through the development of the agricultural tools, through mechanization and through the addition of man-made fertilizers.

It is fundamental to note that the various outcomes of such combinations are determined essentially in a synergic way: they depend less on the nature of each factor involved than on the way each factor *reacts* with the others.

This means that the interaction of *two positive* factors may produce a *negative* result; in virtually no case, will the result be equal to the sum of the two effects. A clear example can be seen in medicine when two different drugs are taken together for a disease: the *combination* may have negative effects. Other examples of positive and negative synergy are detectable all around us.

(e) Depletion and disaccumulation. Any form of accumulation also has a net negative aspect, linked directly to the fact that there is no such thing as a "given" stock of D & P – fixed in time – but that each D & P is in a state of dynamic equilibrium.

We are, then, confronted with a continuous process of natural, biological, cultural and "industrial" disaccumulation and depletion which must be taken into account when considering the dynamics of the D & P equilibrium.

As we have seen, each form of D & P has a different period of accumulation and consequently many D & P assets which have been "produced" over a long period of time (a coal mine, an oilfield) are considered "non-renewable" resources.

The problem is, then, to determine whether cultural and monetary "D & P" (in this case, scientific and technological knowledge) are accumulating fast enough to match – *in real terms* – the depletion of the natural D & P due to current exploitation.

This brings us once again, although from another angle, to the problem of utilization value and of the *real* returns of technology.

3.1.1.2. Accumulation and different forms of discipline

The development and use of our knowledge in assessing different types of accumulation are, in themselves, ways of developing and using "cultural D & P": astronomy, astrophysics, physics, geology, etc. are all specific forms of cultural D & P centered on natural, physical accumulation, in the same way as biology, genetics, zoology, etc. are related to biological accumulation. History, sociology and the arts are the object and subject of cultural accumulation. "Economics", as we have already said, is — or has been at least until now — essentially the discipline of monetarized accumulation in the industrial revolution. All these disciplines have points of interface such as biophysics, psychosomatics, economic history.

In this respect, we take the opposite approach to economists such as Marshall and Becker who see, by analogy, in economic activity, a reference for the study of any other material or cultural behaviour. In fact, the processes they identify (accumulation, equilibrium, cycles, value, etc.), are merely the image (highly miniaturized and specific) within the monetarized D & P of phenomena outside the framework of economics. In their accumulation process, all sciences and disciplines display features and paradigms which mirror a much wider reality. As various psychoanalysts have shown, an individual discipline will frequently, by such analogies, tend to propose that it is the very essence of global reality: such an approach is fed by the individual's ambition to present a "universal" view. If each type of accumulation does, in fact, reproduce general phenomena, the temptation to develop a universal outlook starting from a specific and limited case of accumulation is like using a microscope to study the behaviour of gigantic systems. In certain cases it may develop into organized myopia.*

Joël de Rosnay has pleaded for wider use of the macroscope,[2] rather than the microscope, in studying systems of accumulation processes and their interrelations.

Understanding of the *global* behaviour of D & P is therefore a *premise* for closer examination of monetarized D & P.

Let us now rapidly review some of the various forms of accumulation in the different and interrelated types of D & P.

3.1.2. NATURAL ACCUMULATION: SOME EXAMPLES

(a) Geological accumulation. The natural physical D & P of the universe has taken billions of billions of years to accumulate. The earth has had "only" a few billion years to become the "accumulation system" it now

---

*See Anders Munk: "On Specialism and other Obscurantisms", *Ecoropa Papers*, 1978.

is. Geology is a major discipline which studies this process by analyzing, for instance, vertical sections of sedimentary strata. These simplified images of reality provide a record of the accumulation phenomenon by the superposition and by the succession of consecutive states of a sedimentary sequence.*

However, although it provides physical evidence of the qualitative aspect of accumulation, superficial observation of sedimentary strata is of no use in determining respective ages or in indicating the duration of formation of a sedimentary sequence.

Radioactive dating techniques have made it possible for geologists to replace their previous relative-time dating scale by an absolute-time scale. It now appears that the Earth is 4.6 thousand million years old, as shown in the Table on p. 175.

This Table shows the era at which ore deposits, i.e. the wealth of natural resources containing a part of the D & P drawn on by man, were laid down. In relation to a human lifespan, or even to the duration of man's existence on earth, the lifetime of this stock of services is immeasurable. For the fossil fuels — mainly natural gas, oil and coal — the time scale is appreciably shorter, and yet these deposits are several hundred million years old.**

The notions used above to define the concept of accumulation are applicable to the phenomena of accumulation of natural resources; thus

---

*The expression "sedimentary sequence" implies the non-integration of these states in a regular series of events. It is applied to a method of evaluating time in relative terms so that some object or event is classed as older or more recent than something else; thus, it has been established that the disappearance of the dinosaur antedated the appearance of the human being on earth, without it being possible to state the date of the dinosaurs' extinction but merely that this event preceded man be several million years.

**The oldest known coal deposits were formed about 370 million years ago. Petroleum has been found in rocks of the Paleozoic age, but over 90% of the world's petroleum comes from sedimentary basins of the Mesozoic and Cenozoic ages.

It is interesting to note that the processes which terminate in the formation of oil and natural gas deposits are governed by a sort of natural selection. The extraction of these fluids is, in fact, possible only if three preliminary conditions are satisfied simultaneously:

- Decomposition of micro-organisms inside very fine grained sedimentary rocks, the mother rocks.
- Expulsion of the oil or gas from the mother rocks in the course of their transformation into porous permeable sedimentary rocks, the reservoir rocks.
- Migration of the fluids until an obstacle is encountered against which they accumulate.

TABLE 3.2. *The Geological Time Scale of the Earth*

Era	Period	Epoch	Age in millions of years ago	Generalized biologic continuum	Generalized geologic events (Mountain building for North America only)
Cenozoic	Quaternary	Recent / Pleistocene	2	Paleoindians migrating into North America. Man as a tool user. First manlike primates.	Glaciation on continental scale begins
Cenozoic	Tertiary	Pliocene Miocene Oligocene Eocene Paleocene	25 / 65	Placental mammals common.	Folding and major uplifting of Rocky Mountain ranges
Mesozoic	Cretaceous		135	Major extinctions (dinosaurs, etc.). First flowering plants	Pangaea breaking up, plates bearing continents toward modern locations. Modern Atlantic forming
Mesozoic	Jurassic		190	First birds	
Mesozoic	Triassic		225	First mammals First dinosaurs	Ancestral Atlantic closes, folding and uplifting of Appalachian mountains; Pangaea together
Paleozoic	Permian		280	Major extinctions (trilobites, etc.). First mammal-like reptiles	
Paleozoic	Pennsylvanian		325	First reptiles	Glaciation on continental scale (Gondwanaland) Pangaea forming
Paleozoic	Mississippian		350	First reptile like-amphibians	
Paleozoic	Devonian		400	First land animals (amphibians) First amphibian-like fish First rooted land plants	Acadian mountains rising in New England-Maritime Provinces—subduction zone ?
Paleozoic	Silurian		430	First vertebrates (jawless fish). Nearly all major invertebrate types present.	Glaciation on continental scale. Taconic mountains rising in New York-Quebec region, extensive volcanism-subduction zone ?
Paleozoic	Ordovician		500	Fossils become common as invertebrates develop hard exoskeletons (trilobites, brachiopods).	Ancestral Atlantic closing.
Paleozoic	Cambrian		600		
Precambrian	Late Precambrian		670 --- / 1000	Approximate age of earliest known animals (soft bodied worms, etc.); complexity of forms indicates long prehistory Earliest known advanced cell type (distinct nucleus) / green algae.	Glaciation on continental scale. Ancestral Atlantic opening. Proto-Pangaea breaking up; rifting widespread. Incipient rifting of central North America ?
Precambrian	Middle Precambrian		2000 / 3000	Approximate age of oldest well preserved fossil cells, photosynthetic blue-green algae. Biologically produced oxygen building atmospheric level toward modern atmosphere. Approximate age of evidence of first life, algal structures (stromatolites) in rock, possible bacteria and blue-green algae. ? First organisms evolving ? Oceans with buildup of non-biologically produced complex organic molecules (amino acids, nucleic acids etc.).	Major iron ore deposits of world forming Widespread magmatic activity, major additions of granitic continental crust. Mountain building, widespread volcanism formation of greenstone belts-island arcs
Precambrian	Early Precambrian		3800 -- / 4600	Probable age of earth and other planets. Evidence: radiometric ages of meteorites and lunar rocks, amounts and ratios of terrestrial lead isotopes.	Oldest known earth rocks Oceans and oxygen-free atmosphere forming Initial crust-ocean basins Earth begins differentiating into core-mantle as radiogenic heat builds up.

From: Lawkins, Chase, Darby, Rapp, *The Evolving Earth* A text in physical geology, Second Edition, McMillan Publishing Co. Inc. New York, 1978 p. 109.

selection is inherent in the sedimentation process: no selection — no coal or iron ore. This potential wealth is the result of slow development; the quality of workable natural resources as we know them is due to the millenium-long action of a number of natural factors which have acted together to effect the transformation from quantity to quality.

(b) Biological accumulation. Biology and genetics contain numerous examples of certain aspects of the accumulation phenomenon.

Evolution teaches us that all current forms of life are descended from a very small number of primitive forms and that man, for instance, is the result of a very long selection process. This evolutive process is governed by the rate at which mutations occur, these mutations introducing variations which may or may not be advantageous. Only the advantageous mutations survive, namely those which lead to an ever more successful adaptation of the living organism to its environment, supposed stable in the short term, while the others give rise to unfavourable reactions which lead to loss of adaptability and extinction. Evolution may incorporate a learning process in which the living organisms acquire mastery of their environment and memorize what they have learned in their hereditary D & P.

The fins of fishes, the wings of bats or the single functional digit of horses — responses of these animals to the conquest of various environments — are derived from the same structural type, the pentadactyl extremity of an earlier mammal. Man descends from the same mammal — a fact confirmed by the existence of the vermiform appendix in man whereas in other mammals it is a well developed organ containing enzymes and bacteria that facilitate the digestion of cullulose and other substances which formed part of the human diet at a given point in his evolution.

Such comparative anatomical similarities would be inexplicable without the supposition of adaptive differentiation since creation and the accumulation of differences from a common ancestor.* Selection, the effect of the combined action of the environment and the reactions of the living creature, is at the origin of accumulation.**

---

*Adaptive perfection by the constant use of the organ is another example of accumulation.

**Anders Munk (University of Copenhagen) comments on this point:
"Mutations and selection are the keywords of conventional theory of evolution. However, neither mutations nor selection, as currently conceived, can account for complexity, which is the most spectacular result of evolution found in the living world.
Moreover, complexity can only be described and accounted for in its own terms. It cannot be reduced or transformed to anything else. Analytical-positivistic science describes the world in terms of space and time, matter and energy. Modern science adds a fifth fundamental concept: Complexity.
A complex structure contains information (= negentropy = 'non-randomness'). According to General Systems Theory, several sets of information will most often interact as to generate qualitatively new information on a higher level of complexity, whenever there is an opportunity for such interaction. A genetic code is a set of information. Any organism will encounter other organisms in its environment. Any

Certain biologists consider evolution as the continuous accumulation of small mutations. Others, consider it more likely that major differences occurred suddenly in the course of the evolutionary process. However, these two theses are not contradictory if one accepts that the quantitative accumulation of small mutations (small cycles) culminates in a qualitative jump in the evolutionary process (large cycles).

To this concept of mutation accumulation common to the various evolutionary theses may be added the idea of mutation acceleration at a point in the evolutionary process.

In many cases, the accumulation phenomenon is followed by "disaccumulation" — atrophy and disappearance of redundant organs. Mutation accumulation is thus cyclic as is expressed in a "fundamental law of genetics": Haeckel's "recapitulation law" which states that embryos, during development, recapitulate the characters of the phylogenetic series to which they belong. During this recapitulation, it should be possible to "read out" the evolutionary line which preceded the creature in question.*

What is the origin of these mutated forms? This is a question which attempts to locate the site of mutations.

---

such encounter represents an opportunity for several sets of information to interact. Thus, General Systems Theory permits us to see evolution as a process characterized by an accumulation of ever escalating complexity.

The key operant factor in evolution, its 'generator of non-randomness', is selection. Selection is rarely a simple, one-sided phenomenon. A model example of this utterly simple case is the effect of an arctic climate on birds and mammals, inevitably favouring the development of a thick fur. In most cases, and in all crucial events, selection operates in a complex pattern of mutual interaction (feed-back) between the organism and its environment, including other organisms."

*Modern biology has denounced the exaggerations and extrapolations which this law has caused, but the facts on which it is based would appear to constitute one of the uncontested elements of the theory of evolution.

Anders Munk comments as follows:

"Scientists and many others have speculated about the origin of radical innovations during the evolution process. Qualitative big jumps have been postulated ('hopeful monsters'), but there is no evidence of such events. Moreover, it is difficult indeed to imagine one qualitative jump for a whole population; and all organisms exist in populations. The evolutionary process seems to have been continuous. But it has not necessarily been differentiable. Qualitative jumps may well have occurred, not in the genetic codes, but in the behaviour of animals. A radical shift in the behaviour of an animal means a radical shift in the entire selectional situation, and from then on evolution will take a radically new course. The otherwise smooth curve that represents the course of evolution will display a sharp angle at such an event.

(c) Genetic accumulation and mutation. "At the origin of any living being, there is always one unit which constitutes life, a drop of protoplasm contained in its envelope, that is an architecture which already possesses all the attributes of the living creature."[3] This unit is derived from the previous generations and conveys the "hereditary tendency": "the chromosomes of the father (or mother) constitute half the nucleus of the infant, those of the grandfather (or grandmother) contribute a quarter, those of the preceding tenth generation 1/1024 and so on".[4]

The substance of the chromosome is, as it were, a reservoir of accumulation; the cell is both the summary of past experience of its phylum and the vector of its transmission: "every egg thus contains, in the chromosomes received from its parents, the whole of its own future, the stages of its development and the form and the characteristics of the being which will emerge from it. The organism thus becomes the realization of a programme specified by heredity." This certainly justifies the expression "genetic D & P" and its corollary of information storage.

The same happens if an organ becomes of service for other than its original purpose. A good example is the convex lens of an eye, as found analogously in several phyla of the animal kingdom. Originally, the lens served simply to concentrate light on the retina, thus rendering the eye as a whole a little more light-sensitive. But a convex lens not only can but will inevitably do one more service than to concentrate light: it will form an image somewhere in the roundabouts of the retina. And from the moment when the first blurred image is registered by the retina, there will be an enormous selectional advantage in any improvement of that image (provided there exists an adequate nervous system to process the data from the retina). Hereafter, a completely new trend in evolution takes its course, developing not only the eye, but also the nervous system – if not the whole organism.

Simple or complex, selection has always two important characteristics:

(1) The 'selectional situation' is always the one it is because of what has happened *in the past.*

(2) Selection operates in terms of *'here and now'.*

In other words: selection is a matter of past and present. The future is not within the picture at all.

The amount of Dowry and Patrimony in terms of information stored in the world of living beings is literally unmeasurable: not only has it taken hundreds of millions of years to generate all this information – the only yardstick one could have thought of to measure it – it is also wildly improbable that the evolutionary process will ever repeat itself. Extinction of species represents irreversible destruction of Dowry and Patrimony."

Geneticists have demonstrated the primordial role, in the reproduction of life, of certain acids — deoxyribonucleic acid (DNA) and ribonucleic acid (RNA). DNA is a carrier of coded information and contains the programmes required to synthesize all the proteins a given cell can manufacture. RNA acts as the cell's messenger by copying the programme (gene) information in the nucleus DNA and carrying to the area where the cell manufactures its proteins. The code carried by the messenger RNA is usually a faithful copy of what was found in the DNA; however, if the copy is not faithful it becomes the origin of a variant. If it represents an advance and the environmental conditions are favourable to it, the error is transmitted to the descendants . . . where it accumulates in their genetic D & P.

Selection therefore operates inside the cell itself at three different levels: the gene; the individual considered as a set of genes; and the species. "By a kind of cycle, the substrate of heredity ends up by being also that of evolution."[5]

Feeding, breathing and reproduction are functional requirements common to all living organisms. Continuity is associated with functions, rather than with the means of implementing these functions.

(d) Mutations and value deducted. Do advances in medicine have negative as well as positive effects and do they favour the accumulation of harmful genes in the hereditary D & P? If this should be the case, then this modification of the genetic D & P is quite certainly an example of a value deducted associated with medical technology, since without it the "unfavourable variants" would have been eliminated by natural selection.

Prudence, however, is essential. Genetic studies have shown that over 50 generations are necessary before the incidence of recessive gene occurrence doubles. This is rather negligible.

There is something more serious, however: artificial ionizing radiation and many chemicals have definite if little understood mutagenic and teratogenic effects. These effects give rise to particular concern in the case of radioaction substances with long half-lives. Accumulation occurs and unacceptable levels may be built up in the body. An even more important hazard results from our inadequate knowledge of the mutagenic action of new chemicals. "Less than 7 or 8% of spontaneous mutations are due to ionizing radiation, the rest being essentially associated with the various chemical processes taking place in the cells; any modification of the conditions in which these processes take place can therefore have dramatic consequences. This is only a possibility — most substances, in all probability, are strictly inoffensive as far as our genetic D & P is concerned, yet this is only a hope unsupported by the least objective proof. In face of this paucity of information, the only reasonable attitude is one of prudence; it would appear that this attitude is not always adopted by our society."[6]

Since most of these new substances are synthetic products that nature can not always absorb, the result might possibly be a degradation of our genetic D & P by modification of our chromosome structure; this would be a value deducted following on a technological advance, and must therefore be monitored closely.*

3.1.3. MAN-MADE ACCUMULATION

(a) Cultural accumulation. Human culture and nature are not two separate, unrelated domains. Any culture takes root in the common compost of biological needs (breathing, eating, reproduction, resting, sleeping, etc.) as much as in the aspirations proper to human nature (striving to attain goals, artistic creation, etc). In society, man is, to a very large extent, occupied by his biological survival. The division of labour, the storage and preservation of foodstuffs, progress in agriculture and transport, the expansion of trade up to a certain point, appreciably facilitate man's task of survival. He tends (or hopes) to move from a subsistence existence to an increasingly intellectual mastery of his environment, his relations to that environment, their meaning and their future evolution.

Humankind by responding to its environment, invents behavioural patterns and creates values** and institutions to satisfy certain needs (biological, spiritual and, often, both) by means of individual or joint activities which contribute to the community or social organization. Even in the most primitive societies, gathering food, hunting, keeping the fire

---

*Following this line of considerations, see M. Steinmetz and G. Gonzy "Quelle Révolution Biologique?", *Le Monde,* Paris, April 11, 1979, p. 14.

**Archie Bahm (University of New Mexico) comments: "Our D & P includes not only ethics, but lack of it, not only understanding of ethics, but also lack of understanding of ethics".

alight, cooking food and ensuring the safety of the group, are not left to chance. The very survival of the members of the group is at stake. Shelter, tools, hunting weapons no matter how rudimentary, are just so many cultural responses, their number, variety and complexity depending on local conditions: climate, hydrology, availability and use of natural resources, etc. Once they have appeared, these derived or secondary needs create a type of secondary conditioning. This happens every time a new cultural need appears, whether by invention or dissemination, so that one can talk of cultural sedimentation in respect of this evolutive process: once fire had been discovered, the security, the warmth and the light which it offered and the cooked food it made possible became necessary for man's life and he never stopped improving his original condition by increasing the uses of fire. Similarly, the design and construction of forms of shelter are being constantly perfected to achieve more effective protection, and today considerable losses in welfare and even in human life accompany any large scale and abrupt regression from solid buildings in the direction of the mud hut or thatched hut. These derived needs, in turn, influence biological needs:* consumption of cooked food modifies eating habits and has repercussions on the alimentary functions; from a herbivorous or carnivorous animal, depending on his location, man became an omnivorous animal, increasingly suited to a diversified diet; subsequently, the invention of food storage and preservation techniques ensured him a food reserve which gave him further advantage in the incessant struggle for survival.

Any cultural process is therefore a continuum in the course of which humankind, following a series of adaptations to his environment, tends to replace external constraint by a constraint of which he is simultaneously both the subject and the object. Any culture expresses the capacity of the individual to invest instrumental mediations between himself and his

*The reciprocal interaction of the primary (domain of biological needs) and secondary (domain of cultural needs) environments may be schematically represented as shown below:

Biological needs   Cultural needs
                          (derived, secondary)

The two sets of needs are linked by circular causality.

natural environment and to select them. However, animal societies are also capable of inventing instrumental mediations. Human society is distinguished from animal societies by its ability to transmit acquired or accumulated behaviour by tradition: "One goes from the abilities and the precultural executions of the animal to this stable and permanent organization of activities which we call culture, when habit becomes custom, when instead of instruments that happened to be available, one uses a set of objects specially fashioned and transmitted by tradition, when habits which are constantly lost and found again are replaced by traditional rules and, finally, when the individual sporadic act gives way to group behaviour organized in a permanent manner."[7] In man's transmission and assimilation of professional competence and scientific knowledge, the role of an articulate language is clearly decisive. Moreover, the maintenance and the stability of a culture are conditioned by the vigour of its institutions which set the values of the social group, govern behaviour at the workplace, in school, in the family, etc.: in this respect, the group's cohesion is in part subordinated to its power of integration.

The expression "cultural sedimentation" used above thus implies an accumulation phenomenon.

A person's education, instruction and training are the results of an apprenticeship* which allows him to assimilate the know-how, language and other symbolic tools of his culture and locate himself in a system of institutions that define his setting in life. During this apprenticeship, he benefits from the achievements of his predecessors in preparing the environment which is to accommodate him. This apprenticeship process takes place at both individual and group levels and is both quantitative and qualitative in nature. As an individual or a community expand their knowledge and activity, they refine their perception of their environment, and rise from a sensory level to an intellectual and conceptual level.

In the organized group, cultural accumulation does not mean blind perpetuation of existing lifestyles; new behaviour forms are adopted, new values acquired and new institutions founded which progressively replace and obliterate the previous ones by a process of continuous adaptation. As

---

*The apprenticeship is not limited to knowledge acquired at school, in the university or in the family. "The school of life", the sum of observations, reflections, physical experiences . . . is an essential component of knowledge, if not the exclusive source.

man reaches each new stage in the control of his environment, his capabilities are better served by more appropriate means. The behaviour, values and institutions which previously served as a reference become obsolete, out-moded or unsuitable; in short, they become less operative or even inoperative.

Cultural characteristics, which do not disappear as a result of the evolution of human societies, are survivals.* A survival is "a cultural characteristic which does not correspond to its environment. It persists rather than functions, or its function is out of place in the contemporary culture."[8]

Culture is thus the whole set of values, institutions and behaviours, including material productions, specific to a given human group which, by a series of evolutive adaptations, constitutes a specific D & P comprising a series of accumulations, sedimentations and selections. This process may also frequently be negative and lead to a culture's decline or disappearance. During regressive cycles, certain cultural characteristics are destroyed and not replaced — as when the ancient Greek cities lost their freedom and the pre-Columbian civilizations in America were destroyed by conquest and the spread of new diseases.

---

*"Also in cultural evolution, selection is active, in the mind as well as in material practice: Inadequate innovations are dismissed, either in the mind, on the drawing board, or after unsatisfactory performance. Other innovations come to stay. By what kind of criteria?

1. By criteria of the actual situation. An invention can be introduced in vain, and the same invention can get a break-through for good some years later. It all depends on the actual situation, and that is determined by the past.
2. By criteria of performance here and now, 'now' may include some near future; the distant future is completely out.

So, in terms of cybernetics, there seems to be an important parallelism between biological and cultural evolution: In neither of them is the future really within the picture" (Anders Munk).

We would stress the fact, though, that human culture introduces more and more the future under the form of expectations, hopes, forecasts, myths, religious beliefs, utopias which are all, of course, images lived and acted upon in the present. The present, in human cultures, appears to be more and more mirrored by images of the future, in a rather similar way as images of the past are also "selected" by the present. The philosopher, B. Croce, used to say that history is always "contemporary": we would add that the future is "contemporary" too. They both contribute to our judgement, behaviour, in other words, to our selection system, which operates always — and we agree on this with Anders Munk — in the present. The only real future is now.

Cultural diversity thus proceeds from the variety of the natural environments to which human communities are exposed and the capacity of these communities to invent appropriate cultural responses. The tradition of the Industrial Revolution has been essentially one of attempting to develop or promote ostensibly "universal" models for the organization of society. At least two of these models, the North American and the Soviet ones, are based on an "industrial vision" of development. They postulate the absolute priority of a certain concept of science and technology over all other domains of social life. Technical progress, once initiated, become autonomous and imposes the transformation of social relationships along a linear pathway.

The implicit hypothesis is, therefore, one of cultural evolutionsim which qualifies cultural differences merely as obstacles on the path to "development": in this line of thought, diversities are simply the expression of different evolutionary stages or degrees in the movement toward a unique model.

If, on the contrary, the wealth of mankind stems from diversity and the inter-communication of diversity between our multitude of cultural D & Ps, the radical impoverishment which a uniform "world culture" would engender must be seen as a net value deducted. The utilization value is, in effect, intimately connected with the development of the D & P potential proper to each culture.[9] The cultural responses — relationship to nature, the group, material goods, work, life, etc. — are closely linked with each community's own D & P. Maintenance of the diversity of the particular cultural D & Ps is a guarantee for optimization of the utilization value in each particular case. The accumulation of diversities is a source of wealth whereas sterotyped accumulation is a cause of poverty.

(b) Accumulation by means of money. The possibility of accumulating goods and services in time and space is limited by their very nature (size, weight, location, durability, etc.). It is possible to optimize the systems that increase time–space mobility by inventing tools: the invention of the wheel and the domestication of horses helped in transporting people and goods from one place to the other. The Inca empire had neither wheels nor horses available and therefore, free food was available along the road for people making long journeys; thus the social system — in

this case a communitarian view of food ownership – can, at least partially, replace a specific tool. Using such systems, the scope of travel can be extended – the Inca empire was an enormous one, stretching over 1600 km from North to South.

However, with money which is universally recognized and accepted (which implies a certain cultural adaptation) – one can have in one's pocket enough food, shelter and transport to travel the world for years.

As such, money has been known and used – in various forms – for thousands of years, at least in certain parts of the world. Nevertheless, as the paragraph on economic duality will show in greater detail, up until the beginning of the Industrial Revolution, money was an economic tool of a secondary nature.

When the new technology, as we have seen in the previous dossier, began to require increasingly large concentrations of resources in a given place, money became essential for the very development of the economy itself. From being a partial means of limited exchange, it developed into a means of *productive* accumulation. Without the accumulation and diffusion in time and space that money made possible, the modern world as such would never have existed.

Parallel to the development of technology, financial technology has developed to dimensions which were impossible to even imagine at the beginning of the Industrial Revolution. At that time, personal family saving was the form of accumulation providing the means to concentrate the first simple tools of production. Only in the course of the last century, in response to the need for capital and the limits of individual and family saving, did the corporation (based on the collection of capital through shares) start its great development. As such, it was welcomed by economists like John Stuart Mill but – as we have seen – essentially rejected by Adam Smith who saw it as a destructor of individual enterprise (another point that Karl Marx was to develop further).

It was only later that the banking system developed as an important institute for accumulation and investment lending.

Banks had existed long before the industrial revolution, but they were essentially an aid to trade: at only a very late stage they really became an essential and integrated part of the industrial system. Even today, there still exist in many "advanced" countries, representatives of the old industries (such as the textile sector) who until recently resisted the principle of obtaining investment funds from the banking system.

Banks have now become gigantic institutions but even so, investment projects have grown to such a size and the sums of money involved have become so huge that the banks have had to form consortia to pool their resources to face up to the situation.

Financial intermediation is thus also essentially a cultural tool permitting through capital formation an unprecedented increase in human intervention in overall D & P formation. It is the same synergy process observable in other cases of general D & P formation: new technology makes new resources accessible thus increasing the available and accessible D & P; in the same way money — by the type of accumulation it makes possible — is an essential tool for increasing such accessibility. The money system, as well as any other technology, "creates" D & P, and more directly that part of monetarized D & P we call "capital". Of course, this creation is not necessarily entirely and always positive. Like any other tool or process of D & P formation, it may be directly or indirectly negative. It is inescapable: the production of powerful tools is one thing, but the definition of their goals and their positive utilization is a matter of human choice and responsibility. Power, instead of merely making life easier, does, in fact, oblige man to be more responsible and more "human" than ever. The penalty is the growth of potential deducted values which can ultimately lead to the annihilation of the human race.

3.1.4. THE COMPLEMENTARITY OF D & P AND CAPITAL: THE CASE OF ENERGY

Man's exploitation of natural and useful resources* is the whole set of acts which transform his environment, determining the mutation of the environment, its change from one state to another, the potential D & P of natural resources becoming effective and useful D & P.[10] Put in extreme, schematic terms, man's life on earth is in the last analysis the multiplication of the initiatives tending to make available to him ever more abundant and varied "wealth". Let us take the example of energy.**

*This term does not restrict this exploitation to the extraction of raw materials. It includes the production and distribution processes and their quantitative and qualitative changes, and hence all scientific discovery.

**See also: Georgescu Roegen, Nicholas: "Energy Analysis and Economic Valuation" *Southern Economic Journal,* April 1979, pp. 1023–1058, and "Myths about Energy and Matter", *Growth and Change,* January 1979, pp. 16–23.

The Charts in Figures 3.1., 3.2 and 3.3 below show the considerable acceleration in the rate of energy consumption during the industrial age, and highlight a major factor: the combination of capital and technology, from the time of "industrial man" (Figures 3.2 and 3.3.), has enormously increased the size of the accumulation, and has increasingly shifted its source from renewable raw materials to non-renewable raw materials.

". . . In the United States, total primary energy consumption has grown at the rate of about 3% annually since 1850, although the rate has increased to over 4% during the past 10 years. In 1850, 90% of this energy was supplied by renewable sources — wood, water, and wind power. Currently, more than 75% is supplied by hydrocarbon fuels, petroleum, and natural gas."[11] The real big task of technology in the next decades will

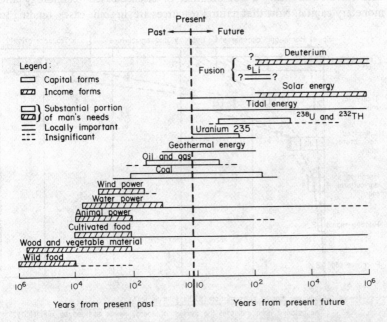

Source: James O'Toole and the University of Southern California Centre for Future Research, *Energy and Social Change,* p. 11, Massachusetts Institute of Technology.

FIG. 3.1. *Man's use of Energy Through the Millenia*

thus be either to try to "renew" the energy basis of D & P, or to find new sources of the renewable type, without, of course, producing other or new types of deducted values.

For the time being, it is obvious that, reduced to a geological time scale, the "disaccumulation" of D & P caused by human activities has no equivalent. What nature has patiently accumulated over millions or even billions of years is being "disaccumulated" in a few decades by human action combined "bulimic technology" as is illustrated by Figures 3.4. and 3.5. on pp. 190 and 191.

Although geological phenomena are measured on a relative time scale, human activities are governed by real time; this time has steadily shrunk under the influence of the technical progress achieved so far by the Industrial Revolution using a combination of science-based technology and monetary capital. Now that natural resources are, in some cases, tending to

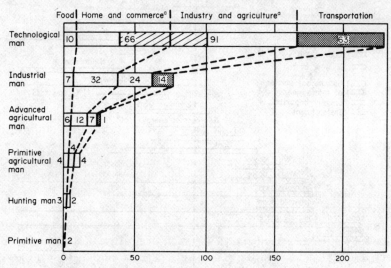

Daily per capita consumption (1000 kilocalories)

[a] The hatched area indicates the portion of energy needs fulfilled by electricity.

Source: James O'Toole and the University of Southern California for Future Research, *Energy and Social Change*, p. 12, Massachusetts Institute of Technology.

FIG. 3.2. *Daily Consumption of Energy* per capita *for Six Stages in Human Development*

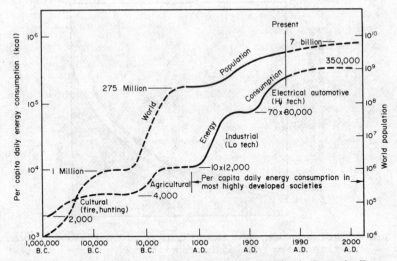

Source: James O'Toole and the University of Southern California Centre for Future Research, *Energy and Social Change,* p. 12, Massachusetts Institute of Technology.

FIG. 3.3. *Population and* per capita *Consumption of Energy 1,000,000 B.C. to 2,000 A.D.*

become depleted,* the temptation is to accelerate exploitation of the D & P through capital investment of very low or even negative real productivity. The prospect of oil scarcity stimulates exploitation of other energy sources. Nuclear energy is an alternative frequently encouraged by certain private and public authorities. Is it an acceptable alternative? How far do the technologies of nuclear-energy production tend to increase the subsidy from other energy sources? Uranium extraction and transport, nuclear-power station construction and operation, radioactive-waste storage, the disposal of worn-out nuclear plants, vulnerability control, etc., are costly

*The concept of natural resources is a fluid concept since the available, useful reserves depend on the level of technology reached. Nevertheless, the distinction between renewable and non-renewable natural resources retains its full validity; the first represent a finite quantity, and new discoveries are exploitable only at an ever-increasing technological cost, generally because of difficulties of access: North Sea oil, Siberian reserves, depth of terrestrial deposits – nodules found on the ocean floor, for instance.

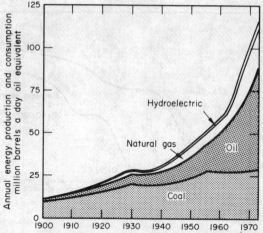

Source: Workshop on Alternative Energy Strategies, *ENERGY: Global Prospects 1985–2000,* New York – McGraw Hill, 1977, p. 17.

FIG. 3.4. *Energy Production and Consumption of the World (Including Communist Areas).*

operations in terms of energy. If the increase of this subsidy is such that these technologies might become major users (directly and indirectly) of energy, the continuation of nuclear power station construction would hit important economic barriers in terms of real value produced. From the point of view of constantly increasing the GNP, the construction of nuclear power stations definitely has a positive effect in accounting terms: but this is at least partly illusory. If the energy-production system would tend to consume a very large part of the energy it produces, its effects on D & P "disaccumulation" should be carefully evaluated.

On a more general level, the concept which regards any increase in the GNP as an improvement in social well-being has masked a major fact: capital accumulation is often no more than an apparent accumulation since, by correlation, the D & P may be destroyed in its substance as the result of industrialized activity. In other words, the concept of value added (VA) must be corrected by a variable which is a measure of this loss of substance. This, as we have seen, is the value deducted (VD). Consequently, the effect of a new investment into the economic circuits should be appreciated only if $(VA - VD) > 0$. This equation neatly expresses the

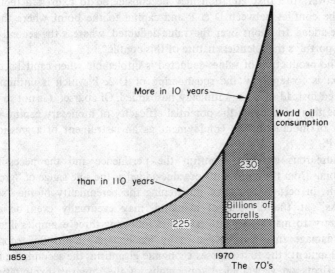

Source: Lawkins, Chase, Darby, Rapp *The Evolving Earth, a Text in Physical Geology,*
Second edition, p. 509, Macmillan Publishing Co., Inc. 1978.

FIG. 3.5. *Diagrammatic Plot to Illustrate the Rapidly Accelerating Trend of World
Petroleum Consumption*

need to properly integrate the value of capital into the value of the D & P
in any strategy affecting our well-being.

3.1.5. D & P DEPLETION

(VA + VD) > 0 and (VA + VD) < 0* are the two aspects, positive and
negative, of a single phenomenon: the evolution of the state of wealth.
The uses of monetary capital cannot have a neutral effect on the overall
D & P. Any economic activity will generate a value deducted: if there is
accumulation somewhere, there will be "disaccumulation" elsewhere.

*Certainly the choice is between (VA + VD) > 0 and (VA + VD) < 0, but this is
not sufficient. The magnitude of VA and VD is not without significance; the greater
the VA and the smaller VD, the more rational is the management of the D & P. The
efficacity of an economic activity would then be measured not so much as a function
of its contribution to the growth of the GNP but rather as a function of its VD which
should tend to be zero.

Moreover, the first equation may be considered to express a reduction in the conflict between D & P and capital to the point where the real value-added triumphs over the value-deducted, whereas the second equation portrays the relentless nature of this conflict.

The production of values-deducted is intolerable when capital accumulation is fostered by the squandering of D & P which is unthinkingly wasted instead of being rationally husbanded. Of course, it is not so much a question of denying the potential efficacity of monetary capital rather than of modulating its employment as an instrument of aggression on D & P.

Numerous examples confirm the pertinence and the necessity of escaping from the constraints of value-added as the sole gauge of "growth" which, in certain cases, by threatening the perenniality of the "service stocks" at the disposal of mankind, may eventually even be acting contrary to man's true interests. The following three examples illustrate the damage that can be caused by inadequately controlled economic development: the first exposes economic gigantism; the second, the harmful effects on geographical topography of the intensive exploitation of underground resources; the third, the ineluctable result of aggressively destructive technology.

In Egypt, the construction of the Aswan dam on the Nile was completed in 1965. The objectives of this project were to control the waters of the Nile, to generate electricity, to develop irrigation and permit the establishment of a fishing industry in the Lake Nasser region. The advantages were incontestable but the wisdom of constructing the dam is now being questioned since a number of negative repercussions have been observed, particularly on the Egyptian fluvial and agricultural systems.

The rich alluvium regularly deposited by the Nile's floodwaters on the Egyptian agricultural plain has been an essential factor in the soil's fertility since the time of the Pharaohs. This alluvium is now held back by the dam and has had to be replaced by chemical fertilizers.

With the Nile's flood controlled by the dam, the river's effect on the Delta configuration has been terminated. The sea, no longer restrained by the force of the river current, is steadily encroaching on the Delta region, the rise in the level of salinity has made the soil unsuitable for agriculture, and the existence of freshwater lakes protected by narrow strips of sand is threatened.

In the lower Nile region, an accelerated process of erosion of the river bed and banks has started. Fishing has declined significantly in the eastern Mediterranean and the Delta lakes region.

Parasitic diseases such as schistosomiasis are spreading along the irrigation channels.

Evaporation from the immense Lake Nasser — 5860 km^2 in area — is intense and the loss resulting from this is estimated at 12% of the annual floodwater of the Nile. It is feared that evaporative loss will be further increased if the lake is invaded by aquatic plants as had happened in the world's largest artificial reservoir, Lake Kariba in Southern Africa.[12]

Last but not least, the dam's entry into service has accelerated land concentration and the exodus of the rural population towards the large towns of the Delta, especially Cairo, which are already overpopulated and incapable of assimilating these newcomers.

The cumulative effect of these values deducted is a refutation of the wisdom of building the dam — monetary capital has contributed to the depletion of D & P. Projects of more modest size and better adapted to local conditions would have achieved the same overall objectives without causing damage on such a scale.* Studies of impact and subsequent effect would have contributed to ensuring a more harmonious balance between VA and VD and to optimizing the utilization value of the Egyptian natural D & P.

A little-known phenomenon is the land subsidence resulting from the intensive exploitation of underground resources. In the Southern part of the Californian Central Valley, the pumping of underground water for irrigation purposes is progressively exhausting the ground water table which has a stabilizing effect on the topography. Very large areas (approximately 7800 km^2) have been affected by land subsidence. Topographical observations have shown that, in some places, subsidence is as much as several meters. Figure 3.6. shows how the affected zones account for a considerable portion of certain California counties. Without going to the extreme of halting operation of all the wells, it would nevertheless be

*In the United States and other countries, concern is now being expressed about the dams built to date, the pressure they exert on the earth crust, and the disaster hazard that they might constitute. This is another example of enhanced vulnerability that has not been taken into account in monetary balances. See "Dam Design — is Technology Faulty?", by P. Williams, *New Scientist,* February 2, 1978, pp. 280–284.

possible to reduce pumping to a more moderate level and continue to exploit only those water tables where there is adequate security or halt building in zones likely to be affected by land subsidence. Massive extraction of gaseous or liquid fluids in numerous areas of the world gives rise to the same kind of problem. In the Po delta, on the Adriatic coast of North East Italy, extraction of the natural gas from poorly consolidated sediments has caused local subsidence of 30 cm per year. The situation has become so serious that cessation of extraction has been envisaged.

In the High Plains region of the United States, water is used intensely in spite of its relative rarity. In the States of Texas, New Mexico, Oklahoma, Colorado, Nebraska and Kansas, tens of thousands of square kilometers of semi-arid land are irrigated, thanks to an immense underground water table, the Oglallala reservoir. Without it, regular harvests would be impossible in this region which currently produces 20% of America's sorghum and cotton, and 3% of its wheat and corn; nor would it be possible to fatten the large herds of livestock now maintained.

It took millions of years for the water in this reservoir to accumulate; however, if exploitation continues at the present rate, supplies will be virtually exhausted by the close of the century. In Texas, for example, the water level is falling at an average rate of 2 to 7 feet a year, whereas in this same region of the High Plains, water infiltrates into the reservoir at a rate of only one tenth of an inch a year. In Colorado, the situation is no better: research workers at Colorado State University have estimated that a pump drawing water from this reservoir at a rate of 2000 litres per minute lowers the water-table level by half-an-inch every two weeks over the equivalent area of the reservoir. Some agricultural operations use 4000 litres per minute for a 4-acre section. At this rate, the level of the water table is falling by half-inch every two days. Since 1948, the exploitation of the Oglallala lake has accelerated continuously: the number of irrigation wells in the High Plains of Texas has increased from 8400 in 1948 to 52,000 in 1963 and 71,000 in 1976; they are of increasing depth and the area irrigated per well is decreasing as is shown in Figure 3.7.

Some farmers are already deprived of water and, faced with the prospects of a shortage in the near future, some of them have increased (!) the rate of pumping. The farmers of this region are squandering a precious D & P, which is non-renewable on the timescale of human life, and,

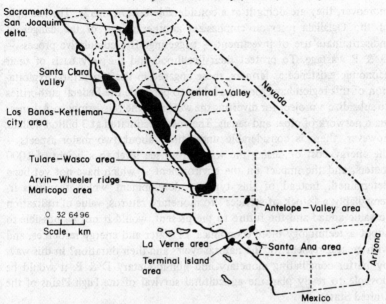

FIG. 3.6. *Sketch Map of Part of the State of California. Darkened Zones Indicate Areas Affected by Land Subsidence Due to Man's Activities.*

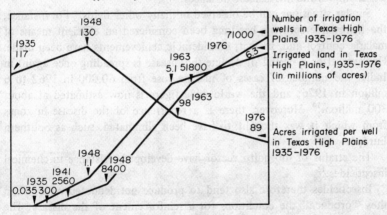

Source: Nicole Ball, Water: "The Real Constraint on American Food Production", *Ecologist Quarterly,* no. 1. Spring 1978, pp. 22–24.

FIG. 3.7. *The Diminishing Returns of Irrigation*

moreover, they are doing it at a considerable cost in energy. The example of the Oglallala reservoir emphasizes another aspect of the danger of indiscriminate use of investment — triggering-off a cumulative process — D & P wastage. To protect their livelihood and the very basis of their economic existence as farmers, those engaged in the agricultural exploitation of this region have formed a lobby to persuade the Federal authorities to subsidize a project for diverting the waters of the Mississippi to Arkansas via a network of pipes and canals. The cost is estimated at 3 billion dollars; however, there is considerable uncertainty about two major aspects — the energy cost of raising the water from sea level to a height of 1000 meters, and the impact on the environment — which have not yet been determined. Instead of this type of development which sacrifices irremediably a "stock of services" to monetary returns, value of utilization to value added and the future to the present, would it not be possible to adopt a technology more economical of water and energy resources, and with greater respect for the natural cycles and their duration? In this way, by better conciliating monetary and non-monetary D & P, it would be possible to really plan the agricultural survival of the High Plains of the United States.

Admittedly, these are all cases of limited extent but they are nevertheless examples and not isolated instances.[13]

Similar situations can be observed in many other fields.* For instance, the insecticide spraying has long been considered an efficient means of malaria control and, in fact, considerable achievements have been made. However after a period of decline the disease is spreading once again: in India, the number of cases of malaria rose from 60,000 in 1962 to 6 million in 1976; and the world wide figure is now estimated at about 300 million.[14] Moreover, there is a recurrence of the disease in zones from which it was thought to have been eliminated, such as Southern Europe.

The strains of mosquito vector have developed resistance to chemical insecticides.[15]

Insecticides therefore also tend to produce net deducted value, when they "produce" the conditions for a reinforcement of the disease. The approach must therefore be rigorously systemic so as to find the best equilibrium level thus enabling disease control to be "optimized".

*The story of the so called "green revolution" is another bitter point in case.

Still more decisive in the long term, in view of its effect on the biosphere, is the thoughtless destruction of the tropical forests. It is estimated that some 40% of these forests may already have been destroyed and "what is left is being burnt or felled at the rate of 20 hectares a minute."[16] What price then the project to "exploit" the Amazonian sub-soil with the concomitant destruction of its vegetation which, according to the experts, is a major source for the renewal of the Earth's oxygen?

The repercussions of this profligacy are unpredictable since once the threshold of the intolerable is attained, curative action may be too late.

3.1.6. WEALTH AND POVERTY

D & P depletion is clearly an index of increasing poverty, even if — and precisely because — it is accompanied by increasing costs in the monetarized economy.

Poverty in the world today has two main roots: "classical" poverty which even the modern world has not succeeded in suppressing completely and "modern" poverty, which is *produced* through increased, industrialized D & P depletion.

"Classical" poverty is measured, in part, in terms of disposable income which determines the solvable demand. Modern poverty is measured in terms of increasing costs which require increasingly high disposable income and effort to provide access to a constant, or even decreasing, level of services.

Official statistics of poverty are generally derived from quantitative analyses of individual income. In 1975, Robert S. McNamara, President of the World Bank, estimated that some 900 million people were living on an income of less than US $75, and provided the following description of absolute poverty:

"They are absolute poor, living in situations so deprived as to be below any rational definition of human decency (absolute poverty is a condition of life so limited by illiteracy, malnutrition, disease, high infant mortality, and low life expectancy as to deny its victims the very potential of the genes with which they are born). In effect it is life at the margins of existence."[18]

In an attempt to define poverty and stimulate action against it, an ILO report entitled "Employment Growth and Basic Needs", divides the relevant populations of Asia, Africa and Latin America into two categories: "seriously poor" and "destitute". These two levels of poverty are defined respectively in relation to the average earnings of unskilled workers in large Indian firms and on the basis of one rupee per person per day. The cost of a typical shopping basket of the goods consumed by the poor is calculated at the equivalent of US $1 in Western Europe, 20 cents in Asia, 23 cents in Africa and 36 cents in Latin America. On this basis, the "seriously poor" poverty level would involve an annual personal income of: US $500 in Western Europe, US $180 in Latin America, US $115 in Africa and US $100 in Asia. The corresponding figures for the "destitute" level would be US $250 in Western Europe, US $90 in Latin America, US $59 in Africa and US $50 in Asia.

These figures, are of course, supposed to represent very low standards of living. Nevertheless, their meaningfulness can be disputed. With a total annual income of US $500, a European could not of course meet even his basic needs: a subsistence level of food, clothing and housing. If he is still alive at the end of the year, it means he must have other sources of revenue, and that his monetary income is only a part of his total income.

By its apparent neutrality, monetary income gives an inaccurate picture of development. "Absolute poverty" would relate to the circumstances of persons reduced to the level of biological survival, and "relative poverty" to the situation of those who had risen above this level but still had no access to the sociocultural services which any *industrialized* country makes available to its citizens. Thus, the difference between absolute poverty and relative poverty would be one not only of degree but also of nature. There is a shift in the scale of values, from the area of basic needs to that of the priority and the legitimacy of industrial development. "Malnutrition is the consequence of poverty, the misfortune which only a society which has arrived at the stage of maturity, the society of mass consumption, as Rostow[19] says, makes it possible to transcend."

If, in reality, there were a mechanical response to this linear scheme of development, the number of destitute would decrease when economic growth increased in real terms. However, despite the rapid economic growth between 1963 and 1972 in most Third World countries, the number of poor has increased by 40 million even though, in view of population growth, the proportion of poor in the total population has decreased slightly during the same period. As for illiterates, according to UNESCO, the number increased, from 700 million to 760 million.

In fact, the division is not between the absolute poverty of the destitute in Third World countries and the relative poverty of the destitute in the industrialized countries. Extreme destitution is the lot of those living at the limit of survival who are subject to all the diseases inherent in deficient nutrition and whose sole preoccupation is their daily search for food to the exclusion of all desires other than the biophysical. This extreme destitution, frequent in the Third World countries of Asia and Africa and, to a smaller extent, in Latin America, has become more rare in the industrialized countries, but has not disappeared. Far from it.

The term "culture of the poor" used by Oscar Lewis in the introduction to his book *Les Enfants de Sanchez,* defines serious poverty in a convincing manner. Serious poverty is, in certain cases, the effect of industrialization and urbanization on private and family life. The victims are the least favoured social classes: unskilled workers, small farmers, plantation workers and what is commonly termed the "Lumpenproletariat". The two main characteristics of the "culture of the poor" are the persistence of poverty, even in industrially advanced social systems, as in the West for instance, and its universal nature. Oscar Lewis, in fact, noted great similarity between the poor classes of Glasgow, Paris, Harlem and Mexico with respect to family structure, relations between people, use of time and money, the hierarchy of values, and community spirit. The main characteristics of the "culture of the poor" are described by Lewis in the following terms.

"The economic facts most characteristic of the culture of the poor are the constant struggle for life, under-employment, unemployment, low wages, a variety of unskilled jobs, child labour, the absence of saving, a chronic shortage of liquid funds, the absence of food reserves in households, the habit of buying small quantities of food several times a day as required, the pawning of personal possessions, borrowing from local money lenders at usurious rates, *ad hoc* unofficial credit systems. . . ."[20]

"Among other social and psychological characteristics, there is that of living in quarters where there is a high density of population, the lack of intimity, the gregarious instinct, alcoholism, frequent recourse to violence to settle disputes, corporal punishment of children, wife battering, precocious initiation in sexual life, cohabitation. . . ."[21]

Albert Tévoédjrè has recently written a book with a paradoxical title: *Poverty, the Wealth of People.*[22] This defence of poverty is the defence of those (utilization) values which constitute an essential basis for wealth and which, too often — since they are not accounted — are sacrificed to the exclusively monetarized notion of wealth.

It must be clear, as it is clear for Albert Tévoédjrè: we all want to be wealthy. What is at stake is real wealth, real *material* wealth as well as cultural wealth. In one word: real maximum freedom.

The reference base here is the availability and accessibility of D & P: a D & P which industrialization can help to increase, but only up to the point at which an equivalent — or even worse — higher level of deducted values is produced.

A major objective of economic policy should therefore be to protect and develop our D & Ps whilst giving due account to all their complexities. To achieve this, D & Ps must first be recognized, identified and their additions and losses accounted for.

We need new ways of assessing wealth and welfare.

3.2. Assessing Wealth and Welfare

3.2.1. D & P AND VALUE

The concept of wealth is identified in economics by a certain notion of value. The notion of added value is very often used to indicate the standard of living and, as such, it is accepted as a more or less adequate definition and quantification of wealth and welfare. The advantage of this notion of added value is that it is easy to define and quantify; even when its limitations are admitted, it is in practice still the most used tool for measuring wealth. Another reason for the practical success of added value is that it fits into a general economic theory.

Over recent decades, it has often been admitted that the concept of added value is inadequate and incomplete for defining real wealth and welfare. As a consequence, many other ways and means of identifying and quantifying wealth and welfare have been discussed: in particular, a large number of so called indicators have been proposed and used in both a socioeconomic context ("social accounting"), in an institutional or company context ("social audit") or even in an individual context ("satisfaction indices").*

The problems and criticism of such indices vary and are briefly resumed and commented below.

The first criticism, coming from economists, is that social indicators are sociological tools which do not directly concern economics: this criticism derives (once more) from the identification of economics with the monetarized economy. In fact, it should be recognized that these indicators are related to the definition of and search for wealth and welfare and that their existence and even proliferation are a sign of the growing dissatisfaction with the traditional tools of economic measurement, precisely in view of economic goals and research objectives.

The second criticism is that the indicators are very often too qualitative and difficult to quantify. This is obvious; however, there are also clearly many cases in which quantification is, in reality, a meaningless process. For example, since value added entails certain deducted values, it can no longer be considered a reliable indication of wealth and welfare even though it can be measured relatively easily: the first requirement is to be sure that the measurement in question has the expected significance. To select factors in a system on the basis of their direct measurability and not in terms of the behaviour of the system in itself and of its goals, will clearly lead to aberrations.

The third criticism relates to the multiplicity and variety of these indicators: the "indicators" movement may seem to be the outcome of different situations; it leads to very different types of measurements, and is, apparently, based on very different types of motivation. Two types of answers can be discussed here. The first is that wealth and welfare can be differently defined in different places and cultures, as well as in different moments in time. It is the very inflexibility of the traditional concept of value in economics, that may constitute an acceptable factor since it presupposes a world in which living conditions, constraints and appreciations are uniform. However, the diversity which, in fact, exists should not be taken as evidence of any

*A recent interesting effort has been made by two economists to "Determine comparative values for unpriced things" under the assumption that "Valid comparisons can be made without always resorting to monetary prices". See J. Snider and A. Worrell: *Unpriced Values"*, New York, 1979.

lack of consistency and logic of the "indicator" movement. On the other hand, the above-mentioned lack of any adequate theory of wealth and welfare has probably impeded a more successful use of such indicators. A more comprehensive theory of wealth and welfare of the kind proposed here tries to provided a basis for a more consistent approach and actually encourages utilization of the indicators. In fact, the whole target of this report can be redefined in the following way:

(a) define first a new theory of value (utilization value)
(b) devise then the most appropriate methods and possibilities of measurement and the judgment (selection of indicators)
(c) open in this way the possibility of defining new operational economic policies (for instance in the fiscal and monetary field as we shall see later).

We will therefore bring together the various ideas on D & P, utilization value, deducted and added value exposed in previous sections and chapters, in an attempt to set out a systematic reference framework for assessing wealth and welfare.

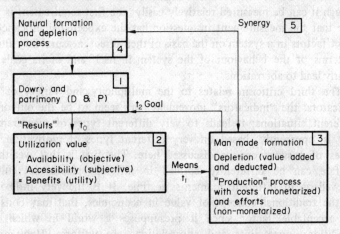

FIG. 3.8. *The Dynamics of D & P*

The above diagram proposes a logical sequence of D & P formation and use in time and space — a prerequisite for any comment as to its general structure.

Central to the notion of wealth and welfare is the concept of Dowry and Patrimony (D & P, Box 1), including every available resource and asset, material and non-material, monetarized and non-monetarized.

D & P, as we have already indicated has a *utilization value* (Box 2) which represents the (objective) availability of D & P (apples on a tree, the music of Beethoven, a bank account) and the (subjective) accessibility to it (both material and cultural: I appreciate Beethoven, I am in a position to use my bank account and to get the apples from the tree). It represents, to use a word much in favour with economists, the notion of utility in its widest sense.

Utilization value allows mankind to live and therefore to produce (positive and negative yields, added and deducted values in their monetary and non-monetary sense). Box (3) relates to *man-made formation and depletion* of D & P and box (4) indicates the *natural D & P formation and depletion* process which influences directly the total D & P, but which develops in *synergy* (point 5) with the man-made process.

Boxes (3) and (4), in their synergy (point 5) determine the level of total D & P.

This *dynamic* sequence entails several implications of considerable interest.

(a) The first is a great apparent paradox: contrary to what is normally assumed in the industrial production process namely that *"production" precedes "consumption"*, we *discover that "consumption" actually precedes "production"*.

Such a paradox is not new in economics, where it is normally admitted, in monetary field, that although the individual needs money first before he can spend it, the creation of money in the general monetary sense is the result of a debt situation.

In the case in question, the paradox is much easier to accept and verify:

— historically, it is intuitively acceptable to imagine that mankind initially exploited the available natural D & P with very little personal effort to build it up. We can consider from this angle the fact that at the start of the Industrial Revolution, Britain was a rather prosperous country which *had* the resources to expand its activity in the new technology: a relatively rich D & P was the *pre-condition* for the start of the Industrial Revolution itself.

— in our personal existence, we start at birth, as consumers and net users and remain so for sometime before becoming "producers".

Moreover society clearly does not consume at any given moment the products it is simultaneously producing – what happens in a given moment is a product *exchange*. An acquisition can be consumed either virtually instantaneously (e.g. a cup of coffee in a restaurant) or over a period of years or even decades (a car, a house, a book, a foreign language). In other words, the exchange act determines the allocation of D & P constituents – it is a form of distribution – in time and space – of the utilization value.

(b) Dynamically, wealth use at a given moment is possible because of *past* wealth production activities (up to the moment of use).

On the other hand, current production (be it positive or negative), relates exclusively to the future.

The only point then at which past and future meet is during the act of exchange; utilization and production are dynamic realities which take place in different relative time dimensions.

All present actions and decisions are therefore constituents of the future, because they have a life-cycle (a behaviour) in the future (from now on): they *make* the future.

Thus, we propose here to consider the problems of planning from a point of view rather different from the traditional one,[23] which consists in defining first a probable or desirable scenario of the future, whereas it is, in our view, essential to start first from the study of the inertias of the present.

In the dynamic perspective, it can be perceived that D & P is not only the starting or reference point of wealth (in time t_0), but that it is also the final objective (in time t_2). At the limit, t_0 can be equal to t_2 but, in fact, t_0 incorporates "eternity until now" and t_2 concerns "now till eternity".

Paradoxically, when "production" is understood as something which precedes consumption, the "goal" or future is in fact inevitably determined by the past and there is no freedom or simple means of escaping a pre-determined and unidirectional mechanism. In fact, this kind of determinism is clearly the result of an optical illusion, linked to the Cartesian fiction of static time dimensions.*

---

*From this point of view it becomes obvious that "Historical Determinism" is "wrong", especially when linked to economic facts and the "production" of D & P.

It can now also be understood why, both philosophically as well as merely psychologically, if "production" is considered as occurring before "consumption", then it is axiomatic to believe that the act of consuming legitimizes the act of producing to the point of believing that traditional added value is "real" value.

It is necessary to underline the concept of D & P as both a goal and a result — the result provides our utilization value, and the goal is determined by our action and interreaction with different types of D & P. The goal is not something which can be determined in an *absolute* freedom: freedom itself is a notion derived from the human D & P, but which is overcome by the constraints imposed by the interrelations with all other D & Ps. The drama of mankind is that this limited freedom is often wasted either because it is consciously relinquished or because goals are defined passively: since all actions are inevitably the expression of a goal (conscious or not, stated or not), one must know whether responsibility is being taken to recognize them as such. Assuming such responsibility is the pathway of civilization.

We can now try to recognize and systematize the different forms of wealth and welfare indicators in this scheme.

3.2.2. ASSESSING WORLD D & P

D & P, as we have defined it, is a very wide concept and its assessment and enlargement is a constant and diverse process. Scientific research, learning and intuitive knowledge (the arts) are all part of human endeavour in assessing and creating D & P. Knowledge can also bring destruction; therefore, certain moral attitudes must also be included in the D & P as a tool for inhibiting this destruction potential.

Going back to the previous chapter where an analogy was made with the electromagnetic-wave spectrum, it is possible to restrict the analysis to that of D & P as a basis for material welfare.

As early as 1957, Bertrand de Jouvenel was regretting that free goods and services on the one hand and commercial values on the other were not integrated into economic analysis. He attributed this to the "intellectual edifice erected by the economists" who had limited their research to the field of well-being in relation to the monetary measuring unit.[24]* The origins of this attitude lie in the distant pass — as was seen in Chapter 2.

The work of Bertrand de Jouvenel did not form part of a new, general, coherent economic scheme but certainly prefigured it.[25]** How could he have gone further, when an era of new technological advance had just started and the multiplication of the fields of investigation hid the degradation of the natural D & P? Hence, a rejection phenomenon occurred and the rigidity of the classical conceptual framework remained intact.

At that time it was not yet possible to talk of the diminishing returns of technology or of value deducted, thereby making it necessary to acknowledge the limits of industrial growth and its dependence on global D & P. But now more and more the recognition — even if often implicit — of the diminishing returns of technology and of the existence of deducted values, is well underway.

For instance, at the level of the State in which the responsibility of preserving the national D & P is to a large extent vested, such new prospects are more and more frequently being outlined:

---

*Bertrand de Jouvenel: "L'Economie politique de la Gratuité", 1957, dans Arcadie, Essais sur le Mieux-Vivre, *Futuribles,* 1968.
Other quotations of importance in this context are:
"Of these (human needs), some are satisfied by the use we make of certain things that nature freely provides, such as air, water, sunlight. We can call these things natural wealth because nature alone is responsible for them. As they are given to everybody, no one is obliged to acquire them at the cost of any sacrifice whatsoever. They have therefore no exchange value" — T. B. Fay:
"Traité d'économie politique ou simple exposition de la manière dont se forment, se distribuent et se consomment les richesses", Volume Two, Chapter 1, 1918 edition, p. 5.
"The natural agents are not charged for since they are inexhaustible and available to all. Thus, the brewer, the distiller and the dyer make constant use of air and water in the production of their goods but since their abundancy is unlimited there is no price attached to their use" — David Ricardo: *On the Principles of Political Economy and Taxation,* Chapter II: "On Rent", published by Sraffa, Cambridge, 1951, p. 69.
**See Bertrand de Jouvenel: "Organisation du Travail et Aménagement de l'Existence", 1958, in Arcadie, Essais sur le Mieux-Vivre, *Futuribles,* No. 9, 1968.
"In the exploitation of Nature, the only thing considered is the expenditure of human effort, so that what we take from the common patrimony of the human race does not leave us open to any revendication — *Arcadie,* p. 244.
"As for energy, it is different, since we are burning our stocks: in this sense, our process of social enrichment is a process of consumption of the patrimony" — *Arcadie,* p. 246.

"The acute problems raised by the transformation of nature have led the governments of the technologically most advanced countries (USA, Europe, Japan, . . .) to consider the *systematic management of the natural environment,* the *source of all wealth,* as a matter for concern. This patrimony, long considered inexhaustible and invulnerable, is showing itself to be limited and fragile once the power of technology, the need for raw materials and energy and the complete transformation in the modes of populating the world affect nature considered as capital. It is probable, in fact, that having previously lived on the interest associated with this capital we are now living off the capital itself."[26]

Is the above statement the prelude to a radical change in our mentality, behaviour and socioeconomic practice? Does it herald the day when we will consider Dowry and Patrimony as our most precious possession?

Governments of the industrialized countries are, at last, accepting the idea of natural D & P accounting. Here again, Bertrand de Jouvenel has proved a forerunner. In a proposal to the "Commission des Comptes de la Nation" (National Auditing Commission), made in May 1966,[27] he suggested no less than an accounting system for the D & P in which he would have included: flows of services which were not the object of any commercial transaction, the negative flows which are nuisances, and drawings on nature.

It is thus an old idea which those responsible for national accounting are attempting to adapt to current needs. According to Paul Cornière "we are entering an epoch where, by fair means or foul, dialectic props will be established between those managing an active Nature and those managing human activities."[28] The table on p. 208 gives some idea of these attempts.

In referring to these examples, the following points should be considered:

· The concept of D & P should not be just parallel and separate from that of monetarized wealth.* The problem is more basic than that of accounting the contribution of nature to wealth: it touches on the very revision of our concept of wealth. It should be the result of a new

---

*Just as the evolution of monetarized D & Ps should not be considered as the ultimate measure of wealth, although such studies are of greatest interest. See "Eléments de Comparison Internationale des Patrimoines des Ménages" by D. Strauss-Kahn, *Economie et Statistique,* INSEE, Paris, September 1979, pp. 119– 125.

TABLE 3.3. *Examples of D & P Components and Resources which should be Included in any D & P Management Strategy*

Components of D & P	Resources	Points to be watched	
		D & P conservation	Resource husbanding
Sun + atmosphere	Solar radiation absorbed by the earth	Composition of the atmosphere (carbon dioxide, ozone . . .) Earth albedo	Solar energy utilization balance sheet
Physical cycles: ocean currents			
Biochemical cycles: nitrogen			
Genetic D & Ps		Disappearance of species	
Animal and Vegetable populations	Biological production (surplus)	— Condition of soil — Biological contamination — Size of populations — Land area devoted to agriculture — Consumption of known natural reserves and reserve substitution — Agricultural and silvicultural practices — Equipment	— Rate of culling — Organic matter balance sheet — Materials balance sheet
	Non-renewable resources (ores, sands and gravels, fossil energy)		
Countrysides			
Groundwater	Water	Water quality	Amount drawn off in relation to replacement flow
Forests	Wood	Areas by categories	Timber and wood products balance sheet

Source: Cornières, Paul. *Futuribles* November 1978

discipline of welfare, derived from the synthesis of economics and ecology.

- The concept of D & P depends very much on the concept of general economic value, and this relationship should not be avoided or considered solved by the acceptance of the idea that "natural" D & P must be protected. Real protection and protection and promotion of "natural" D & P will really become a matter of efficient policy when it will be considered within the general framework of the utilization value.

- Unlike Gross National Income, the concept of D & P cannot be reduced even with the best will, to a specific nation-state dimension: national histories and traditions as well as resources of any kind coincide only very partially with existing political institutions.

At this point in time, the definition and the assessment of world D & P would be a valid activity in itself: by improving awareness of the resources and limitations (utilization value) of our space vessel, goals can be better specified and the means of achieving them defined.

3.2.3. INDICATORS OF WELFARE (UTILIZATION VALUE): SOCIAL INDICATORS

This section will review the various attempts made to measure welfare, bearing in mind that such attempts always relate to an explicit notion of value.

(a) Gross national product (GNP) and the Measure of economic welfare (MEW). The traditional indicator of welfare for economists has been, and still largely is value added, as computed in Gross National Product.

However, some economists have now started to openly criticize this approach. "Gross national product is not a measure of economic welfare. Economists all know that, and yet their everyday use of GNP as the standard measure of economic performance apparently conveys the impression that they are evangelistic worshippers of GNP. An obvious shortcoming of GNP is that it is an index of production and not of consumption."[29] Using these considerations as their starting point, W. Nordhaus and J. Tobin, propose the calculation of a "Measure of Economic Welfare"

(MEW) in an "attempt to allow for the more obvious discrepancies between GNP and economic welfare."

The following graph plots both the MEW and GNP for the United States, and indicates for each major reference year, the extent to which MEW was greater than GNP.

The authors conclude that "MEW has been growing and the progress indicated by conventional measures is not just a myth". The present report too has underlined that real wealth has progressed considerably during this period of the Industrial Revolution. However, the following remarks should be made concerning MEW accounting methods and the conclusions drawn by Nordhaus and Tobin:

- it is striking that MEW increases more rapidly during periods of economic difficulties: during the periods 1929–1935 and 1945–1947, when GNP *diminished,* MEW increased rapidly and even more rapidly than during other periods. One should not, however, necessarily draw conclusion that, in order to boost welfare as measured be "MEW", it is advisable to drastically induce a negative GNP growth rate as was the case in the two above-mentioned periods. . . .
- the accounting method is based essentially on a reclassification of GNP final expenditures and on imputations for capital services, leisure and non-market work.

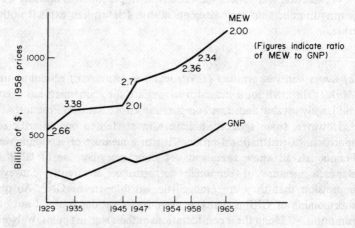

FIG. 3.9. *GNP and MEW from 1929 through 1965 in the United States*

It might be noted here that, although some items regarded as instrumental and intermediate to final output have been subtracted, and even though some external diseconomies have been taken into account, we are still faced essentially with the same type of methodological inadequacies as are encountered in the GNP indicator. The latter *cannot* be improved as an indicator of welfare, essentially because it measures a *flow* of expenditures (and, in the case of MEW, of efforts as well). Welfare can be measured or estimated only from the situation and the degree of access to a *stock* of assets.

Furthermore, welfare — even if limited to material welfare — simply *cannot* be measured on the basis of a concept of value which does not distinguish between "costs adding to D & P" and "costs subtracting from D & P", beyond what are normally accepted as negative externalities.

To measure or indicate welfare, entails the development of new methods, founded on a more adequate notion of value.

(b) Social indicators: the physical quality of life index (PQLI). In their MEW study, Nordhaus and Tobin acknowledge the existence of the trend toward "social indicators"[29a] but also admit that these "still lack a coherent, integrative conceptual and statistical framework".

In fact, this form of "accounting" is the outcome of several factors and different implicit theories: frequently, these are of sociological origin and, as such, they try to constitute a parallel or an alternative to economic analysis. They may also be developed as an extension of existing, accepted economic paradigms — as in the case of MEW. Sometimes they are developed as an application of accounting theories. Finally, and frequently they are produced to meet a need to identify specific situations.

This is a point that must be insisted upon: the proliferation of such indicators, is a clear sign of the inadequacy of the existing, official methods of measuring wealth and welfare. Their overall coherence can be found in a more adequate concept of value which they could use as a reference point.

Elements of this (often implicit) search for a new value theory, can be found in many attempts to construct social indicators, as in the case of the Physical Quality of Life Index (PQLI). In a paper describing such indicators, James P. Grant[30] writes:

- "The indicators are about *ends,* not means" and "the indicators have the advantages that they do not make any assumptions about special patterns of development and that they measure *results* rather than input".
  Ends and results: here are the two connotations of utilization value (case 2 in Fig. 3.8. on page 202) in relation to D & P.
- Furthermore, in an attempt to identify which variable affects individual physical well-being (physical health), J. Grant puts forward the following complex model (p. 213) which inevitably integrates what we called the monetarized and non-monetarized factors.

The development of indicators such as PQLI derives from the fact that, if the correlation between average income and welfare are as close as its devotees suggest, how can one explain the fact that, in Sri Lanka, with an average income of US $130, life expectancy in the 1970s was about the same as that in the State of Washington, where the average income was US $5000. Can there be any doubt that life expectancy is — in most if not all cases — an integral part of welfare?

The table on p. 214 compares incomes with indicators of life expectancy at birth, infantile mortality, educational level and birth rate.

A number of international conferences (the United Nations Conference on Population in Bucharest in 1974, the Conference on Housing in Vancouver in 1976, the Conference on Food in Rome in 1974, and the ILOs World Employment Conference in 1976) have provided a sounding-board for new approaches in this direction. For example, the World Employment Conference defined basic needs in terms of adequate food, satisfactory housing and hygiene conditions, clean drinking-water, access to health services and education, etc.

Substantial progress was made, but still not enough. How indeed is a common specification of basic needs to be achieved when present levels differ between geographic regions and climatic zones and even according to the structure of the basic social unit? This does not mean that indicators are not useful as a yardstick for reducing disparities between the advanced industrialized countries and the Third World countries, or that they are of only minor importance in any policy for improving the welfare of societies and individuals.* It merely means that their limitations as social

---

*Although the Satisfaction of Basic Needs Index has now been overtaken by more recent developments in thinking, the fact that economists have had recourse to this type of index combining data on nutrition, housing, employment and medical services definitely represents something of a breakthrough.

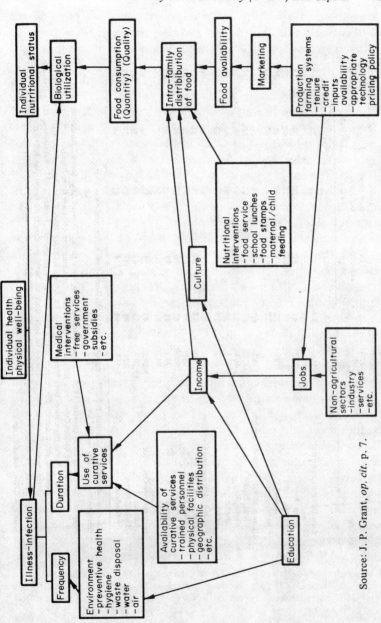

FIG. 3.10. *A Model of Individual Physical Well-being*

Source: J. P. Grant, *op. cit.* p. 7.

TABLE 3.4. *Economic and Social Indicators of Development in Selected Countries, Early 1970s*[a]

	Average per capita GNP 1970–75 ($)	POLI	Life expectancy at birth (years)	Infant mortality per 1,000 births	Literacy (%)	Birth rate per 1,000
Low-Income Countries	156	39	48	136	34	40
Mali	90	14	38	188	5	50
India	133	41	49	129	34	34
Kerala, India	110b	68	61	58	60	27
Sri Lanka	179	82	68	47	81	26
Bangladesh	92	32	46	153	22	47
Lower Middle-Income Countries	452	60	61	95	60	30
China, People's Rep.	350b	68	62	65	60	22
Korea, Rep.	464	82	65	47	88	24
Zambia	415	38	44	159	47	50
Angola	600	16	38	203	13	47
Upper Middle-Income Countries	1,026	67	61	87	65	36
Iran	1,260	52	57	104	37	45
Mexico	996	75	65	66	74	42
Cuba	800b	85	70	27	78	21
Algeria	780	41	53	145	26	48
Taiwan	847	87	70	25	85	26
High-Income Countries	5,272	93	71	17	96	17
Kuwait	13,787	75	69	44	55	43
United States	7,024	95	73	15	99	15
Netherlands	5,558	96	74	11	98	13

[a]Income categories include only the 127 countries listed in the World Bank's "Derived Atlas Series."
[b]Single-year estimates for 1975.

Sources. GNP data are in constant 1974–76 dollars and are from World Bank, "Derived Atlas Series," November 1977, except for China, Cuba, and Kerala. The GNP data for China and Cuba are from Population Reference Bureau, "1977 World Population Data Sheet." The data for Kerala are from John W. Sewell and the Staff of the Overseas Development Council, *The United States and World Development: Agenda 1977* (Washington, D.C.: Overseas Development Council, 1977). The social indicators are based on data from Population Reference Bureau, "1978 World Population Data Sheet." Literacy data are from *UNESCO Yearbook*, 1973 and 1975.

Source: Grant, James P.: *op. cit.*

indicators of development must be recognized. Hence, the interest of indexes which represent aggregate and comparable indicators together, as is the case of the Physical Quality of Life Index (PQLI). This index incorporates data on life expectancy, infantile mortality and literacy.* Because such indexes reflect over-all development and bring together the effects of over-all economic and social policy — including the way in which investment profits are allocated — they provide a better indication of progress in combating the worst evils that result from poverty than can GNP or development-input figures.** Since the factors they measure are more or less universal objectives, they provide a suitable standard for meaningful comparisons between different regions of the globe. The fact that they are valued *per se* does not, of course, mean that all possible directions of development are covered: "welfare" and "standard of living" — and this can never be repeated enough — are not one and the same thing.

Life expectancy at one year and infantile mortality rate are very important indicators of social progress, since they show the combined effect of all the means and types of action employed in the war against poverty: improved nutrition, greater access to health and education services, healthier housing conditions, improved water supply, etc. — whatever the pattern of resource allocation. At the same time, they reflect the situation of individuals *vis-à-vis* the social and natural environment: the

---

*Morris D. Morris: "Measuring the Condition of the World's Poor" The Physical Quality of Life Index, ODC, 1978. See also Morris D. Morris and Florizelle B. Liser, The PQLI Index — Measuring Progress in Meeting Human Needs, ODC; In the PQLI each variable is expressed as an index on the scale from 1 to 100 so that the progress of economic and social development can be observed within a stable framework of upper and lower limits. Thus, an increase of life expectancy from 40 to 45 years over a period of ten years will be shown as an annual rate of 5%; a fall in infantile mortality will appear as a percentage drop from the initial level (from 100 to 85, for example) and progress in literacy will be indicated in a percentage rise (from 60 to 70 or 75%, for example).

**Especially of the contribution made by the non-monetarized sector. Such an index cannot therefore be considered neutral in the sense of implying a nonvalue-judgment regarding the choice of development model. By substituting export crops for food crops (i.e. a monetarized economy for a mainly non-monetarized economy) some governments have made poverty worse and, in some cases, forced part of the population below the absolute poverty threshold where life expectancy declines and infantile mortality rises. In other words, they have opted for a confiscatory type of income distribution, obtaining foreign exchange for industrial development — or conspicuous spending — by destroying the structure of subsistence production that is not compensated by the low level of wages.

level of infantile mortality is affected by the woman's position in society; life expectancy at one year depends on the general environment and the level of nutrition; the degree of literacy is an indication both of the welfare level and of the ability of individuals to accept and spread proposed reforms.

The research group headed by Jan Tinbergen[31] has suggested for the developing countries the following targets for the end of the century: life expectancy of at least 65 years as compared with the present average of 48 years in low-income countries; an infantile mortality rate of 50 per thousand in contrast to the present rate of 125; a birth rate of 25 per thousand as compared with the present 40 per thousand; and a literacy rate of 75% instead of the present 33%. The targets set by Jan Tinbergen and his team are most desirable but one may wonder whether a decline of 3.5% per year in infantile mortality is really possible. Past experience suggests that it is.

In Sri Lanka, infantile mortality was reduced from 218 per thousand in 1911 to 141 per thousand in 1946, and then fell to 71 in 1953, corresponding to an annual decline of 1.3% in the first period and of 10% in the second. In 1963, infantile mortality dropped to 56 per thousand (an annual fall of 2.7%) and then to 43 per thousand in the early 1970s (2.9%).*

In Romania, the number of infantile deaths per thousand births during each five-year period from the late 1940s to the late 1960s was 54, 27, 15 and 13. This remarkable result was achieved with a very low level of *per capita* income (the Romanian average in 1965 was US $440). Taiwan did even better in the period between the early 1930s and the early 1950s.

Nor is it unrealistic to predict that life expectancy will increase from 48 to 65 years by the end of the century. Between 1940 and 1960, life expectancy in Puerto Rico rose from 45 to 70 years. In China and Sri Lanka, it rose from 45 to 62 years.

The aim here is not to exclude entirely the use of average income as an indicator of development but rather to propose that income, when combined with other indicators such as PQLI, would give a truer picture of development in various regions, nations and cities. A quite different

*This may be compared with the fact that, in Mali, over 350 children per thousand die before the age of five years (Claire Brisset "Le désert médical du Tiers-Monde" *Le Monde,* 6 September 1978).

picture of needs is emerging, associated with a renewed emphasis on the mobilization of national resources, including the non-monetarized economy in particular. This is because the total resources comprise more than just the stock of money and imported, capital-intensive technologies. The eradication of poverty and its attendant human evils of infantile mortality, premature death* and illiteracy is dependent only partially — and sometimes *very* partially — on the volume of the money stock and on the number and complexity of the relevant technologies. Consequently, in setting targets for welfare policies, more importance should be attached to social indicators than to GNP data.

Since infantile mortality, premature death, etc. are more common features of daily life in Third World countries, there is a tendency to regard social indicators as something peculiar to these countries. However, it should not be forgotten that the excesses of industrial development (unbalanced urbanization, over-rich and unsuitable nutrition, smoking and various types of public health hazard and nuisance) are also contributory factors in increased morbidity and mortality, especially due to cancer and cardiovascular diseases. Such factors which have an increasing impact on the growing cost of individual health care could be more systematically monitored by adequate indicators taken as the prime basis for national social and economic policies in the more industrialized countries.

(c) The OECD study on social indicators. A recent OECD publication illustrates both the interest of the social indicators to official institutions,

---

*The new WHO doctrine of "primary health care" opens up a new sphere of action for the non-monetarized economy. This proposes a radical change in health policies giving priority to the health of rural populations rather than to the building of hospitals in the towns. Mali had already anticipated this trend by drawing up a plan for systematic medical coverage in the rural areas which have been divided into zones of 100,000 inhabitants, each with a doctor and team of nurses working in the field and using an urban centre as their base. Each nurse has a group of nursing assistants to operate the village pharmacies financed by the local inhabitants. At the lowest level, "primary health officers" chosen by and from the villagers and working under the control of the nursing assistant, are responsible for distributing the medicaments needed to improve health in the district. In the last resort, arrangements are made to evacuate sick persons to the chief town in zone, where the doctor has access to an operating centre. Clearly, the non-monetarized sector is able to make a very substantial contribution since it even covers the whole work of the operating centre at the top of the medical infrastructure.

and the practical difficulties encountered when good intentions stumble on the obstacle of a methodology which still depends on the traditional concept of value.

The publication is entitled: "Measurement of social well-being — Progress achieved in the elaboration of social indicators," and if the content were faithful to the title, it would give an overview of the thought being devoted to the subject of social indicators in the industrialized countries. In fact, the first part of the book does display the same preoccupations as those raised in our research.

The authors have implicitly accepted the concept of D & P. In fact, it is stated that material wealth extends to such resources as: pure water, clean air, silence, ecological equilibrium and open spaces. Scarce resources — and goods having no monetary value — the report continues, are being increasingly exhausted or destroyed as the quantities of products and services traditionally considered as important rise. D & P degradation — value deducted — is therefore accepted as a fact and as the direct consequence of the increase in products and services traditionally considered as important. Analysis based on consumption and production models for the industrialized countries, together with deductive reasoning, provides an insight into the nature of the techniques used.

Human well-being is reinstated as the factor of prime importance, at the nerve centre of man's relations with his fellow beings and the physical environment. A direct link is established between identification of the elements of well-being and the basic question of the scale of values in our existence. Here, the report breaks with the unilateral concept of well-being as directly and automatically related to the level of net disposable income and questions the operational function of disposable income in the light of cultural diversity. It would be tempting to follow up this new approach by affirming that values are as numerous as cultures and consequently have no hierarchy, and to acknowledge that the cultural factor is an essential component of development. Moreover, the report regrets the fact that nothing has been done to elaborate indicators relating to the maintenance and the development of cultural heritage.

As far as development resources are concerned, the report poses three questions, opening the way to the renaissance and redeployment of the non-monetarized sector:

"— What resources permit the acquisition of goods and services?

- How secure are these resources in the event of a crisis? If the inadequacy or precariousness of the monetary resources in uncertain situations were not involved, there would be no reason for this question.
- How can we ensure a minimum of resources? How then can a minimum level of resources be restored?"

In recognizing that choice is an element of well-being and that the accessibility of goods and services has grown more important than their actual use, the report demonstrates clearly that it neither mistakes nor underestimates the rigid structures engendered by the current economic and social system: educational structures, vocational training and promotion systems, constraints to the organization of health-service and staff distribution, and to the production system, etc.

The report also concedes the significance of the subjective element in well-being: "The perception of fundamental aspects of their well-being by individuals and groups is a necessary and important component of a programme of social indicators. This type of information gives a new dimension to reality and may also bring out certain factors relating to objectives which have not previously been recognized as significant.*

Finally, it is stated that the social indicator is "a direct and valid statistical measure which will allow observation of the level and the variations with time of a basic social preoccupation."**

Unfortunately, the remainder of the report reduces these promising premises to mere wishful thinking. Moreover, abandoning the concept of "societal well-being" is an omen: the authors state that this concept, their own invention, encompasses a reform of the institutional structures of society but does not form part of the OECD programme on social indicators. This fortuitous or intentional exclusion of the concept is an admission: the details are changed but the reference basis remains. The role finally attributed to social indicators confirms this intention. These

*OECD programme for the elaboration of social indicators. Measurement of social well-being. Progress achieved in the elaboration of social indicators, OECD, Paris, 1976, p. 22.
**Idem, p. 15.

indicators are completely subject to monetarized logic. Revenue is stated to encompass "all" sources of revenue — but these are all monetary:
— Salaries and payment in cash
— Salaries and payments in kind (cost to the employer of food, housing and working clothes which he may provide free or at reduced cost)
— Revenue of the enterprise (essentially net rental of dwellings occupied by their owner plus the net rental of other buildings, net income from other individual enterprises)
— Property revenue (essentially interest, dividends, farm rents, etc.)
— Current transfers received (social security and accident insurance payments, private pension fund allowances, transfers from other households, etc.).

In such a perspective, wealth and welfare are again based, *de facto,* on the traditional concept of value. A concept which allows that the production of poverty, provided it costs large amounts of money, adds to apparent wealth.

(d) Social indicators at the corporate level. Over recent years, social indicators have been increasingly applied at the micro-economic level. Much research and many specific applications have seen the light.*

It is necessary to pick out the more immediate motives that have, in certain cases, encouraged corporations and other institutions to present a "social audit". Frequently the motive is the need to find a more convincing way of selling the company's or institution's image, or even to find better ways of "controlling" the situation.

Nevertheless, this type of social audit does have a more basic motive:
· there is a growing feeling that welfare can not be measured by distributed monetarized income if this income is accompanied by new and growing direct or indirect costs (monetarized or not).
· there is a need for greater realization that service and investment are closely linked to the "quality" of an increasingly complex environment.

The "social audit" that simply presents the promoter's case in a more skilful way, will eventually give way in the face of the fundamental question

*See for instance: The Study entitled "Corporate Social Audit" of Battelle, Geneva Research Centre. The "Bilan Social" presented in 1978 by the MIGROS in Switzerland.

of how to organize, in every society, a type of wealth based on a more adequate and comprehensive concept of value.

3.2.4. INDICATORS OF COST AND EFFORT: GOALS AND MEANS

(a) Costs and deducted values. Let us now consider case (3) shown in Fig. 3.8. on page 202.

Finally, we come, in due course, to the concept of cost. Gross, monetarized cost, which is often improperly identified with added value, is, in fact, a measure of gross effort in monetarized terms.

Once again, we return to the concept of deducted value that can be applied at two levels.

- if we limit our analysis to the monetarized system, a distinction should be made between the different types of added values normally accounted: those which quantify the financial resources used to increase D & P; and those which are induced by the industrialization process (the monetarized economic organization), itself. The deducted value is, in a sense, the expression of a cost or effort which has missed its objective.
- we can extend the concept of deducted value to the whole synergic process (case 5) by which D & P is depleted by a combination of natural and man-made activity.

In either of these cases, the deducted value applies to D & P and — as was noted in Chapter 2 — necessarily covers both the monetarized and the non-monetarized system.

Some attempts have been made, in the formulation of economic policies for developing countries in particular, to devise and use indicators of effort and thus extend beyond the simple identification of monetarized costs.* "Real" costs are also being approached from other angles: in fact, many indicators that have been devised for ecological purposes are indicators not of D & P and of its utilization value as we have defined them, but rather of non-monetarized costs (i.e. they are part of the general concept of deducted value).

This latter idea of accounting for "ecological constraints" has also

---

*See "Effort-satisfaction analysis (E -) in the formulation of Integrated development policies", Battelle Geneva Notebooks, June 1972. We can also mention a study by the UNCTAD secretariat (New York, 1970) on "The Measurement of Development Effort". Here again the monetarized effort is privileged.

given rise to proposals for specific indicators. The elements considered are essentially: rarity of resources, and their potential hazards.* Each resource is attributed an "equivalence coefficient", which indicates its costs in terms of the ecological equilibrium. Innovations such as this provide evidence of the growing interest in the accounting of deducted values.

(b) Means and goals. In the final analysis, the fact that expenditure and effort can lead to global *negative* results is not such a strange one. What is strange is that the disciplines dealing with wealth and welfare have not previously attempted this type of accounting more seriously. The evidence is there for all to see: a war is a cost, a seismic disaster is a cost too – and yet, when a country is destroyed for one reason or another, no audit is ever made of how many "national income equivalents" have been lost. Paradoxically, a devastated country or region is often presented as providing an "opportunity" for increasing "value added". The concept of value added is thus a strange notion since it sometimes seems to conceal the need to destroy in order subsequently to "increase". How can officialdom continue to insist on the use of a definition of wealth linked to the GNP rather than to the level and accessibility of D & P?

Should we not start to talk about *real* wealth and the cost and effort entailed in attaining our (implicit and explicit) goals rather than believing that goals are identified by their means, even when they are "wrong"?

Money itself is a means, and finally the definition of and convergence towards common (implicit and explicit) goals in D & P formation will mobilize this means better than *any* purely financial plan. We must stress the point that in the concept of value and of D & P proposed in this report, capital is technically different from the capital of traditional economics. In our dynamic system, capital is the part of D & P which exists in monetarized form and which, by this characteristic, renders resources more easily available and attainable in time and space (and increases therefore the global D & P). The only difference between "investment" in a loaf of

*R. Mueller-Wenk: *"Die oekologische Buchhaltung"*, Campus Verlag, Zuerich, 1979. The principles described in this book have been used to establish an "ecological audit" of a food company.

bread to be eaten within the space of ten minutes and "investment" in the purchase of a house, is the *duration* of utilization of the assets purchased. In the same line of thought by traditional standards a house which burns down in ten minutes after being purchased becomes "consumer" goods whereas a piece of bread bought to form part of a collection of different bread types becomes "durable" goods.

Money is then a tool to expand (or destroy) D & P and, as indicated in the paragraph of the "dialogue" dealing with "investment capital" its use should be developed to the extent that it *contributes* to human effort to expand D & P.

The problem of capital formation and mobilization does not exist *per se*, but only within a framework of defined (or implicit) goals — of natural and man-made constraints.

In the face of these limits and opportunities, enormous potential exists for improving the development and the use of the tool itself. This will be the subject of our study in Chapter 4.

3.3. Current Evidence of D & P and Capital Complementarity: The Dualities in the Economic System

In order to complete this analysis of wealth and welfare in their relation to monetarized and non-monetarized factors, we will examine in this paragraph various aspects of economic duality that point to the shortcomings of current-day economics in approaching economic problems exclusively from a monetarized angle. In this, attention will be drawn to qualitative differences between monetarized and non-monetarized economic activities and the duality *within* the monetarized system itself (i.e. the "official" and the "grey"* economy).

3.3.1. THE PREDOMINANCE OF THE MONETARIZED ECONOMIC SYSTEM: A RECENT DEVELOPMENT

Today, in the industrialized countries at least, the monetarized economic system has permeated all exchanges to such an extent that it is almost

---

*Also called "underground" or "dual" economy. See *L'Economie duale*, by J. J. Gershuny, Economie et Humanisme, Caluire, 1979, pp. 66–71.

impossible to imagine that any other type of economic system could have existed. Nevertheless, economic history provides ample proof that the monetarized economy has emerged as a predominant economic system only comparatively recently. Although specific figures are all too often lacking, numerous data exist to show the importance of the non-monetarized sector up until the nineteenth and even into the early twentieth century. In 1775, Adam Smith states that in one Scottish village "it is not infrequent to see the craftsman bring nails instead of money to baker and brewer".

In other regions of Europe at this time, barter was used extensively as a means of exchange. According to Fernand Braudel "Innumerable examples can be quoted: the Solingen cutlers, the miners, the Pforzheim weavers, the peasant clockmakers of the Black Forest, all paid in barter, with victuals, salt, cloth, brass wire, corn measures — all of which commodities were exorbitantly priced. This "barter system" prevailed in Germany, Holland, England and France. Even German Empire "officials", *a fortiori* the municipal ones, were paid partly in kind. And, as late as the last century, how many times were the schoolmasters remunerated with poultry, butter, corn!"[32]

Significantly, in 1791, Clavières and Brissot, well-known personalities of the French Revolution, wrote in their book on the United States: "instead of money, incessantly passing and re-passing through the same hands, direct barter is used as a reciprocal means of supplying the needs in country areas. Tailor and cobbler come to practise their trade in the home of the farmer, who very often provides them with the materials they need and pays for their wares in foodstuffs. This type of exchange extends to a multitude of commodities; parties inform each other in writing of what shall be given and received at the year's end, and thus a very small quantity of currency winds up a great number of transactions which in Europe would only be possible against a large amount of money ... an important means of money-less circulation has thus been established."[33]

In Japan, the monetarized economic system took root only during the seventeenth century, and in some countries, penetration of monetarization occurred even later ... for instance in Corsica not until after the First World War.

This does not mean that, at other times and in other places, money has not been a significant instrument of trade: Fernand Braudel relates that, during the Ming rule in China (1368–1644), silver mixed with antimony was the incentive to a monetary and capitalistic economy, but only for large-scale exchange.

Today, the ascendancy of the monetarized economic system follows several centuries of slow gestation during which the important role of small-scale agricultural and artisanal production is all too often over-shadowed by the priority most historians accord to the spectacular rise of large-scale industry during the first, and later, the second Industrial Revolutions. Nevertheless, the strength of these scattered but numerous, small-scale producers made a major contribution to economic wealth and D & P accumulation.

Thus, after depicting the contribution to general wealth of petty agriculture and craftsmanship in the Grenoble area – made up almost entirely of family businesses or farms – Le Roy Ladurie writes: "a combination of this type is characteristic of a certain growth, which can be defined as lower-middle-class and "non-soiling" and which is visible almost everywhere during the nineteenth century in European countries, more especially in meridional areas. Today, it is gradually disappearing . . . routed by the more "successful" feats of big capitalistic banks and industries which nowadays monopolize far too much of the limelight. And yet it is to this type of "petty" development, efficient and unassuming, that vast sections of modern humanity owe their infrastructure – in the Central and Mediterranean regions of France, in Italy and Spain . . . but not, of course, in smoke-logged areas such as Lancashire, where the "real" Industrial Revolution took place; however, only this latter is recognized by historians, because it gained supremacy in later years. The example of the country doctor gives the true measure of the artisan's progress towards modernization; he stands opposite to Germinal[34] . . . pain-filled epos of another type of growth."[35]

Thus Karl Marx's description of industrial capitalism anticipates by many years the disappearance of a sector economy where "plots, shops and workshops will survive as essential ingredients of Western economy until 1910 or even 1950 or later."[36]

The development of economic monetarization during the nineteenth and twentieth centuries should not obscure our vision of the long-term trend in which it evolves. The return to a subsistence economy, caused frequently by market shrinkage, alternates with a revival of the monetarized economy, which shows that the progression of the latter is a discontinuous process. Thus, "in agriculture: the development of capitalistic seigniorial and physiocratic farming (before 1789) shifted to a strong revival of peasant, family and plot farming and small-holdings, in the nineteenth century."[37]

Clearly, the latter is more conducive than the former to subsistence economy. It can also happen that, in the event of a sudden and short-lived monetarization of the economy, sectors of subsistence may exist side by side with sectors in the throes of monetary flux. Nevertheless, for example, "in the sixteenth century up to about 1560, Upper Normandy farmers were increasingly obliged to enter the market circuit, increase their crop yields and employ and pay a larger labour force. Although in some cases, international market pressures resulted in the introduction of certain crops, e.g. the vine in the Nantes area between 1550 and 1570, subsistence farming predominated in a rural area where 80% of the corn produced was consumed by the peasants who accounted for at least 85% of France's population at the end of the sixteenth century. Even in a country like France which was in the full throes of industrialization, certain areas of the economy were almost entirely untouched by monetarization."[38] Taking the example of Brittany in the nineteenth century, Le Roy Ladurie states "The nineteenth century in Brittany reminds me more of the twelfth century and the mass land-clearance that took place then, of parcelling out: of the burgeoning of family poly-cultivation, of the mass abolishment of fallow and waste land due uniquely to demographic growth, of the maintenance and even the expansion of a menial proletariat lodged on the premises, which accentuated the family aspect of soil cultivation, lastly, of the progression of small property ownership, to the detriment of land where "notice to quit" could be given, and of tenant farming, although this latter was more conducive to the growth of true agricultural capitalism."[38]

One of the main clues to monetarization of the economy is certainly the growth of the towns. Since money is used less in rural areas than in the towns, where industry, commerce and the civil service are predominantly located, the lack of currency is a major factor in the maintenance of a non-monetarized economic system. Emmanuel Le Roy Ladurie in discussing a rich country squire from the West of France states "... but these days, when money from America is oiling the cogs of the most highly commercialized sectors of the economy, a rich gentleman, the likes of our Squire, can never be short of money, certainly . . . at the most lacking "change". In his Journal, expressions similar to the one below occur repeatedly: "bought cloth in Cherbourg; did not pay for it for want of change . . . will pay on Monday."[39] According to Fernand Braudel, the situation was no better in Colonial America where monetary economy was a feature only in the large towns of mining countries such as Mexico and Peru.

Sometimes, currency was not available even in the towns: in 1721, a merchant from Philadelphia, unable to obtain financing because of the lack of means of payment, complained to his correspondent in Madeira that, for this reason, he had been unable to despatch a shipment of corn. That coin was rare in European rural areas as late as the nineteenth century is adequately demonstrated by the expedients resorted to by the rural population of France; Le Roy Ladurie states that, due to the practice of fostering out children, common between 1700 and 1850, "silver pieces made their way into even the humblest homes, which otherwise would only have had an economy of subsistence, hardly monetarized at all."[40]

The structure of property ownership has an importance that should not be underestimated since it may act as a brake or an accelerator to monetarization of the economy. The breakdown of the smallholding structure was an essential factor in the development of agrarian capitalism and the integration of the rural economy into national or international markets, as proved the case in England after the eighteenth century, when agrarian capitalism* reached its peak — i.e., following the take-over of the peasant's common land by the nobility and the conversion of arable land to pasturage. This was accompanied by expropriation of smallholder farmers who following the abolition of serfdom at the end of the sixteenth century had gradually constituted the large majority of the rural population.

Another important factor conditioning the monetarization of the economic system is, of course, the slowness with which attitudes and behaviour are modified.

*In the section entitled "The dual economy and development" (section 3.3.4), we shall illustrate the close link between the evolution of agrarian structures and different forms of income which, in turn, correspond to different forms of economy: the non-monetarized, semi-monetarized and monetarized.

Even after the Bank of France was founded in 1801, the notes it issued evoked practically no interest at all in provincial areas. As late as 1752, David Hume writes of "this new invention, paper money", although the Bank of England had been issuing notes since 1694.

Even today, when monetarization seems to dominate most forms of exchange, we must realize that the adoption of this phenomenon has been gradual, discontinuous and irregular. However, is the non-monetarized economic system today no more than a relic of times past? If islets or even whole areas of activity resist and escape monetarization, should not an effort at least be made to estimate their contribution to individual welfare? The need is all the more acute when we realize that monetarization has its limits and covers only part of the tools contributing to the production of wealth and welfare. Moreover, there is an optimum level of monetarization which, if exceeded, can produce deducted values.

Our intention is not, of course, to propose a return to a barter economy but rather to stimulate recognition of the value of that segment of the economy that is not apparent in the monetarized exchange system.

In theory the need for such recognition may seem self evident; however, in practice it is not the case. Books about money deal only essentially with the history of money and almost *never* with the economic system's *transition* to monetarization.

3.3.2. THE PERSISTENCE OF NON-MONETARIZED ECONOMIC ACTIVITIES IN ADVANCED INDUSTRIAL COUNTRIES

(a) Some examples. Superficial examination may suggest that in the advanced industrial countries monetarization has permeated throughout the entire fabric of the private and public sectors of the economy. However, the "D sector" which overlaps with and extends beyond the non-monetarized sector and has been defined by Yona Friedman[41] as the part of the "non-active" population which performs a socially useful task — albeit not included in the Gross National Product (GNP) — is a major component of economic and social relations, both as a stimulator of the latter and an indicator of social well-being. Let us list some of the related activities which immediately spring to mind.*

*See also: "Le Tiers-Secteur non Marchand", *Recherche Sociale*, N. 67, Paris, July–Sept. 1979.

The usefulness and indispensability of domestic work cannot be denied. The housewife's* many-sided activities have an important bearing on the physical and mental equilibrium of the members of the family circle. If it were possible to determine and measure the importance of domestic work in relation to all the factors that most influence "production" efficiency, it would most certainly prove one of the most decisive. Even when it is recognized and sometimes evaluated,** this socially useful activity never figures in official economic tables.

Is not auto-consumption a relic of the agricultural economy, in which it was normal practice? It is certainly true in the case of farmers who, in almost every instance, consume some part, at least, of their own produce. Even in the cereal and wine-growing regions, the farmer will almost always have a kitchen-garden or small orchard to supply his needs of fruit and vegetables. Many town dwellers have an allotment which provides both indirect income and leisure activity.

These examples reveal that the non-monetarized sector still exists as an economic force and also that conventional indices (e.g. GNP) are not an adequate measure of social well-being.

Is the non-monetarized sector likely to spread or will it die, will it progress or regress? Does its subsequent development depend on political trends or is it, in fact, maintained by economic and social forces, which even help it thrive and expand?

Yona Friedman believes a subsequent extension to the "modernized D sector"*** to be essential based on the fact that, currently, with the slackening in industrial and agricultural growth rates, increased instability, persistent inflation, maladjustment of monetary mechanisms, rising bankruptcy, and the difficulties experienced by more and more sectors of

---

*On the social consequences of the subdivision of the economy into monetarized and non-monetarized activities and its effect on the marginalization of women, age and social minorities and even "ecologists" see Hazel Henderson "The Coming of the Solar Age", *Resurgence*, Vol. 10, N. 2, August 1979, pp. 6–9 and E. Dodson Gray: *Why the Green Nigger*, Wellesley (Massachusetts), 1979.

**The Liberty life insurance company has calculated that, in Great Britain, the cost of replacing a woman working at home and looking after two young children was £90 a week – and even more in London (£114.80).

***Yona Friedman's D sector is wider than the non-monetarized sector since, by definition, it does not exclude moonlighting.

The "modernized D sector" would then cover both monetarized and non-monetarized activities.

the economy, governments are impeded in the efficient implementation of their programmes.

One of the most significant cases in the non-monetarized system is for the unemployed to undertake additional activities in their competence: producing part of the family food, household maintenance (fixing a leaky gutter or a faulty electrical installation), offering services to a neighbour in exchange for fruit, vegetables, or . . . gratitude. All such measures contribute to reconciling a relative shortage of money with the maintenance of a standard of living . . . and habits formed during unemployment may persist when employment is found. Craft work may come within the non-monetarized system if part of the payment is effected in kind. In view of the persistent unemployment in the majority of industrialized countries, the non-monetarized sector would with advantage, make up for the loss of paid jobs, thus contributing, at least partially, to the avoidance of a drastic reduction in living standards. In this connection, a reduction in working hours could possibly be beneficial in two ways: by reducing unemployment; and by giving individuals the time to earn additional non-monetary income.*

These cases are comparable to efforts to obtain partial freedom from the constraints of monetarization – in particular that of having to exercise a paid activity – since such a trend offers the possibility of individual subsistence living – a situation which is now being taken more seriously and is sufficiently rooted in the past for it not to be ascribed to a purely passing fad.**

(b) The diminishing returns of monetarization. In examining the persistence of the non-monetarized sector in advanced industrial countries, one might conclude that although not negligible, this sector is still marginal and assumes importance only in exceptional circumstances such as war.

---

*At the general economic level, serious consideration should be given to the adjustment of other constraints such as the cost of working, on the one hand, and the cost of unemployment on the other.

**It is paradoxical to note in some cases how advanced technology even favours some new developments of barter trade: "The Electronic Rebirth of Bartering". The computer in fact does help information storage and distribution for goods and services exchanged without the use of money (*Business Week*, September 19, 1979, p. 108).

In fact, the monetarization process may also be subject to its own law of diminishing returns. Increased monetarization was essential for the Industrial Revolution; however, is such an increase always positive, or may it also be subject to the law of diminishing or even negative returns and consequently have an overall negative effect even in *purely* material terms?

Accepting that wealth and welfare are derived from D & P and utilization value, it may be profitable to reflect on some current, typical manifestations of advanced "monetarized" countries.

Take first the cost of eating. We can buy the products and prepare them ourselves — the work of lunch preparation being a "non-monetarized", "do-it-yourself" activity. At a restaurant or cafeteria, the meal costs more owing in part to the paid work of those employed there. Thus "free" or "non-monetarized" work has been replaced by monetarized work. There has been no increase in D & P (unless the meal we prepare is very bad in comparison with that offered by the restaurant — although the opposite may apply); non-remunerated work has been substituted by remunerated one. The monetarized component of D & P has, of course, increased (increased GNP) but without necessarily any change in the total real wealth. It is admitted that there is normally a gain in specialization and any economist would immediately identify this.

Let us now take a step further: with the development and concentration of the catering industry, diminishing returns may become apparent. To maintain the monetary system (i.e. to ensure no *monetary* loss), restaurants are obliged to hold down costs, especially those of labour. Labour costs can be reduced by technology offering new cooking and washing processes of real utilization value. However, subsequently costs can often be controlled only by *retransferring* at least a part of the effort to the *non-monetarized* sector e.g. by requiring the client to service the meal himself. The goal of monetarized equilibrium becomes dissociated from an increase in *total* real wealth.

The health sector provides an even more dramatic example. Hospital costs are skyrocketing, not merely as a result of increased equipment and treatment costs but also because hospitals are now less of a community service organization (with a large voluntary benevolent infrastructure) and more a monetarized machine. If today, hospitals are financially often in worse shape than restaurants, it is because they cannot retransfer costs to the non-monetarized sector as easily as can restaurants. Current trends to health care decentralization and domiciliary care constitute a clear indication that recourse is being had to the "non-monetarized" sector.

These two examples show once more that the monetarized and the non-monetarized systems are intricately interrelated. If we do not measure the real increase of total utilization value, we subject ourselves to the monetarized system's partial logic which is illusory especially when the monetarized system needs increasingly disguised "subsidization" by the non-monetarized system. Promotion of "Do-it-yourself" is therefore not just a way of getting people to do more with their hands but often also an outcome of the need to maximize transfer from the "monetarized" to the non-monetarized sector in order to maintain monetary profits. It is not a question of whether "do-it-yourself" is good or bad but of which *combination* of monetarized and non-monetarized activities produces *more* real utilization value. Monitoring the balance between the monetarized and the non-monetarized activities is an important procedure in organizing wealth and in avoiding the negative returns of monetarization, that occur when a single tool becomes identified with the overall goal.

New types of accounting should be used to identify and to stimulate the non-monetarized system's contribution to real global wealth's increase.

(c) Stimulating the non-monetary sector. Expansion of the non-monetarized sector *does not* imply exclusion of the monetarized sector, but rather its coordination. Economic policy might thus be aimed at providing more opportunity for both monetarized *and* non-monetarized production.

In view of the continuing rise in unemployment in the industrialized countries, it might be possible *to offer new occupations* rather than to *create new jobs,* in particular activities in the social sector, where the public's needs are far from being satisfied: help for the elderly, day-nurseries, cultural activities, etc. This cannot, however, be done benevolently unless individuals have the wherewithall to meet their basic needs.

A more liberal approach to authorizations and permits would encourage the appearance of new "small trades" and the proliferation of old ones, the latter being conducive to non-monetary trading. There would be a deliberate policy of encouraging "monetarized" investment in non-monetarized occupations and production.

Certain services could also be developed if, for example, everyone was given elementary medical instruction for the detection and prevention of certain common diseases,* etc., or the technical know-how needed to repair a washing machine or a motor-car; the principle being to augment utilization value by transforming certain monetarized costs into self-produced or self-managed "no-cost" activities.

Non-monetarized sector development naturally implies some modification to the tax system: this is dealt with in the next dossier.

Extension of the non-monetarized sector depends not only on co-operation between State authorities and the public, but also on a change in individual and collective behaviour; currently, food product or consumer goods accumulation is considered an indication of social status, and monetary income is considered, rightly or wrongly, as the most certain means of achieving this objective. The example of social groups initiating non-monetarized activities would, no doubt, be the best stimulus to accomplishing this behavioural change.

World-wide discussion of the concept of value would probably help and encourage this cultural adaptation. Even though the individual and the community are often practically confronted with real deducted values, attitudes and behaviour will not change all the while if they are seen simply as a transient malfunctioning of the traditional — but still "right" — way to consider wealth and welfare. We are in a period in which it might be useful to "recognize" what our real interests are.

Recognizing and searching for our Dowry and Patrimony, both locally and worldwide, as our real basis of wealth and welfare will produce practical actions to increase them, at both the material** and non-material level.

---

*No doubt it is in China that this type of medicine — the barefoot doctor — has been encouraged the most. Why should it not be possible to achieve in the industrialized countries the successful results obtained by a semi-industrial country, even at the expense of certain adaptations?

**French forests are a good example of how the non-monetarized "material" sector could be extended. France has a total forest area equal to that of all the other Common Market countries together, but is unable to meet its own timber needs. Annual wood imports amount to several billion francs. This is due partly to the abandonment of the forest by those who previously tended it: woodcutters, resin-collectors etc., and is marked by the encroachment of brushwood and the gradual disappearance of forest-groves, which are much more suitable for industrial purposes. It might perhaps be possible to plan tree-felling and subsequent reforestation on a non-monetary basis. Taxation in kind might be ideally applicable to reforestation. Similarly, forest-oriented jobs could be re-established, e.g. resin-collection, etc.

3.3.3. THE GREY ECONOMY

Current discussion of the contradictions within the economy centres, in general, on another problem: the existence of economic dualism within the monetarized system itself — the phenomenon of the "underground" or "grey economy". This phenomenon affects activities in the monetarized sector but appears only partially or not at all in national accounts. The reasons behind it are varied but most often linked with tax evasion.

In certain countries, the grey economy is so extensive and so dynamic that it may be considered to indicate the monetarized economy's need to have growing recourse to this type of disguised subsidy in order to maintain itself as the dominant economic system.

How important is the grey economy?

Peter Gutmann, Professor at Baruch College, University of New York, has estimated that, in the USA, the grey economy accounted for US $176,000 million in 1976 and to US $195,000 in 1977,[42] i.e. somewhat more than 10% of the official GNP.

No comparable figures are available for France but the Government estimates that 25% of French workers have a second, undeclared job.

In Italy, the "grey economy" is said to involve 2 million workers — over 10% of the total labour force — and the rhythm is accelerating.[43] ...

The phenomenon is universal, regardless of its name: "fiddling" in England; "travail au noir" in France; "Schwarzarbeit" in Federal Germany; "hidden income" in Japan; "second economy" in the USSR. . . .

In the United States, economists have tried to identify and evaluate the sources of the "grey economy". In *Business Week,* Seymour Zucker[44] added to undeclared wages, the undeclared income of self-employed persons, their income from letting, profits of small companies and interest on undeclared income. . . . He obtained a figure of US $100,000 million. In addition, income from illegal activities should not be underestimated: dealing in drugs, prostitution and gambling (the latter being all the more important because of its public acceptance) probably amounts to US $150,000 million. Similar figures have been advanced elsewhere, for example by James Henry in *The Washington Monthly* (May 1976).*

*Obviously no figures are available for the Eastern bloc countries, but the "grey economy" is just as thriving there as in the Western countries. In Czechoslovakia, for example, a large proportion of the economically active population does a second day's work after the legal working hours.

Who contributes to the maintenance and expansion of this "grey economy"?

Almost all social categories are involved: agriculturists, office employees, manual workers, self-employed persons. In general, anyone who receives cash in payment of a transaction can participate in the "grey economy", and this covers a wide range of activities: retailing, personal services, casual or part-time work, illegal or quasi-legal activities. . . .

The dynamic nature of the "grey economy" owes more, it would seem, to the large numbe. of workers who hold one or more undeclared jobs in addition to their declared occupation, than it does to practice of one or more illegal activities. According to Peter Gutmann, even if the latter were to account for 10% of those contributing to the maintenance of the "grey economy", the official unemployment statistics in the USA should be corrected downward and 820,000 units be added to the number of economically active persons. Moreover, the official figure should be viewed with caution since the authorities have an interest in underestimating the volume of "moonlighting" in order to prevent voluntary payment of taxes being adversely affected by the truth about tax evasion.

Do any indicators exist for evaluating the "grey economy"?

Peter Gutmann proposes observation of movements in two components of M_1 money supply figures, i.e. money in circulation and current accounts.

Up to the end of the Second World War, the historical trend was towards the amount of money in circulation to be small in comparison with the amount in current accounts. In 1892, for each US $1000 deposited in current accounts, US $352 remained in circulation; in 1941, the corresponding figures were US $1000 and US $219 and, by the end of the Second World War, US $1000 and US $363. The earlier decline in extra-bank monetary circulation has been followed by an opposite trend which has continued regularly since 1961. By December 1976, the volume of extra-bank monetary circulation had risen to approximately US $380.68 per person.* It is believed that some of this liquidity goes to sustain the flow of undeclared income and "moonlighting", i.e. a veritable under-

---

*There are two other explanations for the strong growth of money in circulation. The first attributes to the increase in interest rates the displacement of demand deposits to time deposits. The second sees technical innovations as the cause of the reduction in current accounts – e.g. RPs (a type of corporate lending where a company's demand deposits are lent overnight or longer and the demand deposits thus do not appear in Government demand deposit statistics).

ground economy which escapes all taxation and is substantially ignored. Of the US $77,800 million circulating outside the banking system, US $28,700 million are said to be channelled into the "grey economy", enabling US $200,000 million worth of goods and services to be produced.*

Some economists question the value of this indicator. For example Philip Cagan of the University of Columbia states, "But the estimates that you get this way are only suggestive. You can't pinpoint the amount of cash that should be outstanding and then conclude the residual is due to the subterranean economy". Cagan gives the example of liquid money sent abroad.

Let us consider some of the causes of the "underground economy".

The "underground economy" is alleged to be the direct result of income tax, of the complexity and growing burden of the tax system in general, and of limitations affecting the access of specific social groups to legal jobs (foreigners, for example) and prohibitions on certain activities. Its existence is bound up with the impossibility of procuring certain goods or services by other means or with the fact that they are too expensive. Without claiming to be exhaustive, mention may be made of ever higher income taxes and consumer taxes (VAT in Western Europe is a good example) which encourage payments in cash in order to avoid taxes, and the repetition of such payments as often as possible in order to circumvent the statutory tax procedures. Social security beneficiaries whose earnings potential is limited, retired persons and pensioners may also have recourse to the "grey economy". Three factors have a more decisive effect in the medium- and long-term because they indicate that a turning-point has, perhaps, been reached which threatens the equilibrium of the entire political and economic system in Western societies at least: the acceleration in the operating expenses of the State apparatus; inflation which reduces the individual's real income and obliges him to take refuge in the "grey economy"; and the political concept of income redistribution which seems less and less to be a significant preoccupation for the individual.

What are the remedies for the "grey economy"?

The size of the present study must necessarily limit our ambitions in this respect, and we must confine ourselves to indicating some paths that might be followed for further research.

*See the table on the importance of the "grey economy" in the United States, on p. 238.

Taxpayers, today, too often have the feeling that the number of those who pay considerably exceeds the number of those who benefit.* An effective income redistribution policy should, it would seem, increase the number of beneficiaries without diluting the benefits. This would be achieved by concentrating, for example, on services likely to provide advantages for the greatest number: social services, assistance — in the form of subsidies — for the purchase of sites intended for producer co-operatives. Such an approach might, moreover, considerably expand the monetarized economy. In any case, an accounting of effects on the D & P would be essential.

State bureaucracy absorbs an ever growing volume of tax revenue and this excessive growth of the State apparatus is not unrelated to the taxpayer's reticence or refusal to pay his taxes. Decentralization would provide a remedy to the extent that it led to the creation, closer to the citizen, of civil-service posts occupied on a rotation basis, with everyone becoming a citizen-administrator in turn. Moreover, it could be desirable for wage-earning to be replaced gradually and partially by honorary work.

The complexity of tax declaration forms is one of the reasons why people resort to the "grey economy", and consequently simplification of these forms would be a way of not discouraging the goodwill of taxpayers.

The tax system is a blocking factor for social mobility when it becomes a brake on the improvement of social status. Reducing income taxes at all levels encourages social mobility at the upper level. Increasing death duties, taxation on gifts intervivos promotes social mobility at the lower level.

The growing rejection of the way in which society is organized is leading to a monetarized economy which tends to resist all regulation. A manifestation of the monetarized economy, the "grey economy" is working clandestinely towards ensuring its survival as the dominant economic system. Thus, it is not an exaggeration to regard the "grey economy" as a form of disguised subsidy to the legal economy. The remedies mentioned above may correct this deviant behaviour; however, are not more radical changes necessary and why should not the non-monetarized economy provide the inspiration?

The "grey economy" is a phenomenon of sufficient importance that it

*Particularly if payments are in "real" value and if benefits include a larger and larger portion of "deducted" values.

TABLE 3.5. *Importance of the "Grey Economy" in the USA*

| | | 1937–41 | 1976 = M_1 | = % = GNP | |
				(billions)	(billions)
Currency	Illegal	0%	12.7%	$ 28.7 9.4%	$ 176.–
	Legal	21.7%	21.7%	$ 49.1 ⎫	
Demand deposits		100%	100%	$226.2 ⎭ 90.6%	$1.693.–
Total				$304.0 100%	$1.869

(a) The amount of currency required for legal transactions in 1976 is assumed to be the same percentage of demand deposits as in 1937–41. The amount of currency required for subterranean transactions is obtained by subtraction.

(b) The amount of GNP lubricated by one dollar of M_1 — whether currency or demand deposits — is assumed to be the same for both legal and subterranean activities.

Source: *Across the board*, Vol. XV, No. 8, August 1978.

perceptibly affects the true state of the entire economy; in certain cases, it is probably more effective than the measures some governments take to "strengthen the economy" or handle a crisis. It also reveals the limits of the official action in economic policy. Consideration must be given to both the "non-monetarized" and the "underground" economies if a realistic picture is to be obtained of the true economic situation.

3.3.4. THE DUAL ECONOMY AND DEVELOPMENT

Whereas in the industrialized countries, the monetarized economy has absorbed a greater part of the production and distribution of goods and services, in the Third World countries, the non-monetarized economy is still the predominant economic system.

In a study of agricultural workers' incomes in Central and East Africa,[45] J. Freyssinet and A. Mounier identified three main forms of the organization of production and exchange: the self-sufficient economy; the small-trade* production economy; and the plantation economy.

The first is characterized by the absence of trading within the social group: family, tribe, ethnic group, etc. and the direct sharing of the

*It must be clear that "trade", in this research means strictly monetarized exchange.

product among its members. The small-trade production economy is based on sale-orientated crops, side by side with the production of foodstuffs which continue to fulfil main needs and generate income in kind as opposed to monetary income. In the plantation economy, the income issues from trade and assumes monetary form. Even here, autoconsumption based on food production is appreciable.

None of these three forms of economy are pure or exclusive: inter-penetration takes place in various ways and monetarized and non-monetarized sectors co-exist within each other.*

How should this co-existence and its development in time be evaluated? The best method is by application of a criterion reflecting the rate of transition of the economy from one of subsistence to one of exchange, from a non-monetarized to a monetarized economy, the downswing of the one and the upswing of the other. This criterion is the structure of income. In the determination of its components, both kind and money, the latter represents one measure among others, since agricultural workers also take into account direct utilities and costs.

Thus measurement of the actual quantities produced or consumed is better suited to the autoconsumption or trade-in-kind and to social obligations as regards gifts. Human effort involved in acquiring goods or services is a better reference for comparing the level of arduous labour with the utility value that this effort confers on the goods and services in question.

Income is defined by Freyssinet and Mounier as being "the total material assets and services at the disposal of an economic agent to satisfy his needs, either by immediate consumption or by the extension of his patrimony".

The stress placed here on the finality of income, its determination and distribution would be incomprehensible without a knowledge of the mechanisms of solidarity — i.e. the customary system of transfer employed by the individual in his adherence to a specific social group** — which ensure group cohesion.

*François Perroux has noted recently: "Everything pushes us to make a deeper analysis of what exists beyond and under the market (monetarized) economy.... The new development makes economic thinking younger", in *Le Monde*, Paris, October 9, 1979, p. 21.

**Gifts and taxes pertaining to ritual festivities or family celebrations at births, weddings and deaths.

Is a reduction of the non-monetarized sector desirable? Is it possible? This last question is bound up with an examination of the expansion factors of the monetarized sector and of the resistance factors of the non-monetarized sector.

The expansion factors of the monetarized sector include:

— easier communication tends to expand trade zones, leads to dealing in new commodities and generates a demand for a general equivalent.

— in numerous Third World countries, during the harvest period the peasant may have difficulty in making ends meet and consequently appeals outside the group to an agent with monetary savings.

— the trade economy uses bush commerce channels to introduce products manufactured in rural zones. Demonstration creates demand which encourages seasonal and even permanent migration to stable, salaried work.[46] What is the impact of this migratory movement on the traditional economy? The monetarization it generates would seem to favour the breakdown of traditional social structures. However, experience shows that cash inflow can also act as an "oxygen balloon" providing protection against external disruptive influences.*

The role of the State in reducing the non-monetarized sector should not be underestimated. In Central and East African territories, over 30% of State resources originate from taxes levied on the product of agricultural activity. Since export-oriented crops are the sole important currency generators, it is feared that the State will encourage the development of big plantations to the detriment of the self-consumption sector.**

One sign of this trend is the replacement of bush commerce by public commerce offices which are directly opposed to the dispersion of production locations and accelerate the shift from a subsistence to a plantation economy.

Some authorities believe that the non-monetarized sector has such resistance factors that a big monetarized sector should not be expected to emerge in the foreseeable future. Progressive replacement of non-monetary by monetary circuits does not necessarily result in de-structuri-

*Resistance to external disruptive influences probably depends on the quantity and density of the solidarity networks that ensure group cohesion.

**The fear is a very real one since this policy does, in fact, lead to a reduction in the farmer's disposable income. Monetary income increases but overall income decreases because monetary income does not compensate for the resultant shortage of foodstuffs for local consumption.

zation of the traditional environment, at least not in the short or medium term.

Robert Badoin claims that this duality, far from weakening the existing system, infuses it with new creativity and vigour. We would not go as far as this but, nevertheless, admit that customs, hierarchies and structures can be absorbed and beneficially assimilated. Contrary to today's most prevalent theories, increased income would not necessarily lead to additional productive effort: as soon as the customary needs have been fulfilled, productive effort often loses its object.

This has been the experience in Senegal, where those who introduced harnessed tillage have increased the income; however, surplus income has not been invested in new production facilities but rather squandered on enhancing the splendour of ritual festivities and on offering more valuable gifts to religious chiefs.* In Senegal, the act of saving does not have the same significance as in an industrialized economy; it is subordinate to the logic of the traditional system which possesses a rationality of its own. The concept of D & P is based on different cultural values.

Can it be said that a reduction of the traditional sector is desirable? Yes, if economic development is thereby favoured, as depicted by Arthur Lewis[47] and Barber.[48] The theories of these two authors run on the following lines.

According to Lewis, the labour supply in the modern sectors of the economy is generated by its relationship with the traditional economy. Proceeding from a marginalist concept, he shows that, as marginal productivity is weak or non-existent in the traditional spheres of economic activity, and high in the modern sectors, the pay level in the latter spheres depends not on the difference in productivity but on the difference between the average incomes in the two spheres. The difference necessary for a population shift from the traditional to the modern sectors is estimated by Lewis at 50%. Until the traditional economy has been demolished by complete resorption of the traditional sectors, this afflux of cheap labour will support the international competitivity of Third World

*However, one cannot definitely state that the lower the needs, the quicker the labour offer starts to decline; generalization of this behaviour would generate the reversal of the desired effect, i.e., the higher the income, the lower the productive effort. It should be remembered that no mechanism is absolute and that other factors may intervene to counteract the above pehnomenon. The effect of demonstration is certainly not the least influential.

countries in relation to industrialized countries, where, says Lewis, dualism (i.e. the antagonism between traditional and modern economy) has disappeared.*

Barber's theory, essentially the same, corrects Lewis on one point: traditional forms of activity are not reduced to the point of extinction; when modern forms extend beyond a certain point, the traditional sector is reduced through slow conversion. He estimates that if the manning of the traditional system were reduced by 50%, the human resources necessary for it to function properly would no longer be available and that a transformation of the agricultural system through the introduction of harnessed tillage and fertilizer would then become inevitable.

However, to procure the means of increased production it is necessary to buy, and buying . . . means selling!

Though it is true to say that low salaries are an important factor in the industrial competitivity of Third World countries and that the average incomes in the traditional sectors partly determine the salaries in the modern sectors of the economy, Lewis' theory can be criticized on several heads: it is based on an assumption and implies two hypotheses. The assumption is the comparison of income in the modern and traditional sectors on a monetary basis. The study by T. Freyssinet and A. Mounier advises the greatest caution in this respect: the estimation of income by the sole means of a monetary criterion is not sufficient in economic systems which are still largely non-monetarized; other criteria are required here: the physical quantities produced and consumed, the human effort involved. . . .

The two implied hypotheses are the abusive faith in the absorption capacity of the modern sector and the prejudice about the structural weakness of the traditional sector. In fact, demographic growth** and the

---

*This theory has been developed partially in "The Theory of Economic Growth" and more systematically in Lewis' article "Economic Development with Unlimited Supplies of Labour".

**The population growth rate in African countries is reckoned to be in the region of 2.3% to 2.5%, and the population doubles from one generation to the next. Today the under-fifteen age-group represents approximately 45% of the total population.

A disastrous consequence of the demographic increase is the unbounded growth of numerous Third World towns, which is characterized more by slum accumulation than by the construction of areas providing decent living conditions. Concentration-linked industrialization clearly induces the production of relevant "deducted values".

too frequent choice of capital intensive techniques* in Third World countries set a double limit, objective and subjective, to the modern sector's absorption capacity. Moreover, we have stressed the recuperative powers of the traditional sector, and its effects should not be minimized, at least in the initial stage of monetarization of the economy.

Barber's theory is more convincing. It gives a truer reflection of the effects of monetarization: a slow and discontinuous process which leaves large, non-monetarized sectors intact. Hence the structure of income as defined by Freyssinet and Monier becomes an excellent criterion whereby to judge the real economic trend and estimate the degree of interpenetration of monetarized and non-monetarized sectors.

The monetarization of agricultural incomes renders farmers more and more dependent on their productive effort when this is accompanied by the replacement of foodstuff cultivation for subsistence by large-scale plantation crops. The latter, grown for export, submit farmers' incomes to exogenous factors over which the farmers themselves have no control.

We have enumerated some of the factors which, in Third World countries, hinder the absorption of agricultural labour by capital-intensive industries. Extensive farming and agrobusiness, based on agricultural mechanization also seem to be unsuitable for absorbing an appreciable portion of the population from the non-monetarized sector.

Normally, the agriculture of small-trade production or of plantation farming does not seem to be generated by a transformation of the traditional system: rather they are merely grafted onto the traditional system since the peasant does not develop such innovations unless they can co-exist with self-sufficient production. This attitude is justified by the labour supply made available by the agricultural cycle and by the low practical efficiency of modern systems. Commercial practices also have an important effect. "The price of groundnuts, in husk and seed is highest at the beginning of the farming cycle, when the peasant is unwilling to

---

*The choice of capital-intensive techniques could be considered reasonable if the profits were and could be locally re-invested so as to have a diffusive effect which would encourage the implantation of processing industries. This process has already started in some Third World countries – some oil-producing Arab States are a case in point – but it is still too rare for other development alternatives to be desirable. A policy of income distribution' deliberately aimed at creating a vast *domestic* market would still be the best vector for monetarization of the economy.

part with his produce. The price falls by half after the first harvest and declines progressively the nearer the approach of the trading period; the peasant who decided to sell part of his harvest at lower prices a few weeks before the trading season only does so when in dire straits. The merchant is well aware of this and uses it to lower the prices."[49]

Thus the shortcomings of self-sufficient production would not be compensated by a monetary income, which, in the same way as income in kind from the non-monetarized sector, appears to be more a complementary income of subsistence than one of accumulation.

All these factors combine in favour of maintaining a large non-monetarized sector in Third World countries, in the most of which it may remain the predominant sector for some considerable time to come.

Even though the non-monetarized sector must be considered with care in the framework of any development policy, it does not mean, of course, that monetarization of the economy is undesirable. The current indebtedness of Third World countries illustrates, though, the dangers inherent in a mass appeal to outside monetarized savings, not to mention the fact that savings formation and utilization are strictly related to cultural pattern.

A UNESCO report observes the important relation between savings and their "squandering" (in light of western economic rationality) on religious and family festivities, in some Third World countries.

"The sums spent on different ceremonies represent, in rural areas in India, 7.2% of the income per inhabitant. An even more significant figure reveals that, if the money spent in these areas on wedding and funeral ceremonies were used to acquire productive goods, it would swell the total investments by 50%. . . ."

"The money spent by one family in the course of its existence on wedding and funeral ceremonies represents approximately one fifth of the total non-renewable spendings."[50]

On the other hand, taking into account monetarized and non-monetarized saving, accumulation in low-income countries is underestimated.*

Real saving is, in fact, effected by accumulation of durable goods, non-monetary circuits here being considered by economic agents as a

---

*Simon Kuznets claims that the share of savings in the national product is much higher than in the developed economies, *Economic Development and Cultural Change*, July, 1960.

means of protection against wastage, when the latter is stimulated by liquid assets. The monetarization of the economy, therefore, also runs the risk in certain cases of generating increased consumption rather than the growth of the mobilizable real savings potential. Such forms of behaviour, which normally escape macroeconomic analysis, are absolutely rational on the microeconomic scale. Nevertheless, the classical economic concepts make it impossible to comprehend the behaviour of economic agents in Third World countries.

G. Abraham-Frois[51] provides a good example in this context when he observes that if savings are a function of the liquidity preference, it is not because the economic agents save more the higher they are paid, but because of their tendency to transform the structure of their assets. Seen in this light, the interest rate would not be the price of savings, but that of renouncement of net assets, or more precisely, the price of conversion of non-mobilizable real assets into mobilizable financial assets, i.e. the price of the conversion of treasury to capital.

Once more, wealth is a question of a well balanced Dowry and Patrimony.

Bibliography

1. GEORGESCU-ROEGEN, N.: *op. cit.*
2. DE ROSNAY, Joël: *Le Macroscope, op. cit.*
3. JACOB, François: *La logique du vivant, une histoire de l'hérédité,* Paris, 1970, p. 171.
4. JACOB, François: *op. cit.,* p. 238.
5. JACOB, François: *op. cit.,* p. 245.
6. JACQUARD, Albert: *Eloge de la différence, la génétique et les hommes,* Paris, 1978, p. 51.
7. MALINOWSKI, Bronislaw: *Une théorie scientifique de la culture,* Paris, 1968, p. 114.
8. GOLDENWEISER, A. A.: *Early civilization. An introduction to anthropology,* London, 1923.
9. PREISWERK, Roy: *Relations interculturelles et développement,* Paris, 1975.
10. ZIMMERMANN, Erich: *World resources and industries,* New York, 1933. In this important work, the difference between effectively available resources and unusable resources is fundamental.
11. O'TOOLE, James; and the University of Southern California Centre for Future Research, *Energy and social change,* M.I.T., Boston, Mass., 1976.
12. The example of the Aswan dam is cited by HAWKINS, CLARK, DARBY and RAFF in their book *The evolving earth, a text in physical geology,* New York, 1978, p. 473.

13. On the more general question of diminishing returns of technology in agriculture, see also *The Worldwatch Papers,* 1977–78, Washington D.C.
14. SEE, James A.: *News and views from the World Bank Report,* July/August, Washington D.C. 1978.
15. AGARWAL, Anil: "Malaria makes a Comeback", *New Scientist,* February 2, 1978, pp. 274–277.
16. *Prospective et Santé,* No. 7, p. 115: "La dégradation de la biosphère".
17. McNAMARA, Robert: "Address to the Board of Governors", World Bank, Washington D.C. September 1975.
18. Report of the Director-General of the International Labour Office: "*Employment, growth and basic needs: A one-world problem*". International Labour Office, Geneva, 1976, p. 21 and 22.
19. ROSTOW, W. W.: *The stages of economic growth,* Cambridge, 1960.
20. LEWIS, Oscar: *Les enfants de Sanchez,* Paris, 1963, p. 31.
21. LEWIS, Oscar: *op. cit.,* p. 31.
22. TEVOEDJRE, A.: *Poverty, the wealth of people,* Oxford – New York, 1978.
23. GIARINI, Orio and LOUBERGE, Henri: *The diminishing returns of technology, op. cit.* page 77–79.
24. DE JOUVENEL, Bertrand: "L'économie politique de la gratuité", dans "Arcadie, Essais sur le Mieux-Vivre", *Futuribles,* 1957.
25. DE JOUVENEL, Bertrand: "Organisation du travail et aménagement de l'existence", 1958, dans "Arcadie, Essais sur le Mieux-Vivre", *Futuribles,* 9, 1968;
26. CORNIERE, Paul: "Vers une comptabilité du patrimoine naturel", *Futuribles,* No. 18, Novembre–Décembre 1978, p. 733.
27. DE JOUVENEL, Bertrand: "Proposition à la commission des comptes de la nation", 6.5. 1966, dans "Arcadie, Essais sur le Mieux-Vivre".
28. CORNIERE, Paul: "Vers une comptabilité du patrimoine naturel", *Futuribles,* No. 18, Novembre-Décembre 1978, p. 733.
29. NORDHAUS, William, TOBIN, James: "Is Growth obsolete",*Economic Growth,* (Fiftieth Anniversary Colloquium V), National Bureau of Economic Research, New York, 1972.
29a. Among various studies and books referring to this subject see:
   • the studies on social accounting by the United Nations.
   • *Social accounting* by Lee SEIDLER and Lynn SEIDLER, Los Angeles, 1975.
   • DELORS, Jacques: *Les indicateurs sociaux,* Paris, 1971.
   • *Societal accounting,* by Trevor GAMBLING, G. Allen & Unwin, 1974.
30. GRANT, James P.: *Targeting progress in meeting basic needs,* Overseas Development Council, Washington, internal paper 1978.
31. TIMBERGEN, Jan: *Reshaping the international order,* a report to the Club of Rome, New York, 1976.
32. BRAUDEL, Fernand: *Civilisation matérielle,* p. 340 (Material Civilization) Paris, 1967.
33. CLAVIERES et BRISSOT: "*De la France et des Etats-Unis*", Londres 1787.
34. ZOLA, Emile: *Germinal,* Paris, Various Editions.
35. LADURIE, Emmanuel le Roy: *Le territoire de l'historien,* p. 196–197, Volume IV, Paris, 1973.
36. LADURIE, Emmanuel Le Roy: *op. cit.,* p. 197.
37. LADURIE, Emmanuel Le Roy: *op. cit.,* p. 445.
38. LADURIE, Emmanuel Le Roy: *op. cit.,* p. 261.

39. LADURIE, Emmanuel Le Roy: *op. cit.,* Volume I, p. 195–196.

40. LADURIE, Emmanuel Le Roy: *op. cit.,* Volume II, p. 181, 182.

41. FRIEDMAN, Yona: "The D. sector of the economy", *Futuribles,* No. 15, May/June, 1978.

42. GUTMANN, Peter: *Off the books, across the board,* Vol. XV, No. 8, August, 1978.

43. "The fast growth of the underground economy", in *Business Week,* 13 March, 1978.

44. Economics Editor of *Business Week.*

45. FREYSSINET, J. and MOUNIER, A.: *The incomes of agricultural workers in eastern central Africa,* International Labour Office, 1975.

46. DIOP, A.: *Société Toucouleur et migration,* IFAN, Dakar, 1969.

47. Cited in the article by BADOUIN, Robert: "La réduction du dualisme; l'example de l'Afrique Noire" p. 17 et suivantes, in the book *Structures traditionnelles et développement,* de Maxence Petit-Pont, Edit. Eyrolles, Paris, 1968.

48. BADOUIN, Robert: *idem.*

49. ROCHETEAU: "Pionniers mourides au Sénégal" (ORSTOM, Dakar, 1969), cité par J. Freyssinet *et al.,* Mounier, A dans *Les revenus des travailleurs agricoles en Afrique centrale et occidentale,* ILO Genève, 1975.

50. LAMBERT, R. D. and HOSELETZ, Bert F. (Eds.): *Rôle de l'épargne intérieure et de la richesse en Asie du Sud-Est,* UNESCO, Paris, 1963.

51. ABRAHAM-FROIS, G.: "Epargne, intérêt et sous-développement économique", taken from *Structures traditionnelles et développement* by Maxence Petit-Pont; Editions Eyrolles, Paris, 1968.

CHAPTER 4

Dossier for an Analysis of the Monetarized Accumulation of Dowry and Patrimony (D & P): Some Issues in World Capital Formation and Needs

> Je ne dirai pas de mal de nos outils.
> Mais je les voudrais utilisables.
>
> I shall not speak ill of our tools.
> But I would want them to be usable.
>   Denis de Rougemont
>   (Penser avec les mains)

"It is obvious that the present-day world is witnessing a drastic acceleration in the pace of history: it is equally obvious that our financial machinery and systems are bound to be affected by these radical changes. Nevertheless, I am convinced, especially now that our experience extends over several decades, that we are still treating financial matters in accordance with conventional concepts whereas there are other forces at work which are more dynamic than our current monetary and financial parameters. In my view, analysis of the problem is hampered by the fact that short and medium-term financial policies, whether international or national, are in the hands of experts whose opinions are hard to contradict. This is a field which the social sciences, with their more comprehensive approach, normally avoid."

"The current theory and machinery of finance, more than any other

248

aspect of development, is unmistakably 'Western' in character. In view of the world-wide crisis in concepts of development in relation to other cultural models (Islamic, Hindu, Chinese, etc.), it is quite conceivable that in this respect also, we shall witness changes resulting from the reactions of what has been called 'cultural identity'."

"My personal experience is that there is a real crisis in the financing of international operations. One only has to observe the debates on the budget of any international organization. This is completely absurd when one thinks that mankind is spending a billion dollars a day on armaments."

". . . Would it not be advisable to accept the need for a new stage to ensure that public international financing machinery is at least equal to its task? . . . This report should state not only how much is required but also its purpose."

These statements are from Dr. Felipe Herrera* and they fit particularly well within the outlook proposed by this overall report. In the three previous Chapters, we have tried to show how the process of accumulating and using money is integrated in a much wider sphere – physical, natural, cultural – which inter-reacts with the monetarized world – and this to such an extent, that the inter-reactions become *the* essential explanatory factor, particularly in periods of diminishing returns of technology.

A further consequence of considering capital as a monetarized part of D & P is that – as we have seen in Chapter 3 – it becomes much clearer that capital accumulation is a means, a tool, used for the purpose of producing wealth and welfare. It cannot be confused, even "in practice", with the goal, since – being a tool – it may help not only to achieve goals but also to destroy them.

4.1. The Determination of World Capital Requirements

This report has been drafted under the assumption that the primary goal of economic activity is to increase wealth and welfare. It recognizes that wealth and welfare, in order to be defined, require an agreement on the definition of value. It recognizes furthermore that the concept of value is not unique and that no one exclusive definition can be universally

*Seminar organized by the Spanish Chapter of the Club of Rome in Granada, October 1978, on the prolematique discussed in the present Report.

accepted: moreover, the fact that the definition of value is different in different parts of the world is a value in itself.

Within this frame, the role of money and, in particular, the role of capital (accumulated money) is to contribute to the increase of wealth and welfare, by making it possible through monetarization, to better mobilize "real" resources in time and space. In such a way, resources can "increase", because they are made available more easily (and at less effort).

Table 1.4. in Chapter 1, section 1.4. shows the shift from a simple world where mankind uses only his body as a tool, to a world where the tools are contrived (machines, domesticated animals, etc.), and to the modern world where money is a new way to organize tools. The same Table proposes the idea that there is an *optimum* balance between the amounts of labour, tools and capital which contribute to produce wealth and welfare *together*. This optimum varies according to human technological constraints.

In Chapter 3 and, in particular, in Sections 3.2. and 3.3. an attempt was made to explain that this optimum balance depends on the relationship between all economic activities, whether they are monetarized or *not*.

In Chapter 2, and, in particular, in Section 2.2., an effort was made to establish a very close link between the process of monetarization and of that type of technology developed by the First and, even more so, by the Second Industrial Revolution.

One might now ask how far "capital formation" is necessary to increase the wealth and welfare of the world.

Attempts may be made to give an "objective" answer, but this answer can never be of the "as-much-as-possible" type: the limit is reached when the monetarization has the effect of decreasing the total utilization value of D & P instead of increasing it. Subsequently, in Chapter 3, it was proposed that specific indicators be used to monitor this situation.

There is also a subjective approach defining the amount of "capital formation": this depends on expectations of the future yields of *total* D & P. If there is evidence, or at least a hint, that monetarized investment will produce higher real yields, there will be greater incentive to save money than to acquire "intangible" assets (e.g. the learning of a foreign language which can be carried out during "free time" that might otherwise be sold).*

*See note opposite.

In practice, this means that, once monetarized investments are desirable enough for a community, this perception will motivate the necessary monetarized investment. The problem is one of time required for adjustment and of adequacy of stimulus, motivation and technical ability to attain specific goals. In most cases, "inadequacy" of capital investment depends on:

· the time needed to adapt savings attitudes to investment goals (often defined as "necessities"): this gives rise to short or medium term fluctuations in capital availability (shortage or excess situations)
· the fact that capital "necessities" (which are in fact goals) do not correspond to social perception
· the need to develop resource utilization and, in particular, technology.

The first two factors are rather subjective conditions: the first can be overcome by better functioning of the financial intermediation systems; the second depends on the recognition of the need to optimize monetarized *and* non-monetarized efforts.

The third is more of an objective condition, linked to the real returns of technology. As mentioned in previous Chapters, when technology has diminishing real returns, the overall need for capital investment diminishes.** This can be observed currently in many industrialized

---

*This reasoning is in line with the modern theory of money, as elaborated by J. R. Hicks, J. Tobin and M. Friedman: factors determining the demand for money are the same as those determining demand for any other asset — financial, physical or human capital. This means that the optimum quantity of an asset depends on the analysis or perception of the economic agent (a person or an institution) who tends to optimize his "portfolio", towards a maximum yield of all assets together.
We quite agree with such analysis (which derives from the subjective notion of value as we have seen in Chapter 2) under a certain number of conditions.
— First, the notion of assets must include all that we have defined as monetarized and non-monetarized economic values: this means that the optimization will never be adequately achieved by monetarized standards only;
— Second, it should be acknowledged that such subjective analysis depends on the fact that it is done at point 2 of Figure 3.8., where the decisions on the types of means (point 3) are taken. Such decisions are then also filtered by objective phenomena which depend on natural, cultural, and technological constraints and their inter-reactions. In other words, one cannot dispense with objective conditions of value formation, as the neo-classical notion of value tends to do.
**Many cases of "demand saturation" are of this type. It is not real demand for better welfare or for more wealth which is saturated. It is the utilization value of products and services offered (including their monetarized and non-monetarized characteristics), which is close to zero.

countries where the real cost of capital (the real rate of interest, after deduction of the inflation rate) is extremely low and investments are "inadequate". The inadequacy is not simply a matter of investors' subjective "expectations", but rather negative feedbacks of experience of the real returns of new technology in the last decade.

The problem of world capital needs and formation is primarily one of defining *desirable* and *possible* objectives. Mobilization, collection and utilization of monetarized savings depend on a clear consensus as to the desirability of the goals. Bankers often say that a really good project will always find money; we would add that a really good project is the one that adds to real wealth and welfare, and increases D & P with the help of the "monetarized" economic system, provided it integrates well with the "non-monetarized" one.

4.1.1. GLOBAL PROJECTIONS OF CAPITAL NEEDS

It is first necessary to emphasize that the defining of capital needs is subordinate to the definition of goals.

As stressed in Chapter 3, indicators should be used first to determine the levels of real wealth (monetarized and non-monetarized) to attain. The synergy between the monetarized and the non-monetarized system should then be analyzed and monitored. Only then, is it possible to introduce monetarized indicators and the logic and strategy of monetarized-system management.

Most general analyses of capital needs follow a different pattern, which was summarized in Chapter 1, Section 1.3. (page 14): increased wealth depends on increased industrialization and therefore on absolute and relative increases in investment, as shown by "past evidence". Therefore, the future is essentially an extrapolation of the past, with very little scope for modifications.

4.1.1.1. The Leontieff scenarios[1]

The United Nations study carried out by Leontieff, is a typical example of the current approach to economic problems, which assumes that wealth and welfare is best aimed at in terms of national income. The value paradigm is the value-added discussed in Chapter 2.

Goal-setting is presented in a number of different scenarios.

The following table indicates the expectations for growth rates and shares of world gross domestic product, by region, for the period 1970–2000.

TABLE 4.1. *Regional GDP (1970–2000)*

Region	Average annual growth rate (percentage)	Regional GDP as a percentage of world GDP	
		1970	2000
Developed market		66.1	50.9
North America	3.3	32.9	21.0
Western Europe (high-income)	3.7	22.6	16.7
Japan	4.9	6.2	6.5
Oceania	4.5	1.3	1.2
Southern Africa	7.5	0.5	1.1
Western Europe (medium-income)	7.0	2.3	4.4
Developed centrally planned		18.6	20.7
Soviet Union	5.2	13.5	15.4
East European	4.9	5.1	5.3
Developing market		11.1	22.0
Latin America (medium-income)	7.1	3.5	6.9
Latin America (low-income)	7.2	1.2	2.5
Middle East	9.0	1.1	4.0
Asia (low-income)	6.7	3.8	6.6
Africa (arid)	5.5	0.8	1.0
Africa (tropical)	6.5	0.7	1.0
Developing centrally planned	6.3	4.2	6.4
Developing as a whole, including Asia (centrally planned)	7.2	13.3	28.4

This would imply the changes in gross fixed investment, including both private and public investment, shown on p. 254 (Table 4.2).

The report states clearly that: "The extent of the increase of the investment ratio is largely determined by the growth rate of GDP. Growth rates of 4–6% can be accomplished with an investment ratio of about 20%: growth rates of 7–8% to investment ratios of about 30%, while sustained

TABLE 4.2. *Gross Fixed Investment as percentage of GDP (1970–2000)*

Region	1970 %	2000 %
Latin America (medium-income)	20	33
Latin America (low-income)	17	31
Middle East	20	41
Asia (low-income)	15	21
Africa (arid)	15	20
Africa (tropical)	15	21

growth rates of 10% or more cannot be accomplished unless the investment ratio goes up to 40%."

The reader might wish to refer to the Leontieff Report which contains various interesting analyses and indications that cannot be summarized here. It can be accepted that the investment figures presented above might constitute a rule of thumb in this context: it is reasonable to expect, in the modern world, that total monetarized investment will tend to oscillate between 18 and 30% of GDP and that, with some intuition and practical knowledge of a specific country and of a specific situation, one can give an overall figure for the total amount of monetarized investment which is or should be envisaged. However, it is also clear that the strategy suggested by our report is based on rather different assumptions and value paradigms.

The first is that goals should be defined by appropriate indicators — GDP figures can only be indicators of part of the costs involved in achieving the given goals — they cannot be considered goals in themselves. GDP accounting deals with the means to an end — not the end itself.

Secondly, we do not share the assumption that the more the use of "modern" technology (through capital investment), the faster the rise in GDP (taken as a measure of wealth). From the discussion in our previous Chapters, it is obvious that an attempt should be made to achieve a monetarized investment *optimum* (given the relevant cultural, environmental and technological constraints) rather than adopt, in models, a mode of thought which would lead to the "inevitable" but absurd conclusion that the highest growth rate would be achieved if *all* the GDP were to be invested. We are, here, clearly in the heaven and hell paradox mentioned in Chapter 1.

4.1.1.2. The World Bank scenarios[2]

The scenarios the World Bank has proposed for the developing countries are as follows:

TABLE 4.3. *Growth rates of GDP, 1975–1985*

	Average annual percentage growth rates, 1975–85		
	Base scenario	Low growth scenario	High growth scenario
GDP*			
Developing Countries	5.7	5.2	6.1
Low Income Countries	5.0	4.8	5.1
Middle Income Countries	5.9	5.3	6.3
Gross Investment	5.3	4.4	5.7
Low Income Countries	6.5	5.8	6.7
Middle Income Countries	5.1	4.2	5.6
Imports	5.6	4.8	6.5
Low Income Countries	5.7	4.8	6.3
Middle Income Countries	5.6	4.9	6.5

*For developed countries, the global annual growth estimate is 4.2%.

It should be noted that, in 1975, gross domestic investment was between 19% and 26.4% of GDP and, according to such scenarios, these rates are not likely to change very much in 1985.

An important aspect is, of course, the contribution from foreign sources to investment in developing countries. This aspect will be considered in greater detail in Section 3.

4.1.1.3. The Bariloche Foundation Study (A. Herrera)[3]

This study defines the goal as that of satisfying the basic needs of mankind, considered as "invariable needs, because they exist in every human being, independently from their being a specific culture, origin, race or sex". But it is clear that "the concept of invariable basic needs is linked to the needs as such and not to the way of satisfying them, by means of different cultural methods, available means, historical developments. . . ."

Having said that, the study goes back to the traditional economic method of monitoring wealth by the indicator of national income. Thus, the cultural tool of the Industrial Revolution is taken as such to define the rates of growth (in national income) necessary to satisfy basic needs, as shown in the following table.

TABLE 4.4. *Rate of Growth by the Year 2000*

	Rate of growth between 1966 and 1970	Rates of growth needed in order to satisfy basic needs in the year 2000
North America	4.5	5.3
South America (more developed part)	5.3	9.9
South America (less developed part)	5.2	10.5
Western Europe (developed)	4.6	5.7
Europe (less developed)	6.7	7.9
Soviet Union	7.0	4.1
Eastern Europe	5.7	3.4
Japan	10.6	5.9
Far East and India	5.3	10.5
Middle East (oil countries)	8.5	10.4
Africa (more developed part)	4.1	11.5
Africa (less developed part)	5.1	11.8
South Africa	6.0	12.8
Australia/New Zealand	4.9	5.6
China	4.4	no indication

Consequently, no real attempt is made to determine, by means of a coherent set of indicators, the real level of wealth, the possible contribution of investment, under specific conditions, in increasing value-added, and the effects of deducted value.

The investments which go together with such scenarios are based on two assumptions. The first (a) the "normal" development of technological progress, and the second, (b) the "diminishing" returns of technological progress starting in the year 2000 (and affecting projections up to 2060).

This implies:

TABLE 4.5. *GNP Growth*: Developed Countries*

		1960	1980	2000	2020	2040	2060
(a)	GNP *per capita*	1402	2962	4778	5984	7512	9470
	Investment rate (% of GNP)	21.6	25	11.9	10.2	9.2	8.1
(b)	GNP *per capita*	1402	2755	3966	5156	6291	7676
	Investment rate (% of GNP)	20.6	23.16	29.14	28.11	32.9	39.85

TABLE 4.6. *GNP Growth: Latin America*

		1960	1980	2000	2020	2040	2060
(a)	GNP *per capita*	.372	.530	1107	2247	3822	5746
	Investment rate (% of GNP)	18.3	21.2	25	25	25	25
(b)	GNP *per capita*	371.8	489.1	688.7	.901	1050	1173
	Investment rate (% of GNP)	18.2	20.78	25	25	25	25

TABLE 4.7. *GNP Growth: Africa*

		1960	1980	2000	2020	2040	2060
(a)	GNP *per capita*	.137	.167	.387	.911	1728	2657
	Investment rate (% of GNP)	15.1	16.7	25	25	25	25

		1960	1980	2000	2010	2020	2030
(b)	GNP *per capita*	136.9	157.3	184.4	186.7	133	109.8
	Investment rate (% of GNP)	15.1	16.47	20.36	20.01	5.02	5.08

TABLE 4.8. *GNP Growth: Asia*

		1960	1980	2000	2020	2040	2060
(a)	GNP *per capita*	89.7	135.6	262.8	450.7	707.3	
	Investment rate (% of GNP)	16	17	25	25	25	

		1960	1980	2000	2010	2020	2030
(b)	GNP *per capita*	89.7	126.5	150.5	153.1	114	89.23
	Investment rate (% of GNP)	16	16.63	25	23.64	10.72	6.39

All these tables reveal what we would call fundamentally a hidden assumption, or an intuitive rule of thumb, which is roughly consistent with the figures of the previous studies and which leads to the conclusion: investment should be or tend to be around 25% of GNP.

This model also takes into account the hypothesis of the diminishing returns of technology, but only for the year 2000. This is just about the opposite type of hypothesis that would be considered in our report.

Furthermore, a technology which produces diminishing returns would be considered disastrous by the Bariloche model in terms of bridging the world's wealth and welfare gap. On the one hand, the developed countries would be obliged to invest more, on the assumption that higher investments are needed to compensate for technology's lower productivity: the history of the Industrial Revolution shows that in practice the opposite is the case. On the other hand, technology that produces diminishing returns is assumed to cause trouble for the rest of the world. Here too, the opposite is probably happening: it is precisely because the increased levels of technology cannot be pursued in developed countries at the same rates of return as in 1947–1970, that investment in developing countries has tended to be accelerated* as a result of not only the financial changes that have occurred since 1973, but also of the drive to find investment locations and situations in which the diminishing returns of modern

*See the summary report of Prof. José Ramon Lasuen at the Colloquium on Intercontinental Financial Cooperation in the 1980s (Madrid, November 1979), published by Instituto de Cooperación Intercontinental (Madrid).

technology are unlikely to produce the type of constraints encountered in developed countries.

Once again, we are compelled to propose that investment be defined and practiced in a way that takes into account the *indicators* of wealth, an optimization between monetarized and non-monetarized economic activity and utilization value.

This does not mean that a monetarized investment of 20–25% would not eventually be desirable: it does mean, though, that it would be used more efficiently and fruitfully within the frame of the analysis proposed in previous dossiers.

4.1.1.4. Sectorial projections: The UNIDO* Model

The UNIDO study on world investment needs was carried out using the following target: the UNIDO Second General Conference in March 1975, adopted the Lima Declaration and Plan of Action, proposing that the developing countries' share of world industrial production should be increased from 7% in 1975 to 25% by the year 2000. The study itself is based on the LIDO (Lima Industrial Development Objective) Model, which uses a set of conditional scenarios of manufacturing input.

The total investments projected by the LIDO model for the year 2000 (in billions of constant 1972 dollars) are shown in Table 4.9.

TABLE 4.9. *Investment projections by world region*

Africa	123.73
Asia	327.71
Latin America	725.60
Middle East	171.10
Total developing countries	1348.14
Industrialized countries	2093.76
World Total	3441.90

Source: LIDO Model (UNIDO, mimeo, May 16, 1973)

*United Nations Industrial Development Organization.

It is projected that, in the developing countries, 36% of total investment will go into manufacturing as compared to a figure of 46% for the
developed countries. This would mean a doubling of the investment going
to industry in the developing countries in 1972 as shown in Table 4.10.

This, of course, presupposes a definition of *industrial* investment and
that can, in practice, be solved case by case. However, considering the
changing structures of the economy, as discussed in Chapter 2 — it would
perhaps be useful to verify the consistency and practical use of the
definition of the "industrial" sector.

In any case, the developing countries' projected manufacturing investment of 491.9 billion dollars, in the year 2000 is about 17% of manufactured output in the same year. The corresponding figure for industrialized countries would be slightly over 10%.

TABLE 4.10. *Growth of Investment for Industry in
Developing Countries*

(1972 constant $ billion)	1972	1985	2000	Annual rate of growth (%)
Total developing countries' investment	82.1	300.5	1348.1	10.5
Manufacturing investment	14.6	71.5	491.9	13.0
Manufacturing investment as percentage of total investment	18.0	24.0	36.5	

4.1.1.5. The regional projections: the ECE and UNCTAD Studies

Mention should also be made of studies done by various regional organizations of the United Nations, whose work on future economic development necessarily implies forecasting of capital needs.

The European Commission for Europe[4] has forecast economic development up to 1990 and states that "the spectacular growth of the 1950's and
1960's is likely to give way to a slow-down of overall growth rates both in
market and centrally planned economies during the period to 1990".

In our view, widespread slow-down is a consequence of the diminishing-returns cycle described in Chapter 2.

The ECE ascribes this slow-down to:

(a) diminishing labour supplies in centrally planned economies and labour excess in the market economies;

(b) capital requirements which are likely to grow in most countries as compared with output in general. It is stated that "This is mainly due to the growing need for investment to be carried out in sectors with low returns such as energy, basic products, agriculture, infrastructure, improvement of environment, housing, etc.", which is another way of admitting a situation of diminishing returns of technology;

(c) energy and basic products growing scarcer and/or relatively expensive – which confirms our last comment.

In terms of capital requirements, the investment ratio (to GDP) is as follows:

TABLE 4.11. *Investment Ratios in Europe 1953–1990*

| | | | 1990 | |
	1953	1973	Scenario A	Scenario B
North Europe	19.9	23.6	22.8	22.6
West Europe	17.8	23.9	21.5	21.6
South Europe	16.8	27.3	27.5	25.7

This demonstrates a very cautious approach, consisting in forecasting for 1990 a capital needs situation comparable to the present one.

The United Nations Conference on Trade and Development (UNCTAD) also produces studies on economic development and capital needs in developing countries.* A growth objective of 6.4% of GDP is set for the period 1974–1980 for Africa, South and East Asia and of 6.8% for Latin America. The calculation of capital needs for 1980 varies according to the different growth rates taken into account for the economies of the OECD countries which are supposed to grow by 4.8% per year. If growth in the

*See for instance "Commercial perspectives and capital needs of developing countries, 1976–80", UNCTAD, Geneva 1976, and "Measures of development efforts", UNCTAD, Geneva, 1978.

OECD area is 1% lower than the projected 4.8%, this would mean an increase of 12 billion dollar investments for the non-oil-producing developing countries (if growth were 1% higher, there would be 9 billion dollars less investment).

For the period 1975–1980, the developing countries would need a net external contribution to investment of 65 billion dollars per year (at 1975 prices) against an effective availability in 1975 of 43 billion.

These figures are consistent, in their order of magnitude, with those in the UNIDO study. The specific point made by UNCTAD concerns the poorest developing countries: "for a large number of them, the pro capita income – in real value – in 1980 will probably be lower than in 1973". Consequently, in our view, it is even more urgent to achieve an immediate real increase in wealth and welfare by stimulating the contribution of the non-monetarized local economy and to control any step towards monetarization.

4.1.2. THE GEOGRAPHICAL EXTENSION OF INVESTMENT AND THE DISSEMINATION OF THE INDUSTRIAL REVOLUTION

UNCTADs analysis that slower growth in the OECD countries may be

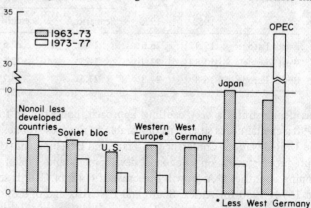

FIG. 4.1. *Annual Percent Change in Real Gross National Product*

Source: U.S. State Dept., Organization for Economic Cooperation & Development. U.N. Economic & Social Affairs Dept., BW estimate

combined with more rapid development in the developing countries, has been confirmed by recent experience.

An article in *Business Week** stated: "Since OPEC price hike, overall economic growth has slowed down relatively little in LDCs" (Fig. 4.1, p. 262).

Specific events such as the acceleration of industrialization in China are adding impulse to this movement. *Business Week,* again, talks of the "start of a 350 billion dollar march".**

As noted in Chapter 2, the tide of worldwide industrialization is there: this is an additional reason for stimulating a worldwide strategy on wealth creation, based on a new, pluralistic notion of values.

4.1.3. STUDIES ON CAPITAL NEEDS IN THE UNITED STATES

In the last decade, the economic debate on capital requirements has been an important one in the United States and has resulted in a multitude of studies at different levels. Mention should first be made of the studies by Edward Denison of the Brookings Institution on the contribution of capital to the postwar growth of industrial countries.[5] These are an important contribution to the study of the role of capital in economic growth, within what we would call the traditional paradigm. It is interesting, for the purpose of our present Report, to note Dr. Denison's statement that "The years 1974 and 1975 witnessed (in the United States) a sharp and rare decline in NIPPE (national income per person employed in the non-residential business sector). Although part of the decline was attributable to the recession with which it coincided, most was not. In 1976, NIPPE increased, but only about as much as is usual in a cyclical recovery of the 1976 magnitude. As a result NIPPE is *much lower* than it would have been *if the past trend had continued.*"

Of this drop of 3.3 points (by Denison's measurements) 1.6 points are specifically allocated (for instance, to pollution abatement and crime prevention — which by the way, in our terminology, are deducted-value costs). He continues: "A drop of 2.1% points appears in the residual series for advances in knowledge and not elsewhere classified. . . . Why this sudden change? My investigation does not say. Some writers suggest that advances in knowledge have contributed less to recent growth, either

**Business Week,* 24 July, 1978.
***Business Week,* 6 November, 1978.

as a delayed reaction to the end, in the mid-sixties, of the previous long rise in R and D spending or due to a mere happenstance that important new developments have not come along recently". He then prefers to leave "much of the drop unexplained" as he feels that the "sudden impact in 1974 should have appeared gradually if linked to basic changes in the advancement of knowledge".

Our comment here is to take the example of a rope which, by reason of its elasticity can be subjected to increasing tensile stress for some time before it suddenly breaks under the strain:* the long term cycle of the diminishing returns of technology can, as indicated in Chapter 2, be counterbalanced by shorter-term compensatory movements, even at the technological level. The tension released in 1973–74 had, in fact, been accumulating since the middle sixties at the latest. Furthermore, we are not sure that the precise effect of delays and transition-times between fundamental research, applied research, development technology and utilization is adequately measured in *any* current economic model or analysis.

It is, in any case, significant that the problem is now more and more coming to the surface as many other studies and articles show: Peter Clark speaks of "extraordinary productivity downturn" in the United States in 1973–75.[6] Michael McCarthy advances the hypothesis that "New technologies which are energy intensive may also have become obsolete before they were introduced. Because of this, the rate of introduction of new technologies may have temporarily (Ed.: why temporarily? . . .) slowed."[7]

The question of the diminishing returns of technology is then coming to the surface in different ways. However, before it could start to be linked with capital requirements and investment problems, the discussion, in the United States as to the adequacy of investment in the economy had already been going on for some time.

In 1975, the Brookings Institution had issued a study entitled Capital Needs in the Seventies,[8] which concluded that "Capital needs – though large – will be manageable in an expanding economy with a growing capacity to supply savings".

---

*The very low price of energy until 1973, and excessive expectations engendered by the "promise" of even cheaper energy from nuclear reactors, have helped to conceal the problem for a while.

The Council of Economic Advisers, under the direction of Beatrice Vaccara, had produced in 1975 a report for the US Department of Commerce,[9] which was also based on the normally accepted economic paradigms. It assumes fixed coefficients of production and a model which is moved from the demand side. It leads to the conclusion that, in 1980, in order to meet the needs of a full-employment economy and the requirements for pollution abatement and for decreasing dependence of foreign sources of petroleum, private investment needs to total 11.4% of the periods 1965–1970 and 1971–1974".

This need for an increase in the share of GNP devoted to investment is attributed to:

"(a) technologies in sectors where the capital/output ratios have been increasing;

(b) investments in petroleum mining and other industries resulting from the energy situation; and

(c) pollution abatement."

The report states further "If it were not for these factors, the 1971–1980 cumulative investment requirements would total only 9.9% of GNP". Of these three factors, the third is a deducted value resulting from the negative returns of technology, the second is an admission that new technology does not compensate enough for geographical, political and physical constraints, the first one means diminishing returns of technology, when more money has to be invested in order to get the same benefits. In this latter case, further study is required to determine whether the increase of capital per unit of output is in fact an indicator of diminishing productivity, which would then lead to *reducing* the demand for capital instead of increasing it. This is a very basic issue: on the one hand over recent years in the United States there has been wide discussion about capital inadequacy and the capital crunch;[10] on the other hand, the experience, at least to date (October 1979) has been one of capital excess, in both the United States and most other industrialized countries where the problem for many governments has been more to stimulate the absorption of available finance, rather than the other way around.*

*For an evaluation of the controversy about "capital shortages", see also: Arnold Sametz and Paul Wachtel. "Understanding capital markets, Volume 2: The financial environment and the flow of funds in the next decade." Lexington, Massachusetts, 1977.

Most research centres in the United States have studied the question of capital availability and requirements, and a comparison of these studies carried out by the Stanford Research Institute[11] is given in Table 4.12.

We can observe from this Table how, in three cases, a specific capital shortage is foreseen. More of a consensus can be found on the point that gross private domestic investment during 1976–1985 will probably exceed the average level of the last 20 years. In our view, it is necessary to determine the extent to which this is more an effect of increasing deducted values than of net added values.

The problem of capital requirements has also attracted the attention of the United States Congress, whose Joint Economic Committee has sponsored extensive research on long-term economic growth leading to the publication of a number of reports over the last three years. One of these, by Carl Madden,[12] was referred to in our Introduction and has been a major reference and inspiration for our own report.

4.1.4. THE GROWING FINANCIAL NEEDS OF THE LARGE-SCALE PROJECTS

Specific projects or products in advanced technology are often characterized by huge investment requirements.

Several types of "machine" have already passed the billion dollar barrier, e.g. nucleus reactors, estimated (in 1978) at 1.5 billion dollars for 1000 MW capacity.[13] The biggest North Sea oil rigs also cost around 1 billion dollars. A plant for efficiently producing synthetic gas from coal costs about 1.2 billion dollars.[14]

We have become accustomed to reading statements such as that recently issued by the civil aircraft transportation industry at the end of 1978,[15] that some 80–90 billion dollars worth of aircraft will have to be purchased by the end of the 1980s. One company alone, United Airlines, envisages buying 9 billion dollars worth of civil aircraft.

A Chase Manhattan Bank study has forecast that the rising cost of new oil sources will have an impact on the investment needed. From 1966 to 1975, the oil industry invested 272 billion dollars (of which 118 billion were for prospection and production); between 1976 and 1985, it expected to invest a further 900 billion dollars (470 billion for prospection and production and the rest for refineries and transport).

TABLE 4.12. *Comparison of Investment and Saving Forecasts*

	Historical	SRI[a]		NYSE	Chase Bank	Brookings	DRI	Chase Econometrics	General Electric
Time period	1955–74	1976–85		1974–85	1975–85	1973–80	1975–85	1975–84	1974–85
Assumed or projected real GNP growth (per cent)	3.4	3.8	3.5	3.6	—	4.3	4.5	3.6	3.2
		(As a percentage of GNP)							
Nonresidential fixed investment	10.0	11.2	10.9	12.1	14.9	11.6	10.6	10.6	12.3
Change in business inventories	0.9	0.8	0.8	0.3	0.4	0.9	0.7	0.7	0.7
Residential construction	4.2	4.0	3.8	4.0	3.7	3.3	4.0	3.1	3.5
Total Investment	15.1	16.0	15.5	16.4	19.0	15.8	15.3	14.4	16.5
Personal saving	4.6	5.0	5.2	4.0	4.5	4.9	5.4	6.2	4.8
Business saving	11.2	10.7	11.0	10.7	9.6	10.2	11.0	10.2	11.2
Government saving	−0.4	−1.4	−0.7	−0.6	−0.7	0.2	−0.8	−2.0	0.1
Net foreign inflows	−0.2	0	0	0	0	0.3	−0.2	0.1	0.3
Total Saving	15.2	14.3	15.5	14.1	13.4	15.6	15.4	14.5	16.4
Capital shortage	—	1.7	—	2.4	5.6	—	—	—	—

[a]The first column presents the average of the independent projections. The second column presents the average of the reconciled projections.

Notes: Saving and investment may differ slightly due to statistical discrepancy. "Capital shortage" equals the difference between saving and investment when each has been projected independently. This table is derived from material presented in "Capital Shortages: Myth or Reality?", *Journal of Finance*, May 1976, and "Investment Requirements and Financing: 1975–1985," National Bureau of Economic Research, October 1975.

SRI   – Stanford Research Institute
NYSE – New York Stock Exchange
DRI   – Data Resources Inc.

The cost of bringing the oil resources of Prudhoe Bay in Alaska into production is estimated at 11—12 billion dollars, in view of the very delicate and vulnerable transportation system.

Assuming a 10% inflation rate, dividend, debt reimbursement and other financial costs, the oil industry is expected to drain off a total of 1345 billion dollars of investment for the period 1976—1985.

The Grigg Field and St Fergus Gas Terminal II in Scotland were first estimated at 700 million pounds sterling but finally proved to cost 2 billion pounds.[16]

The construction of huge dams in Brazil (several times the size of the Aswan dam in Egypt), will cost several tens of billions of dollars.

By comparison, in 1977, Switzerland's total GNP was about 63 billion dollars; and there are still 67 countries with a total national income of under 10 billion dollars,[17] of which 27 are under 1 billion dollar mark (either the very small and/or the very poor).

The problem, of course, is to know how much is too much (as well as sometimes also how much is too little): one way of measuring it is the cost of all the deducted values, including direct and indirect vulnerabilities.

The 64,000 dollar question is then: does the cost of such "big projects" indicate that we need more and more investment capital or — quite the contrary — are they indicative of greater financial uncertainty and finally of *less* total capital needs? The answer depends essentially on the assessment of their utilization value.

4.1.5. INVESTMENT AND COST OF DEDUCTED VALUES

Over recent decades, the notions of risk and vulnerability have undergone fundamental change, as a result of the structural modifications of the industrial system.

Whereas modern technology has become very efficient, it has also become — paradoxically — increasingly vulnerable, as was discussed in Chapter 2.

The frequency of accidents has often decreased, but their amplitude has increased, to such an extent that a single accident may constitute a catastrophe. The fact that catastrophes are rare but may occur immediately or only in 50 years time, adds to the uncertainty: from an actuarial point of view, this becomes in practice an uncontrollable risk, normal insurance becomes inoperable and huge sums of money have to be invested to try to reduce the accident incidence to zero.

This type of risk, linked with increased vulnerability, have grown so important that industry is increasingly involved in "risk management" which deals precisely with these new dimensions of vulnerability. Twenty years ago, the main concern of most companies was to develop new technologies, find new markets and improve financial techniques: today, a major task is preventing and controlling the vulnerability of a machine or process, the indirect effects of an accident to the production process[19] or, finally, the undesirable effects of a product.[20]

Although the incidence of any *single type* of risk has diminished, the number of different fields in which widespread damage and catastrophes can occur has multiplied. The thesis has been advanced that the specialization of risks has impaired their manageability, and increased the *total* probability of widespread damage and catastrophes occurring.[21] This means not only that there is a trend towards greater vulnerability and uncertainty for industry (clear evidence of the diminishing real returns of technology): this situation also has negative effects on the work of service industries, such as insurance in intervening and coping fully with the development. The situation becomes self-evident when many projects and investments exceed the limits of insurability. The result is a kind of indirect nationalization of certain typical insurance activities when governments intervene for technical reasons related to the level and severity of the risks to be covered. "The principal impediment (to obtaining sufficient capital for huge, new investments) stems from the necessity . . . to expand new sources and new technology at rates that are far riskier than private investors alone can accept. The solution lies in using the government's capacity to assume or alleviate a major part of extraordinary risks."[22]

Government intervention such as this, in substitution of normal mechanism for risk taking and risk protection, can be justified in terms of national policy: the only trouble is that if more and more sectors enter the category of "intolerable" risks, they will simply be placed in a single basket — the government one — which finally, becoming a sort of reinsurer of last resort, will itself be in the most vulnerable situation. The tendency is therefore to pile up engagements against natural catastrophes (and an earthquake in Tokyo today, could cost more than 200 billion dollars), protection for nuclear power stations and help for pollution disasters, including contributions for different types of social security — the system directly concerned with individual vulnerabilities.

This complex growth of vulnerability is central to the question of capital needs and should stimulate study of this problem not in terms of past ratios between economic growth and investment, but in terms of optimal control of risks, particularly where increasing vulnerability gives way to evident deducted values and, therefore, to a diminished real wealth.

It is within this framework that we can consider also investments for pollution control and abatement. Many official studies have already been done in this field.[23]

Many of the models and studies on capital needs and requirements now take into consideration such expenditures. In Leontieff's study for the United Nations, the current costs of pollution abatement are calculated at much less than 1% of GDP for all countries in the world and for all periods between 1970 and 2000.

Such accounting, in terms of deducted-value analysis is clearly inadequate: it covers only the very limited type of investments *officially* devoted to pollution abatement. The model clearly does not consider the link between type of technology and economic structure and the amount and quality of pollution it produces.

Everybody knows how much higher pollution costs are even when the non-monetarized aspect is left aside. One merely has to evaluate the cost of household garbage disposal for a single family, or pollutant disposal for a single company, or the control and protection of dangerous products or processes. The economic cost of fire alone in industrialized countries, is equivalent to about one full percent of national income: and the increasingly expensive consequences of fire are linked to the vulnerability of the systems or premises at risk.[25] Of course, the actual costs of pollution are a matter of definition; but this should not be used as an excuse for hiding the problem. In studying an economic problem, the main question is the maximization of wealth and welfare on the basis of a definition of value. Insertion of the "economics of pollution" into the traditional frame of economic analysis is — in our view — another compelling reason for clarifying the concept of value on which the analysis is based. It is then probably inevitable to define the concept of deducted value, a concept which goes beyond the monetarized economy.

What counts is not only how much money is invested in pollution abatement, but how much value is deducted by the destruction of any sort of goods or services. It is from this angle that a wider economic view should be taken of the real wealth and welfare costs of such losses (as they result from the increase of disasters, cropland wastage or forest destruction).[26]

Last, but surely not least, of the major investment "needs" is armament; we will leave the analysis of utilization value, read added value and real deducted value open for discussion. One might just bear in mind though that currently world armament investment is running at around a billion dollars per day and still growing.[27]

To conclude, the problem of capital needs and capital requirements is primarily a matter of goals within the definition of what we have called "D & P". It is a problem of trying to approach a situation of optimum equilibrium at which the capital investment — as a monetarized tool for increasing D & P — has real positive and accepted effects.

The method deriving capital requirements from general economic models based only on monetarized assumptions, and not taking into account the real dynamic behaviour of technology, is of very limited value. It is surely of much greater value, *once* objectives in wealth increase are clearly and reasonably defined, to approach capital formation as a part of D & P formation. The real problem is to verify whether — in a given situation — D & P formation is really best served by monetary formation (normally defined as saving), and then if the technical mechanisms for saving are functioning adequately (through various financial intermediation mechanisms). If the wealth objective is clearly stated and widely adopted, there should not be a problem of capital needs. There is the problem of mobilizing for Dowry and Patrimony formation. This mobilization must have "worth" and be sufficiently perceived as such. In the long run it is impossible to mobilize simply by means of public relations campaigns, etc., if no answer is given to the fundamental question of "what for"?

For this reason, discussion of value and wealth and welfare objectives is likely to be the most "efficient" tool in really tackling what is defined as "capital requirements problems". It is then at the specific, operational level that the question of capital needs can be most profitably answered and acted upon.

4.2. Accumulation and Capital Formation

Saving is a matter of present and future accumulation of Dowry and Patrimony.

On the one hand it concerns the controlled, optimal utilization of D & P, including monetarized D & P: in this sense it is the opposite of waste. On the other hand, saving — in specific forms — concerns the accumulation of man-made tools directed towards the future increase of D & P. One of these tools is monetary saving.

In a well balanced and properly optimized system recognizing interdependence of the monetarized and of the non-monetarized facets and aimed at the optimization of the utilization value, saving relates to that general human behaviour which conditions D & P formation.

Monetary saving is one of the most important foundations of industrialization. One of Adam Smith's merits was to attribute to monetary saving the connotations of a virtue — an essential step in dismantling the attitude by which money saving — in a non-industrialized world — is often the sign of avarice and backwardness rather than of a constructive attitude tending to D & P formation. Today such negative attitudes as avarice are relegated to strictly individual connotations with no necessary implication for society: financial intermediation and financial policy can easily compensate for such individual negative attitudes. Maynard Keynes struck the final blow when he obtained acceptance for the idea that excessive saving could be compensated by deficit spending.

The real problem is still that of promoting or optimizing monetarized savings in such a way that capital formation contributes in a positive way to D & P formation. Here again, there is large scope for developing appropriate indicators.

As already mentioned, the main advantage of monetarized accumulation, which, from now on, we shall simply call "saving" is its ability to transmit value in time and space.

The first problem that monetarization encounters is the availability of a unit of account — money — which is sufficiently stable in time, and widely enough recognized in space that its functions can be adequately performed.

Stabilization in space, by the adoption of a specific monetary unit in a given geographical area, is something which has been achieved at the level of the modern State. This process is by no means complete; even in the most modern state, the same amount of money does not buy exactly the same amount of goods and services at every point throughout the country. However, it is worth underlining that establishment of a common unit of account and control of the issue of national currency is *the major* attribute of the modern State and is the best starting point for an analysis of the differences between the modern political organizations and those that existed in the pre-industrial era. Since monetarization is the key element in mobilizing modern technology, it can be seen that the Industrial Revolution, technological development, monetarization of the economy *and* the organization of modern sovereign states — most often under the form of a Nation State — are aspects of the *same* system.

In other words, the modern state has been an essential premise or condition for the organization of a situation in which money can achieve — even if imperfectly — uniformization in a given space.

The transition of this space from a national to an international dimension gives rise to the problems of an international monetary system which will be examined in the third part of Chapter 4.

As to uniformization in time, no currency has really achieved perfect stability: far from it. The history of money is usually a history of varying rates of inflation and deflation. When inflation is so high that it destroys the advantages of money, namely the facilitation of transfers in time and space, then money itself is destroyed.

It is not our intention to analyze the current inflation phenomenon; the literature on this point is more than abundant. We would simply like to make a few observations concerning the general problem of D & P and capital formation.

The first is that modification of the value of money in time, only partially affects the *amount* of the community's D & P, but rather more its *distribution*; i.e. it affects *individual* D & P. Such variations are therefore, implicitly or explicitly, an equivalent of the fiscal system.

As such they produce the same effect as a negative income tax when inflation is of benefit to the debtor.

The second observation is that money apparently maintains its function as a store of value in time, even in periods of relative high inflation. The reasoning is apparently as follows: today, 1 franc will buy 1 kilogramme of bread; as a result of inflation, next year, this same franc will buy only half a kilo; and perhaps in three or five years time only 100 grammes. Increased effort is required to save money to buy as much bread as possible in the future. A degree of inflation introduces more uncertainty and, apparently, stimulates more saving, up to a certain point at least. Indicators should therefore be used to evaluate in detail the effects of monetary instability not only on D & P formation, but also on the modification of its accessibility in relation to different "economic agents" and categories of population.

The third observation concerns the proposed use of a generalized system of indexation to maintain — in a period of inflation — the value of money in time: in other words, imposing the same rate of inflation for all priced and paid goods and services, including incomes. The obstacle encountered by such proposals is that the decision to index uniformly cannot be put into practice: the price of a kilo of bread may rise 10% today; the employee's salary will increase only when he is paid (even a month later); because of legal and technical delays, the payment of accident damage may not be paid until years later. There are enormous opportunities for speculation in the delay differentials that occur in adapting to a "common" inflation rate. On the other hand, if indexation is only partial (and we do not know how it really can be efficiently totally generalized), it may easily become a method not of preserving D & P, but rather of modifying its accessibility for different population groups, and not necessarily in a desirable way.

The fourth observation is that the total quantity of money available — which depends on its circulation velocity — must be in some relation to the size of the monetarized economy. From the moment that Karl Marx launched this discussion by linking the level of prices to the quantity of money, until the present time when the money supply is considered a conditioning factor for price levels, a wealth of economic literature has been produced.

The point that must be emphasized here is that the problem of monetarized saving is primarily one of having a type of money that performs in an optimal manner the function of transferring value in time and space. This function is far from perfect but it is a cultural tool which still has to be developed at a national and even more at an international level.

Saving is then an individual as well as a collective process, subject to different degrees of freedom and compulsion.

From spontaneous individual saving, through compulsory saving imposed, for instance, by a social security scheme, to collective saving organized by the public authorities through the fiscal system, the number of variations is enormous.

We shall limit ourselves to some considerations concerning savings formation and distribution in the world and the problem of adapting fiscal policy to the objective of D & P preservation and augmentation.

4.2.1. SAVINGS FORMATION

4.2.1.1. Savings in the developing countries

There is a wealth of literature, both informational and theoretical, on the subject of savings in the industrially developing countries.*

Mention should however be made of the UNCTAD studies** from which has been taken the following table which summarizes domestic savings, external resources and total savings in developing countries from 1970 to 1976 (see Table 4.13, p. 276).

The comments presented by UNCTAD in this study confirm, in practice, many of the views we have proposed in previous Chapters.

For example the study states that "in countries with very low income, the increase in consumption of goods of first necessity results not only in an increase of the standard of living, but can be considered as an *investment* in the quality of manpower". This comment, which can be extended

*For example:
- United Nations: "Policies and techniques for mobilizing personal savings, in developing countries", Report of an Inter-regional Workshop, ESA/OTC/SM7713.
- Programme des Nations-Unies pour le Développement", projet: "Mobilization de l'epargne", Cotonou, June 1974.
- Economic Commission for Asia and the Far East: "Seminar on the Mobilization of Private Savings, under the auspices of ECAFE in cooperation with SIDA and ISBI", Bangkok, Thailand, August, 1974.
- Economic Commission for Asia and the Far East: "Problems encountered in the mobilization of personal savings in urban and rural areas: a case study of India."
- Mikesell, R. F. and Zinser, E.: "The nature of the savings function in developing countries: a review of the theoretical and empirical literature with special reference to Latin America," OAS, 12 October 1971.
- Moltura, P.: "Savings mobilization in African developing countries", International Savings Banks Institute, December 1972.

**United Nations Conference on Trade and Development: See "Internal savings in developing countries", UNCTAD, Geneva, October 1978 (TD/B/C.3/153) and the other texts mentioned in this paper.

TABLE 4.13. *Domestic Savings, External Resources and Total Savings in Developing Countries*
(Expressed as % of GNP^a) 1970–1976

Country groupings	Domestic savings				External resources[b]				Total savings[b]			
	1970–73	1974	1975	1976[c]	1970–73	1974	1975	1976[c]	1970–73	1974	1975	1976[c]
Countries with a *per capita* income[d] in 1975												
Over $800	21.9	30.4	28.2	28.6	0.4	−7.2	−4.1	−3.9	22.4	23.2	24.1	24.7
of which:												
Oil-exporting countries	46.4	67.2	66.5	59.9	−27.3	−52.7	−52.6	−35.7	19.1	14.5	13.8	24.2
Others	18.7	19.2	18.1	19.5	3.3	5.9	5.7	3.4	22.0	25.1	23.8	23.6
$300–800	16.3	21.5	18.3	19.1	3.3	0.8	6.9	4.7	19.6	22.4	25.2	23.8
Under $300	14.3	14.1	11.4	14.4	2.5	3.1	5.0	1.0	16.7	17.2	16.3	15.3
of which:												
Least developed countries	8.6	4.2	3.4	3.5	4.2	7.8	12.5	9.5	12.8	11.9	15.9	13.0

Source: UNCTAD Secretariat estimates based on United Nations and other international sources.

a For some countries, for which GNP figures were not available, GDP figures have been used instead.
b External resources are the excess of imports over exports of goods and services including factor income payments. Total savings equals gross domestic capital formation.
c Preliminary.
d *Per capita* GDP in current dollars.

far beyond the specific example given, is an illustration of the sequence of D & P utilization and investment/effort presented in Chapter 3, Section 2. This is even more significant if such consumption can be met — at least in part — by the non-monetarized economy. Furthermore, the same study points out that "internal savings, and income tax are different in various countries essentially as a result of the structure of the countries themselves, and only very partially due to the 'effort' done by each of them".

In 1974—1976, the average level of savings in the developing countries with a *per capita* income of over 800 dollars was 29% of GNP, a relatively high figure. Of course, this is due largely to the oil exporting countries converting their non-renewable resources into financial assets. However, even the non-oil countries, in this income category, manage to provide over 80% of their total savings by their own national means. The very low income countries, with a national *per capita* income of less than 300 dollars, manage to provide only one-third of total savings by their national means, the rest being provided from external sources.

The relative success of the first group and the difficult situation of the latter, show that the priority is, first, to increase internal saving capabilities, and, thereafter, to optimize the management of external contributions and help. We consider briefly the first point in the following pages.

*Savings accumulation in developing countries.** Because of certain subjective factors which influence the formation of savings, there are no immutable savings coefficients that can be related to income per inhabitant. Accordingly, an economic policy directed towards the growth of collective capital is insufficient if it is confined to promoting the expansion of the national income and of the average income per inhabitant.**

The propensity to save is more a family and social phenomenon than a matter of personal inclination. Any attempt at an in-depth study of the phenomenon connected with the saving process will require an examination of the structural characteristics of the households forming part of the population concerned.

The theory that it is the well-to-do classes which accumulate the major part of the savings in a country, and that a régime which accentuates social disparities through a very unequal distribution of the national income favours the formation of savings, is totally unfounded.*** It is contradicted

*For this section, the African case has been taken as basic reference.
**This mistake is nevertheless a frequent one.
***This argument is commonly used to justify the inequality of incomes in developing countries.

by the rapid and enormous increase in the number of savings books reported by credit institutions in regions of rapid growth — books taken out by ordinary workmen from the various sectors of production.

Moreover, because of the difference in savings elasticity between different income categories, and because this elasticity is greatest where middle incomes predominate, it is in the national interest, with regard to the formation of savings, to foster the emergence of a large middle class. Why is this? Because incomes that are too low or too high are insensitive to economic stimuli: too low incomes because they leave no margin for savings; too high ones because, having reached saturation point in consumption, a form of automatic savings is already achieved which are not likely to increase significantly and which have a marked tendency to go abroad.

Domestic households remain the basis of all formation of savings in a community, for even public savings and the savings of enterprises are derived from household incomes. This is particularly true in the developing countries where family savings account for the largest share of national-savings formation and exhibit great stability.* As will be seen later, the main problem is that of channelling these savings towards productive investment.

Saving is neither a phenomenon pertaining to the realm of mere financial technique (e.g. manipulation of interest rates) nor a phenomenon isolated from the socio-cultural context in which it occurs. It is influenced, in particular, by the following factors:

— The age of the populations forming the national community.
— The state of traditional practices and beliefs.
— Family structures.
— The level of financial and economic education of the people concerned.
— The vision which people have of economic development.
— Monetary-income levels and rates of growth.
— The degree to which the economy is monetarized.
— Price stability.
— Investment habits.
— The influence of imitation factors.

*This is true, more so, in view of the fact that 70—80% of the savings in India are attributed to the household sector and the major increase was recorded by this sector, Saving and Economic Development, Calcutta, Scientific Book Agency, 1967, p. 112.

– The level of investment opportunities.

Now, on all these points, the African socio-cultural environment, for example – although the remark can be equally applied to many developing countries in other regions – does not favour the formation and accumulation of savings for production purposes: low average age; low level of life expectancy; traditional beliefs and practices which encourage hoarding and the collective dilution of savings; extended family structure within which ties of solidarity are maintained; illiteracy and total absence of financial and economic education; fragmented vision of economic development; instability of prices; social imitation habits which favour ostentatious consumption; lack of investment opportunities.

A savings policy is inseparable from a general economic policy. This statement is true: it is not possible to promote the formation and accumulation of savings and their utilization for productive purposes if one ignores the African economic fabric, which is marked by economic dualism. In order to make the best possible use of this economic dualism, one must:

– Encourage the geographical dissemination of technical progress and of infrastructures; foster a coherent conduct in Government bodies to endeavour to derive maximum benefit from local resources – natural and social:

– Expand exchanges in the internal market, a thing which is not possible with poor and under-employed populations:

– Stimulate a broad differentiation of productive activities in order to derive maximum benefit from all local circumstances in the technical and human fields.

At present, the specialization of production exposes the developing countries to wide fluctuations in income, investments, consumption, exchanges, savings and foreign currency reserves. It thus creates obstacles to the achievement of the objectives stated above.

The State has its share of responsibility in the promotion of an effective savings policy, from at least two points of view:

– By its ability to define the legal system in force (which determines the kind of legal safeguards for the ownership of property and for the circulation of all forms of wealth).

– By its capacity to create conditions of security for the protection of vested interest in property. The absence of security is apparently one of the reasons which explain the prevalence of hoarding in the developing countries.

There must be no mistake with regard to the effects of the dissemination of the use of currency. The cultural features of African societies cannot be safely ignored. It is true that the dissemination of the use of currency tends to increase the formation of household savings and opens a wide range of choices for investments, but the phenomenon of hoarding finds, in currency, a means of manifesting itself. The hoarding of coins and of national and foreign banknotes is thus added to the pre-existing hoarding of consumer goods and that of capital goods.

The main problem is therefore that of the effective mobilization of savings and *this mobilization depends on the determination of objectives which take into account the real incomes in the developing countries.*

In point of fact, there are three sources of error in the evaluation of incomes in the developing countries:
- The share of the subsistence economy in the formation of the national income is systematically underestimated;
- Unrealistic rates of exchange are being adopted to ensure a homogeneous expression of incomes in terms of the national currency: these rates are based purely on the logic of a monetarized economy;
- The importance of climatic advantages in certain regions must not be ignored, for they constitute elements of income: they correspond to the additional consumption that would be necessary for survival in less-favoured climates.

According to Arnaldo Mauri,* if allowance is made for these sources of error in the evaluation of incomes in the developing countries, the relative gap between the two extremes (represented by the average levels of living in the most advanced countries and those in the most backward countries) is actually less than one-third of the apparent gap.

The mobilization of savings cannot be dissociated from a good credit system. How can the inert wealth constituted by sterile hoarding of available capital in the developing countires, be turned into a driving force in the social life of these countries? The credit system must fulfil at least two functions:
- Reconcile the economic concentration of capital with the fragmentation and dispersal of legal ownership;

---

*Arnaldo Mauri: "The promotion of savings and of savings banks in the developing countries", p. 53, in *The mobilization of household savings; an instrument of development,* Cassa di risparmio delle provincie lombarde (Savings Bank of Lombardy), Milan, 1978.

— Ensure the rapid mobilization of savings, for the speedy movement of available savings transformed into investments means that a smaller amount of capital will be necessary to obtain a given volume of production.

In Africa, the financial machinery is ill-adapted to this function.

The commercial banks inherited from the colonial era the practice of collecting funds in the form of deposits in current accounts and on long term. They show no interest in small savings deposits. It is the Postal Savings Banks which cater for this type of saving but they do so in an inefficient manner: the interest paid is low, bearing in mind local credit conditions (2.5% in Ghana, Kenya, Nigeria, Tanzania and Uganda; 3.75% in Zambia; 3.5% in Cameroons and Senegal; 3.25% in Ivory Coast). Furthermore, there is generally very high inflation.

As for the development banks, their structural and functional characteristics prevent them from playing the desired role, since they channel public funds, as well as any capital obtained as assistance or loans, towards investment in industry and agriculture. They play little or no part in the collection of household savings.

Any effective savings policy in Africa must take into account the dual credit structure.

The credit markets of the developing countries have in common their dualistic structure, i.e. the coexistence of modern and archaic forms of credit and their separation into two distinct and almost watertight compartments.

In the developing countries, the low rates of interest practised by the modern sector benefit mainly the high-income groups. Economic operators offering risks, due dates or profitability rates at variance with the conditions in which official credit institutions function, are excluded from this benefit.

These operators accordingly resort to the indigenous associations which handle a considerable mass of funds. They practice what might be termed capillary collection of savings.

In the developing countries, personal savings make little contribution to the crude formation of internal capital (CFIC): the attitude of economists and planners contributes to this result when they emit the following judgements:

— That personal savings are weak and dispersed;

— That their mobilization would entail prohibitive costs;
— That the growth in the volume of private savings is allegedly connected with the average income per inhabitant.

The first of these statements is contradicted by:

— The number and volume of business of the indigenous savings and credit associations;
— The sizeable demand for the services of custody of funds, in rural areas;
— The widespread habit of hoarding among low and middle income groups;
— The large overall volume of prestige spending by individuals and by households.

There exist certain statistical indicators which can give at least a rough idea of the dimensions of personal monetary savings.

One indicator is the considerable number of banknotes and coins brought to the banks for exchange every time the Treasury and the Central Bank issue new banknotes and coins.

The total volume of legal tender in circulation outside households can be related to the total number of households (amounts held by high-income households should not affect materially the ratio obtained, because the liquid assets of such households are usually deposited in banks).

On the second point, the mobilization of small savings is undoubtedly onerous if one bears in mind the organic structure of commerical banks, and if one relates the unit cost of this mobilization to the real and expected operational receipts.

It is however, necessary to develop *ad hoc* institutions and methods of financial intervention, without trying at all costs to reproduce the type of structure which is appropriate for highly industrialized countries. If the criteria accepted in those countries were applied to banks of Renaissance Europe, none of them would have been considered profitable.

We have already seen what one must think of the last point which forms part of a set of worn-out clichés; in any case, the various considerations set forth in the present Chapter show that the relationship between private savings and average income per inhabitant is not an automatic one.

With regard to the mobilization of public resources, it must be borne in mind that, in the African countries, less than 1% of the population pays any direct taxes; the taxpayers are mainly public officials and the staff of large firms. In order to minimize both the costs and the problems of tax collections, the emphasis has been placed on customs duties, sales taxes and State monopoly charges.

Experience shows, however, that smuggling is rife, particularly owing to the permeability of frontiers. Public savings are thus patently inadequate to ensure economic and social development.

The subject of external resources will be examined in Section 3 of the present Chapter.

What seems to us important to emphasize here is the fact that there is *a margin available for mobilizing local capital formation,* an observation based on a conception of economic development implying a definition of wealth which is less reductionist than the one prevailing so far.

This vision of things is essential in order to develop usefully the function of financial intermediation.

In any case, many of the problems we have discussed are clearly in evidence and are much more apparent in the controversy which opposes the neo-classical model of growth to the structural approach* in the efforts to frame a policy aimed at developing the function of financial intermediation in the interests of a better economic development.[28]

4.2.1.2. Some data on monetarized savings in Western industrialized countries

The comparison between the Tables 4.14 and 4.15 show the development

TABLE 4.14. *Gross National Saving 1900–1950* (in % of GNP)

Country	Period	1896–1900	1904–1908	1911–1914	1921–1924	1927–1932	1938	1949
United States		11	13	12	12	6	14	18
United Kingdom		14	12	15	–	–	10	14
France		9	12	10	–	–	13	20
Sweden		20	20	16	–	–	20	17
Denmark			12	15	–	20	18	19

Sources: Jeanneney, J. M.: Rapport Général. Congrès International pour l'Etude des problèmes de l'épargne. Paris 30–9/3–10–1957. Imprimerie Nationale 1957, Tome III, Tableau pp. 128–130; Goldsmith: A study of savings in the United States; Reports of O.E.C.D. (for 1948 and 1949).

*See Chenery, H. B.: *The structuralist approach to development policy,* AEC (Vol. 65), May 1975.

TABLE 4.15. *Gross National Saving* (in % of GNP)

Country/Period	1958 to 1962	1963 to 1967	Country/Period	1958 to 1962	1963 to 1967
Germany	27	26	Ireland (1963–66)	15	17
Austria	26	26	Italy	25	23
Belgium	20	22	Japan	35	36
Canada	21	31	Luxembourg		
Denmark	20	20	(1963–65)	30	28
Spain (1964–67)	–	23	Norway	27	28
United States	18	19	Netherlands	28	26
Finland	28	27	United Kingdom	17	18
France	20	21	Sweden	24	24
Greece (1963–65)	19	21	Switzerland	26	28

Sources: O.E.C.D., National accounting of OECD countries. 3rd part. Table per country. Percentages are taken from Table 10. (National gross capital formation) and 1 (GNP of market prices), OECD, Paris, 1969.

TABLE 4.16. *Household Savings* (including individual entrepreneurs) as a % of gross national saving

Country/Period	1958 to 1962	1963 to 1967	Country/Period	1958 to 1962	1963 to 1967
Germany	(34)	(33)	Ireland (1963–66)	40	42
Austria	46	44			
Belgium	(43)	(44)			
Canada	45	43	Japan	44	44
			Luxembourg		
Spain	–	(35)	(1963–65)	(32)	(30)
United States	43	40			
Finland	35	42	Netherlands	31	35
France (1959–62)	43				
(1966–68)		44	United Kingdom	26	30
Greece	(43)	(55)	Sweden	30	29
			Switzerland	(24)	(33)

Source: OECD: National accounts of OECD countries.

of gross national saving, which, in the course of the years after the Second World War, has risen to over 20% of GNP: a slow increase, in relative terms, can be also observed in the period 1963—1967 over the period 1958—1962.

Households are still a very important source of savings — often the major one — even if their contribution to national savings, which was about 70—80% around 1900, has decreased to about 40% in the industrialized countries since 1950.

In terms of *net* savings (excluding depreciation), personal savings clearly remain the most important as can be seen from the graphs shown on p. 286.

It is therefore with some apprehension that a marked decrease in personal saving has been observed in recent years in countries such as the United States, as indicated in the next graph.* (Fig. 4.3.)

This tendency is often deemed even more delicate in consideration of the general trend of net saving as related to total gross saving. In fact, during the years around 1970, national net saving experienced a period of stabilization in many major countries. Since then, net saving as a part of gross capital formation, has declined rapidly in favour of depreciation, as is shown in the study of Albert Coppé,** from which Table 4.17 is taken.

In the United States, the great importance of depreciation can be seen from Figures 4.4 and 4.5: the first analyzing the components of business savings; and the second, giving the total gross savings.

If depreciation is left aside, business saving has been diminishing in the last decades in many of the important industrial countries, which has seen the decreasing reliance and importance of self-financing:

— in 1954, own funds of German industrial companies were 46.3% of the total sources of finance, as against 31.5% in 1979;

*This situation has provoked a great debate and many studies in the United States on savings and capital formation, and the major factors affecting them, such as inflation, government policies, social security etc. See, in particular, the studies of Martin Feldstein, President of the National Bureau of Economics and the study directed by George von Fürstenberg and published in 1979 on "Capital investment and saving" sponsored by the American Council of Life Insurance. See also G. von Fürstenberg "Social security versus private saving and insurance", Geneva Papers on Risk and Insurance, November 1978.

**Coppé, A.: "Epargne, revenu, inflation", dans Epargne et Nouvelle Croissance, Colloque international pour l'Etude des problèmes d'épargne.

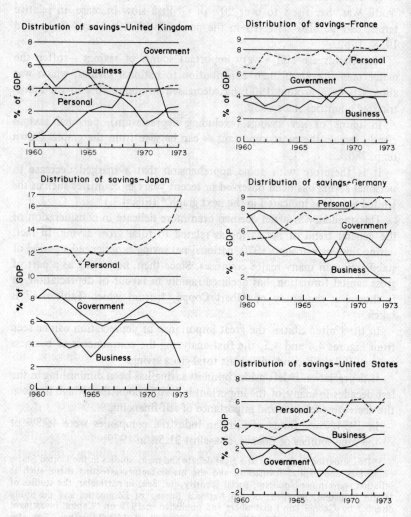

FIG. 4.2. *Distribution of Savings in Selected Developed Countries*

Source: Baron, D. C.: "Capital availability", Research Report 586, Stanford
           Research Institute, 1977.

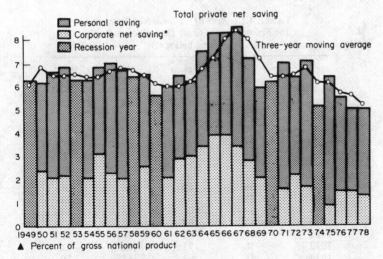

FIG. 4.3. *Total Private net Saving*

Source: Commerce Dept., Data Resources Inc., BW estimate
Reprinted from *Business Week*, 11.12.1978, by special permission, © 1978 by
McGraw-Hill Inc. All rights reserved.

— in Switzerland, self-financing, including undistributed profits and pro-
visions, has decreased from 40% during the fifties to 20% in 1975;
— in Italy and Japan, own capital of industrial corporations in 1974
and 1975 accounted for 13 and 17% of the total, respectively.

The reasons for these situations and trends vary. In Italy, for instance,
one must take into account the dominant role of State holdings, which
are relatively poor in own funds, and their apparent influence on private
enterprises as well. In Japan, Manfred Munch attributes the situation to
the past inadequacy of the financial market.[29]

Among the causes which have a more general impact, mention is
frequently made of the diminishing returns of capital, the rules for
depreciation and profits tax.

Figure 4.6 gives a picture of the sources of funds for US corporations
for the period 1950–1975.

TABLE 4.17. *Role of National Net Saving in the Foundation of Gross Capital* (excluding external balances)

	FRG (%)	Belgium (%)	UK (%)	Italy (%)
1960	70	48	54	65
1961	69	53	56	67
1962	66	55	53	67
1963	63	52	53	64
1964	65	59	58	64
1965	63	60	59	63
1966	61	59	57	63
1967	56	60	56	64
1968	61	57	57	64
1969	62	61	58	64
1970	62	63	58	65
1971	59	62	56	62
1972	58	73	50	61
1973	58	63	51	60
1974	54	64	39	52
1975	44	58	35	49

Source: Coppé, A.: "Epargne, revenu, inflation", dans Epargne et Nouvelle Croissance, p. 80.

The growing role of financial intermediation must also be underlined, in what is called the passage from the "auto-economy"[30] to the "overdraft economy", which means the passage from liquidity based on easily negotiable financial assets to a liquidity based on borrowing capacity.[31]

Finally, the contribution of the government as the direct saver (or dissaver as in the case of the United States – as shown in Fig. 4.6.) must also be taken into consideration: this is another immense subject which would need research of its own.

As with capital needs, so also with savings, there has been considerable discussion and numerous studies to determine whether savings are adequate or not.

Here again, the problem is first to know how much and how far it is possible to increase D & P – how much monetarized capital is needed in *this* context.

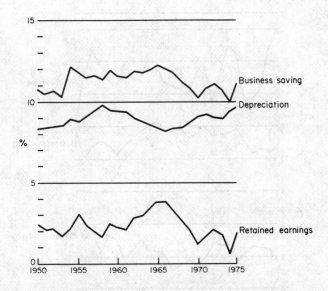

FIG. 4.4. *Business Savings and its Components (% of GNP), in U.S.A.*

Source: Baron, D. C., *op. cit.*

The points dealt with above were intended merely to open the debate and indicate the overall dimensions of the savings problems today. It would subsequently be necessary to carry out an in-depth study starting from the definition of D & P, and aiming at defining the proper equilibrium levels for monetarized savings within this framework.

4.2.2. FISCAL POLICY AND CAPITAL FORMATION

After the problems of *accumulation* (and saving) in capital and wealth formation, the next important issue is that of choosing a fiscal policy and determining the way in which it can affect the quantitative and qualitative process of accumulation (and saving).

The following discussion is based essentially on the analysis of previous

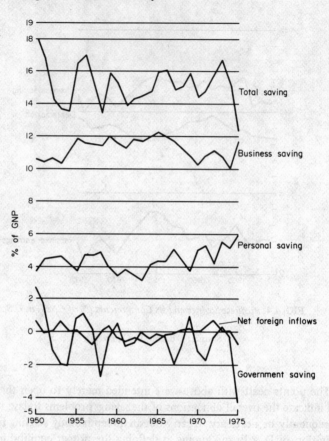

FIG. 4.5. *Total Saving and its Components (U.S.A.)*

Source: Baron, D. C., *op. cit.*

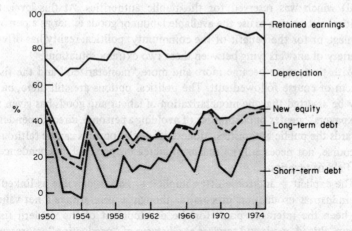

FIG. 4.6. *Sources of Funds for US Non-financial Corporations*

Source: Baron, D. C.: "Capital Availability", p. 4 Research Report 586, January 1977.

problems and concepts, confronted with the views of some economists specializing in fiscal policy.*

4.2.2.1. Taxing values: which values?

In the pre-industrial and essentially non-monetarized society, values were mostly "free" (unpaid) and this applied to labour as much as to goods. The fiscal system was then inevitably largely dependent on getting some quantity of both: it often took the form of compulsory labour and of the delivery of a certain percentage of production (essentially agricul-

---

*These economists are chiefly Nicolas Kaldor ("An expenditure tax", George Allen & Unwin, London, 1955), Firmin Oulès who succeeded to the chair formerly held by Pareto at Lausanne ("Les impératifs fiscaux dans les pays occidentaux" in Revue économique et sociale, Lausanne, July 1959 as well as a series of articles published in the Revue Comptable from October 1959 to February 1960) and most of the authors mentioned by them (Keynes, Mill, Fisher, Marshall, Pigou, etc.).

For a more recent series of references and debates see *The government and capital formation,* by von Fürstenberg, G. and Malkiel, B., American Enterprises Institute, Washington, 1977.

tural) which was reserved for the public authorities. At this level, the political option was to use the available labour or goods either as a personal privilege or for the benefit of the community: political reality has offered a variety of answers lying between these two extreme situations.

With time, value became more and more "monetarized" and the fiscal system of course followed suit. The political options are still there, but it may be asserted that the monetarization of labour and goods has given the "taxpayers" greater opportunities of avoiding a personal, direct dependence towards the public authorities. Monetarized relationships can be (although, of course, not necessarily) a means of increasing personal independence in the field of taxation.

The explicit — and more often implicit — notion of value as linked to the industrial production process (as though it were always a net value), has been the reference point for the development of the modern fiscal system. Priced goods and services at all stages of "production", represent a "value" and they can be taxed as such.

It soon became apparent, however, that this notion of value was concealing the fact that it represented at the same time a cost; among others, Stuart Mill underlines the fact that savings have to be protected, since they are an important tool in ensuring the running of the production machine. Taxing savings would mean placing a burden precisely on a necessary requirement of accumulation for investing. Building capital through saving should not be penalized or restricted by an excessive fiscal policy. It is not inappropriate to recall that Stuart Mill was not a politically conservative mind but, for his time, a man "of the left".

The need to preserve and encourage "saving" has succeeded, in some cases, in avoiding the consequence of being considered within the logic of the "production value" and as such fully taxable, either through tax exemptions (for instance in the case of life insurance policies), or via loans to industry at reduced interest rates (where the subsidy given by the government becomes a sort of compensation for what is taken in the "saving" process), or in many other ways. But these have been "technical" solutions, to face a reality which was not in the mainstream, fundamentally, of the basic economic paradigms.

There are other fundamental reasons why the issue of not "taxing costs" has not gained momentum until recent years. One is historical and another is linked to theoretical thinking in economics.

The historical reason is connected with the fact that, during most of the past century, technology was more "productive" — as we have seen — than people (entrepreneurs and economists) recognized, so that demand was not really adapted to needs, *deflation* was prevalent most of the time and capital requirement moved only from a need for a saving of 4–6% (of GNP) at the beginning of the nineteenth century to 10–12% at the end of that same century. Most of this saving was still taking place within the framework of the family enterprise, favoured by "moral" reasons. In fact, all the available savings, as Keynes detected and explained (it was a revolution in economic thinking), were not used for investment, and this was supposed to be the key reason (oversaving and underinvestment) for the economic cycles.

The Keynesian theory thus consists of stimulating demand in order to push the level of equilibrium of the economy to the full employment level. This will produce investment, and the savings can be taxed, in order to curb their tendency to remain idle.

All this seems to us quite acceptable, subject to a fundamental assumption: the rate of innovation and of productivity of technology must be high enough (the elasticity of supply must be high enough), to regulate the economic equilibrium almost at will from the demand side. Real investment possibilities (real saving) are produced by advancing technology at higher rates of return.

One can then tax savings, because the advances in technology compensate (and in some cases more than compensate) the tax burden on the production costs.

The absence of inflation is an indicator that technology is absorbing this burden well: the increasing costs of production are inevitably passed on in the final price of the product (in the end, most taxes are paid by the final consumer, whatever the illusion of the "income" direct tax). When technology enters a phase of diminishing returns, the increase in productivity is no longer able to absorb the tax burden on the costs of producing values: here we have one of the mechanisms which explain inflation.

4.2.2.2. Added value and utilization value from a fiscal point of view: the fairness factor and the time factor

Almost every student who has taken a normal course in economics has been taught that the basis of fairness in the taxation system is essentially an emphasis upon direct income taxes. Very often the ratio between direct taxation and indirect taxation is quoted as evidence of the degree of modernity and of progress of a country, where this ratio is in favour of direct taxation.

This clearly represents a progress since historical experience proves that often the poor have been taxed mainly through the goods of primary necessity.

However, even a "progressive" economist like Kaldor has felt that the taxation of income is the taxation of a flow, and that it does not reflect necessarily a "just" sharing of the tax burden. Kaldor proposes that the actual "power of expenditure" should be estimated and that it should replace income as the reference amount of "value" for taxation purposes. Some of Kaldor's objections have been taken care of by the introduction of a tax on personal wealth (as in Switzerland). We think, as Keynes has also said, that it would be very complicated to make an estimate of a personal "expenditure" value.

Furthermore, as Professor Oulès has explained in his writings, and as much common sense experience has shown in the last decades, the system of direct taxation (through income tax) is itself the source of a new and growing social injustice.

Professor Oulès stresses that evey theory should be verified by its possibilities of practical application: personal income tax has been essentially a tax, in the application of which, justice is proportional to the extent to which everybody's personal income can be verified. This acts as a stimulus, as we have seen in the previous chapters, to the development of the "grey" economy.

We would also add that the direct tax system is blind to non-monetarized values.

This discussion on tax fairness is of course very complicated and we can only outline it here.

From an economic standpoint, however, it seems to us of great importance to revert to some of the basic points we have mentioned in previous Chapters.

The first is linked with the notion of utilization value as a *dynamic* notion, as opposed to the notion of traditional value.

As we have pointed out in previous chapters, economics is still essentially tied to a static — which, in practice, means short-term — notion of equilibrium.

In reality, elasticity has two dimensions: in time and in space. When, in economics, one speaks of elasticity, one normally measures elasticity in the short-term: this concerns prices, productions and substitutions. But, as we have seen, as more modern technology penetrates the economy, the adaptation process takes longer and longer. This phenomenon is today much more important than at the time of Marshall who clearly pointed out the delays of supply. The first result is that all elasticities seem to tend to disappear and to be substituted by more and more rigidities. In fact, it is the behaviour of the elasticity in time which changes. We have seen, in this case, that the attempt to speak of "dynamics" in economics (see Hicks and Samuelson[32]) is normally simply the confrontation of given periods of time (frozen pictures) with one another. The *behaviour* of elasticity is not a problem of *one moment in time,* it is the behaviour in a *period* (continuous period) in time.

The taxation system is, in principle, fundamentally tied to the static notion of economics and value. We propose here two fundamental cases for discussion.

The first concerns the problem of adjusting short-term to long-term equilibrium. The short-term market situation in oil production and consumption may be such that prices tend to fall. Furthermore, as we have seen in our book on *The Diminishing Returns of Technology,* the more the market is gigantic (as in oil, fertilizers, many raw materials, etc.), the more it is sensitive to a minimum disequilibrium between demand and supply. In the case of fertilizers, an excess of total world supply over demand of just 1% can disrupt the market enormously, because of "service" constraints (storage, distribution) and difficulties in time spread. So, a small over-supply of oil at a given moment (or, at most, in a period of a few months) determines the price. This same product may be exhausted in 20 or 30 years' time, and/or become much more costly to extract in the next 5–10 years. Short-term elasticities work against long-term elasticities.*

The fiscal system could have the function of filling more specifically *the time gap,* in order to prepare a smoother adaptation to the long-term

---

*We recognize that this point can be very controversial for economists, who could object by the way they analyze supply and demand curves, making the difference between curve elasticity and curve displacement.

situation. This will be possible after serious research becomes available on actual *elasticities in time* (and their trends) in the major economic fields.

Another case, which results from the "short-term" view and the static assumptions of economics, concerns the very reference basis for all economic activities: the fiscal time basis is generally one year. Economic thinking and action is in this case still determined by the agricultural, pre-industrial experience.

It is obvious that there must be some contradiction between investment needs and planning which require computations over 10 or even 20 years and a fiscal instrument which is based on one year only. This very basic and simple fact, is one among several factors which contribute at present to transforming the financial game more and more into a hazardous short-term game.

This touches upon the very fundamental problems of facing risks in a modern society. An example taken from the insurance business provides a very good illustration: modern technology concentrates risks more and more, which means that it also concentrates possible damages in space (see the Amoco Cadiz catastrophe, the risk of an offshore oil-well explosion, or the risks of a nuclear power station). At the same time, the probability of damage diminishes in time, so that for instance one can assure that a major catastrophe due to a nuclear reactor will happen only once every 20–30 years. At first sight, what appears to be an advantage (the diminished frequency) becomes an important element of uncertainty when the size of the likely damage is catastrophic. The very fact that it can happen next year or 20 years from now, introduces a fundamental element of uncertainty in the management of such a risk. This uncertainty is aggravated by the fact that the fiscal system, applied to the financial management of such risks, normally knows only the annual logic. The result is that the fiscal system contributes to the uncertainty of the whole economic system, as in the above case.

The fundamental point is always the same: economic realities are less and less short-term. Short-term management becomes more and more the fool's court, where all the walls are more and more rigid and do not permit any real decision. It becomes more and more simply the other side of the coin, where every economic activity is rigidly constrained under a compulsory long-term plan.

In between, we have the reality, comprising facts which are adaptable and which have a specific life cycle.

Elasticity measurement becomes more and more like measuring how many moments in the year the temperature at the North Pole is over 10 degrees Centigrade; if this occurs only very rarely, the danger is to conclude either that the thermometer is wrong or that the era of warm times is finished. In fact, the space/time dimension has to be "rediscovered" (as it has become in reality), and we must proceed to manage elasticities as they are, i.e. with varying time characteristics. Fiscal policies are a very important tool in this direction, even if, of course, not the only ones.

4.2.2.3. The preservation of wealth and of non-monetary services

What we have said about the usefulness of employing fiscal policy in order to bridge the gap in time between short-term equilibrium and long-term elasticities, applies not only to time, but also to space.

Going back to the notions of "utilization value", "stock of services" and D & P (including services), an effort should be made to devise a fiscal policy which has the effect of increasing real values (non-monetary and monetary). The taxation of any element of costs which contributes to the "production and life-use" of a "stock of services" should be so as to optimize the utilization value, and care should be taken not to go beyond the substitution possibilities among different elements of costs: a tax which stimulates production as against maintenance could have the effect of stimulating the reduction of the life period of the "stock of services". A tax on the cost of disposals could have the opposite effect: there are clearly cases in which more "value" is "produced" by controlling waste than by subsidizing production.

An investment policy (backed by fiscal policy) which adds to the transfer of non-monetarized activities into the monetarized field (hospital health care as opposed to home health care), will not necessarily solve welfare problems and will increase maladjustments: more taxes will be needed in order to pay for public health, labour shortage (because of delays in training and costs) can be produced in the hospital sector, while the "manpower" released at home will perhaps be in search of a paid job in a sector where there is already full employment.

It is clear again that all these cases become more and more frequent when economic-technological productivity is no longer such that the increases in costs (monetarized *and* non-monetarized) are more than offset by the overall productivity gain.

In the advanced industrial sectors of today, the issue becomes pretty clear when one thinks of the problem of pollution and waste. This is not the result of the last few years of ecological susceptibility. Town sewage, the disposal of more than one kilo of waste per person per day, is a cost (of the "deducted" type) that thousands of administrators have had to face for many years with increasing anxiety. Why should a more specific tax not systematically be imposed on the amount of waste produced? Why is it that in practice, very often those who produce less waste have to pay through their income taxes for those who produce more waste.

In addition to the waste problem, there is the more general problem of the preservation of all the "free" D & P. This is a case in which more "monetarization" could help to preserve a · greater number of non-monetarized assets: i.e. taxes to preserve the total D & P.

Disregarding the fact that the present system, based largely (although far from exclusively) on an inadequate notion of value, introduces into the economic system (especially in a period of diminishing returns) a series of subtle subventions that detract from the real problem which is: how to increase real welfare in terms of utilization value.

4.2.2.4. The case for taxing consumption

All the above cases would seem to lead to the conclusion that there are more and more reasons today to tax the final expenditure, i.e. the final consumption at the level of its utilization. We are not very far here from the idea of Professor Oulès who has been proposing for years a "differentiated tax on expenditures". Probably such a tax cannot be applied globally in substitution for the present income tax. At the same time, there are today many reasons which militate for a reduction in direct taxes, not only from the point of view that it is somewhat illogical to tax efforts to produce and not willingness to consume, but also for other reasons such as the demotivation of initiative and work itself.

Today, the question of fairness should not be taken as a serious reason to justify direct income taxes. If values in the present world are increasingly recognized as being of the monetary and of the non-monetary types, it is obvious that there will be an increasing trend towards a shift to non-monetarized activities. Looking closer at the life style of the very rich, one can observe that their abundance of money is often a hedge to protect their non-monetary advantages and values. We even suspect that there is a tendency to discharge more and more of the costs of modern life on to the monetarized sector, by giving money to those who are condemned to spend it to catch up for lost "free goods".

The moment when monetarization of the economy reflects the increase of deducted values, those who get more values of this type, are in fact losing in the deal: the housewife or househusband who now needs a compacting machine — is she or he any richer? The man who obtains a subsidy for going back and forth to work — has he got something "more"? Those who have succeeded in getting an anti-noise wall because they are close to a highway or an airport — are they now "better off"?

Furthermore, there is another fundamental point to discuss: the great majority of taxes, one way or the other, are inevitably reflected in the final price of goods. There are many channels through which a direct tax becomes, in fact, a disguised indirect tax: and here we have more and not less inequality. There is a real discrimination between the costs which affect the production of essential goods and services and that of luxury ones.* The indirect taxation already at work is very often only a partial compensation.

By increasing the burden of taxes on "the utilization value" (what is generally called the tax on consumption) it should be possible to achieve a better control of demand (in the short-term and for long-term considerations); this could also help in the fight against inflation. In some cases, a negative consumption tax could also be envisaged.

It should be possible, by setting as a priority the maximization of the creation of a "stock of services" or of "utilization values", to start a new period of "real" economic growth.

All these points of course require very thorough investigation and analysis both at the level of the general theoretical assumptions (the switch in the notion of value) and at the level of practical applications.

In any case, traditional analysis of the fiscal policy/capital formation/

---

*Obviously the notion of luxury varies in time and space, according to various subjective *and* objective criteria.

capital needs relations seems to us difficult and perhaps even impossible to pursue today in a situation of altered economic structures.

To put it simply, most economists, particularly in the United States, have been writing about the future capital crunch (reasoning in purely extrapolative, monetarized terms, and ignoring the diminishing returns of technology). At the time of writing these lines, *Business News* reports the availability in the United States industry of 80 billion dollars which can be invested right away. Where is the capital crunch? Why then is there still so much unemployment (even in the United States)? Why is inflation still there and even tending to accelerate as soon as there is a tendency for the economy to be stimulated?

The point we make of an economic situation which has now basically new characteristics and where traditional explanatory paradigms and theories do not apply as one would wish, is thus perhaps justified.

4.2.2.5. Non-monetary fiscal policy

We have suggested in the foregoing paragraphs that fiscal policy should take more into account the effects that taxation has on non-monetarized activities.

On the other hand, a non-monetarized fiscal policy, based on requiring from individuals and/or institutions the "free" supply of goods and services, could also be examined and in certain cases proposed.

It is clear that some premises must be set here, in order to avoid any negative or counter-productive manipulation of these concepts: we have observed already that the "monetarized" fiscal policy has been a step in the promotion of greater freedom, bearing in mind situations in which the non-monetarized fiscal system can in some cases, simply serve to swell bureaucracy and, in others, serve as an excuse for promoting modern forms of compulsory labour and other medieval forms of oppression. But neither can one dismiss the principle of non-monetary fiscal measures, once it is clear that, in some specific cases, it can represent a net advantage from both a social and a personal point of view.

After all, some forms of non-monetarized fiscal systems do exist: compulsory military service is, at least partly, a case in point (the remuneration is generally only partial as compared with that of a normal job; the learning of some new activities during military service is an example of benefits distributed in a non-monetary form).

In a previous Chapter, we have recalled the case of forest exploitation, where a specific tax as a percentage of real product could be considered. Deeper research into a variety of similar cases is necessary before going further along this path.

Looking back at the functioning of an advanced society, one could examine the possibility of developing some sort of generalized social services, where people would contribute with a limited amount of free time to various activities in many fields.

On the one hand, free service given in fields other than that of their normal daily activity, would give people a more open view of their society.

On the other hand, the specific activity of each person could be used for teaching and other purposes for the benefit of the rest of society.

It could be considered, for instance, whether instead of taxing a physician (which implies the cost of the various operations at the level of the declaration, payment, collection and redistribution of the tax), he may be required to perform a certain number of unpaid operations; this could be feasible and useful (if the collection and costs of such unpaid activities really prove, at least in certain cases, to be more efficient than in the "monetarized" case).

Probably, the most "productive" utilization of "free" time would be in education and in some sectors concerned with social and health activities (helping disabled persons, providing contacts to the isolated and to aged people, etc.). In the case of education, it would probably be very useful if every worker, businessman, commercial agent, actor, writer, etc. could go into the classroom and explain his activities to the students (both for normal school up to university and for "permanent" education). Of course, all these people would experience difficulty in "teaching": but this problem could be overcome if the professsional educators would accept more and more the role of monitors and specialists in communicating between real people. This role has, in any case, to be developed with the increasing use of TV lectures and other modern systems of information transfer. In all these cases, the quality of the information can become better and better updated, but it has to be understood by the audience and here is where the teacher/monitor has to work and check the assimilation of the subject proposed.

This contribution by people active in all sectors of "real life" could probably help to integrate society better and to counterbalance the excesses of specialization in our culture, where the people "outside" (in "real life" or in "another sector") are considered more and more as outsiders. Practitioners would rediscover the necessity of theory, and people at school would face reality in a less abstract way. In any case, if the problem of "permanent" education has to be realistically solved in the future (without being obliged to recognize that it will "cost" too much), and if the traditional education will evolve more and more in the sense of being a preparatory phase (in particular the university) for the permanent education system, some sort of contribution from everybody in his field of activity will be necessary.

This all the more so, if it is better understood that teaching and research is the best way of learning.

Finally, the "free" (or partially "free") service activity, has some relevance in the international sector and as such it is sometimes already performed (in the fields of learning, relief organizations, etc.). An assessment of experiences in this field would be useful, in particular with regard to the notion of global welfare.

4.3. The international Transfer of Capital

Money is used essentially to transfer economic values in time and space. Therefore the greater the space, the more need there is to use money to organize and promote transfers of all sorts. Money is the expression of unifying tendencies, whereas the non-monetarized values are the expression rather of local and specific assets. A good equilibrium of the two is an optimization which maximizes benefits from pluralism and from unification.

We have already mentioned how, in the Industrial Revolution, one of the major problems has been the creation of national currencies and how national currencies are also the expression of national sovereignties.

At the international level there is no "world currency", although paradoxically it is at this level that such a unit of monetarized exchange would be even more necessary than at the national level. The economic rationality has to cede in front of prevalent political preferences.

Gold has often been used and proposed as a "world" unit of monetary exchange, being "non-national". In fact, gold mines are not distributed equally among countries and extraction costs are not the same everywhere: far from that. It is still used by Central Banks, although it is no more the "standard" of the international monetary system. But it will hardly become the "money" of the world; as a substitute for present national currencies.

Some national currencies have, in practice, established themselves at least in some areas, as the real international reference currency: the pound, the French franc and particularly now the dollar. The regional units of accounts, *like the ECU (European Currency Unit), will survive* and develop only if political will can match the economic ambition, and we shall consider this point in detail at the end of the chapter.

In fact, instead of introducing the problem of the world currency unit, we are still obliged to analyze the "world monetary system", which has to be seen as an artisanal system which exists for want of a world currency system. The day such a system comes into being, there will be much less confrontations potentially leading to nuclear wars, because of oppositions between international and national economic problems of development: all problems will become more of *our* problems and nationalism will hopefully cease to be the determinant and leading ideology of the present world, of the "pre-civilized" world.*

What is very important to note here from a methodological point of view is that the more we move from the local and/or national system to the international one, the more our analysis tends to return to what we

---

*For this paragraph, several other points have been studied, but omitted from this dossier, either because other publications have been exhaustive enough, or because they finally require a very specific and detailed study, which would have made this dossier excessively heavy. These points were:

- Problems and perspectives of collaboration between public and private institutions in international intermediation.
- Regionalization of the financial intermediation at the continental level and its contribution to the world financial system. See on this point in particular Felipe Herrera: *Aspects of the External Financing of Latin America*, November 1979, Instituto de Cooperación Intercontinental, Madrid.
- International taxes: a detailed report by E. Steinberg and J. Yager was published by the Brookings Institution, Washington, in 1978.

called the conventional economic analysis. In fact — as we have already remarked — the monetarized system tends to become more and more important in relation to the non-monetarized economic system when distances and dimensions increase. The major effect of the non-monetarized system is then indirect rather than direct: the equilibrium of national and local entities and states depends on the integration of the local monetarized *and* non-monetarized economies. Local or national disequilibria of the two are then at the origin of the disequilibrium at the larger international level even though at such a level the economic relationships tend to be more monetarized in nature.

4.3.1. THE TRANSFER OF SAVINGS AND THE BALANCE-OF-PAYMENTS PROBLEM

In a world where the different nations lived in complete autarchy, in each nation there would necessarily be equality between savings and investments, since price mechanisms and the variations in interest rates would allow the necessary adjustments to take place. For example, if *ex ante* it was noted that savings were inadequate with respect to investment demand, the interest rate would increase thereby encouraging savings and discouraging investment. Moreover, there would be an increase in the prices of goods and services, notably those serving for equipment, thus provoking a fall in both investment demand and consumption. *Ex post*, the

---

- the question of aids to development: it may be recalled here that, in 1977, aid from the OECD countries was 0.31 of their GNP (it was 0.33 in 1976). Many publications are concerned with the forms of this aid (which is, in most cases, bound by the "donor" country). A new form of aid is the cancellation of the debts of very poor countries (in 1978 the total amount of such aid was about 6 billion dollars).
- The question of bilateral versus multilateral development policies (see a recent summary of the situation in *Intereconomics,* January 1979, Joachim Betz: "The internationalization of development policies).
- The various forms and potential of export credit insurance and export credit guarantee facilities (see the documents prepared by UNCTAD for the Manila Session of May 1979 as well as L. Kramar "Quelques aspects de l'assurance dans les relations economiques internationales", in *The Geneva papers on risk and insurance,* July 1978).

result would necessarily be that national savings became identically equal to national investment.*

On the other hand, in a world where international trade and international payments are more or less free, savings may diverge from investment. To the discrepancy between savings and investment there then corresponds a discrepancy between exports and imports. If the savings of a nation are not sufficient to allow it to carry out its investment plans (i.e. to allow it to attain the desired rate of creation of capital) and if there is no further possibility of mobilizing the non-monetarized economy, it may have recourse to imports. Imports of consumer goods will enable it to make more national resources available for the production of capital goods; imports of capital goods will enable it to make good the lack of national resources available for the production of these goods. Conversely, if savings are more than adequate, there remains an exportable surplus after national requirements in consumer goods and capital goods have been satisfied.

Thus, the excess or lack of savings with respect to the investment needs manifested gives rise to an excess or a deficit respectively in the balance of current transactions (balance of goods and services and factor income).

The transactions which are entered in the balance of goods and services (exports and imports) take place between resident and non-resident economic agents. The corresponding settlements or credits therefore cause a change in the world distribution of currency credits and debts. This change is entered somewhere in the balance of payments account, under a heading other than those which form the balance of current transactions. If, to make things simpler, it is supposed that the balance of payments account contains only the two main entries constituted by the balance of current transactions and the balance of capital movements, any entry in the balance of current transactions — to account for a flow of goods or for services rendered — will give rise to an entry in the capital balance account — to deal with the settlement or credit corresponding to this transaction. For example, a purchase of British equipment by an American

---

*The same result is arrived at in a planned economy, even though the mechanism of prices and interest rates cannot function correctly in this case. If the State-planned investment is not compatible with the consumption desired, it will not be fully realized or else consumer products will be lacking. Since the resources are limited, it is not possible to produce as much butter and as many guns as one would wish.

firm constitutes an import for the balance of payments of the United States. If the settlement is made in dollars, the foreign debts of the United States increase. If the settlement is made in pounds sterling, the foreign assets of the United States decrease. In both cases, it is a matter of a capital import for the balance of payments of the United States.

The economic agents may simply adapt to the new distribution of currency credits and debts caused by international trade. However, it is more probable that the new distribution will differ from the one they want. In this case, an adjustment will have to take place so that there is convergence towards the point where there is identity between the effective distribution and the desired distribution. This adjustment takes place in part by means of interest rates but it also takes place more immediately by the price mechanism. In this case, since the exchange rate between two currencies represents the relative price of the credits held on each of the currencies, the adjustment would take place by means of variations in the exchange rate.

Thus, in the above example, it may be that the British exporter does not wish to keep the dollar credit he has acquired. He may then sell it, for pounds sterling for instance, on the foreign exchange market. There, it will be acquired by an economic agent wishing to increase his net credit in dollars – whether for investment purposes or to repay a loan or to finance imports payable in dollars. In particular, it may be that this economic agent is the Bank of England, purchasing dollars for sterling as part of its policy of intervention in the foreign exchange market.

If the supply of dollars by the British exporter is not compensated by any demand, because no holder of sterling wishes to increase his net credit in dollars, the price of the dollar in terms of sterling falls. It falls until an adjustment takes place, that is until the dollar is sufficiently cheap to induce holders of sterling to modify the distribution of their wealth and to substitute for sterling credits an investment in dollars or a purchase of American products.

It can thus be seen that international trade causes variations in the stock of currency credits which may lead to changes in the exchange rate. The other important source of changes in the exchange rate, for a constant stock of currency credits, lies in the changes in the desire to hold this stock. However, in so far as variations of the first type are caused, in the last analysis, by excessive or insufficient savings at the national level, and in so far as the flow of net savings of a country represents the desire of the residents of this country to increase their stock of credits in the national currency, it can be said that the exchange rate of a currency is determined by the relation between the available stock of this currency and the desire to hold this stock. If the supply of dollars increases without this leading to an increase in the supply of products in the United States there will be a resulting fall in the dollar exchange rate, unless Amercian residents decide to increase their savings (in dollars) in the same proportions — in which case, the external supply of dollars does not increase — or unless people not resident in America desire to increase their net dollar holdings in the same proportions (or a combination of the two phenomena).

The above analysis may also be extended to a particular case. This is the case where the exchange rates do not suffer appreciable fluctuations because the central banks declare themselves ready to intervene — and in fact do so — to reabsorb any excess supply or demand resulting from a lack of equality between the stock of credits in their national currency and the desires to hold this stock. A system of fixed parity then obtains. The imbalances which arise from the divergence between savings and investment and which are translated by a non-zero balance of current transactions, have repercussions at another level: in the absence of movements of capital they give rise to more or less appreciable variations in the currency reserves held by the central banks. If these variations should assume unacceptable proportions or if they are amplified by movements of capital, there is then a series of abrupt devaluations or re-evaluations in an atmosphere of crisis.

However, whatever the exhange system adopted — the system of flexible exchange rates or a system of controlled exchange rates — the divergence between savings and investment at the national level gives rise to a balance of current transactions problem. As this problem generally has repercussions at the level of exchange rates or at the level of the official reserves, it is possible to speak — to misuse the term — of a balance of payments problem. The system of international payments represents the set of rules and usages to which one has recourse to resolve this kind of problem.

4.3.2. THE SITUATION OF INTERNATIONAL PAYMENTS SYSTEM

Since February 1973, on which date the principal world currencies ceased to have a relationship of fixed equivalence to the dollar, the system of international payments entered a new era. The previous era started in 1944 at Bretton Woods on the occasion of a conference where the rules for a new international order in matters of currency were drawn up, and where it was decided to create institutions responsible for seeing that this order was respected: the International Monetary Fund (IMF) and the International Bank for Reconstruction and Development (IBRD).

The spirit of Bretton Woods drew its inspiration from two sources: the economic and military power of the United States immediately after World War II and the desire for international economic cooperation in order to avoid the errors of the past and their disastrous consequences. The exchange system instituted at Bretton Woods was not that of a flexible exchange rate. In the minds of the participants in the conference, such a system was in fact associated with the period of monetary crisis of the thirties. At that time, no distinction was made between erratic speculative movements leading to lack of stability and movements of capital, the direction and magnitude of which reflected the instability of the internal macro-economic conditions.*

The terms of the Bretton Woods agreement defined a gold standard system but they also left the way open for a gold exchange standard** based on the dollar, and it is the latter system which finally imposed itself in practice.***

The parities of the different currencies, defined in gold or in dollars, were to remain fixed, allowing for a tolerance of ± 1% for the margin of fluctuation. They were adjustable, but the signatory countries undertook to make changes in parity only in the event of a fundamental imbalance.****

---

*See Willett[33] p. 4.

**In a gold exchange standard, the participating countries are divided into satellite countries and a central country. The reserves of the satellite countries in international liquidities are constituted by the currency of the central country which itself is convertible into gold (L'Huillier[34], pp. 31–35).

***See L'Huiller[34] p. 119–124.

****Experience has shown that a "fundamental" imbalance could be defined as an imbalance in face of which internal stabilization measures proved inadequate or too costly in jobs (L'Huillier[34], p. 125).

Otherwise, a network of financial assistance organized under the aegis of the IMF would allow them to get through difficult periods without devaluation.

The gold exchange standard had been proposed for the first time by the United Kingdom in 1922 at the Conference of Genoa and was introduced in practice between the two World Wars, the central banks adopting the practice of keeping their reserves in both gold and currency (pounds sterling and dollars). Unfortunately, it led to the devaluation of the pound and the collapse of the monetary system in 1931.

In 1944, the soundness of the American economy appeared to offer better guarantees than the Great Britain of the twenties, but the adoption of a gold exchange standard concealed the dangers inherent in this system; it can function long-term only if the requirements in international liquidities and the deficit in the balance of payments of the central country evolve harmoniously. Otherwise, there results a shortage or an excess of the key currency.* This is what happened with the Bretton Woods system; it went through four phases in turn: two phases of transition and dollar shortage; two phases of breaking up and excess dollars. It is worthwhile to pause to consider the history of such phases.

1. A phase of acute dollar shortage (1945–1949). During the period in which the European economies, seriously affected by the War, were being built up again, currency parities were fixed to comply with the terms of the Bretton Woods agreement, but as the satellite countries lacked currency to intervene at the limits of fluctuation on the foreign exchange market, they were obliged to severely restrict payments destined for foreign countries.** This bending of the rules of the Bretton Woods charter was authorized by the IMF for a transition period (Clause XIV).

Payments were then made on a bilateral basis, that is the surpluses noted by country A in its trade with country B could not be used to compensate the deficit of A with respect to C. In the framework of their respective exchange controls, pairs of countries were obliged to reach agreement for balancing their reciprocal payments. For inter-

---

*This problem had been raised at the beginning of the sixties by Rueff[35] and Triffin[36].

**This did not prevent the flourishing of currency black markets, where exchange rates varied freely.

national payments, the currency used mainly for settlement was the pound sterling, since the central banks hoarded their precious dollars which were reserved for paying for imports from the United States.* In other words, the dollar-based gold exchange standard was not yet functioning.

2. A phase where the dollar was relatively scarce (1950–1958). During this period, the economies of the industrialized countries quickly made up for lost time and were able to organize their international payments on a multi-lateral compensation basis in the framework of the European Payments Union. The main currency used for compensations became the dollar. This became the predominant international currency, particularly as the collapse of the old colonial powers (Great Britain and France) caused the abandoning of the use of sterling and the franc as reserve currencies in numerous Third World countries.

Exchange controls remained but, with the progressive disappearance of the dollar shortage, they were gradually relaxed. In each country, the commercial banks were able to resume their activity on the exchange market, the central banks no longer constituting the market but having the role of operators on the market, where they intervened to cause the limits of the margin of fluctuation to be respected. In 1958, the external convertibility of the main currencies was re-established; freedom of payments, the general rule of the Bretton Woods agreements (Clause VIII) thus became the effective rule.**

The three rules of convertibility of a gold exchange standard were thereafter observed: free negotiation of currency on the market; convertibility of each currency into the currency of the central country and of the currency of the central country into each currency at the central banks of the satellite countries (at the limit of fluctuation of the exchange rates); convertibility of the currency of the central country into gold. The Bretton Woods system was ready to function but the

*See Tew[37], Chapter 1.

**It is remarkable to note on reading the extremely well documented work of Willett[33] that the liberalization of the movements of capital had not really been considered as a plausible hypothesis by the authors of the Charter of Bretton Woods. The idea prevailed that controls would continue to exist in this domain and this is one of the reasons why the stability of the system in the face of the speculative movements had not been subjected to criticism (see in particular pp. 7–10).

symptoms of its collapse were already starting to appear.

3. A phase of abundance of dollars (1958–1971). Figure 4.7. shows that despite an excess of current payments, the balance on official accounts of the United States was in deficit for practically the whole of the sixties. The capital outflows caused a reversal of the tendency which

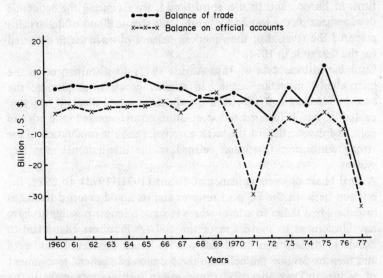

FIG. 4.7. *The Balance of Payments of the United States, 1960–1977*

Source: Tew (1977) and B.I.S. (Annual Reports).

had prevailed during the fifties. The scarcity of the dollar gave way to its abundance and then started to sustain the fears regarding the future of the dollar and the viability of a monetary system based on the confidence shown in the dollar by those who held it. Despite numerous

*Relation between United States gold reserves and liquid external liabilities in dollars:

Year	Gold reserves	Liquid liabilities
1949	24.5	6.9
1969	11.0	40.0
1971	10.0	65.0

Amounts in billions of dollars.

attempts to staunch it (gold pool, Roosa bonds, swap agreements, measures to limit the export of capital from the United States) the outflow of dollars did not stop. It was swelled by an official source — the military aid given by the United States to numerous countries — and by a private source — the investments of American multinational firms in Europe and in the Third World. By favouring the economic development of the rest of the world, this second flood of dollars also prepared the reversal of the American balance of trade which occurred for the first time in 1971.

Until the historic date of 15th August 1971, the disturbances on the international monetary scene had steadily grown in amplitude: the excess of dollars had provoked the appearance of a mass of "floating capital"[38] which fostered the speculation on an increase in the price of gold, the devaluation of the weak currencies and the revaluation of the strong currencies. Confusion reigned in the international monetary system.

4. A final phase of overabundance of dollars (1971–1973). In 1971, the relation between the US gold reserves and its liquid external liabilities in dollars had fallen to a level where it was no longer possible to have any illusions as to the health of the dollar.* President Nixon had to decide to declare that the dollar was no longer convertible into gold and then to devalue the dollar on the occasion of a general realignment of parities in December 1971 (Smithsonian Institute agreements). The Bretton Woods system gave way to an ephemeral dollar standard system.

Fixed rates of exchange had become an unmaintainable system since the central banks had no longer the material capacity to oppose market movements. After the second devaluation of the dollar (February 1973) and the flight from the American currency which accompanied it, the authorities of the principal countries resolved to allow their currencies to float with respect to the dollar.

Since 1973, the world has had to adapt itself to flexible exchange rates. The work on the reform of the international monetary system which had been initiated in 1963 under the aegis of the Group of Ten and in 1973 under that of the Committee of Twenty did not have a great effect in face of the pressure of events. Thus, the topics which had been excluded from the discussion in 1963 — the official price of gold and the floating of exchange rates — were just those which have been in the news in recent years on the international monetary scene. The sole tangible result of the discussion of the sixties — the creation of SDRs — plays only a minor part in the present situation of international payments.

Rather than continue chasing after an improbable reform of the international monetary system, the leaders of the Western world ended up by ratifying the current system during their meetings held in Washington (September, 1975), Rambouillet (November, 1975) and Jamaica (January, 1976).

The Jamaica agreements left each country free to act as regards rates of exchange. The new Clause IV stipulates that the countries can notify the Fund of any prescriptions they intend to apply regarding exchange rates — whether fixed or floating — with the exception of any system of parities linked to gold or a currency. However, although the decision has to be taken with a majority of 85%, the Fund may "recommend general prescriptions relating to the exchange rate" or decide that the situation "allows" the setting up of a generalized system of exchange rate prescriptions based on stable but adjustable parities.

According to the experts of the BIS, these new exchange arrangements are the opposite of the old ones:

"In the Bretton Woods system, the rate of exchange was a fixed point intended to ensure internal stability by means of discipline in the balance of payments. In the new scheme, it is the internal economy which must give stability to the balance of payments, no exogenous aid being expected from the exchange rate. The philosophy of this new system may be expressed in another way by saying that the authorities will not oppose the free play of the main market forces. As regards the forces which they would resist, the participants at the Rambouillet meeting agreed that their monetary authorities would act to counteract market disorder or erratic fluctuations of exchange rates."*

The last sentence of this quotation indicates that we have not moved to a system of completely free exchange rates but to a system of "unclean floating", that is a system where the central banks intervene more or less regularly on the currency markets, without being in any way obliged to. Moreover, floating is by no means general (even though it nevertheless applies to the principal currencies):

*46th Annual Report of the BIS, p. 131.

"Since March 1973, the great majority of the members of the Fund have continued to link their currencies in one way or another. Thus, fifty-three currencies are currently linked to the Eurodollar, thirteen to the French franc and five to the pound sterling. Moreover, six European currencies form part of the bloc floating together with respect to the dollar and maintaining a margin of 2¼% each side of the exchange rates fixed for each of these currencies with respect to the others. Finally, twelve members of the Fund express the exchange rate of their currency in terms of SDRs. The present system is, in fact, essentially a system of floating blocs with, in addition, a few major currencies floating independently."*

In fact, all this clearly shows that floating has not been the result of a voluntary choice. It was adopted reluctantly and with resignation because no other alternative seemed to exist.

The gold exchange standard system had shown its fragility, the United States would not hear of a return to the gold standard and the sophisticated systems which had been proposed in the late sixties, notably the so-called "crawling peg" or sliding parities system, did not seem necessarily bound to introduce a decisive advantage. It was therefore necessary to decide between flexible exchange rates and a return to protectionism together with exchange controls.

However, experience with floating in the course of recent years is not necessarily negative. It can frequently be read in the newspapers, and even in articles by certain economists, that the floating of currencies is responsible for the current economic difficulties. In our view, this is not correct. The current economic difficulties have much deeper roots;[39] [40] the fluctuations of exchange rate are only the reflection (and not the cause) of the internal macro-economic imbalances.

As Haberler[41] points out, it is not difficult to imagine what would have happened during the crises of recent years if the fixed parity system had still been in operation:

"Given these adverse factors, the present system of widespread floating surely has worked much better than the former system or the adjustable peg would have. It is not hard to visualize what would have happened under the earlier arrangements: huge flows of dollars into Germany, Switzerland, Japan, and so forth; ministers of finance and presidents of central banks rushing around from one emergency meeting to another; a

*46th Annual Report of the BIS, p. 133.

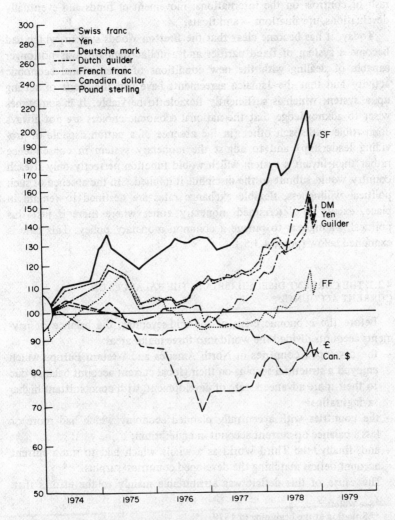

FIG. 4.8. *Percentage Change of Major Currencies versus the Dollar*

Source: Bank Pictet & Cie.

rash of controls on the international movement of funds and eventually devaluations, upvaluations – and floats."

Today, it has become clear that the Bretton Woods system, which had become a system of fixed parities and a dollar standard, was no longer capable of dealing with the new conditions of international economic activity and that the Jamaica agreements have had the merit of setting up a system which is sufficiently flexible to be viable. It is sometimes wiser to acknowledge that the national economic choices are not always compatible with each other (in the absence of a nation capable of providing leadership) and to adjust the monetary system in consequence rather than invent a system which would function perfectly only if each country would submit to the discipline it implied.* In the absence of such political willingness, flexible exchange rates are destined to remain in place, except in determined monetary zones where there is just this political willingness to pursue a common monetary policy. This case is examined below (point 4.3.5.).

4.3.3. THE CURRENT DISEQUILIBRIA IN THE BALANCES ON CURRENT ACCOUNTS**

Before the economic crisis of the mid-seventies, the balance of payments accounts divided the world into three major areas:
– the developed countries of North America and Western Europe which enjoyed a structural surplus on their global current account balance due to their more advanced state of development, with concomittant higher savings ratios;
– the countries with a centrally planned economy which had more or less a balance on current account in equilibrium;
– and, finally, the Third World as a whole which had to run a current account deficit matching the developed countries' surplus.***

The cause of this deficit was attributable mainly to the efforts that

---

*See Willett[33], p. 78.
**Situation at the beginning of 1979.
***However, close study of balance-of-payments statistics shows that the deficits are not completely matched by the surpluses. This seems to be due to errors in the measurement of invisible trade. The fact that this statistical discrepancy is growing over time has led the OECD to start a study on the problem (see OECD Economic Outlook, July 1978, p. 48).

TABLE 4.18. *Imbalances on Current Account by Major Areas*
(in billions of US dollars)

Period:	1971–1973 (cumulated balances)	1974	1975	1976	1977	1978[a]	
		8.2	8.1	13.5	18.6	28.7	"Strong" developed countries[b]
Developed countries	26.3	−0.5	11.7	−1.4	−20.6	−18.0	United States
		−42.6	−31.2	−39.8	|−31.6[d]	−11.25	Other developed countries
Centrally planned economies	1	−3	−9	−5	−1		Centrally planned economies[e]
Developing countries	−10[c]	65	35	40	34	11	Oil exporting countries
		−25	−29	−19	−15	−34	Other developing countries

Source: BIS

[a]Estimated values, published by OECD in December 1978.
[b]Germany, Switzerland, Japan, Netherlands, Belgium.
[c]The surplus of the oil exporting countries for these three years was 10 billion US dollars.
[d]Other developed countries minus Israel, South Africa and Yugoslavia.
[e]OECD statistics are not comparable with BIS statistics for this group of countries.

these countries were making in their process of industrialization: their global investment needs were far in excess of their savings capacity. Moreover, numerous economists have put forward extensive evidence that this imbalance was aggravated by the adverse trend in the terms of trade.

Table 4.18. shows that this traditional pattern of payment flows has changed dramatically since 1973 when oil prices rose savagely. Today there are six groups of countries in the balance of payment statistics:
— the United States;
— the developed countries, with a surplus;
— the developed countries, running a deficit;
— the centrally planned economies, showing a deficit;
— the oil-exporting countries, with a huge combined surplus;
— and the other LDCs who have remained in deficit.

Let us sketch briefly the situation in each of these groups:

1. The group of developed countries with a surplus comprises the Federal Republic of Germany, Switzerland, Japan, the Netherlands and Belgium which have in common the basic strength·of their economies. These countries have, on the whole, been able to match up to the challenge created by the rise in oil prices and the contraction of the world trade brought about by the recession. Their export industries have been able to consolidate their position on the world markets, and/or the regulation of internal demand has succeeded in cutting down the total value of imports. The best example of these countries is Germany, which registered a surplus in its trade with oil-exporting countries for 1974.

   On the whole, the situation of these "strong" countries seems to have "improved" since 1975; however, it must be realized that overall figures do not reflect specific trends in each country.

   (a) Four countries have shown remarkably steady performances: these are Germany, Switzerland, the Netherlands, each with a surplus of around US $0.2—4.0 billion (except for a surplus of US $9.8 billion in 1974 in Germany), and the BLEU (which is around the equilibrium point).

   (b) Japan has shown a constant improvement, starting with a deficit of US $4.7 billion in 1974 and ending with a surplus of US $11.0 billion in 1977.

2. In the United States, the situation has been rapidly deteriorating. Table 4.19. shows that the 1975 current account surplus of US $11.6 billion for the United States has been replaced by a deficit of US $20.2 billion in 1977. The latter has been aggravated by a persistent deficit on the capital account, so that an overall deficit of US $45 billion had to be financed by an increase in liabilities to foreign official dollar holders. Table 4.20 points to the fact that, in recent years, the US trade balance has deteriorated *vis-à-vis* the whole Western and developing zones — a consequence of the efforts to permit nominal growth to start again in a country where the structures have not yet been adapted to the new conditions of the economic environment.

3. The group of developed countries showing a deficit comprises five countries belonging to the Group of Ten: Canada, France, Italy, Sweden and the United Kingdom. These countries and the others in a

TABLE 4.19. *The Balance of Payment of the United States 1975–1977* (in billions of US dollars)

	1975		1976		1977	
	D	C	D	C	D	C
I. Current transactions						
1. Trade balance		9.04	9.32		31.24	
2. Services and transfers		2.50		7.89		11.03
(1 + 2 = Current balance)		11.55	1.42		20.21	
II. Private capital transactions						
1. Non-bank capital balance	6.77			0.86	7.13	
2. Net short-term external position reported by US banks	8.06		8.17		6.50	
III. Net change in the US official external position (credit = an overall deficit)		3.28		8.53		33.84

Source: BIS.

similar situation have been severely hit by the economic crisis and the rise in oil prices. Their economies were not sufficiently flexible to permit swift adaptation to the new conditions of the world economic scene, and the necessary internal adjustments have been postponed for various reasons such as political uncertainties or the indefectible optimism of their governmental leaders.

Since 1976, however, various measures aimed at reducing internal demand have been carried out, with some success, in several countries of this group. The improvement is particularly noticeable in Italy, France and the United Kingdom, where the combined deficit has been curbed form US $10.8 billion in 1976 to US $0.9 billion in 1977, and where a combined surplus of US $7 billion has appeared in 1978.

4. The improvement in the position of countries with a centrally planned economy is attributable mainly to measures aimed at a reduction of imports. The exports to the developed countries did not rise, owing to

TABLE 4.20. *Foreign Trade Balance of the United States by Area*
1971–1977 (in billions of US dollars)

Balances *vis-à-vis*	1971–1973 average	1974	1975	1976	1977
Western developed areas	−3.2	4.2	10.0	4.6	−3.5
of which:					
EEC	0.4	3.0	6.2	7.6	4.4
Canada	−2.5	−2.0	0	−2.1	−3.6
Japan	−2.9	−1.6	−1.7	−5.4	−8.1
Other	1.8	4.8	5.5	4.5	3.8
Oil-exporting countries	−0.2	−8.9	−6.3	−12.4	−19.2
Non-oil developing areas	0.8	1.9	5.2	0.9	−5.9
Eastern Europe and USSR	0.6	0.6	2.1	2.6	1.6
Unidentified	0.2	0.5	0.5	0.4	0.3
Total trade balance	−1.8	−1.7	11.5	−5.7	−26.7

Source: BIS.

a slackening of economic activity in the West. The deficit was covered, to a large extent by gold sales from the USSR, whereas borrowing on the international financial markets fell back sharply.

The large surpluses of the oil-exporting countries are the most prominent event in the pattern of current balances since these surpluses have to be met by a net deficit in the rest of the world. These surpluses give rise to an enormous financing capacity on the international markets and therefore to substantial purchases of long-term and short-term financial assets, as can be seen from Table 4.21.

However, the trend recently has been towards a reduction of these surpluses, especially so in 1978. Several causes are at work here: first, the low level of economic activity throughout the world and especially among the developed nations does not favour massive oil imports, the more so since energy conservation measures have been taken in most countries; second, the increase in oil prices has opened the door to the exploitation of alternative energy sources and to the viability of recovering high-cost oil from the North Sea and Alaska; third, the oil-

TABLE 4.21. *Oil-exporting Countries: Estimated Deployment of Investible Surpluses* (in billions of US dollars)

Items	1974	1975	1976	1977
	In billions of US dollars			
Bank deposits and money-market placements:				
Dollar deposits in the United States	4.0	0.6	1.6	0.4
Sterling deposits in the United Kingdom	1.7	0.2	−1.4	0.3
Deposits in foreign currency markets	22.8	9.1	12.6	11.9
Treasury bills in the United States and the United Kingdom	8.0	−0.5	−2.2	−1.0
Total	36.5	9.4	10.6	11.6
Long-term Investments:				
Special bilateral arrangements	11.9	12.4	10.3	11.7
Loans to international agencies	3.5	4.0	2.0	0.3
Government securities in the United States and the United Kingdom	1.1	2.4	4.4	4.3
Other*	4.0	7.0	8.5	5.9
Total	20.5	25.8	25.2	22.2
Total new Investments	57.0	35.2	35.8	33.8

Source: Bank of England.
*Including equity and property Investments in the United States and the United Kingdom, and foreign currency lending.

exporting countries are spending an increasingly large percentage of their oil-income on purchases of capital goods and armaments from the Western world. For certain oil exporters, the burden of this last factor has become so great that they had to become net borrowers on the international financial markets in 1977 (Table 4.22.). This was the case for Algeria, Ecuador, Nigeria and Venezuela, in particular. Further rises in oil prices might not necessarily change this normal process of absorption, unless dramatic and sudden events take place.

5. The group of non-oil-producing developing countries has been severely hit by developments on the world economic scene during the past years, since they had to suffer both on the import and export side. On the import side, the impact came naturally from the increase in the oil

TABLE 4.22. *OPEC: Evolution of the Balance on Current Account*[a]
(in billions of US dollars)

	1975	1976	1977	1978[d]	1979[d]
(1) *Low-absorbing countries*[b]					
Commercial balance	·35.5	45	42	33	31.5
Current balance	26	33.5	32.2	23	21
(2) *High-absorbing countries*[c]					
Commercial balance	14	22	19.5	9.5	9.5
Current balance	1.2	3.5	−0.7	−12	−13.5

[a]Source, *OECD Economic Outlook,* December 1978, p. 133.
[b]Bahrain, Kuwait, Libya, Oman, Quatar, Saudi Arabia, United Arab Emirates.
[c]Algeria, Ecuador, Gabon, Indonesia, Iran, Iraq, Nigeria, Venezuela.
[d]Estimated figures.

price, but also from the inflation experienced by the developed countries which supply them with consumer and durable goods. On the export side, they have had to face a reduction in Western demand for raw materials as an immediate consequence of the economic recession. Moreover, political developments in the Third World have contributed to increased military expenditures in the countries of this area (see Fig. 4.9). Last but not least, even before the crisis, these countries had made large dollar borrowings to finance their capital needs; therefore, the servicing of these loans is now severely affecting their balance on current account (see below, *The debt issue,* p. 329).

It can be seen from Table 4.18. that, notwithstanding these adverse developments, the global current account deficit of this group has been halved between 1975 and 1977. This was the result of the austere demand policies that even these countries have taken, in an effort to restore equilibrium. The richer countries in this group have been the most successful in this respect, but this also means that the burden of the deficit has fallen more and more on the shoulders of the poorest countries, especially those in Africa. In spite of these efforts, the estimated results for 1978 and the projections for the years to come tend to show that the improvement is not durable and that the financing needs of the developing countries would widen in the years ahead, if no regulating forces or no basic change in development policies took place.

Although it may be still too early to disentangle all the origins of the present crisis, some remarks about the causes of the current account of disequilibria are due here.

It cannot be disputed that the oil-price increases of 1973–1974 have been a real exogenous shock for the economy of the world that necessarily had to give way to different processes of real adjustment. Therefore, the current account disequilibria reflect in part this real adjustment and in part the monetary discrepancies that accompanied it. But in fact, the world economy was already weak and unbalanced before this shock and the current account disequilibria helped to better unveil the deep vulnerability of the world economy.

As a matter of fact, the first lesson from the oil-price increase was that the modern economies had become very rigid. We no longer live in an economic framework in which there is rapid adjustment to external shocks. This applies in particular to technological progress: the experience of past decades has imbued most of us with a faith in the capabilities of science, and in its ability to replace something performing badly by something better suited to the needs of the moment. There was immense delusion when it was discovered that this faith was unfounded, that a delay of several decades was necessary if oil was to be substituted by an alternative efficient energy source. (Nevertheless, people go on assuming implicitly that there can be no limit or setback to the power of science and technology.)

This weakness of our industrial societies (and of the societies in the process of industrialization) made the current account surplus of the oil-exporting countries unavoidable in the short-term because the import capacity of these latter countries (or, at least of the most important of them) was limited. As a consequence, a deficit for the rest of the world was inevitable.

There appear at this point three series of considerations showing that the present state of balance of payments disequilibria is due not only to the oil-trade account but also to other factors: first, the imbalance of economic power and monetary wisdom between the various nations of the world; second, the constraints placed upon many developing countries by the political uncertainties by which they are faced; third, the trough of the long-term cycle, in which the world economy now finds itself.

The first factor made the problem all the more serious because some countries were able to respond positively to the challenge of the oil-price increase. They attempted to correct their disequilibrium, and, because they were best able to succeed, they did, in fact, succeed. They are now proud of their ability to face the difficulties: in spite of the oil-price increase and the fact that they continue to import huge quantities of oil, they are running a current-account surplus because they managed to create an exportable surplus — and sell it. However, although we consider their success is far from reprehensible and that on the contrary it should provide a stimulus to many other countries, there is no disputing, in the short run, that this success forced the other non-oil-exporting countries into a still worse position. These latter countries did not have the same capacity (or, in many cases, even the will) to correct their disequilibria and their approach was rather one of trying to finance their deficits by creating money, internally, and by international borrowing, externally. Therefore, instead of the oil surplus now being compensated, more or less equally, by all the other nations, there is now an even larger surplus that has to be borne by a smaller number of deficit countries. This is the ransom to be paid to the inequalities of life, and to the fact that the world is divided into a large number of countries all competing against each other.

Competition among nations is not limited to the economic sphere, and this is at the origin of the second factor that aggravated the disequilibrium. The developing countries are now the theatre of armed competition between different socio-political concepts. Therefore, in addition to running a current-account deficit because they cannot dispense with their manufactured-goods imports from the developed nations and their oil imports from the oil-exporting countries, the developing countries have increased the size of this deficit by purchasing vast amounts of military equipment. Third World arms imports are estimated at US $3.78 billion for 1974, which is equal to a third of the development aid received by these countries.* The graphs and table

*See Strahm, R. H.:[42] p. 17.

on pp. 326–7* show that many developing countries devote to military expenditure a proportion of their national income out of all relation to their political influence, and that their arms imports display a correlation with political instability: whereas the arms imports of East-Asia are steadily decreasing, those of Africa are rapidly rising. For the Third World as a whole, it has been calculated that the increase in GNP has averaged 5% per annum since 1950, and that, over the same period, the increases in military expenditure and arms imports have been 7% and 9% per annum, respectively.**

Clearly, the arms imports of one country are the arms exports of other countries and consequently, from a viewpoint strictly limited to "monetarized economics" considerations, there would be little to say against arms imports when they are made by a surplus country: the rise in arms imports by OPEC countries helps to ease the balance of payments problems for a few developed countries. But when these imports are flowing to LDCs who are already experiencing difficulties in their balance of payments, they tend to add to the difficulties of the world at large because, even if a deficit country is the exporter, they transfer the burden of adjustment to a weaker country.

A third aggravating factor, and, we dare say, one which is, without doubt at the origin of the whole situation, is the evolution of the economic system. It is now generally accepted that the 1973 oil-price increase merely precipitated a crisis that many signs were already announcing. There was the tremendous upsurge in inflation rates at the beginning of the seventies and the collapse of the international monetary system in two stages: in August 1971 with the inconvertibility of the dollar, and in February 1973 with the move to flexible exchange rates. (These developments were, in fact, the main reasons behind the OPEC decision.) They were unparalleled by the onset of stagflation at the end of the sixties in the United Kingdom, by its spread to the United States in the early seventies and by the decline in the level of profitability in all industrial nations since the mid-sixties. Also, the cultural movements in the Western World and the attention devoted to the First Report to the Club of Rome showed that the

*Source: World military expenditures and arms transfers, 1966–1975, US Arms Control and Disarmament Agency, Washington, DC.

**See Steffens, D.: *Military spending costs US jobs,* Economics Committee Chair, Economic Forum, *Philadelphia Inquirer,* October 1977.

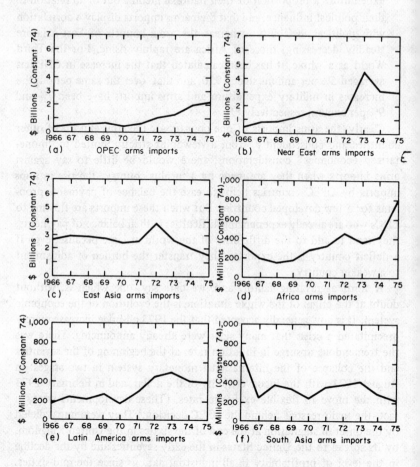

FIG. 4.9. *Arms imports*

TABLE 4.23. *Relative Burden of Military Expenditures, 1975*

Military Expenditures as % of GNP	Per capita GNP							
	less than $100	$100–199	$200–299	$300–499	$500–999	$1,000–1,999	$2,000–2,999	More than $3,000
More than 10%	Cambodia North Vietnam	South Vietnam	People's Rep. of China Egypt	Jordan North Korea	Syria	Iran Iraq	Israel Oman	Soviet Union
5–10%	Chad Laos Somalia	Pakistan Yemen (Sana	Yemen (Aden)	Albania South Korea	Rep. of China Cuba Malaysia Mongolia	Bulgaria Portugal Romania	Greece Hungary Poland Singapore	Czechoslovakia Germany (GDR) Qatar Saudi Arabia United States
2–4.9%	Burundi Ethiopia Mali Rwanda Upper Volta	Burma Central African Rep. Guinea India Indonesia Tanzania Zaïre	Equatoiral Guinea Mauritania Sudan Uganda	Bolivia Congo Morocco Nigeria Philippines Rhodesia Thailand	Algeria Angola Brazil Chile Guyana Nicaragua Peru Turkey Uruguay Zambia	Argentina Cyprus Lebanon South Africa Yugoslavia	Bahrain Italy Spain Venezuela	Australia Belgium Canada Denmark France Germany (FRG) Kuwait Netherlands Norway Sweden United Kingdom
1–1.9%	Afghanistan	Benin Haiti	Cameroon Honduras Kenya Madagascar Togo	Colombia El Salvador Ghana Senegal	Dominican Republic Ecuador Guatemala Ivory Coast Paraguay Tunisia		Gabon Ireland	Austria Finland Libya Luxembourg New Zealand Switzerland
less than 1%		Bangladesh Gambia Lesotho Malawi Niger Nepal Sierra Leone	Sri Lanka	Botswana Liberia Mozambique Swaziland	Costa Rica Fiji Mauritius Mexico Panama	Barbados Jamaica Malta Surinam	Trinidad and Tobago	Iceland Japan United Arab Emirates

Source: BIS.

industrial nations were more or less dissatisfied with the course of their evolution, and that, somehow, the roots of Western success were undermined. The proofs of a profound evolution are evident, and there is no point saying as some economists still do, that the true origin of the crisis lies in the balance of payment problems encountered by the oil-importing countries.

Further evidence of the profundity of our problems may be found in the fact that the countries that have restored their balance of payment positions are unable to let growth start again. They see that any restimulation of economic activity would merely result in a renewed outburst of inflation. Any attempt to vigorously increase the pace of the economy provokes a spurt of price increases because the economic machinery is now running at an increasing marginal cost. Moreover, when one speaks of increasing marginal costs, it means that the law of diminishing returns is somewhere at work. Therefore, although the current stagflation may be attributed to many individual causes, it is becoming increasingly clear that these causes are but manifestations of the profound origin of the present crisis: the law of diminishing returns now applies to the factor that has made economic progress since the end of the last century so amazing — the success of science-based technology.[40] Or at least, the industrial world is now living in the trough of a Kondratieff-cycle in technological innovation.[39]

The result of this is the sluggishness of economic activity. In part, this sluggishness helps in some cases to ease the balance of payment problems because the oil requirements of the industrialized countries are reduced. However, on the other hand, the problems of the developing countries are becoming more acute because these countries face a stagnation in their exports. The recession does not favour the evolution of the economic structure: protection is often preferred to adaptation, and thus the LDCs can no longer profit from the gains in international trade that could be attained in a period of rapid economic growth — at least not to the same extent.

Stagflation also leads to current-account disequilibria because of the different responses to it. Stagflation is a combination of inflation and sluggish economic activity leading to unemployment. More and more governments are becoming aware that there can be no trade-off between these two evils, because more inflation will lead, sooner or later, to more unemployment (and increasingly sooner). However, some still believe that their economies can be driven out of recession by the good old Keynesian principle of demand stimulation that proved relevant in previous times. But times have changed: a stimulation of demand no longer leads to a capital-expenditure boom. The old economic structure still at work is energy-intensive (and leads to oil imports), and domestic supply is inelastic because entrepreneurs feel that the conditions for healthy growth are not being met, and they are unwilling to risk money on expanding capacity. Instead they prefer to wait for future technological advances to become a reality and, in the meanwhile, play the currency game. When an economy such as that of the United States aims at more rapid economic growth, the outcome is inflation, a deficit *vis-à-vis* the oil-exporting countries and the wiser industrial nations, and a fall in the dollar exchange rate that precipitates the latter nations into a more severe depression and the former into a loss of purchasing power.

Redemption is not to be found, as some claim, in a global stimulation of demand by all the industrialized nations. This would lead merely to an increase in the OPEC surplus *vis-à-vis* the rest of the world, and to an expansion of the gap between the strong, developed nations and the weaker ones who would bear a major portion of the deficit.

A fresh look must be cast at the evolution of the economic system, and this is what this book tries to do.

4.3.4. THE DEBT ISSUE*

Since the persistent balance of payments deficits of the economically weaker countries of the world are financed through capital imports there is an unbroken accumulation of international debt. Much has been written in recent years on this phenomenon.** It is therefore hardly possible to present a fresh idea on the subject. However, most of the writings have originated in the circles directly involved in the debate (developing

---

*Situation at the beginning of 1979.

**See among others: "Internationale Verschuldung", a special issue of *Aussenwirtschaft*, No. 1 and No. 2, 1978; Wellons, P. A.: *Borrowing by developing countries on the eurocurrency market*, OECD, Paris, 1977; Solomon, R.: "A perspective on the debt of developing countries", *Brookings Papers on Economic Activity*, 2, 1977, 479–510; and Banque Interaméricaine de développement: *La dette extérieure de l'Amérique latine: situation actuelle et perspectives*, May 1977.

countries, banking community, international organizations), and this is the reason why it seems worthwhile to present here a short synthesis of the problem and to put the debate more in perspective, taking into account the ideas expressed in this book.

The debate has centred on the debt of developing countries (including the debt of high-absorber oil-exporting countries). However, the debt is not limited to those countries: some Western developed countries, and the Eastern European countries have also accumulated an important amount of debt since their balances on current account ran into sizeable deficits in 1974.

In the case of Western countries the deficits seem to be essentially of a temporary nature; they have been linked to the sudden oil-price hike, and although the situation of some of them, such as Spain, Greece, Portugal, and Norway is still giving rise to some concern, the basic situation of their economies, their potential of industrial organization, of human and natural resources make them low-risk countries in terms of global solvability. There is especially a common agreement that the difficulties of these countries can be rapidly brought back to modest proportions by resorting to severe measures of internal demand policy. Italy is an outstanding example in this respect: a rapid improvement of its payment situation has allowed an advance repayment of debt contracted against Germany in the years of deep deficit.

The situation deserves more attention in the case of Eastern European countries: Table 4.24 shows that their net indebtedness to the eurocurrency market amounted to US $17 billion at mid-1977, and their net global indebtedness in external currencies has been estimated at around US $35 billion, by OECD experts at the end of 1976.* The concern here arises from the fact that the deficit of these countries is not directly linked to oil-imports. This area is a net oil-exporter, and is expected to remain in this position in the years ahead. The deficit is essentially due to a structural imbalance in the trade with Western developed countries, and could very well last for a long time, especially if the recovery in Western countries falls short of expectations. According to *Business Week*** "many businessmen, bankers, and government officials worry that the West will find itself in a position where it must

*See OECD, *World Financial Outlook*, No. 2, February 1978.
**See *Business Week*, 9.1. 1978, p. 14.

continue to lend to protect what it has already lent. This is similar to the bind imposed by loans to LDCs. The main difference is that the West does not have the same political leverage with CEMA that it presumably has with the LDCs."

In spite of this, the debt of Eastern European countries is deemed to be much less serious than that of LDCs. Even if a country like Poland is not very far from being insolvent, experts generally agree on the fact that the centrally planned economies are able to drastically cut their imports from the West if they judge it necessary.* And above all, they are backed by the USSR which has huge gold reserves** and which would not permit the image of financial probity given up to now by communist countries to be damaged by the default of one of its satellite countries.

For all these reasons, the debate on international lending centres mainly on the developing countries.

TABLE 4.24. *Eastern European Countries and the Eurocurrency Market* (in billions of US $)

	Movements				Amounts at end-June 1977
	1974	1975	1976	1977/1	
Deposits	1.4	0.3	1.0	−1.9	4.5
Borrowings	2.7	5.8	4.9	0.6	21.4
Net position	−1.3	−5.5	−3.9	−2.5	−16.9

Source: OECD.

The debt problem of developing countries is not really a new one. In discussions on the subject, it is often even argued that there is, in fact, no problem at all because indebtedness is a normal stage in the development process. Countries trying to industrialize have to cover their capital requirement in excess of their saving capacity by making use of outside loans.

It is however undeniable that the situation now is very different from the situation that prevailed in the sixties. The attitude of benign neglect

*For a dissenting opinion, see Portes, R.: "East Europe's debt to the West: interdependence is a two-way street", *Foreign Affairs*, July 1977, p. 751–782.
**See Schoppe, S. G.:[43] pp. 44–48.

has here also been replaced by an attitude of perplexity, and this is due to the following factors:

- It is no longer certain that the payment problems encountered by developing nations will be transitory. Faith in development has faded away. Only little progress has been made in this respect during the last decade, and the miracles expected of modern technology have not happened: the green revolution, the expansion of fisheries, etc. have proved very disappointing.

- The creditors of developing countries are increasingly private banks rather than official institutions (see Table 4.25). Even before the 1973 oil-price increase the coming recession in developed countries had provoked a surplus of loanable funds that the international banks channeled to the developing countries. At that time, these countries seemed to offer an attractive combination of low risk and high return, and banks were thus eager to do business with them. The movement out of debt to public institutions and into debt to private banks has been all the more rapid since the developing countries were thus offered the opportunity to escape the stringent conditions that the official lending organizations tied to the granting of loans.

- The oil-price hike and the recession in the developed countries have

TABLE 4.25. *Total Debt of Developing Countries (Disbursed) at Year-end, by Type of Debt* (billions of US $)

	1960	1965	1970	1973	1975	1976
Bilateral ODA and IDA type	5.4	14.4	28.7	38.0	51.5	57.0
Other international organizations	2.8	4.0	5.3	7.9	11.6	13.4
Export credits	7.2	13.2	26.0	34.3	49.3	61.5
Private debt	2.4	5.3	12.0	30.9	59.0	73.5
Unallocated	0.1	0.2	0.9	1.2	1.5	1.6
Total	17.9	37.1	72.9	112.4	172.9	207.0

Source: UNCTAD.

multiplied the capital requirement of the developing world. As the current-account deficit of these countries approximately trebled, they were compelled to tap very heavily the world financial markets. From US $112.4 billion in 1974, their total debt almost doubled to US $207 billion in 1976. The debt increase in 1976 has been comparable to the total amount of debt outstanding in 1965. Debt-service costs rose from US $15.9 billion in 1974 to US $32 billion in 1976 (see Tables 4.26 and 4.27). The rate at which debt accumulated was far higher than the 15% or so that had prevailed in the 1960s and early 1970s. Some

TABLE 4.26. *Total Annual Debt Service of Developing Countries by Type of Debt* (billions of US $)

	1960	1965	1970	1973	1975	1976
Bilateral ODA and IDA type	0.4	0.9	1.4	2.0	2.2	2.6
Other international organizations	0.2	0.5	0.8	1.2	1.6	1.7
Export credits	1.7	2.5	4.9	7.7	11.3	14.0
Private debt	0.3	0.9	1.8	4.8	10.7	13.5
Unallocated	–	0.1	0.1	0.2	0.2	0.2
Total	2.6	4.9	9.0	15.9	26.0	32.0

Source: UNCTAD.

TABLE 4.27. *Distribution of Total Debt Among Developing Countries* (in billions of US $)

	1967	1974	1975	1976
Low-income countries	11	24	28	31
Middle-income countries	31	89	116	141
Oil-exporting countries	6	24	29	35
Total	48	137	173	207

Source: OECD.

developing countries thus became high-risk debtors, but the banks were trapped by their previous loans. They had to grant new ones in order to prevent a complete collapse of the financial system, and one must say that they experienced no difficulties in doing so as their job was to find large-scale investments to use the surpluses that the oil-exporting countries were pouring into the international financial market.

The result of these developments is that many countries are now in a position of negative foreign exchange reserves (see Table 4.28), and their prospects for a return to a sound situation are very gloomy as the debt-service burden imposes upon them additional foreign exchange needs. A study by Helen Hughes* shows that the ratio of debt to exports has increased from 184 to 200 for low-income countries in the period 1967—1976, and from 77 to 80 for middle-income countries in the same period. This compares with a lowering of the ratio from 52 to 40 for the oil exporting countries. To illustrate the fact that the process of accumulation is not coming to an end, one can indicate that the combined current account deficit of LDCs has been estimated at US $45 billion for the year 1978. This deficit will be covered in the following way:

- US $21 billion   through ODA (Official Development Assistance)
- US $ 6 billion   through other official aid
- US $ 2 billion   through IMF loans
- US $ 8 billion   through capital income
- the rest, US $8 billion, will require a decrease in foreign exchange reserves and further loans from private banks.

This places the world financial system in a rather insecure position. A major default by one of the debtor countries could precipitate the world into a catastrophic liquidity crisis.

However, while many authors consider the present situation as very serious, others think that the views commonly expressed on this problem are unnecessarily alarming. The arguments of both parties are summarized in the following two paragraphs.

The factors of concern
- The industrialization of Third World countries is less and less financed

*Hugues, H.:[44] pp. 22—25.

through direct investments coming from the developed countries, but rather through medium-term capital imports financing too many and too risky projects initiated by the developing-country governments themselves.

- The statistical studies show that the deficits in the developing countries are due to the recession in the Western developed countries and not to the oil-price increase or to errors of economic policy;* therefore, a return of deficit figures to more limited levels seems to be beyond reach so long as a lasting recovery has not taken place in the industrialized countries.

- The amount of indebtedness and the concomitant, huge debt-servicing burden threaten to place several developing countries into a situation where they will be forced to suspend payments. Banks are already obliged to reschedule some debts, or to grant new loans in order that previous loans may be repaid. The years until 1983 might be especially difficult as the medium-term loans of the mid-70s and long-term loans of the late 60s and early 70s will all attain maturity during that period.

- "Within each income group, borrowing is highly concentrated in a few countries: India, Pakistan, and Zaïre have been the principal low-

TABLE 4.28. *Countries with Negative Foreign Exchange Reserves at End-77* (in millions of US $)

Australia	−	1,735	Mexico	−	11,999
Bolivia	−	96	New Zealand	−	177
Brazil	−	10,113	Nicaragua	−	217
Chile	−	308	Norway	−	1,937
Congo	−	44	Peru	−	2,251
Denmark	−	4,195	Portugal	−	228
Dominican Rep.	−	29	South Africa	−	6,025
Ecuador	−	290	Sudan	−	290
Finland	−	2,534	Sweden	−	1,667
Gabon	−	212	Turkey	−	1,396
Iceland	−	81	Zaïre	−	290
Japan	−	3,133	Zambia	−	131

Source: International Reports (12.5.1978). Figures computed from BIS and IMF Statistics. Official foreign exchange reserves do not include foreign exchange assets of the private banking sector. They are especially large in leading foreign trade countries, notably Japan.

*See: Cleveland, H. von B., and Brittain, W. H. B.:[44] pp. 732−750. See also: Brittain, W. H. B.:[45] pp. 365−380.

income borrowers. Argentina, Brazil, Chile, Korea, Mexico, Peru and the Philippines were the principal middle-income country borrowers, with most of their debt owed to private creditors. Algeria, Indonesia, Iran and Venezuela were the principal oil-exporting borrowers."* Together with Turkey and Egypt, these 14 countries account for around 80% of all the debts of developing countries.

· Most lending now occurs through the banks rather than through official institutions. The banks are performing financial intermediation on a world scale; they use their short-term liabilities to oil-exporting countries and multinational firms in order to grant medium and long-term loans to countries experiencing balance of payment difficulties. As their expertise lies primarily in the field of domestic lending, i.e. in microeconomic financial analysis, they are often in an uncomfortable position to judge the macroeconomic situation of the countries to whom they lend, and cannot properly adjust their rates to the risks they are assuming.

· In the past years, lending to developing countries has been performed mainly through the American banking system. In 1972, foreign assets in the 4679 American banks totaled US $55 billion, against a total asset base of US $500 billion. At the end of 1977, total assets had expanded to US $770 billion, but foreign assets swelled to US $145 billion. This means that the rise in foreign assets accounted for one-third of the overall increase. Now, when a bank has started to be involved in lending to a high risk country, it experiences difficulties in trying to disengage itself when the situation of this country becomes critical. Thus, three major US banks have been heavily involved in the fate of three major debtor countries: Citybank with Zaïre, Manufacturers Hanover with Peru, and Morgan Guaranty with Turkey.**

The factors of optimism
· The past experience of lending to LDCs has been overwhelmingly positive; there have been very few losses in comparison to the business in domestic corporate and personal bans.

*Hugues, H.:[46].

**Among the methods proposed to face such situation see "A Proposal for the Establishment of an International Deposit Insurance Corporation", by Herbert G. Grubel, Essays in International Finance N. 133, July 1979, Princeton University, New Jersey, USA.

- Not all the loans are used up by the borrowers; in 1976, the non-oil developing countries borrowed in excess of their financial needs, and thus added to their reserves.
- The banks are only performing their usual business of financial intermediation between areas of excess surplus and excess demand of loanable funds. Since the early 70s, the softness of industrial loan demand had been a factor of concern for them, and they welcomed, as a blessing, the demand from developing countries. They are not worried — quite to the contrary — to *see that the fresh-capital requirements of these countries will* not come to an end soon. Therefore, the discrepancy between short-term liabilities and longer-term assets depends on the conditions of the market. In 1978, as the markets were highly liquid, the borrowing countries have been in a favourable position to renegotiate lending terms and obtain longer-term loans at a low spread over LIBOR.
- The countries that are most indebted to private institutions are the richest among the developing countries: they are the large trading countries of Latin America such as Brazil, Argentina and Mexico, rather than the poorer countries in Africa, which were compelled to draw on the facilities instituted by international organizations. One can best make a distinction between the commercial LDCs, which are making use of their ties to the international banking system, and the aid-dependent countries which do not have this possibility. Now, the flexibility of commercial countries is greater: "The current account of a commercial developing country can often be brought into balance if growth is slowed. Capital goods imports account for 30–40% of total imports in most commercial developing countries. For example, capital goods imports represent 33% of total imports for Brazil, 37% for Turkey and 39% for Algeria. Capital goods are generally a discretionary import as opposed to items such as food and raw materials necessary to keep the economic machinery running. When it is said that creditworthiness depends on the ability to right the current account, this means that growth may have to be curtailed."* The case of Argentina in 1976 is a good example of the resiliency of such countries and the rapidity with which they can react.

*Beim, D. O.:[47] p. 720.

- Although it is right to say that foreign assets in American banks are growing rapidly, it is fair to add *that loans to LDCs are only a small part of these assets, that most of them are guaranteed, and that they are often expressed in local currency*: "Based on data published by a subcommittee of the Senate Committee on Foreign Relations (Church subcommittee), 21 larger US banks that account for nearly all the foreign lending, had each invested over one-third of their consolidated assets in foreign countries at the end of 1975. More than one-quarter of these credits went to non-oil LDCs, or roughly 10% of the 21 banks' total assets. No single LDC accounted for more than 2.5% of the total. The major part — some 75% — of the loans to non-oil LDCs were either covered by the guarantee of a US Government agency or a large US firm or were short-term credits (less than one year) or credits in local currencies. In other words, only one quarter of the loans to non-oil LDCs were term loans in US dollars or other strong currencies, without special guarantees. At year-end 1975, such unguaranteed term loans to non-oil LDCs totaled US $10 billion, or 2.5% of the 21 banks' total assets."* Although these figures are already a little ancient, it is unlikely that they have deteriorated widely since then.
- The total amount of debt seems to increase very rapidly because it is calculated in nominal terms. If the figures are adjusted for inflation, the increase is far from being so amazing, as can be seen from Table 4.29.
- While the size of the risk premium contained in the rates charged to LDC borrowers is often only a fraction of a percentage point, when it is multiplied by the principal amount of the loans involved, it yields a substantial addition to a bank's earnings stream which serves to insure the bank's capital and its depositors against loan losses."**
- The banks are progressively increasing their expertise in country risk evaluation by using macroeconomic indicators such as GNP, exchange reserves, inflation rate, export and import structure, debt service, etc. and by trying to construct ratios of solvability taking these different indicators into account.*** In this respect the international organizations such as the World Bank, the IMF, and the BIS may have an important

*Cleveland, H. von and Brittain, B.:[44] p. 736–738.
**Cleveland, H. von and Brittain, B.:[44], p. 736.
***See Puz, R.[48] pp. 67–71.

TABLE 4.29. *Developing Countries Debt Adjusted for Inflation*

Year	Nominal debt	Amounts actually used	Real amounts actually used	Variation in %
1970	74.23	53.92	53.92	+8.3
1971	87.05	62.84	59.85	+11.0
1972	101.23	75.59	64.24	+7.3
1973	122.04	87.49	62.94	−2.0
1974	151.40	105.53	50.74	−19.4
1975	176.00	123.00	55.41	+9.2
1976	210.00	150.00	61.00	+9.8

Source: Musy, G.: "Croissance et endettement des pays en voie de développement" SBS − Le Mois, 1/1978, p. 7−10.

(Whenever possible, the import price index of developing countries has been used as deflator).

role to play in providing assistance to the private banks in their effort to measure borrowers' soundness. And already now, when the banks provide credit to Governments in financial distress, they no longer make the loan amount unconditionally available to the borrower. Disbursements of loans are increasingly made in installments and are conditional upon certification by the IMF that the terms and conditons of its loan agreements continue to be met.

· Since some financial alerts were experienced in 1976, the banks have also learnt to help their debtors out of a liquidity crisis. Rather than abandoning Zaïre, Peru and Turkey to the aid of international organizations they stood by their side in trying to restore their credit-worthiness, in close cooperation with the IMF.

· The monetary authorities are beginning to enforce regulations aiming at a more even distribution of lending risk. The decision of the US Comptroller of the Currency, early in 1978, that the American banks are no longer authorized to lend more than 10% of their capital and surplus to a single foreign government and its dependent agencies goes in that direction. As a consequence non-American banks will be encouraged to penetrate this market and will relieve their competitors of part of the risk.

· The governments of industrialized countries are well aware of the danger of the present situation and have been active, first in setting up security arrangements in order to prevent a financial crisis from developing (the so-called "safety nets"), then by trying to alleviate the burden that debt service imposes on LDCs' balance of payments. From 1956 to 1978, twelve developing countries have sought and received debt relief in an official multilateral context, involving 37 debt renegotiations and over US $9 billion or rescheduled debt service. In addition, some 60 developing countries benefitted from bilateral debt relief extended by DAC (Development Assistance Committee) governments, involving over US $1.4 billion of renegotiated debt service, of which a quarter was cancelled and the remainder rescheduled in equal parts. Since the Manila Declaration in 1976, discussion on a general alleviating of debt is taking place under the auspices of UNCTAD. The Group of 77 (i.e. the LDCs) is asking for a cancellation of official debt in the case of the least developed countries — the commercial countries, which have accumulated debt against banks — they claim a consolidation and rescheduling of debt. In their eyes, a general approach is imperative, as the debt problem of these developing countries has generalized causes and cannot be split into individual cases of debt default.

On the contrary, the developed countries are in favour of financial facilities on a case by case basis, and limited to the poorest countries. Among the developed countries, Sweden has the most advanced position with a proposition of converting retroactively into grants all existing ODA credits. But most developed countries are not yet prepared to subscribe to this proposition as they fear that such debt relief would cause chain reactions and lead to a loss of financial rigor among developing nations.

The existence of such discussions nevertheless reveals that the industrialized nations would not remain impassive if a major failure should happen.

The perspectives. Based on the above analysis of the debt problem and our own assessment of the global economic outlook, a number of conclusions may be drawn.

It appears first that a sharp distinction between aid-dependent countries and commerical developing countries must be adopted. Once this has been made, the likely development and the accompanying dangers can be assessed in each case.

The aid-dependent countries are the poorest countries in the world and they are not greatly involved in international trade. They import means of subsistence rather than modern technological equipment and their exports are marginal in the import basket of developed countries. Their debt is mostly owed to official institutions as these countries are not technically "creditworthy" enough to have access to the private financial markets. For them, development along the Western pattern — even admitting its desirability — is presently, and for a long time to come, out of the question.

In accordance with the Swedish proposal and in view of the support it has received from some European countries, the debt of these countries will progressively be transformed into grants. This does not mean, as is sometimes argued,* that the cancellation of debt will permit these countries to import more from the industrialized world and thus relaunch economic activity. First, the impact of these imports would probably be negligible on a world scale, and second the debt would rapidly bounce back to its previous level. On the contrary, a more sensible policy would be to couple the debt relief with the adoption of measures aimed at the self-reliance of these countries, in order that:

1. The economic forces of these nations be directed towards the production of their basic needs;
2. The delusion of "modern" development be avoided and the D & P of the countries maximized;
3. Balance of payments problems may vanish thanks to the reduction of imports.

Such a course of action means a complete abandonment of the common development policy followed until now, but the above analysis in this book argues that this is a sensible step for a better future, and more and more experts of development problems are thinking the same way.[50]

Even if the countries concerned are wealthier, the debt problem seems to be more acute in the case of commercial developing countries. These countries are indebted both to the official institutions and to the private

*Angelopoulos, A.:[49] pp. 9–10.

banks. Because these countries are relatively wealthy, it can be accepted that their debt will not be cancelled. They are not even *asking* for such cancellation since they want to keep the door of private financial markets open to them. Their demands do not go beyond some limited rescheduling and renegotiation of debt.

As these countries are very much involved in international trade, and as they are often pressing hard to increase their wealth and welfare in comparison with the industrialized world, there is no question that these countries could easily turn to a different path of development: they can at least avoid increasing deducted values too fast, and try to develop industrialization whilst maximizing their own Dowry and Patrimony.

Unitl now the deficit problems of these commercial countries have been handled through the banking system, and it seems that this arrangement has worked to the benefit of both parties. If some failures should happen in the near future, and this eventuality cannot be readily dismissed, a reasonable expectation is that governments in developed countries as well as international organizations would help to find an acceptable solution, even if such intervention would raise some internal political turmoils ("Poland but not New York City?").

But even if the financial intermediation system functions relatively smoothly, the main factor of concern remains: the debt is accumulating, and it will accumulate as long as the current account deficits of these countries continue to exist. Now, all forecasts up to the year 2000 and beyond are counting on a persistence of the developing countries' deficit.*

If — contrary to the main expectations of this report — the economic recovery were to be strong in the industrialized countries, the perspectives for the exports of the developing countries would be more favourable. But at the same time, a boom in industrial loan demand would occur, and the tightening of credit conditions could then force certain debtor countries into default. The extent of the crisis would depend on the number of borrowers experiencing such difficulties and on the reaction by official institutions.

If, as is more probable, economic activity remains sluggish in the developed world, the banks will be able to go on performing their process of financial intermediation on a world scale. Then the accumulation

*See for example, Leontieff, W.: *The future of the world economy,* Oxford University Press, 1977.

of debt will doubtless become more and more a factor of concern. Maybe the banks, backed by the international institutions, will try to make the loans conditional upon more stringent regulation of internal demand in order to cut imports. But this will mean:

1. A partial renunciation of rapid economic growth in the commercial developing country — and austerity programmes could fail through political troubles;

2. A fall in developed countries' exports, followed by an aggravation of the recession in these countries, and a feedback effect on the commercial developing countries.

Therefore, even in this case, debts will accumulate. The fact that banks are taking all sorts of precautions to limit their exposure will have little weight against the growth of figures. Even if these figures are given in nominal terms and do not reflect the real evolution, it may well happen that some kind of money illusion will work here and destroy confidence in the banking system. Then, a crisis is likely to occur, sooner or later, unless some major political or economic event changes the course of the socio-economic evolution in this group of countries.

On the other hand, it has to be remembered that a debt need not necessarily be repaid, and that it can go on accumulating as long as debt servicing encounters no problem: "The non-OPEC developing countries will be unable to repay their debt anytime soon — but this is equally true to the US Government and General Motors, to cite two examples. The issue is not whether developing countries will be able to repay their debt, but rather whether they will continue to be able to service their debt — that is, to pay interest — and to roll-over the principal on their existing debt and arrange additional financing."*

Developing self-reliance and organizing development through a better integration of the monetarized and of the non-monetarized economy is clearly a way of building progress and stability.

4.3.5. OPTIMIZING THE BENEFITS OF CAPITAL UTILIZATION: THE FUTURE OF THE WORLD MONETARY SYSTEM

The analysis of the world monetary scene presented so far underlines the unsatisfactory situation at this level. Even if the international level is

*Goodman, S. H.: quoted in *Aussenwirtschaft, op. cit.* p. 42.

par excellence a level of predominance of monetarized D & P, of maximal utilization of the advantages offered by the flexibility and fluidity of capital, opportunities for improving welfare are largely misused. This cannot be traced back only to the difficulties originating at the national level from the failure to realize that welfare is a function both of our monetarized activities and of the structure offered by a wide stock of non-monetarized assets. The difficulties encountered at the international level may also be attributed in part to the lack of a world currency unit.

An international monetary system relying on various national currencies (or on one of them) is basically unsound. Its limitations are due to the fact that the management of national monies is *primarily* inspired by the pursuit of domestic objectives, such as full-employment and price stability. This runs sooner or later against the desire of a smoothly functioning system of international payments, with the consequences that we have been used to learn.

Clearly, the solution to the problem of optimal utilization of capital at the *international* level lies in the successful design of a world currency. Most likely, this is still a long way off. But the following pages will remind us that some tentative steps have already been ventured in that direction, and they try to define simple guidelines for future action.

4.3.5.1. The main monetary source of worldwide inflation

Admittedly, the root causes of the worldwide inflation in which we are now engulfed lie outside the field of monetary policies and institutions, national or international. The unprecedented growth of material production, and consumption, initiated some 200 years ago by the *Industrial Revolution* undoubtedly helped meet real needs for food, shelter, health, transportation, etc., and remains essential to the attainment of decent health and living standards in the poorer, less-developed countries. This growth was later sustained and accelerated, however: first, by the *advertizing revolution* which created new needs unperceived before; second, by the *Keynesian revolution* which, in the postwar years, warded off the cyclical recessions which previously interrupted or reversed periodically the growth process; third, by the fantastic explosion of *military expenditures* to a level of US $400–500 billion a year; and fourth, by the limits recently reached by the fuel of past growth, i.e. modern scientific technology.[40] *These non-monetary factors are the basic roots of worldwide inflation.* They have brought within our horizon increasing scarcities of essential foods and raw materials, and environmental problems, which can be overcome only by huge investments and rising costs of production. These latter are further accelerated by collective bargaining and pressure groups, and spread from the scarce sectors to the others.

It is at this point that monetary policies enter the inflationary process. They may accommodate it by expanding bank credit to the official and private sectors of the economy, thus financing increases in wage, costs, and prices; or they may refuse such financing, but at the risk of slowing down not only inflation, but economic activity itself, at least temporarily.

The evolution of the national monetary systems and of the international monetary system itself has tended, over the years, to eliminate former constraints on the inflationary proclivities to be expected from both the public and the private sectors of the economy. This, we believe, is the crucial issue in the acceleration of national and international inflation since the First and the Second World Wars, and particularly at the present juncture. Obvious as it may be, it deserves more emphasis from the economic profession.

Most of the academic and official debates concerning the recent evolution of our international monetary system have unfortunately centered on two secondary issues, rather than on the most crucial one:

1. The explosion of oil prices, which occurred only in the last months of 1973, and cannot therefore be blamed for the suspension of the dollar convertibility in 1971, nor for the doubling of world reserves over the years 1970–1972;

2. The merits and demerits of floating vs. stable (but adjustable) exchange rates. Interesting as it is, this debate obscures the fact that world reserves have grown, under both systems, at a wildly inflationary rate incompatible with the proper functioning of either;

3. Far more significant is the inflationary proclivity of any reserve-currency standard — convertible as well as inconvertible — enabling the reserve-currency centre to finance huge and persistent deficits — internal as well as external — by the flooding of world reserves with its own IOUs.

Not to drown the reader in an ocean of statistical estimates, let us merely mention the highlights of world reserve creation in the last six years (1973–1978) of the floating exchange rates regime under which we live today. Measured in dollars, at current market prices, world reserves have tripled over these six years, increasing by $380 billion, from $191 billion to $571 billion, at an average pace of 20% per year, a multiple, of course, of any feasible growth in world trade and production in real terms.

What are the sources of this increase?

1. World physical monetary gold holdings, measured in SDRs (or in ounces) contributed less than nothing to it. Indeed, they declined slightly as a result of official sales to the private market by the IMF and the United States;

2. There were no SDR allocations over this period (their resumption in 1979 is unlikely to account for more than 3% of reserve increases from then);

3. Net IMF credits contributed about 2%;

4. The remaining *98%* were derived from the following two sources:

   (a) 33% from central banks' accumulation of *national* currencies (overwhelmingly dollars and eurodollars) as *international* reserves, i.e., to the financing of a few rich countries, primarily the United States;

   (b) 65% (nearly two-thirds) from the rise in the market price of gold as measured in SDRs (34%) and from the rise in the value of the SDR itself in terms of the US dollar (31%).*

A major portion of these reserve increases valued in dollars undoubtedly reflects book-keeping profits rather than acquisition costs – and *realized inflationary impact* – of reserves accumulated in the past by the monetary authorities, and to which SDR-valued reserve increases of 133 billion provide a closer, although very imperfect, approximation. These book-keeping profits will, however, be passed on to Governments, and are practically certain to elicit in many countries *in the future* fiscal and monetary policies which are more expansionist that would have otherwise been the case.

---

*Soaring gold prices were the major source (82%) of a further $58 billion increase of world reserves in the first five months of 1979. Revaluing the end of May reserves at the October 1st London price of $414.75 per ounce would account for 97% of a total increase of world reserves by $218 billion to $787 billion since the end of 1978.

TABLE 4.30. *Size, Sources, and Distribution of World Monetary Reserves: 1917–1978*
(in billions of US $ or SDRs)

End of	1913	1937	1949	1959	1969	1972	1975	1978
SOURCES								
I. *World gold* in billions of SDRs at 35 SDRs per ounce throughout	4.1	25.3	34.4	39.9	40.8	41.2	41.1	40.1
II. *Credit* in billions of SDRs	0.7	2.4	11.1	17.0	37.9	105.3	152.7	239.3
A. Foreign exchange	0.7	2.4	11.0	16.1	33.0	95.9	136.9	220.8
B. SDR allocations and IMF credit	–	*	0.2	0.9	4.8	9.4	15.8	18.5
1. SDR allocations	*	*	*	*	*	9.3	9.3	9.3
2. IMF credit	–	–	0.2	0.9	4.8	0.1	6.5	9.2
III. *Impact of Gold – $ Fluctuations*			−0.3	0.1	0.2	44.2	149.6	291.5
A. On gold valuation			−0.3	0.1	0.2	35.2	123.6	219.0
1. Gold–SDR rate			−0.3	0.1	0.2	29.2	99.6	158.8
2. SDR–$ rate			–	–	–	6.0	24.0	60.2
B. On credit valuation (SDR–$ rate only)			–	–	–	9.0	26.1	72.5
Total reserves, in billions of $	4.8	27.7	45.2	57.0	78.9	190.7	343.4	570.9
DISTRIBUTION								
Total Reserves, in billions of SDRs	4.8	27.7	45.5	57.0	78.7	146.6	193.8	279.4
I. United States	1.3	12.8	26.0	21.5	17.0	12.1	13.6	15.0
II. Other countries	3.5	14.9	19.5	35.5	61.7	134.4	180.2	264.4
A. OPEC			1.2	2.5	4.1	10.0	48.3	46.2
B. Other countries			18.3	32.9	57.6	124.4	131.9	218.2
1. Developed			11.0	26.3	45.7	104.7	105.9	165.4
2. Less developed			7.3	6.6	12.0	19.7	26.1	52.8

Notes

1. For 1913 and 1937 estimates, see footnotes to Table 8, pp. 66–67 of [51]. Gold holdings in 1913 are valued at US $20.67 per ounce. Its revaluation to US $35 per ounce in 1934 accounts for US $11.4 billion of the US $25.3 billion 1937 world gold estimate.

2. All other estimates are calculated from the international reserve tables of the annual issue of *International Financial Statistics 1979*. Note that IFS tables show the *composition* of *countries'* reserves, rather than the origin, or *sources* of reserves. They include therefore under "Reserve Positions in the Fund" the impact of gold and SDR transfers by countries to the Fund, attributed here to world gold and to total SDR allocations. Estimates for IMF credit, as a source or reserves, include only the "Use of Fund Credit" *plus* IMF gold deposits and investments in US Government obligations (only from March 1956 through January 1972) and *minus* a slight discrepancy (rising to about $1 billion in 1972–78) arising mostly from the Fund's undistributed surplus. Slight discrepancies in the IFS total for reserve distribution in 1949 and 1959 have been ascribed to the "Less Developed" Group of countries.

Reserve investments, in the United States (mostly in Treasury securities and bank deposits) account for the major portion of world foreign exchange reserves, and of their growth. Direct and indirect (through US banks' branches abroad) US liabilities to foreign official holders, as reported in the *Federal Reserve Bulletin*, total more than two-thirds of these reserves, both in 1972 and in 1978, the remainder being accounted in part (about 12%) by eurodollar creation by foreign banks, and in part (about 20% of the total, according to IMF sample estimates) by other foreign

TABLE 4.31. *Composition of World Foreign Exchange Reserves:*
1972–1978 (in billions of US $, and as percentages of total)

	End of 1972	End of 1978	1973–1978 Increases	% of Total 1972	% of Total 1978
I. *US Liabilities*	70	194	124	67	67
A. Direct	62	162	100	60	56
B. Foreign Branches of US Banks	8	32	24	8	11
II. *Other* (III–I)	34	94	60	33	33
A. Other currencies	21	58	37	20	20
B. Euro-dollars (other than I.B)	13	36	23	13	13
III. *Total Foreign Exchange Reserves*	104	288	184	100	100

Sources and Notes:

I.   US Liabilities: Tables 3.14 and 3.13 of *Federal Reserve Bulletin*, Washington 1979.

II.   A. Other Currencies: Rough estimates of 20% of total foreign exchange reserves (line III), based on sample estimates published in *IMF Survey*, May 28, 1978, p. 155.

Lines II and II.B. are obtained residually: II = III − I and II.B = II − IIA (Line II.B eurodollar estimates of US $13 billion in 1972 corresponds closely to the estimate of "identified eurodollars" reported in the *IMF Annual Report 1978*, p. 53, converted into dollars, *minus* I.B).

III.   *Total Foreign Exchange Reserves: International Financial Statistics*, August 1979, p. 32 estimates, converted from SDRs into US $s.

currencies: Deutsche marks, Swiss francs, etc. It is probable that few economists are aware of the full inflationary impact of this financing upon the rest of the world.

The first — and most widely understood — is that it gave the United States, under floating as well as under fixed rates, what de Gaulle called the "extravagant privilege" of financing most of their deficits with their own IOUs. Their reported direct and indirect liabilities to foreign official holders totalled $194 billion at the end of 1978, i.e., nearly 15 times their total reserve assets of $13 billion at the end of 1972. The increase of $124 billion (from $70 billion at the end of 1972) was of course the main feeder of huge, persistent and increasing deficits which the US would have been unable to sustain if — like other countries — they had been required to finance them from their own reserves.

What is less understood is that the combination of floating exchange rates with the flooding of world reserves by paper claims on a few reserve centres has also suppressed a major restraint on domestic inflationary policies by all countries alike. As long as world reserve increases remained moderate — i.e., until the end of the 1960s — domestic inflationary policies were sanctioned by balance-of-payments deficits and reserve losses, entailing fairly rapidly the inability of the more inflationary countries to avoid a devaluation, or depreciation, of their currency. This was a traumatic experience, especially under a legal system of fixed rates, since it involved an obvious failure of official policies, exposing responsible officials to the danger of not being retained, reappointed or reelected to their jobs. Daily floating rates have greatly weakened this trauma and its consequent *political* deterrent to persistent inflationary policies. Floating rates speed up the readjustment of exchange-rates to competitive levels by the more inflationary countries, but tend also to facilitate the continued pursuit of inflationary policies by them.

Concern about the domestic and external impacts of inflationary policies has not vanished. It has indeed increased with the acceleration of inflation, but the most effective — *because unavoidable* — barrier to them has practically disappeared. The United States was not restrained by gross reserve losses, because the acceptance of its own currency — which it can produce without limit — by other countries enabled it to finance enormous deficits, before and even after the dollar became inconvertible. What is less perceived so far, in most of our economic debates, is that the size and persistence of these deficits, together with floating exchange rates, have practically eliminated any substantial losses of reserves, even by the most inflationary countries. Significant reserve losses were experienced by about a dozen countries only in the first years following the explosion of oil prices, but gross reserves, even expressed in SDRs rather than in dollars, and with gold valued throughout at 35 SDRs per ounce, more than doubled on the average, for countries other than the United States and the oil-exporting countries over the three years 1970–1972, and have nearly doubled again (a 75% increase) since 1972. Even the non-oil-exporting less developed countries increased their reserves by 65% from 1969 through

1972, and by 168% in the following six years. Reserve declines of more than 50 million SDRs are reported by *International Financial Statistics* (in its annual 1979 issue) for only two countries other than the United States from 1969 through 1972* and nine countries over the following six years.**

This does not mean, of course that all other countries were in surplus on current account, but merely that the current account deficits of even the most inflationary ones could be financed — and indeed over-financed — by international borrowing.

The flooding of world reserves by dollar and eurodollar creation has added new dimensions to this financing. As already examined before, it has increased the cash reserves of commercial banks, enabling them to expand their own foreign lending at a pace which they could not have sustained otherwise.

4.3.5.2. Resuming the aborted drive toward indispensable reforms

(1) The EMS breakthrough

The most hopeful sign of possible progress toward reform, since the breakdown of the Bretton Woods System, is the breakthrough finally achieved in March 1979 with the initiation of the *European Monetary System* (EMS for short).

The scepticism — and often outright opposition — of many American economists to this new and crucial development is inspired primarily by the conviction that commitments to exchange-rate stability are premature, harmful, and bound to fail, as long as the participating countries do not succeed in reducing the wide divergences still prevalent today between their national rates of inflation. What they fail to understand is that this conviction is fully shared by the EMS negotiators themselves and that the new system aims indeed to accelerate, rather than prevent, the exchange-rate readjustments still expected to be inevitable in the years immediately

---

*Zambia and, curiously, South Africa, with losses of SDR 200 million each.

**Losses of SDR 3,800 million are reported for Australia, 2,065 million for Canada, 685 million for Portugal, 523 million for Turkey, 521 million for South Africa, 420 million for New Zealand, 107 million for Zambia, 106 million for Jamaica, and 51 million for Greece.

ahead. Full monetary union — and even irrevocable commitments to exchange-rate stability — is only a hope, still relegated to the future and conditional upon the harmonization — hopefully downward — of inflation rates and the consolidation of this harmonization through ambitious reforms — not yet full agreed or even formulated — transferring adequate jurisdiction from national to Community authorities and institutioris.

Let us mention briefly three crucial features of the system most attractive to its promoters:

1. The system restores for the participating currencies, a *common denominator* — or numéraire — sadly lacking in the reformed IMF Agreement. This common denominator is the ECU, defined as a weighted basket of the participating currencies. Unsatisfactory as this definition may be, it is a more realistic benchmark for exchange-rate calculations, readjustments, and progress toward stability than a widely fluctuating dollar, since trade, services and capital transactions among the countries of the European Community and others — in Western Europe, the Middle East and Africa — likely to gravitate around the ECU, encompass two-thirds to three-fourths of their total external transactions, i.e., close to ten times their transactions with the United States.

2. One of the first consequences of this definition is to give, for the first time, an *operational* significance to the principle formulated in Article 107 of the Rome Treaty: "Each Member State shall treat its policy with regard to rates of exchange as a matter of common concern." Since each country's official rate is defined in terms of the ECU, and since the ECU itself is defined as a weighted *average* of member currencies, it is impossible for any one currency to revalue upward — or downward — in terms of this *average* without a compensatory depreciation — or appreciation — of one or more of the other participating currencies. Any readjustment of mutually agreed exchange rates can thus be effected only by mutual consent.*

3. Two other exchange-rate commitments are also central to the EMS agreement.

The first is taken from the former "snake" agreement: the monetary authorities of each country are committed to intervene in the exchange

*As demonstrated by the first readjustment of this sort — and certainly not the last — on September 24, 1979.

market — through sales or purchases of their own currency — in order to limit bilateral exchange fluctuations between any two currencies to a 2.25% margin (temporarily enlarged to 6% for Italy).

The second, and totally novel one, is to calculate for each currency a so-called *"divergence indicator"* reflecting its market fluctuations in terms of its officially agreed central rate *vis-à-vis* the ECU. When these fluctuations reach a certain percentage of the maximum divergence authorized under the bilateral margins system, the monetary authorities of the issuing country are automatically presumed to take appropriate action (market interventions, internal monetary policy measures and/or other economic policy measures, and/or readjustment of its central rate *vis-à-vis* the ECU) or, if they fail to take action, to explain and discuss with their partners the ways in which the situation should be corrected. Thus, in total contrast to Bretton Woods and all other traditional monetary "sovereignty" rules, consultations on desirable exchange-rate readjustments may be forced upon a reluctant country, rather than left exclusively to its own initiative.

4. Beyond its "numéraire" and "divergence indicator" functions, the ECU also serves not only as a unit-of-account for an increasing number of Community operations, but also as a real money of settlement and reserve accumulation.

Central bank stabilization interventions in the exchange market should be conducted, as far as possible, in member currencies rather than in dollars. Since, however, central banks do not in principle accumulate member currencies as reserves, such interventions require mutual credit operations between the two central banks concerned, the issuing bank of the strong currency accumulating claims against the issuing bank of the weak currency. Central banks grant each other through the EMCF (European Monetary Cooperation Fund) *unlimited* very short-term financing for their interventions and short-term monetary support, which can be supplemented further by medium-term financial assistance, granted by the Council under appropriate conditions.

These short and medium-term arrangements now entail lending commitments totalling in theory 38.7 billions of ECU, but not all of which could in fact be simultaneously utilized.

The lending central banks must accept ECUs in settlement for *at least* 50% of their claims, the remaining 50% being settled also in ECUs or any other forms agreed to with the debtor, or – as a last resort – in reserve components, in the same proportions as those in which the debtor central bank holds its reserves.

But how do central banks acquire such ECUs? They are credited in ECU accounts on the books of the EMCF against equivalent transfers of gold and dollar reserves for amounts equal to 20% of each country's gold and dollar assets. The conversion of these gold and dollar transfers into ECUs takes place at current or (for gold) average market prices over the preceding six months. They totalled initially, in June 1979, about 26 billions of ECUs, i.e. about US $35 billion and, at the end of September 1979, ECU 29 billion, equivalent to nearly US $40 billion.

(2) *The ECU and the dollar*

1. One of the first and most urgent problems confronting non-member countries as well as member countries is the insertion of the EMS into the world monetary system, and particularly the uneasy relationship between the ECU and the dollar in international settlements.

A close, two-way, cooperation between the EMS and the US authorities will be necessary, in any case, to prevent a further weakening of an already undervalued, overcompetitive dollar. If this trend were allowed to proceed much further, it would inevitably trigger protectionist reactions abroad against so-called "foreign exchange dumping" by the US, and possibly panicky reactions in the United States itself.

The fear of such a disastrous course of events is a powerful stimulus to cooperation between the US and Europe, and the EMS provides new and unprecedented instruments to make such a cooperation more feasible and effective than in the past.

It will, of course, require from the United States a fundamental correction of huge and persistent balance-of-payments deficits, totally unacceptable for one of the richest countries in the world. The correction of these deficits will, in turn, require determined anti-inflationary policies and energy programme on the part of the US Administration, Congress, and private sectors of the economy. There is full agreement on these fundamentals today, on both sides of the Atlantic.

Even in the best hypothesis, however, results will not be instantaneous. Several years are likely to elapse before US deficits can be totally eliminated, and replaced by the substantial surpluses on current account required for financing the real capital exports, befitting the external relations of the relatively most capitalized country in the world today. These tapering-off deficits will have to be financed by the surplus countries and/or other high-reserve countries if further and excessive depreciation of the dollar is to be avoided.

The measures put into operation since 1 November, 1978 should make such financing easier. The United States authorities now stand ready to intervene massively to defend acceptable dollar rates. They also stand ready to borrow from the private market, rather than from central banks only, and to contract their borrowing in the lenders' currencies rather than exclusively in dollars. Alternative borrowings in ECUs would be *financially* more advantageous, since exchange risks would be lessened thereby. They would also, and foremost, be far more attractive *politically* since they would give a most dramatic demonstration of practical co-operation between Europe and the United States, rather than make the dollar appear as a satellite of the mark, the yen or the Swiss franc.

Moreover, the EMCF would enable the participating central banks to *consolidate* in ECUs their excess dollars while preserving the full liquidity of their reserve assets. This apparent squaring of the circle would result from the fact that the central banks acquiring ECU accounts in the EMCF against transfers of dollars, could draw on these ECU accounts to settle any later payment deficits, the EMCF merely reshuffling its ECU liabilities accounts between their holders, debiting the payer and crediting the payee. This would not, in general, require any liquidation of the claims on the United States received by the EMCF in exchange for its ECU liabilities. Those claims could be exchanged into the most prestigious form used in the past by the British and French Government for much of their borrowings: "consols" or "rentes perpétuelles", made attractive to the holders by appropriate interest-rates and exchange guarantees (the "ECU" denomination providing such a guarantee), but with no imperative repayment maturities. The United States would, of course, be free to reimburse their indebtedness whenever desirable, and obliged upon demand to accept their "consols" in payment for their own surpluses in the future.

This technique would have the enormous advantage of adapting to the realities of life the financial gadgets that now conceal those realities. Indeed, it is plainly impossible for any debtor country to make any "*real*" repayment as long as it remains in deficit. The only way in which it can repay, *in real terms,* is by running surpluses. Similarly, the only way in which a creditor country can obtain real repayment is by running deficits. The pretended reimbursements called for in the financial clothing — or verbiage — to which we are accustomed can only, otherwise, *redistribute* claims and debts among different lenders and borrowers, but without effecting a true reimbursement either to the former, or by the latter. Unfortunately, the illusions created by those financial gimmicks tend to hide the realities of life and to drive lenders and debtors to adopt, or continue, policies totally ineffective, or even highly damaging internationally.

Some mechanism of this sort should ideally emerge also from the forthcoming discussion of SDR "substitution accounts" with the IMF. ECU substitution accounts with the EMCF should be viewed in a similar light; they might be more acceptable to some of the holders, and more quickly negotiable. SDR and ECU substitution accounts should both complement each other.

2. A second major development will be the consolidation of existing EMS arrangements and institutions (notably the EMCF) into a *European Monetary Fund.* The Bremen resolution states that this should take place "not later than *two* years after the start of the scheme", and the problem is already under active discussion at the technical level in the Community and in member countries.

The EMF should integrate into a much simpler system both the complex credit arrangements briefly described above and the market interventions which they are designed to finance. It should ultimately evolve, in fact, toward a European Central Bank, entrusted with the management of a single European currency.

The first step in this direction should be to make more permanent arrangements regarding the conversion of 20% of participating countries gold and dollar reserves into ECU deposits. This conversion is now effected through three-month revolving swaps, renewable at the beginning of each quarter and leaving to each depositing country the risks of gains or losses on the gold and dollars deposited. The effective coordination of intervention policies would call, of course, for a joint assumption by the EMF itself of such exchange risks. The swap technique should be replaced, as soon as possible, by financial transfers of ownership.

Each central bank would have full ownership of its ECU deposit accounts and could use them freely for the settlement of future deficits. The EMF, on the other hand, would manage jointly, in the common interest, the gold and dollar assets transferred to it and be able to use them for interventions on the exchange market, which are still very imperfectly concerted today between member central banks.

Such interventions, however, would require adequate holdings by the EMF of the national currencies of member countries, as well as of dollars. This necessity dictates a second step, implementing the Bremen resolution which specifically foresaw the ECUs should also be created against deposits of member currencies in amounts roughly equal to the gold and dollar deposits of members. Such deposits would replace – and simplify enormously – the complex network of mutual credit rights and commitments described above, and which are indeed roughly equivalent in amounts to the initial gold and dollar deposits of members last June. The simpler deposit technique has been objected to as potentially more inflationary than the combination of automatic and *conditional* credits of the present system. This objection could be met, however, by distinguishing two types of ECU deposits:

(a) freely usuable – and fully convertible – deposits, in amounts equal to gold and dollar deposits, *plus* the present *automatic* short-term debtor quota of each member;

(b) blocked deposits equal to the excess of each member's national currency deposits over and above this debtor quota; the actual use of these blocked deposits would be subject to conditions roughly similar to those now governing the use of "rallonges" and "medium-term financial assistance" by prospective borrowers.

Looking further into the future, we should hope that the successful functioning of the initial EMF will induce gradual increases of the present 20% gold and dollar deposits of member central banks, culminating eventually into 100% deposits of each country's gold and other foreign reserve assets with the EMF, in exchange for ECU deposits. This would obviously be necessary anyway, at some stage, to the ultimate attainment of full monetary union, but it should be emphasized that it would not require a "pooling" of reserves, but only of their management. France could not draw on the ECU account of Germany, nor vice versa. All that would be required is that the foreign reserve assets of members be held in an institution (the EMF) jointly managed by them, rather than *directly* with foreign institutions on which they can exercise far less influence individually than jointly.

3. Far more immediate is the prospect of a popularization of the ECU with the private sectors of the economy most averse to exchange risks on alternative foreign assets in national currencies and eurocurrencies.

The *European League for Economic Cooperation* approved unanimously in May 1978* a proposal encouraging commercial banks to offer to their customers loans and deposits denominated in ECUs as an alternative to *national* currencies (eurodollars, euromarks, etc.) which expose lenders and borrowers to far greater exchange-risks of windfall gains for some, but losses for the others, than on the ECU weighted average of all the EMS currencies. Some lenders and borrowers, fully confident − or "overconfident"? − in their forecasts of future exchange rate fluctuations will undoubtedly continue to lend or borrow in Deutsche marks, dollars or sterling, but those who have been sufficiently burned in the past, or wish to be relieved from daily preoccupation with, and reshuffling of, their foreign currency portfolio, should prefer the ECU to national eurocurrencies. ECU-denominated operations should take their place on a broad and dynamic market, whose gross size is estimated to have risen from about $110 billion in 1970 to well over $900 billion today. Various banks have understood this, particularly in Belgium and begun to open ECU-denominated deposits and loans to their customers. Whenever − as is usually the case − deposit demand exceeds loan demand, the banks are forced, in order to avoid exchange risks, to reinvest the difference on the national money markets of the Community, *pro rata* of each currency's proportion in the ECU basket.

So far, the official authorities have generally been very cool to the private use of the ECU. This attitude may reflect in part the fear of nationalists that the ECU will become a dangerous competitor for their national currency. Yet, the same nationalists should welcome the use of the ECU as a substitute for the *foreign* currencies or eurocurrencies so widely used − and with little control by the authorities − in international trans-

---

*In their document No 2819, entitled "A European Parallel Currency as a Shelter against Exchange Rate Instability" obtainable from the ELEC, 1, Avenue de la Toison d'Or, Bruxelles, 1060 Belgium. The proposal was made by Robert Triffin.

actions for which the use of the national currency is obviously impossible *simultaneously* for both contracting parties.

A growing use of the ECU in such transactions should be greatly encouraged by its official use in the issue of bonds and other market operations by the national — or local — authorities and by the Community itself. As noted above, commercial banks are anxious to find in this respect a *borrower* even more than a lender *"of last resort"*.

4. This popularization of the ECU in private market operations would, of course, pave the way for, and facilitate immensely, the final step toward full economic and monetary union, i.e. the merging of the present national currencies of members into a single European currency. The ECU would already be known and widely used in all foreign transactions for which the monetary and exchange authorities already authorize the legal use of foreign currencies or eurocurrencies.

This legal use would merely have to be gradually extended to other operations, including finally all domestic as well as foreign payments, as each country makes sufficient progress to ensure the stability of its currency toward the ECU. When that stage is reached, however, its *irrevocable and irreversible* character should be consolidated through appropriate transfers of jurisdiction over money creation from *national* to federal *European* authorities and institutions.

4.3.5.3. Progress toward worldwide reforms

Some people still view regional monetary cooperation as the antithesis of worldwide monetary cooperation. The *European Payments Union* provided in the 1950s a most spectacular demonstration of the *complementarity* of these two approaches. The EPU did much more, indeed, than the IMF in those years to restore convertibility between the participating currencies and the dollar, as well as among themselves.

The success of the EMS experiment toward its basic objectives, and of the indispensable cooperation between the EMS and US authorities, might at long last break the deadlock which has paralyzed, since Jamaica, the previous determination to restore a workable world monetary order.

1. First and foremost, of course, should be the actual implementation of the oft reiterated, pious wish to substitute a reformed SDR for the

dollar as well as for gold in international reserves and settlements. The latest IFS estimates show how far we are from that goal: SDRs and Reserve Positions in the Fund accounted each, in May 1979, for less than 3% of world reserves, as against 44% for gold (valued at market prices) and 51% for foreign exchange holdings.

Let us hope that the IMF resolution regarding SDR "substitution accounts" will prove a first step on the long road still ahead. The mopping up of outstanding gold and dollar holdings through "substitution accounts", however, would be useless — and difficult to negotiate — if it were not complemented by the radical reforms to which it should be a mere prelude, i.e., those that will: (i) limit the *future* expansion of the world reserve system to what is needed to make it an engine of world stability rather than of world inflation; and (ii) attempt to earmark this growth for the financing of high-priority economic and social objectives commonly agreed, rather than for the haphazard financing of US or other reserve centers' deficits.

As a way to meet the first of these objectives, a simple but only *presumptive* rule à la Milton Friedman would be desirable: the IMF should be directed to expand its total lending and investment portfolio at a rate of 4 to 6% a year, consistent with the reserve requirements of non-inflationary growth of world trade and production. Weighted voting of two-thirds, three-quarters, or even more, should be required to authorize substantial departures from this presumptive target. For this procedure to have the desired effect, moreover, the monetary authorities should invest *all* of their future surpluses in SDRs — rebaptized, of course, and made more attractive to members — and eschew any purchase of gold and foreign exchange, except for minimum working balances in foreign currencies still needed for interventions in the market until SDRs are made available — as they should be — to commercial banks, and even other holders.*

Particularly encouraging in this respect are the forward-looking *"Thoughts on an International Monetary Fund based fully on the SDR"* of the Economic Counsellor and Director of the Research Department of the International Monetary Fund: J. J. Polak.**

*To the extent that more substantial dollar accumulation were deemed necessary in a transition period, it should be deducted from the authorized Fund lending and investment operations.

**Recently published by the Fund as No. 28 in its Pamphlet Series.

As for the second objective, it would flow automatically from the fact that all reserve growth would become the result of agreed Fund decisions. These should include the type of operations financed in the past by the Fund — including those covered by the "General Agreements to Borrow" — but add to them those now made possible by the substitution of SDRs for gold and foreign exchange reserves, and not necessarily limited — as brilliantly explained by Professor Machlup[52] — to short-term lending. An expansion of IMF operations consistent with the first objective above should leave room for such operations. They might take the form of IMF investments in long-term bonds, *or even consols,* issued by various agencies such as the World Bank, its affiliates, other Regional Development Banks, and even by other international agencies such as the World Health Organization, etc.

2. Two further aspects of this reshaping of the international monetary system deserve a few comments.

The first is the need to take into consideration the incredible mushrooming of international credit financed by private sectors, particularly through eurocurrency credits and eurobond issues. The rough and incomplete estimates reported by the BIS* show a *net* increase of about $330 billion in these private lending operations over the last three years ($535 billion gross), *i.e.* more that 2 ½ times the reported increase of $127 billion in the foreign exchange investments of central banks, and 60 times that of SDR allocations and IMF lending.

Some distinguished economists — from Academia as well as from the US Treasury — have been arguing on this basis that the reforms previously advocated as necessary to arrest the inflationary explosion of reserve creation have not only been made unnecessary by the generalization of floating rates, but have also become irrelevant anyway in view of the ease with which countries can now finance continuing deficits through their borrowings from the private market, rather than through reserve losses or borrowings from the IMF. We would draw from the same facts the opposite conclusions, i.e., that any meaningful attempt to reduce persistent world inflation and balance-of-payments disequilibria must deal with both of their two major sources in recent years:

(a) The disordinate financing of reserve-centre borrowings, which floating rates have failed to reduce significantly;

*In its June 1979 Annual Report, p. 104.

(b) The disordinate growth of private financing, which could not have reached such proportions, anyway, if the US dollar had not acquired unwittingly the privilege — and burden! — of being accepted by central banks as well as by commercial banks and their customers as a "parallel world currency".

The second, and final, observation is that the reform path outlined above should — and undoubtedly will — modify fundamentally the distribution of functions and responsibilities between the IMF, the EMF, and other regional monetary groups already in existence and likely to emerge in the future. The financial, economic, and most of all political, scope for monetary cooperation and mutual commitments is obviously much broader among highly interdependent countries — keenly conscious of this interdependence — than that conceivable at this stage on a worldwide scale between more heterogeneous groups of countries less interdependent from one another.

A few figures illustrate the point. For the European Community members as a whole, exports to other Community countries account for 52% of total exports, ranging from a near-high of 72% for Belgium to a low 38% for the United Kingdom. This is certainly part of the explanation of the greater degree of enthusiasm shown in Belgium than in the United Kingdom for economic and monetary union, particularly if one considers also the greater dependence of GNP on exports for Belgium (50%) than for the United Kingdom (30%). Merchandise exports to the Community account for 33% of Belgium's GDP as against 9% for Britain.

Yet exports to the Community are for all its members a multiple of their exports to their main outside customer: the United States. They are about 4 times as large for Britain, at the low end of the spectrum, and as much as 17 times for Belgium. The crucial importance of the United States — and of the dollar — in Community policies and institutional arrangements derives primarily from other reasons, such as:

(a) The difficulty of changing deeply embedded psychological attitudes, market habits and bureaucratic routines inherited from the past;

(b) most of all, the enormous weight of the United States as an economic, political and military power in the rest of the world, as well as in Europe.

Similar observations could be made — and documented — for other areas of the world. A more decentralized structure of monetary cooperation than that of Bretton Woods is long overdue. It would have a triple advantage.

1. To permit a fuller exploitation of the wider potential for realistic co-operation that can be elicited on a regional rather than a world scale;
2. To relieve the IMF of unnecessary responsibilities, and enable it to concentrate its time and attention on those which cannot be discharged as, or more, efficiently on the regional scale;
3. To make wholehearted participation in the IMF more attractive and feasible to disaffected countries, such as many less developed countries, and particularly to make it possible for the Communist countries, unable to adjust their mutual relations to rules and norms derived from the market (less-centrally-planned) economies of the capitalistic world, but that would not always make sense for their own economies.

These are, in our view, concrete ways to ameliorate the performance of the world monetarized economy, for the benefit of general welfare.

Bibliography

1. LEONTIEFF, W., CARTER, A. and PETRI, P.: "The future of the world economy", A United Nations Study, New York, 1977.
2. World development report, World Bank, Washington, DC, August 1978.
3. HERRERA, A.: *Un monde pour tous,* Paris, 1977.
4. "Overall economic perspective for the ECE region up to 1990", Economic Commission for Europe, Geneva, 1978.
5. DENISON, E. F.: *Accounting for United States economic growth, 1929–1969,* Brookings Institution, Washington, DC, 1974.
   The contribution of capital to the postwar growth of industrial countries, Brookings Institution, Washington, DC, 1977.
   See also his: "Discussion" in *Journal of Finance,* June 1978, page 1006, after the article of G. von Furstenberg, "The long-term effects of governmental deficits".
6. CLARK, P. K.: "Capital formation and the recent productivity slowdown", *Journal of Finance,* June 1978.
7. McCARTHY, M. D.: "The U.S. productivity growth recession: history and prospects for the future", *Journal of Finance,* June 1978.
8. BOSWORTH, B., DUESENBERRY, J. and CARRON, A.: *Capital needs in the seventies,* Brookings Institution, Washington, DC, 1975.
9. *A study of fixed capital requirements of the U.S. business economy,* Washington, DC, December 1975.
10. "The peril of a credit crunch", *Business Week,* 24 July 1978.
11. BARRON, D. C.: *Capital availability* SRI Business Programme, 1977.
12. MADDEN, C.: *U.S. economic growth from 1976 to 1986,* Volume 8, "Capital formation: an alternative view", Studies prepared for the use of the Joint Economic Committee, Congress of the United States, Washington, 1976.
13. *Business Week,* 25 December 1978.
14. LINDSAY, F.: "Financing high-cost, high-risk energy development", *Harvard Business Review,* November 1978.
15. *Aviation Week and Space Technology,* 23 October 1978.
16. *Financial Times,* 9 May 1978.
17. *1978 World Bank Atlas,* Washington, DC.
18. See *The Geneva papers on risk and insurance,* No. 2, Geneva, August 1976.
19. See: "Nature and importance of economic losses due to the utilization of the computer", *The Geneva papers on risk and insurance,* No. 3, Geneva, October 1976.
20. See: Economic analysis of products liability, *The Geneva papers on risk and insurance,* No. 9, Geneva, July 1978.

21. HENDERSON, H.: "Risk, uncertainty and economic futures", *The Geneva papers on risk and insurance*, No. 9, Geneva, July 1978.
22. LINDSAY, F.: "Financing high-cost, high-risk energy development", *Harvard Business Review*, November 1978.
23. *Economic implications of pollution control*, OECD, Paris, 1974.
    Macroeconomic evaluation of environmental programmes, OECD, Paris, 1978.
    The seventh annual report of the Council on Environmental Quality, US Government Printing Office, Washington, DC, 1976.
24. LEONTIEFF *et al*: *The future of the world economy, op. cit.*
25. WILMOT, T.: "European fire costs", *Etudes & Dossiers* No. 27, The Geneva Association, Geneva, 1978.
26. ECKHOLM, E.: "The other energy crisis: firewood", *Worldwatch Paper* No. 1, Washington, DC, 1975.
    ECKHOLM, E. and BROWN, L.: "Spreading deserts", *Worldwatch Paper* No. 13, Washington, DC, 1977.
    BROWN, L.: "The worldwide loss of cropland", *Worldwatch Paper* No. 24, Washington, DC, 1978.
    ECKHOLM, E.: "Forestry for human needs", *Worldwatch Paper* No. 26, Washington, DC, 1979.
27. See on this subject:
    STEFFENS, D.: "Economic Committee Chair, military spending costs US jobs", *Philadelphia Inquirer*, October 1977.
    · Updated report of the Secretary General *Economic and social consequences of the arms race and of military expenditures*, Department of Political and Security Council Affairs, United Nations Centre for Disarmament, New York, 1978.
    · *The social and economic aspects of disarmament in ending the arms race – The role of the scientist*, World Federation of Scientific Workers, 1977.
    STRAHM, R. H.: "Pourquoi sont-ils si pauvres", *La Baconnière*, Neuchatel, 1977.
    · *World military expenditures and arms transfers, 1967–1976*, US Arms Control and Disarmament Agency.
    · *Données économiques et financiéres concernant la défense de l'OTAN*, OTAN, Brussels, 1977.
    · Stockholm International Peace Research Institute (SIPRI), "World armaments and disarmaments", *SIPRI Yearbook*, 1978, Taylor & Francis Ltd., London, 1978.
    CADIX, A.: "Stratégies, commerce et développement", *Le Monde*, 2 May, 1978.
    SAMPSON, A., CAHN, A., KRUZEL, J., DAWKINS, P. and HUNTZINGER, J.: *The arms bazaar*, London 1977.
    · *Controlling future arms trade*, 1980, Project, Council on Foreign Relations, New York, 1977.
28. DERREUMAUX, P. and PELTIER, G.: "Monnaie, intermédiation financière et développement économique", *Banque*, March 1979, Paris, as well as the various bibliographical references indicated in that study.
29. MUNCH, M.: "L'aménuisement des capitaux propres, un danger pour les entreprises allemandes", *Euroépargne*, May 1978.
30. HICKS, J.: *The crisis in Keynesian economics*, Basil Blackwell, 1973.
31. TOULLEC, C.: "Economie de marché, economie d'endettement et politique monétaire", *Banque*, March 1979.

32. HICKS, J.: *Capital and value*, Oxford, 1974 (1st edition: 1939).
33. WILLETT, T. D.: *Floating exchange rates and international monetary reform*, American Enterprise Institute, Washington, DC, 1977.
34. L'HUILLIER, J.: *Le système monétaire international – aspects économiques*, Armand Colin, Paris, 1971.
35. RUEFF, J.: *Le lancinant problème des balances de paiements*, Payot, Paris, 1965.
36. TRIFFIN, R.: "L'étalon monétaire du XXe siècle", in: *Inflation et ordre monétaire international*, IUHEI, Genève, 1967.
37. TEW, B.: *"The evolution of the international monetary system, 1945–1977"*, Hutchinson, London, 1977.
38. BOURGUINAT, H.: *Marché des changes et crises des monnaies*, Calmann-Levy, Paris, 1972.
39. MENSCH, G.: *Das technologische Patt*, Fischer Verlag, Frankfurt, 1977.
40. GIARINI, O. and LOUBERGE, H.: *The diminishing returns of technology*, Pergamon Press, Oxford, 1978.
41. HABERLER, G.: "International aspects of US Inflation, in: *A new look at inflation*, American Enterprise Institute for Public Policy Research, Washington, DC, 1973, pp. 79–105.
42. STRAHM, R. H.: *Pourquoi sont-ils si pauvres?*, *op. cit.*
43. SCHOPPE, S. G.: "Myth and reality of the Soviet gold policy", *Intereconomics*, No. 1/2, 1978, pp. 44–48.
44. CLEVELAND, H. von and BRITTAIN, W. H. B.: "Are the LDCs in over their heads?" *Foreign Affairs*, July 1977, pp. 732–750.
45. BRITTAIN, W. H. B.: *Developing countries' external debt and the private banks*, Banca Nazionale del Lavoro, December, 1977, pp. 365–380.
46. HUGUES, H,: "The external debt of developing countries" *Finance & Development*, December 1977, pp. 22–25.
47. BEIM, D. O.: "Rescuing the LDCs", *Foreign Affairs*, July 1977.
48. PUZ, R.: "How to find out when a sovereign borrower slips from A-1 to C-3", *Euromoney*, December, 1977, pp. 67–71.
49. ANGELOPOULOS, A.: "L'allègement de la dette des pays pauvres: un moyen de relancer l'économie mondiale", *Le Monde de l'Economie*, 28 March, 1978.
50. TEVOEDJRE, A.: *La pauvreté, richesse des peuples*, Ed. Sociales, Paris, 1978.
51. TRIFFIN, R.: "The evolution of the international monetary system: historical reappraisal and future perspectives", *Studies in International Finance*, Princeton, No. 12, June 1964.
52. MACHLUP, F.: "The cloakroom rule of international reserves: reserve creation and resources transfers", *Quarterly Journal of Economics*, August 1965.

Remarks for a Provisional Conclusion

This report, based on a "dialogue" and three "dossiers" has tried to convey a message: an "ecological-economic" notion of value — the "utilization value" — which could become a better general reference than the traditional notions of economic value, for the purpose of defining and promoting wealth and welfare of the world's nations today.

A notion of value is essentially a vision, a strategic vision: as such it scans wide and varied horizons. It has to be consistent and coherent from many angles. History, philosophy, cultural diversities and choices, economics, scientific and technological development, material constraints and ethics are only some of the major elements which constitute the background and facets of values. Values, whether implicit or explicit, form the centre of gravity of any society and are, at the same time, the production factors of goals. In the present predicament of mankind, every possible effort must be made to achieve a minimum level of consensus on values, in order to actively organize survival and future development of humanity. Economic values are a most important component of the total values system and are closely interrelated with it.

This report is first and foremost an attempt to place the concept of value in its widest context: the broad approach was essential since to refrain from discussing the distant origins of the concept of economic value (such as philosophy) or the distant effects (such as fiscal policy), would have undermined the document's overall consistency. It was necessary to run the risk of being criticized for superficiality in having tackled so many issues related to so many different disciplines. If the general concept of value that has been presented is to prove of any worth, then each section of this report will act, as presented in the dossiers, as an introductory reference for more in-depth studies.

Moreover, for most of the subjects that have been dealt with, more specific and detailed analyses already exist, often with very similar pers-pectives — and these are to be found in the bibliography.

Practically all the ideas put forward in this report — even those which might strike the reader as "new" — will be found, in one form or another, somewhere in the present turmoil of world culture. This may somewhat better clarify and justify why this book was written: to help pull all the loose strings together and thus stimulate a much demanded and much needed synthesis, particularly in the field of "economics".

This synthesis will be evaluated by its capacity to produce not only a vision of action, but also certain specific and immediate actions. And since it is necessary to stimulate quickly the discussion on possible actions, we have simply listed here some of the major issues presented in the various parts of the report.

(a) *Issues in economic policy*

- the evaluation of utilization value implies the accounting of all costs incurred by the use of a product or service during *its life-time*: the optimization of such costs should lead to a *reduction of energy and raw-materials consumption* as compared to an economic system based on the accounting of the added (exchange) value;
- at the same time, optimization of the lifetime of products and services (taking into account the real, increasing or diminishing returns of technology), provides a sound basis for stimulating the increase of "productive" occupation (both monetarized employ-ment and free activities) and real wealth and welfare;
- the determination of value deducted should make it possible to identify and measure those economic actions which, while *increasing* GNP (gross national product), in fact tend to diminish *real* wealth;
- the evaluation of overall returns of technology (as well as detailed sectorial analysis), starting from the constraints of fundamental research, inertias of all sorts and utilization value, should become a fundamental exercise in determining the real level of capital needs;
- the analysis of the causes of inflation will become much more significant and action productive when economists will accept the idea that inflation depends mainly on the rigidity of supply, which

is in turn conditioned by the diminishing returns of technology;

- fiscal policy, using the concept of utilization value as reference paradigm and bearing in mind growing expectations of social justice, should swing towards indirect taxation (the reasons — and probably the motivations — are rather different from those proposed by neo-liberal economists);
- savings policy is very much dependent on the situation in the economic non-monetarized field. In particular, in those countries which still have a wide margin for future industrial development, autonomous development of monetarized saving is both a priority and a possibility, provided the interdependence between the monetarized and the non-monetarized sector has been accurately analyzed;
- in all countries, policy level study of the non-monetarized economic system and integration of the monetarized system into the non-monetarized one would probably be a key factor in promoting the stability and progress of real wealth;
- at the world level, the monetarized economic system has still a long way to go; the report, after considering the conditions of economic equilibrium on the basis of the real level of returns of technology and of the relations between the monetary and the non-monetary system (the evolution of the utilization value) underlines the importance of gradual development of world regional entities reinforcing and reinforced by regional monetary systems leading the way to regional monetary units.

(b) *Issues in economic thinking*

- Gross National Product (and any other measure based on the concept of added/exchange value) is a measure of a *flow,* restricted essentially to the monetarized economic system, which does not *necessarily* increase wealth and welfare. At most, it is a (partial) measurement of costs, not all of which have a net productive value;
- wealth is a *stock* of assets (which we have called Dowry and Patrimony — D & P), of which only part is monetarized. Welfare is derived from the level of this stock and from the degree of access to it. *Productive* activity is that which *adds* to the stock of wealth: an industrial activity *is not productive by nature,* but

only if it is wealth-creative and not wealth-destructive, the latter being measured by the deducted value;

- value is provided by an asset during its lifetime: it is its utilization value. Everything which contributes to the formation and maintenance of an asset represents a cost or an effort. In this sense, industrial production, services of all sorts, maintenance and recycling, as well as all the non-monetarized contributions (qualitative and non-remunerated contributions) are all on the same level: they contribute to utilization value. This is the opposite of the traditional economic concept of exchange/added value and of the underlying notion of what is productive and unproductive, where priority is given to industrial, monetarized activity;

- "economics", for the last two centuries, has been the "economics of industrialization" and not of the economy, which includes all assets and efforts that contribute to welfare;

- the reduction of "economics" to industrial, monetarized assets has been possible and maybe inevitable, because of a dominating analytical philosophy, favoured by major advances in science and technology, with limited production of deducted values. Today, the increase of added value at the expense of free-use value, *even when the latter is not scarce enough to be monetarized,* is a mushrooming phenomenon and leads to a new concept of wealth and economic strategy;

- ecological and other current movements (e.g. women's lib., etc.) are all directed at the rehabilitation of non-monetarized assets and activities which contribute to wealth and welfare and which have been marginalized or left out of account in the traditional economic (and socioeconomic) system. Ecology is the base for a new enlarged economics. The question put, for instance, by Ivan Illich are those which were widely discussed at the time of such founding fathers of economics as Adam Smith. Their reference context was the nascent Industrial Revolution: our present context is the nascent, post-industrial, world society;

- indicators (for evaluating and measuring *results* and/or *goals* as well as costs and efforts) should find in the concept of utilization value the theoretical basis for their existence as tools for monitoring wealth and welfare and as instruments in wealth and welfare development. Added value is thus reduced to the level of an indicator of monetarized effort (and of monetarized results if one also calculates the deducted value);

· integration of the concepts of monetarized and non-monetarized economy should fit into more adequate visions and strategies for development policies;

· the planning procedure for developing future scenarios should be reversed: planning should commence with an evaluation of the inertias and life cycles of all current economic factors, of all decisions and lack of decisions and of their interactions. Only after this will it be possible to define possible scenarios. The choice is not one for or against planning: all decisions, lack of decisions or even fortuitous events "plan" the future. The choice is between conscious or unconscious acts or decisions and their impact on the future. In this way, emphasis is placed on the responsibility of the present.

(c) *Issues on the cultural foundations of values*
· the orientation of this report is clearly systemic rather than analytical. This also coincides with the trend to integration of the "two cultures" as identified by the social and by the natural sciences. At a time when "natural" sciences are confronted with growing indeterminacy and complexity, the clear-cut, "Cartesian" boundaries that separate them from the social sciences become less and less distinct;

· if "unique" value exists anywhere, it is the respect of *plurality* of values; an economic value is a goal, and as such it cannot be predetermined "scientifically" in *abstracto* out of contact with its specific (cultural) connotations in time and space. There is no objectivity in the traditional notion of economic value, which measures development of industrialization and *presupposes* a cultural acceptance of this process without adaptation, when its success is measured by GNP accounting instead of specific indicators;

· "science", said Pascal, "is like a ball in a universe of ignorance. The more it grows, the more we are confronted with ignorance." The yardstick to measure the growth of science is the quantity of ignorance and not the quantity of knowledge. If, in a more or less "vulgar" Cartesian way, we believe that every iota of knowledge advances us on our path towards "truth", it means that we are ready to use science as a substitute for religion or metaphysics. Or ideology;

· the great debate initiated by the Club of Rome on "The Limits to Growth" is implicitly connected with the limits of knowledge and of science and technology. Accepting the existence of such limits and making an effort to identify them clearly, is tantamount to setting new goals. The scientific process is a process of discovering ignorance and identifying limits and ways to overcome them. Denying limits, denying ignorance is all too often a sign of superstition, when science is equated to a powerful form of magic. And superstition is at the service of human weaknesses.

Index

373